A Vine of God's Own Planting

A History of Houghton College from
Its Beginnings Through 1972

Richard L. Wing

wesleyan
publishing
house

Indianapolis, Indiana

Copyright © 2004 by Houghton College
Published by Wesleyan Publishing House
Indianapolis, Indiana 46250
Printed in the United States of America
ISBN 0-89827-292-0

Library of Congress Cataloging-in-Publication Data

Wing, Richard L., 1935-
    A vine of God's own planting : a history of Houghton College from its beginnings
through 1972 / Richard L. Wing.
        p. cm.
    Includes bibliographical references.
    ISBN 0-89827-292-0 (hardcover)
1. Houghton College—History. I. Title.

    LD2281.H732W56 2004
    378.747'84—dc22

2004018612

This book is dedicated to the hundreds of heroes of the faith
who labored with dedication, zeal, and conviction on behalf of Houghton
Seminary and Houghton College over the many years.

Contents

Curriculum

Consequences of Houghton

Financial Effects

Houghton and The Wesleyan Church

Staying the Course

A General Summary

List of Tables and Illustrations

Tables

Illustrations
Illustrations follow page 256.

- How did the peculiar religious climate of nineteenth-century western New York shape the institution?

- How did the institution evolve?

- How did the curriculum develop, and in what ways has it changed?

- Who served as faculty?

- Who made up the student body? What did its graduates do?

- What happened on campus in terms of questions and interests peculiar to each era?

- How did World War II affect the college?

- What role has The Wesleyan Church played in the life of the institution?

- Has Houghton remained a Wesleyan institution?

- How has the secularization of other one-time Christian colleges affected Houghton?

- To whom did Houghton College award honorary degrees?

- How has Houghton moved toward the ideal of a great Christian college of liberal arts?

Another standard historiography practice involves great selectivity to boil a complex life history into a limited volume. Only a brief review of the history of Methodism and of Wesleyan Methodism is presented. Similarly, anyone who ever spent a block of time at Houghton in the years before 1972 will note that much from his or her experience has been omitted. Because so many people were doing so many things over so many years in such a changing setting, only a little of what happened could be presented. Therefore, the author requests from the reader a special courtesy: to understand the demands of choosing what seemed to be essential aspects of Houghton's history for mentioning here. Also, because part of this text is chronological, part biographical, and part issue-oriented, there is a modest degree of overlap for in-section clarity.

From its theological beginnings in the work of John and Charles Wesley, its educational launching in the 1844 policy statement by the

Wesleyan Methodist Connection, through its immediate parentage by Williard J. Houghton and Dennison S. Kinney in October 1882, Houghton Seminary and College was built on the dream for an institution that would serve local youth economically and effectively in a morally positive environment. A charter was obtained, funds were raised, a building was erected, and the first students entered in the winter of 1884. Thus began, in the Genesee Valley, the initial era of this school with a vision

The retirement of Houghton president Dr. Stephen W. Paine in 1972 served to conclude the era from college chartering and accreditation by Middle States. In the words of Dr. Alan Graffam, "By the time of Paine's retirement in 1972 the college was well established; its buildings were in place and its identity well known. The major curricular and campus life decisions had been made and the institutional perspective established."[1]

While to some historians the lapse of only a third of a century between any historical milestone (such as Dr. Paine's retirement) and its analysis may appear to be too brief a span for true objectivity, it seemed propitious to those guiding the study to capitalize on the living presence of many individuals who could provide first-person testimony reaching back into the regime of Dr. James S. Luckey and even to Houghton's chartering as a college in 1923.

Transcriptions of the interview recordings (and the recordings themselves) are deposited in the Doezema Archives of Houghton College, housed in the Willard J. Houghton Library. A list of those interviewed appears in the bibliography. Also, all materials assembled as part of this effort have been placed in the Houghton archives.

Acknowledgments

The author greatly appreciates—

- Daniel Chamberlain, Houghton's president, who conceived the idea of producing an analytical history and persuaded the trustees to fund it.

- Jane Miner, master scribe and administrative specialist, who voluntarily made typescript transcriptions of about 150 hours of tapes through the goodness of her heart and the magic of her flying fingers.

- Dean Liddick, retired Houghton writer and administrator, who has been my alter ego of blue pencilage for over two decades.

- Richard Gould, Houghton archivist, who found great treasures (some hidden) and made them readily available for research. Kudos also to William Clark, archivist at Wesleyan World Headquarters, who provided encouragement and great volumes of minutes.

- Willard Smith, former treasurer and business manager, who kept voluminous records, wrote the first Houghton College history, kept a diary that led to a 560-page single-spaced autobiography, and granted me five-plus hours of interviews and numerous private conversations.

- Oswald Ratteray, ace staffer at Middle States, who broke through the crimson tapes of bureaucracy and located several very helpful documents.

- Paul Shea, professor of religion, who contributed the section on missionary work.

- Maxine Seller, my long-ago dissertation adviser at SUNY at Buffalo, who schooled me in the joys of historical research and writing.

- Historian Stanley Sandler, who reviewed a late draft and made numerous helpful suggestions.

- Donald Cady, Lawrence Wilson, and Mandy Rutherford at the Wesleyan Publishing House, who patiently and persistently convinced the author that their way was a better way.

- The three members of my advisory team—Katherine Lindley, Melvin Dieter, and William Brackney—who helped shape and guide the project.

- The many folks with Houghton connections who donated time for interviews—you provided about four thousand pages of transcripts, all now lodged in the Houghton archives.

- And especially the former Lois Magdalena Griffen, my sweet spouse of nearly half a century, who insisted that we make no retirement snowbird trips until the book was done.

ONE

Houghton's Story

An Overview

Prologue

M ay 22, 1972, was graduation day for the class of '72. Spring was
rounding into summer. Lilac and redbud blossoms had come and
gone, and the oaks and maples of the campus were in full leaf. On the
wide shoulder of a small plateau on the western edge of the Genesee
River, roughly half way between the Pennsylvania border to the south and
the shore of Lake Ontario to the north, the sturdy buildings of Houghton
College—many of them faced with stone reclaimed from neighboring
creeks—surrounded the neatly clipped grass of the quadrangle. Parking
lots overflowed, and the new John and Charles Wesley chapel was
packed.

Trumpeter David Johnson presented the processional, and the Rev.
Bert C. Krellar led in the invocation. Pianist Ramon Cooklis played
Prokofiev's "Sonata No. 7 in B-flat," then Illinois Congressman John
B. Anderson challenged those assembled with his answer to the question,
"How Do We Build a Christian Society?" Baritone John Thompson
rendered Corelli's "Sonata No. 9." And then it was time. Graduation time.

One by one, the men and women of the graduating class of 1972 stepped with wide grins and shimmering gowns across the chapel stage to receive leather folders containing their Houghton College diplomas. The venerable Dr. Stephen W. Paine, presiding at his final commencement, greeted them by name, a feat his carefully-cultivated, prodigious memory might well have allowed him to accomplish even without Dean Clifford W. Thomas's reading of the graduation list.

"January graduates: Robert John Batdorf, *summa cum laude,* Mary Beth Burdick, Thomas Preston Coffan . . . May graduates: Dorothy Jean Abbruzze, Wilma Jean Alessi, Judith Carol Amber . . . Peggy Colleen Iles, Robert John Illback, Calvin John Johnson . . . Larry Nimitz, Dorcas Faith Nussey, Kathleen Lois Oehrig . . . Frances Lois Woods, Roberta Ann York, Karen Ann Zimmerman . . . August graduates: Linda Louise Storms, Bradley Paul Taylor, Kathy Ann Vandenbergh." The list in the graduation program included 229 names. Almost all were present.

Honorary degrees were awarded to commencement speaker John B. Anderson; evangelist Thomas Skinner; Wesleyan pastor and Caribbean district superintendent A. Wingrove Taylor; and Houghton's own retiring business manager and treasurer, Willard G. Smith.

A century earlier, the locale for 1972's moving and thoroughly religious convocation had been a tiny hamlet known from Buffalo to Albany as the wildest, roughest spot on the entire Erie Canal system, a center of overnight rest and rowdiness for the canal-boat men. Three booming taverns stood among the meager handful of houses, and so many horse races were held on the long, straight stretch of dirt road south from the center of town that the community was known as "Jockey Street." Hundreds of dollars in bets changed hands every week, liquor flowed freely, and the major social activity seemed to be street fighting. From the early days of the Genesee Valley Canal until that waterway was shut down in 1878, it is said that there existed no more deeply sin-drenched locale in all of western New York and perhaps in all of the Empire State than Houghton Creek.

But here, in May of 1972, behold the scene: hundreds peacefully assembled for a highly moral, strongly academic, totally dry, clear-minded convocation. The initial change toward morality had taken place in less than a decade before 1883, partly due to the burgeoning railroad net, partly due to the perfectionist gospel message of the local Wesleyan Methodist church, and partly thanks to the evangelizing efforts of the Sunday school man, Willard Houghton.

And now, for retiring Dr. Paine, and for Houghton College, this graduation ceremony represented the culmination of an eighty-nine-year educational expedition and shift in community morality that began in the post-Civil War dream of the Reverend Houghton—and had roots even earlier in the history of Wesleyan Methodism, of western New York, and of America.

The Creation of Houghton College

"Where does the story of Houghton College begin?" asked one-time Houghton faculty member Kenneth Wilson in the local history he edited, *Consider the Years: Houghton College 1883–1958*, for the seventy-fifth anniversary celebration.[1] "Who, placing a finger on a date in history, can say, 'This is where it started'? For always there was something before . . ."

Because the reader exists in the present, with a memory that reaches back but a few years or decades, perhaps the place for us to start is nearer to the end of our story, with the Houghton College of 1972. Consider these words, written about another college but ringing true to Houghton readers:

> Sometimes I think of [this college] as an island, with all the island qualities: a sense that everything is connected, nothing is ever over, and everything that happens ought to be taken personally. The kind of place that, on its good days, can feel like the heart of the universe, the perfect center of a well-spent life. On other days it's simply nowhere squared: not just a small college but a small rural college, a small rural college in the Midwest, a lightly-endowed, wrist-slicingly isolated college with English roots and eastern airs, national and international aspirations, some wishful, some warranted, a college poor but proud, less conservative than old fashioned, less elitist than peculiar, not a pushy, voguish college, not this one, but a college that stands at the edge of the party and waits and waits politely, sometimes it seems like forever, to be recognized and remembered and appropriately introduced . . . A place I sometimes love, with a history that rolls like the seasons, down through the years, and moods that change like the weather.[2]

These are the words of novelist P. F. Kluge, a 1964 graduate of Kenyon College in Gambier, Ohio, who returned there in 1991 for a year as a visiting teacher of writing. Combining his teaching experience and his memories of four years as an undergraduate, he wrote *Alma Mater—A College Homecoming*. Because Kenyon is somewhat similar in size, ruralness, and

situation to Houghton College, Kluge's descriptive summary may well pro-
voke comparable images in the minds of Houghton alumni.

When Williard J. Houghton talked with Rev. D. S. Kinney in October
1882, General Robert E. Lee had surrendered his cause and his forces at
Appomattox Court House just seventeen years earlier. Now, the Wesleyan
Methodist church was trying to adjust to the loss of one of its prime focal
points (anti-slavery), to the re-defection of many members to the Methodist
Episcopal church, and to the leadership and educational needs of a denomination with but 480 churches and fewer than seventeen thousand members.
America was alive with visions of national destiny, of the marvelous opportunities in this rich and sparsely populated land. And Wesleyan Methodists
wanted to offer affordable, high-quality, Christ-centered education in a
place of unsullied isolation.

Both D. S. Kinney and Willard Houghton shared a dream for an institution that would serve local youth economically and effectively in a
morally positive environment. As Willard recorded, "We as a denomination
very much needed a school in western New York, as it was a central place
where we as a church would school our children away from the influences
[evils] of the large towns and cities."[3] The hamlet of Rev. Houghton's birth
offered such a location, the local church began a subscription drive, and the
Lockport Conference of the Wesleyan Methodist Connection endorsed the
venture. Willard Houghton's dream for the school was translated into the
motto, "Low in expense, fundamental in belief, and high in scholarship."
But as 1883 began, there was nothing at hand—no money, no land, no charter, no teachers, no students. There was, however, a clear and powerful
dream, and that dream was the beginning of the era that led to the creation
of a seminary and then a college.

In like manner, the retirement of Houghton president Dr. Stephen
W. Paine in 1972 served to conclude the era from college chartering and
accreditation by Middle States through Houghton's great expansion in
enrollment and facilities.

Note at the outset that this was an institution that changed in many ways
over the years, and not just in growth of curriculum, buildings, enrollment,
faculty credentials, and funding. Organized as an entity of the Wesleyan
Methodist Church, in its early years it was thoroughly Wesleyan from top

to bottom, even though students readily were admitted from other denominations, and it even accepted non-Christians who agreed to abide by "The Rules": at first the Prohibitions, later The Pledge, and still later the Statement of Community Responsibilities. By 1972, it was still distinctively Wesleyan above the president, and uniquely non-denominational (though still strongly evangelical) below that level. Part of Houghton's story involves the challenges faced by successive presidents to walk that Christian liberal education tightrope.

Long-time Houghton English faculty member Josephine "Doc Jo" Rickard identified these factors as the sources of Houghton's strength:

- Being permeated with the conviction that God planted the college.

- Strong leadership, particularly in the two men whose presidencies spanned sixty-four years.

- High scholastic standards, maintained through a faculty well trained with the ideals of progress. Nearly half of them [circa 1981] have doctor's degrees.

- Prayer of faculty, students, alumni, and other supporters.[4]

This book will follow the development of Houghton College through historical documents, administrative records, extracts from dissertations, and evidence from first-person accounts, material that will allow the reader to witness the growth, observe the travails and successes, and encounter some of the personalities that shaped and were shaped by the college.

Before the Founding

The Beginnings

The Beginning

W hen and where did Houghton College begin? In a legal sense, it
began in April 1883 when the Lockport Conference of the
Wesleyan Methodist Church incorporated the Houghton Seminary. But,
like any other living thing, the seminary did not spring entire from a church
resolution or some denominational board action. It had a long genesis,
stretching back almost two centuries.

In essence, the origin of Houghton College may be traced to the birth of
John Wesley in 1703 and Charles Wesley in 1707, for the Wesleys' concepts
of a faith built on the Bible and illuminated by personal regeneration and
holiness stand at Houghton's foundation. (The contributions of the Wesleys
will be developed further in the section on John and Charles Wesley.)

In another sense, Houghton began in 1842 when Orange Scott had
taken all he could from the dictatorial bishops of the Methodist Episcopal
Church, and he and a few others walked away to form the Wesleyan
Methodist Connection in 1843.[1] This spirit of independence and grass-roots
activism framed the perfectionist inspiration that led Willard Houghton to

yearn for and provide a suitable secondary-education opportunity for the youth of the church and the region.

Likewise, one might argue that the college began when Willard J. Houghton, born in 1825, surrendered his soul to his Lord and began his life-long quest to improve mankind (at least in the local area) through establishing Sunday schools and by helping to provide better education for area youth.

The historical documents record that Houghton as an educational institution began in the conversation of Willard J. Houghton and Wesleyan connectional agent Dennison Smith Kinney[2] when they met, following the re-dedication of a church in nearby Short Tract in December 1882, to discuss establishing a Christian school in western New York.

Let us consider each of these aspects: the role of John and Charles Wesley and their spiritual heirs, the early history of the Wesleyan Methodist Connection, the burgeoning secondary education movement, and—in the next chapter—the life of Willard J. Houghton.

Influence of John and Charles Wesley

John Wesley was born in Epworth, England, to the Reverend Samuel Wesley and his wife, Susanna, on June 17, 1703. The birth of his brother Charles followed in 1707. Both lads were in the younger half of the couple's children; one reference listed John as tenth of nineteen;[3] another said he was fifteenth of nineteen.[4] A current Houghton Wesley scholar reported that there were but seventeen progeny. The essential point, however, was that the boys were born into the household of a Church of England priest who was a pietist and a nonconformist. In fact, both grandfathers, John Westley (original spelling) and Samuel Annesley, were non-conformist preachers.[5] From their earliest days John and Charles were exposed to strong Biblical teaching, especially from their mother.

According to Wesley biographer A. S. Wood, "John Wesley appeared on the scene when faith and morals in England were at low ebb. For this, of course, the [Anglican] Church itself must shoulder a considerable share of the responsibility."[6] The message of the church was wrapped in formalism, in ritual, and in prayer books. Said Wood, "It was not a religion which had much appeal to the men and women living brutal and squalid lives in the disease-ridden slums of the new towns and mining villages.[7] But it was religion of which John became an active part: he studied at Oxford for five years and completed his bachelor's degree there, then was ordained as a deacon in the Anglican Church in 1725. He completed his master's work in 1727, was ordained as a priest in 1728.

In 1735, John Wesley was appointed as chaplain to James Oglethorpe, governor of the newly chartered colony of Georgia, where, as he served the "fifty poor families," he would also minister to the Indians. His younger brother Charles also journeyed in Georgia, to serve as secretary to General Oglethorpe. On the ship enroute to Georgia, John met some Moravian missionaries and learned of the Biblical standard of justification by faith and the need for personal conversion. He admired the Moravians' joy in living, peace in the face of death, and abnormal poise when facing a violent storm.[8] His disappointing and frustrating experiences during his two "missionary" years in Georgia led him to a painful awareness of his own lack of conversion.

After his return to England in 1738, John participated in a series of meetings and conversations with Moravian missionary Peter Boehler in Aldersgate. On May 24, John Wesley experienced a dramatic conversion as he surrendered to the gospel message and felt "strangely warmed"[9] as he experienced "the regenerating grace of God."[10] Following his conversion, Wesley's preaching began to center on Christ's status as the only foundation of faith and affirming that "by grace are we saved through faith."[11]

With his brother Charles, George Whitefield, and some others, John formed a small pietist-influenced group devoted to Bible reading and prayer. The members of the group, which became known as the "Holy Club" (among other, less charitable, appellations), espoused the ideas of repentance, faith, and personal salvation before a person could be sanctified, and of exercising holiness in daily living. To him, sanctification was a lifetime process built on God's sustaining and edifying love, resulting in the progressive development of a state of holiness. The methodical nature of the religious practices of John and his fellow worshipers gave rise to the term "methodism."[12]

When the Church of England limited their preaching opportunities because of their outspokenness on salvation and piety, the Wesley brothers took their ministry outside, John preaching wherever the opportunity was presented and Charles preaching and writing great hymns of revival.[13] (Despite this exclusion from Anglican churches, John Wesley "remained a Church of England man to his dying day, with a strong sense of discipline and a desire to bring about reform from within. . . . His overriding concern was for the good of souls, and where existing church order stood in his way, he did not hesitate to set it aside."[14])

Slowly, over the next three decades, the Methodist movement gained numbers and territory in England, and in 1766 Methodism spread to

America. In 1770, Wesley sent Richard Boardman and Robert Pilmore as missionaries to the American colonies, and the next year two more were appointed: Robert Willams and John King. They were followed by Francis Asbury and Richard Wright in 1771, Christopher Hopper and Joseph Benson in 1772, and Thomas Rankin and George Shadford in 1773.[15]

Methodist missionary work was somewhat sidetracked by the American Revolution, though the number of American Methodists nearly doubled from 1776 to 1781. Later, and partly due to the independence of the new American states, the Methodist Episcopal Church of America was organized in 1784. It was followed in 1787 by the establishment of the African Methodist Episcopal Church, an offshoot organized in protest to the parent church's discriminatory practices toward blacks. Then, in 1828, a second fracture occurred in the church facade: the Methodist Protestant Church was formed by persons expelled from the parent church for holding anti-episcopal sentiments.[16] Fifteen years later, another great schism led to the formation of the Wesleyan Methodist Connection.

The Wesleyan Methodist Church

Houghton College officially began in 1883 as the Houghton Wesleyan Methodist Seminary, and throughout its entire existence, Houghton Seminary and then College has been under the direction of The Wesleyan Methodist Church in its various appellations: first as the Wesleyan Methodist Connection, then the Wesleyan Methodist Church, and more recently (following its 1968 union with the Pilgrim Holiness Church, discussed in chapter 11) as The Wesleyan Church. Consequently, a review of the history of the Wesleyan Methodist Church since its creation in 1843 will enhance understanding of the development of the college.

Northern leaders of the Methodist Episcopal church of the late eighteenth century viewed slavery as the worst of moral evils. John Wesley had called it "the sum of all villainies," and Thomas Coke, regarded as the founder of American Methodism, was bitterly attacked in the South for preaching against it. The initial American Methodist Episcopal Christian Conference, held in 1784, concluded that slavery must be abolished and adopted rules requiring members who owned slaves either to free them, withdraw from the church, or face expulsion.

But Methodism's subsequent numerical growth was in the South, prompting an increasingly pro-slavery attitude within the church and a softening of denominational condemnation. In 1804, in an effort to appease the southern churches, the Methodist Episcopal rule against private church members holding slaves was rescinded, and nothing was ever enacted to replace it.[17]

By the time of the General Conference of 1808 all penalties for slave-holding among private members of the church had been erased from the denominational literature. In the place of a definitive, total church rule, decisions regarding the holding of slaves were left to each annual conference. The only restriction which remained prohibited slaveholders from holding official church positions in instances where they refused to free their slaves when state laws permitted.[18]

Noting with alarm the reversal of the anti-slavery position as defined by founder John Wesley, many Methodist Episcopal members agitated for a return to his teaching. As the abolition group within the church gained support, pressure increased on its leaders to confront the problem directly. Their refusal to do so raised the additional problem of use of episcopal power, which proved to be the proximate cause for the defection of a number of Methodist Episcopal congregations and pastors.

The episcopal structure of the Methodist Episcopal Church in America clearly showed its roots in the hierarchy of the Anglican Church and even in that church's predecessor, the Roman Catholic Church. Atop the hierarchy were the bishops, who, though different from Anglican bishops, were elected for life and held absolute power over ministerial appointments, committee assignments, and church conferences. As the division in the church over the slavery question became more pronounced in the early 1840s, the bishops used their ecclesiastical power to suppress abolitionist opposition in an effort to promote a united church and placate the southern majority.[19] Their efforts had been foreshadowed in the "advice" given by the Anglican Bishop of Bristol to John Westley, John Wesley's grandfather: "There must be a unity without divisions among us, and there can be no unity without uniformity."[20] When the anti-slavery movement developed and gained strength in the Northeast, the New York Anti-Slavery Society was formed in 1833. But the anti-slavery position, later solidified as the Abolitionist movement, was nowhere near universally accepted throughout the North, even in the anti-slavery hotbeds of New York and New England. In fact, there were twenty thousand slaves in the state of New York in 1825.[21]

According to regional historian Floyd H. Benham, "The opponents of anti-slavery in the North were not so much in favor of slavery as they were in fear of the results of open discussion of the subject, anticipating that if the issue were raised that it would result in the division of the Union."[22]

In 1836, the Methodist Episcopal bishops had formally declared that "ministers and people" must wholly "refrain from agitating this subject [abolition]." Orange Scott and his fellows were abolitionists of the most radical type and could not accept such counsel. Said Jennings,

> They could not stand against slavery without standing against episco-
> pal authority which formed the great ecclesiastical bulwark of slavery.
> The emphatic fact of this whole history is that the episcopal power in
> the Church was employed to suppress freedom to speak and write upon
> a subject which thousands regarded as a moral evil. Had a wiser course
> been pursued in this matter there is little probability that there would
> have even been a secession from the Methodist Episcopal Church.[23]

As the tension grew, some pastors and lay leaders in the Methodist Episcopal Church attempted to insert a discussion of the anti-slavery issue in the agendas of the quarterly and annual conventions of the church. But they were strongly rebuffed by the bishops, and several pastors were banned from the church for disobeying the bishops' orders by speaking against slavery and by attending anti-slavery meetings. First Orange Scott, then Jotham Horton, La Roy Sunderland, and Luther Lee withdrew from the church in November 1842.[24]

In disgust, other individuals and congregations of dissenters also withdrew from the Methodist Episcopal Church, and the leaders of the dissenters called a convention in Utica in May 1843, at which time they began the groundwork for organizing the Wesleyan Methodist Connection. A notice in *The True Wesleyan* for January 14, 1843, sounded the call to assemble: "All, both ministers and laymen, who are in favor of the formation of a Wesleyan Methodist Church, free from Episcopacy and Slavery, are invited to attend."[25] Wesleyan Methodism thus joined the roster of new groups seeking to combine "democratically methodist doctrine (individual free will) with democratically baptistic polity (congregationalism)."[26]

In a document titled "Pastoral Address of the Convention Assembled at Utica, N. Y., May 31, 1843, for the Purpose of Organizing the Wesleyan Methodist Church," a team of founders offered this thought:

> Most of those who at present compose the New Connection have
> been members of the M. E. Church, and have for years been looked
> upon as refractory children, rebelling against the lawful authority of
> our mother's family government; but this charge can no longer be

preferred against us. We are now of lawful age and have entered upon the responsibilities of a distinct community, to be governed upon principles more in accordance with our views of primitive Christianity, and we believe better adapted to the security of individual rights, and to the general development of Christian zeal and enterprise throughout the ministry and membership.[27]

The new sect was to be conducted according to a document called *The Discipline* (Wesley conceived the organization of Methodism according to a "discipline"), which cited and explained the Biblical points espoused by John Wesley. While it included most of the doctrinal points of the Methodist Episcopal Church, it emphasized three special aspects:

- Slave-holding and the buying and selling of slaves were prohibited.
- All contact with intoxicating liquors, including manufacturing, buying, selling, and using, was prohibited (with exceptions made for mechanical, chemical or medical uses).
- Ministerial and lay members, in equal numbers, were to be elected to the annual and General Conferences.[28]

The reaction of the Methodist Episcopal Church to the secession of so many individuals and congregations led to a major rethinking of its pro-slavery stance and the ill-used power of the bishops. At three Methodist Episcopal conventions in New England, anti-slavery resolutions were permitted on the agendas and adopted.[29] While this kept others from defecting, it helped trigger the split that led to the formation of the Methodist Episcopal Church in America, South, in 1844.

According to Houghton College historian Willard Smith, "The government of the new denomination was weak and decentralized, because the leaders of the Wesleyan group sought to avoid the least vestige of the episcopacy of the Methodist Episcopal Church."[30] But the vision of the Wesleyans was clear: to conduct the religious life of each cooperating church as close as possible to Biblical standards and the precepts of John Wesley.

Upon the creation of the Wesleyan Methodist Connection in America, six conferences were formed:

- The New England Conference embraced the New England states, except that portion of Vermont lying west of the Green Mountains.

- The Champlain Conference included that part of Vermont west of the Green Mountains and that part of New York State north and east of Black River and a line running from Carthage to the southwest corner of Vermont.

- The New York Conference comprised all that portion of New York not included in the Champlain Conference, and eastern Pennsylvania and New Jersey.[31]

- The Allegheny Conference included all that part of Pennsylvania west of the Allegheny Mountains, and that part of Ohio east of the Scioto River, and Western Virginia [West Virginia had not at that time been set off as a state].

- The Miami Conference included the State of Ohio west of the Scioto River, the states of Illinois and Indiana, and the Territories of Wisconsin and Iowa.

- The Michigan Conference embraced the State of Michigan.[32]

In their very first quadrennial convocation in 1844, the assembled representatives of the church approved the report of their Committee on Education.[33] Although the traditional credentials necessary to be a Wesleyan Methodist pastor were the possession of a Bible and a Divine call (and in some measure the same was true of Baptists), the committee stated:

> We allude to the cause of literature—sound, sanctified learning. While we would not make mere literature a test for ministerial calling . . . we would regard it as affording increased means of usefulness to its possessor. The world—our work especially—is demanding an educated ministry. If we cannot supply this demand, others will. . . .
>
> Our members generally . . . have learned to appreciate the benefits of education. . . . Your committee would recommend that each conference take early and vigorous measures to establish, as soon as practicable, a seminary for both sexes within its limits.

Thus, some forty years before its founding, the need for the Houghton Wesleyan Methodist Seminary had been stated. (The full text of this 1844 document appears in appendix B.)

Growth of the Wesleyan Methodist Connection was steady though not particularly rapid, and when the Civil War brought an end to formal slavery, membership took a downturn as a number of individuals and congregations returned to the Methodist Episcopal Church. One of the causes of this defection was the rejection of a proposed union with the Methodist Protestant Church, and the defectors included Luther Lee and several other founders of Wesleyan Methodism. McLeister reported church membership as 16,466 in 1848[34] and then as 15,807 in 1868 (in-between figures do not seem to be available). It climbed to 17,807 in 1879, then regressed to 16,321 in 1883 and inched upward to 16,949 in 1887.[35] One reason for the slow growth of the denomination may be deduced from a note found in the papers of denominational leader Rev. Francis R. Eddy:

> When they created the new form of [church] government . . . they transferred the emphasis from evangelism that had swept across the mountains and was sweeping across the plains, to reform . . . a moral reform and a governmental reform. They transferred the emphasis from evangelizing to save men, to legally compelling them to do things certain ways. For forty years our church did nothing but argue. They did nothing but promote reform, conducted more debates than revivals.[36]

The Holiness Movement and Perfectionism

Two hundred years into the great American experience, two forces were developing that would help to shape American education. One was the holiness movement, a key doctrinal aspect of the Wesleyan Methodist Church, and the other was the growing national belief in the perfectability of mankind.[37]

Concurrent with the flowering of the anti-slavery crusade in early nineteenth-century America was the growth of the holiness movement. The doctrine of holiness was traced to John Wesley and his adherents, who drew the concept directly from Scripture. It came to the United States via the Wesleyan revivals and gained strength through lay-led home gatherings and in camp meetings dedicated to the preaching of entire sanctification. This era also saw the beginning of a shift from sanctification as an extended process in which the individual moved towards a state of holiness, towards being an instantaneous, crisis-triggered event where sanctification was received as an immediate state. In the early nineteenth century, great revivals broke out as evangelists—including Charles G. Finney, in western New York—preached thousands to conversion. "Soon the emphasis turned to teaching the 'second blessing'—holiness and discipline—as the new nation witnessed 'the rise of the holiness revival' before the Civil War."[38]

This also lead to a time of increasing holiness social activism, with anti-slavery at its core but also encompassing women's rights, foreign missions, and action against the evils found in society. Describing this social gospel dimension of the holiness perfectionists (to whom he applied the label "ecclesiastical abolitionists"), Donald Strong said, "[They sought to bring] greater democratization [to] African Americans—and eventually to other marginalized people, such as women, Native Americans, and industrial laborers.[39]

Whitney Cross, writing in *The Burned-over District*, observed:

Across the rolling hills of western New York and along the line of DeWitt Clinton's famed canal, there stretched in the second quarter century a "psychic highway." Upon this broad belt of land congregated a people extraordinarily given to unusual religious beliefs, peculiarly devoted to the crusades aimed at the perfection of mankind and the attainment of millennial happiness.[40]

Concurrent with the blossoming of the holiness movement and the concept of personal soul freedom was the shift away from Calvinistic theology to the doctrines espoused by Jacobus Arminius. Curtiss Johnson observed,

By the early nineteenth century Calvinist ideology was incongruent with the experience of most Americans. The doctrine of election, held dear by Presbyterians, Congregationalists, and Baptists, did not fit the image most citizens had of themselves. . . . By the late 1820s universal white suffrage was a reality. Men could choose their leaders and, through representative government, establish public policy. Why, then, could they have no control over their own salvation? . . . [Through the movement toward Arminianism] thought and experience were once again brought together, and religion was revitalized.[41]

Mark A. Noll, in his introductory essay to William Ringenberg's book, *The Christian College,* offered a brief overview of the forces shaping the new nation:

In the years between the administrations of presidents Thomas Jefferson (1801–1809) and Abraham Lincoln (1861–1865), Christian values and the values of American public life joined in a popular cultural synthesis. The revolution had brought the United States into existence; its ideology of liberty provided a powerful impetus for constructing a new nation. Similarly, the Second Great Awakening [approximately 1800–1835] had witnessed the conversion of many people; its twin engines of evangelism and reform also offered means to reconstruct society. When these two influences came together—as they did so clearly for the great revivalists like Charles G. Finney, the great reformers like abolitionist Theodore Dwight Weld, the great organizers like Lyman Beecher, the great educators like Noah Webster, and the great politicians like Lincoln—the result was a singularly powerful set of cultural values which decisively shaped the character of America's Christian higher education.[42]

Robert Fletcher, in his history of the early days of Oberlin College, provided a sketch of the vision that inspired the men and women who founded secondary schools, seminaries, institutes, and colleges in the nineteenth century.

In the first half of the nineteenth century militant Protestantism saw itself marching to the conquest of America and the World. Rank on rank they advanced with flying banners: the revivalists leading the way, the missionary societies, the Bible societies and Sunday School societies, and the tract societies. Combined in the same great army and under the same staff were the anti-slavery societies, the temperance societies, the physiological reform and moral reform societies. Closely allied were the educational reformers whose task it was to train a generation for Utopia. In the heavens they saw the reflection of the glorious dawn, which was just beyond the horizon, when all men should know Christ, should serve him in body and spirit, and acknowledge their universal brotherhood.[43]

According to educational historian Frederick Rudolph, "College [and academy] founding in the nineteenth century was undertaken in the same spirit as canal-building, cotton-ginning, farming, and gold-mining. . . . All were touched by the American faith in tomorrow, in the unquestionable capacity of Americans to achieve a better world."[44] Helping to shape the environment in which institutions were founded were the post-Civil War American attributes of national ambition, democratic aspirations, regional isolation, and romantic imagination.

Rudolph went on to state the following:

Inspired by the results of the second period of religious awakening and revivalism . . . the churches looked forward to the new day when Christianity would prevail in the lives of men.

. . . The last of the denominations [to found institutions] were those with a dedicated hostility to learned clergymen . . . particularly the Methodists and Baptists.[45]"

Willard J. Houghton shared this spirit of improving individuals and through them improving America in general, and he expressed this clearly in his closing of a letter to his good friend and seminary benefactor, O. T. Higgins: "Yours for fixing up this world."[46]

Growth of Secondary Education

The American tradition, especially in the first half of the nineteenth century, was to attempt to found colleges even before adequate local secondary schools existed. Wesleyan Methodists likely shared some of this enthusiasm, but their vision leaned more toward establishing private secondary schools (often called seminaries).

Since the time of the founding of Harvard College in 1636, secondary-education institutions that would generate college students have been an important component of American life. According to educational historians,[47] the earliest American secondary school was the Latin grammar school, created in Massachusetts to prepare young men for entrance to college, where they would study theology, medicine, or law. In essence, this was an upper-class institution imported from England by the Puritans.

Because the Latin grammar school was narrowly elitist, it never achieved widespread popular enrollment or support—even as the idea served as a pattern for curricula in many academies. In contrast, members of the growing American middle class sought schools that would prepare young men for commerce and government, and this led to the development of a system of private academies. While the coursework often embraced the traditional Latin and Greek, other offerings included practical subjects such as surveying, navigation, and bookkeeping, and students were expected to master English, history, science, and mathematics. Operated most typically as boarding schools, some of these academies were highly sectarian in nature while many others were proprietary and taught whatever studies were in demand. One source reported that by 1850 there were more than 6,000 academies with total enrollment of over 250,000.[48]

Dissatisfaction with academies developed due to a number of factors: tuition charges, private control, a growing emphasis on Latin-school curriculum, admission of students at too early an age, and lack of focus on preparation for earning a living.[49] The American dream of widespread and equal educational opportunity demanded publicly-funded local secondary education, and thus began the public secondary-school movement.

While American public high schools were being organized widely in the years following the Civil War to satisfy a perceived need, their genesis was necessitated by a unique American phenomenon. On one hand, communities had long realized the importance of providing a basic education for the boys and girls who would become the workers and parents of the future, and thus since the days of the first colonists they provided district or common schools. On the other hand, the new and growing communities of the frontier embraced a philosophy of seeking the benefits of higher education and of fostering community pride and status by having a local college. This led to the founding of many small colleges. But between the two sets of institutions there was a vast educational gap: district school graduates were not ready for college, and colleges were not particularly successful with the preparatory departments they added at the edge of the colleges.

While the founders of the new public secondary schools had some idea of what they wanted to accomplish, they were not sure how to go about it. What curriculum should be offered or required? What ages should be served? How many years should students spend in the schools? As a result, public high school programs tended to copy in some measure both the Latin school curriculum and that of the private academy.[50] But the local institutions were as variegated as anything else that developed in an uncontrolled climate, and colleges soon instituted entrance exams to establish the degree of preparation of matriculating high school graduates.

A reasonable standardization of secondary school curriculum did not occur until after 1900. The first major step was through the deliberations of the Committee of Ten, a team organized by the National Education Association in 1892. The committee's report led to establishing the secondary school duration as four years and to adopting the definition of high-school courses in terms of Carnegie units of five recitations per week for an academic year. (Incidentally, the structuring of course offerings and credits in American colleges and universities only slightly preceded this same general era.)

The second major step was the development of regional accrediting associations for colleges and secondary schools. These agencies (such as the Middle States Association of Colleges and Secondary Schools, which in 1935 accredited Houghton College) were organized as cooperative regional examining and certifying bureaus for member schools and colleges. The first regional agency, the North Central Association of Colleges and

Secondary Schools, was organized in 1895 using a model created by the University of Michigan, wherein all secondary schools in Michigan were seen as branches of the university and were individually examined before being certified and "accredited." Graduates of secondary schools accredited by the regional association were accepted for college entrance.[51]

Throughout the nineteenth century, there was a growing belief that education was an essential component of many dimensions of life: scriptural understanding, moral perfection, national development, and personal achievement and success. To offer youth an opportunity to study in a good secondary school or academy, and later in a college, was a social investment, and society would be well-served through the lives of dedicated graduates. Also, for Methodists and Baptists, providing such an education was a part of "that apparently endless American process of coming to terms with an essentially middle class society."[52]

The net effect was the organization and erecting of large numbers of seminaries, union schools, and free academies in western New York and elsewhere. Citizens wanted local, high-quality education, and denominations and other agencies worked to provide these schools, but adequate funding was always a problem. It was into this milieu of marginalized academies and burgeoning but unstandardized public secondary schools that Houghton Seminary was born.

Early Academies in Western New York

Houghton Seminary came into existence some sixty-five years after the first private secondary school was established in western New York. Middlebury Academy was founded in 1817 in the hamlet of Middlebury in Genesee County (later renamed as the village of Wyoming and now in northern Wyoming County, organized in 1843). According to historian Lawrence B. Davis, Middlebury Academy was coeducational and enrolled about 150 students per year. It offered a classical education and numbered among its graduates seven college presidents, many ministers and college professors, and a number of prominent politicians. Baptists and Presbyterians vied for control of its board; other denominations were also represented. Middlebury Academy became a public secondary school in 1884 and was the ancestor of the present Wyoming Central School.[53]

The desire to provide local secondary schooling was reflected in a number of other regional attempts, including short-lived institutions in Angelica, Belfast, Centerville, Friendship, and Rushford. Some closed;

others became union schools. The institution begun in Alfred in 1836 survived to become something greater, the Alfred University of today.[54]

Another private academy, the Pike Seminary, was built even closer to Houghton. Founded in 1856, it grew from classes sponsored by Pike's four churches when a local citizen raised funds to erect a building. Initially assisted by the Genesee Conference of the Methodist Episcopal Church, the seminary came under the control of Free Will Baptists in 1859 when the Methodist group failed to provide support. Its program resembled the one that would be developed at Houghton Seminary: daily chapel exercises, weekly prayer meetings, mandatory attendance at classes, regular hours of study, weekly church attendance, and the banning of smoking, drinking, card playing, and dancing. It too produced leaders for the region, including educators, lawyers, physicians and even the future president of Stanford University, David Starr Jordan. It too maintained a non-denominational posture, encouraging all who would benefit from its curriculum and agree to abide by its rules to attend.[55]

Pike Seminary ceased to exist as a school in 1903, and the old seminary building was destroyed by fire in December 1904. A new structure built on the same site became the Pike Seminary High School, a union free school.[56] This building likewise met its demise by fire in February 1946, just as Pike was uniting with four other local districts to form Letchworth Central School.[57]

Early Wesleyan Methodist Schools

It should come as no surprise to any student of Wesleyan educational history that Houghton Seminary grew out of a strong Wesleyan educational tradition that dates from the founding of the denomination. The men who founded Methodism were well educated for their generation. John Wesley, trained at Oxford, urged his co-laboring ministers to preach education and promote learning among the laity. American Methodism leader Francis Asbury wrote that "The obstinate and ignorant oppose [education] among preachers and people, while the judicious in church and state applaud."[58] Likewise, the founders of Wesleyan Methodism were active proponents of education. The Rev. Lucius Matlack wrote in 1843:

> If our public instructions are adapted solely to the unintelligent, all other will be unprofited, and in this way the mass of society will be repelled from our altars, for the masses are intelligent . . . The promotion of intelligence, the cultivation of the mind, the cause of

literature, shall form a prominent object of effort in the Wesleyan Methodist Connection everywhere.[59]

In their book, *Conscience and Commitment: the History of the Wesleyan Methodist Church of America* (4th ed.), Ira Ford McLeister and Roy Stephen Nicholson offer the following:[60]

> The educational interests of the denomination claimed early attention, and efforts were made to provide schools for the education of the rising generation, free from the pro-slavery influence which was common to most schools of other denominations.
>
> The First General Conference heard and approved the report of the Committee on Education, which proposed as a general policy the opening of a seminary for both sexes in each annual conference, and a "Wesleyan Collegiate Institute" for literary and theological training, to be located at a suitable center. These high hopes were not realized, but they reveal a determination on the part of the Church fathers to assure the denomination of a trained and capable ministry.

Luther Lee, one of the founders of the Church, wrote:

> In this their zeal run [sic] beyond the means they could command, and there were some failures, yet there has been large success, and we believe the Wesleyan Connection has educated more persons than any other denomination, in the same time, in proportion to their number and means.[61]

While the educational focus of the Wesleyan Methodist Connection was far-sighted and commendable, the implementation of that vision suffered from a number of problems. The greatest, of course, was financing: the Wesleyan Methodists were not large in number and many were tied to the agricultural economy which suffered from regional droughts, limited access to markets, and national financial crises. Organizational problems and weak planning also led to some fiascos. Because of these factors, several early Wesleyan Methodist attempts to establish schools ended in failure.

- Dracut Seminary in Massachusetts was opened in 1844 but closed two years later.

- Royalton Academy, planned in 1845 in western New York, never even opened.

- Wesleyan Methodist Seminary in Wasioja, Minnesota, organized in 1839 under the Free-Will Baptists, passed to Wesleyan sponsorship in 1873 and closed in 1891.

- The Leoni Theological Institute and Seminary, in Michigan, was started in 1845, and a college department was introduced in 1851. The incorporation was changed in 1857 to Michigan Union College, and the school was abandoned in 1859.

- Adrian College, in Michigan, was incorporated in 1859 with one half of its self-perpetuating board of trustees composed of Wesleyan Methodists. The involvement of the Adrian College Wesleyans in the ill-fated movement for union of the Wesleyans and the Methodist Protestants in 1866 caused the Michigan Conference to discontinue its financial support. The trustees, driven by the desperate necessity for adequate funding, turned the college over to the Methodist Protestants in 1867.

- The Illinois Institute at Wheaton, Illinois, was organized about 1850, and college courses were introduced in 1855. Unable to support the school, the Illinois Conference transferred the institute in 1860 to the Congregationalists, who rechartered it as Wheaton College.

- The Wheaton Theological Seminary, the first educational project sponsored by an agency of the central denominational body, was created in 1881 when the Wesleyan Educational Society signed an agreement with Wheaton College to sponsor a theological department. This arrangement ended in 1889.[62]

Williard Smith summed the factors contributing to the failure of these school projects as primarily financial.

The colleges and Wasioja seminary engaged in the unsound practice of selling scholarships to raise money. The Panic of 1857 intensified the financial distress of Illinois Institute and the Leoni school. In two cases, Dracut seminary and Wasioja Seminary, the bad location contributed to the failure. The conferences that sponsored the various schools lacked sufficient membership to carry the financial burden and they found no effective means of gaining church-wide support. The church-union activities of the Adrian College leaders caused the withdrawal of Wesleyan support.[63]

Edmund Palmer

Traditionally, the names of Willard Houghton, James Luckey, and Stephen Paine are cited as primary individuals in the life and growth of Houghton College. But another figure deserves at least brief mention in Houghton Seminary's pre-history: one-time canal boatman and area lumberman Edmund Palmer.[64] Edmund's prayers are believed to have had an effect in helping shift the social climate at Houghton from vice and violence to temperance and morality.

Edmund was born down-river from the hamlet of Portageville, near the middle falls of the Genesee River, in 1826. By his testimony, he came under conviction at the age of eight, though he was not baptized until his later sojourn in Iowa. His father was a lumberman, and Edmund got his early waterman's training by helping his father raft logs down the Genesee to Rochester. With the opening of the Genesee Canal as a connector to the Erie Canal and the markets of Albany and New York City, Edmund became a canal-boat captain. Sensitive to the admonitions of his father, he never ran his boat on Sunday.

Later, after four years in Iowa and in Colorado and as the Civil War began, he felt his family would be safer back in New York. In the fall of 1862, Edmund, with his wife and three surviving children, returned via mule-drawn covered wagon to Allegany County. Some years later, in a camp meeting in nearby Eagle, Edmund received his baptism of the Holy Spirit, and in 1879 the Wesleyan Methodist Church gave him a license to preach.

In the eyes of Edmund and a few others, the same canal that brought economic progress to the Genesee Valley unfortunately had also opened Houghton to rowdy canal men (who wintered over when the canal froze), adding them to stagecoach drivers and herd drovers. The traffic at the three village taverns boomed. Local tradition says that Edmund Palmer one day ascended a hill overlooking Houghton Creek, where he prayed, "Let this place some day be as noted for its righteousness as it is now for its wickedness." Through his efforts as a churchman, local congregations grew in strength, and when the railroad replaced the canal in 1882, the departure of the boatmen brought a great change in the moral life of the village and helped set the stage for the organization of the seminary.

A variety of factors set the stage for opening a seminary in Houghton Creek. Willard Houghton's grand vision was the catalyst that combined Wesleyan Methodist theological tradition, the village's remoteness from negative urban influences, access via the newly established railroad, site availability, and the craving of western New Yorkers for affordable and careful secondary education. With the granting of a charter in 1883, the little vessel of education was launched.

On This
Solid Rock

Willard J. Houghton

Anyone who has attended a fire safety lecture knows that three ingredients are needed to start a blaze: fuel, oxygen, and an ignition source. Similarly, any gardener must combine a proper environment of soil, water, and air with well-planted seed if he is to grow a good crop.

Both metaphors may be used to enhance our understanding of the immediate pre-history of the Houghton Wesleyan Methodist Seminary. The people of the community of Houghton Creek and its surrounding lands and their religious proclivities provided the fertile (or combustible) environment, while Willard J. Houghton, the seed-planter for the seminary, was the "ignition source." Let us consider them in turn.

The Houghton Environment

John Minard, author of *Allegany County and Its People: A Centennial History 1795–1895*, has been identified as the source of the following essay from a Rochester newspaper shortly after the start of the twentieth century. It is offered here in its entirety because it provides an interesting depiction of "Houghton in Days of Yore" and introduces the reader to Willard J. Houghton.[1]

The writing style is quite reminisencent of the lexicon and patterns used in the era when Houghton Seminary was founded.

About 1817, Luther Houghton, a typical Yankee, from the Green Mountain state, settled in the southeast part of Caneadea, Allegany County, N.Y., with his family, which consisted, in part, of three sons, whose names were Warren, Leonard and Luther, the last two being twins [born in 1797]. The boys married and settled in the immediate neighborhood. The sons of Leonard were Samuel, Willard J. [born in 1825], Stephen W. and James. The place of their settlement was almost directly opposite the historic old Indian village of Gaoyadeo, or Caneadea, for long years the "western door" of the Long House of the Iroquois Confederacy, and was then a town of considerable importance in the Seneca nation.

The relations of the Houghtons with the Senecas were most friendly. Their log cabins were always open to their red neighbors across the river, and they were always welcome to the huts or council house of the Indians. Shongo, Hudson, Big Kettle, Long Beard and others less-noted often shared their hospitality, and occasionally they were visited by such celebrities as Red Jacket, Governor Blacksnake and Cornplanter. On occasions of Thanksgiving or Christmas shooting matches or "turkey shoots," the old Indian village furnished marksmen who made it interesting for their white neighbors, and a good share of the bird trophies found their way over the river, and on occasions of green corn dances, or their annual festival, when the white dog was burned, the Houghtons were always welcome visitors.

Distilleries went up along the valley, at which the Indians could trade their corn for their favorite snick-e-l (whisky) and some of the white man's corn was disposed of in like manner. Wayside inns, the first of course of logs, became frequent along all the main roads, and in a short time three were located in the immediate neighborhood of the Houghtons, all within a distance of half a mile.

Liquors, of course, were sold at all these places, and the settlers of the vicinity were in the habit of visiting them to take a social drink with their neighbors. On the long winter evenings, in the cheerful light of the crackling fire in the old-fashioned fireplace, they would gather and crack jokes, sing songs, tell stories, do tricks, and sometimes the revelry would be extended far into the night. Everybody, even the clergymen, drank, and if one was found who did not, he was a subject for unfavorable comment. It was not long before the place became noted as a resort for horse traders and jockeys and offering the longest straight stretch of road anywhere about, horse racing became frequent, and so, very naturally the place took the name of "Jockey street."

The Houghtons were not immune to the drink habit, though perhaps with a single exception, they were not known to drink to excess, as excess was regarded in those times. Sam Houghton, as he was called, was known by all far and near, to possess rare qualities at the bowl and a capacity for enduring treats, which was considered truly marvelous. In that particular respect, he was the acknowledged champion of the whole region, he was indeed par excellence, unapproached and unapproachable, and it was a delight to others, even to the few who were averse to drinking, to survey his countenance, and witness the inexpressively felicitous and appealing smile which would illumine his features when some free-hearted fellow was about to stand a treat; and it would have taken a heart of adamant to refuse to ask him to drink.

Sam knew all those from "down North," Rochester and other places, who occasionally passed through, such as the drovers, peddlers, mail carriers and stage drivers, none of whom could pass through the place without seeing him, for he was always visible and so became an institution so to speak peculiar to "Jockey street."

The construction of the Genesee Valley canal [starting in 1836] which passed through the place, brought with others, an influx of toughs who did much of their drinking at "Jockey street," and helped largely to create tumult.

The Sundays were dedicated to horse racing, card playing, drinking and fighting, and bloody noses and blackened eyes were familiar sights in "Jockey street." When the canal was completed and opened [in 1851 as far as Oramel; in 1856 to Olean], "Jockey street" became the winter quarters of a number of boatmen, who would tie up their boats at the place, which circumstance added not a little to the conviviality and increased perceptibly the number of fights and amount of disorder.

Finally, to crown the whole list of iniquities for which the place had become noted, a gang of counterfeiters made their headquarters there, or at least such was popularly claimed to be the case.

Willard J. Houghton, whose name has now become a household word in the Wesleyan church, was a brother next younger to Sam. Willard for a period danced. He liked to "trip the light fantastic toe," and those still linger, including the writer, who mingled with him in the "giddy mazes of the dance," to the bewitching music of Bona DeRock's violin, or Benson's "Full Band," which consisted of Geo., ex-clown and all-around circus man, and song-singer, and his brother Isaac, the gunmaker, all of Hume. On one Fourth of July occasion, while they were "cutting it down" to the best of their ability, the ball-room floor gave way and they went down with it. Willard was one who went down. But Willard had a finer sense of the proprieties than most of his associates, and tho it must be admitted, that he was occasionally a little "frisky," he was never known to overstep the bounds of good-hearted and good-natured jollity, with possibly a single exception.

There came a time, however, when Willard became convinced that the horse-racing, especially Sunday racing, card playing, drinking, and other practices for which "Jockey street" had become so distinguished, were wrong, and he set about a reform in those directions. Many years before, good old Elder Ephriam Sanford, he of the bearskin cap and buckskin coat and trousers, had in his quaint way expounded the gospel truths at Suckerville and Ewersville (places nearby to the south, now Caneadea and Oramel), and Rev. John Watson, the leading dissenter in all these parts, from the old Methodist Episcopal church, and one of the pioneer Wesleyan preachers, had occasionally discoursed in the "Jockey street" schoolhouse.

Good seed had been sown in good soil, and though perhaps a little tardy in germinating, the roots had taken a stronger hold. Willard decided to make a public profession of religion [in 1851], join the church of his choice, which was the Wesleyan Methodist, and lead a better life.

He was not an educated man, but by diligent study and careful reading of the Scriptures and religious books and papers, he qualified himself for a highly successful career as a Sunday-school worker, became an exhorter, and after a time began to preach. He visited the school houses for miles around, organized and conducted Sunday schools, and had stated times and places for preaching, all the while extending his acquaintance, not only with preachers of his own denomination, but of others as well. One day in October, 1882, Rev. D. S. Kinney, one of the leading preachers of the Wesleyan Methodist church, and then agent of its publishing house at Syracuse, remarked to Mr. Houghton: "We as a denomination very much need a school in Western New York."

This agreed exactly with Mr. Houghton's ideas in regard to the matter, and he at once determined to be first in the field to accomplish this desirable object. So effective were his labors that by the next February, the necessary funds to warrant the first steps towards incorporation were secured, and in the following April the articles of incorporation were filed in Albany.

Willard J. Houghton, the Sunday School Man

Willard Houghton, born in the village of Houghton Creek on July 19, 1825, was a descendant of the original river-valley family whose name became attached to the little settlement where they lived. The arrival of the family was reported in Beers's *History of Allegany County:*

In 1817, Luther Houghton move in from Centreville, and located in the northwest part of the town [Caneadea] near the river. His family consisted of a wife and four sons and one daughter. They were originally from Linden, Caledonia county, Vt., and settled in Centreville six years before.[2]

Sources such as Minard (above) and Smith (below) indicate that Willard was a sturdy post-frontier farmer, given to enjoying his labors as well as the limited social life the community presented. Typically, in the early era, one building served jointly as school house, community center, and church building. While the local church was in many ways a highly constraining institution, the local congregation nevertheless offered in its regular assemblies one of the few social focal points for the community, and anyone submitting (even in modest measure) to its strictures opened the gates of its fellowship. Though there is little documentation to suggest great religious involvement on Willard's part before 1851, it must be presumed that he was quite aware of the local church and its events. It was not until a more mature point in his life that Willard truly fell under the power of the gospel and began what would be a remarkable crusade for a man of such limited education.

Willard G. Smith provided a verbal sketch of Willard Houghton via a Houghton College chapel talk he presented in April 1958.

The life and labors of Willard J. Houghton, the Sunday School man, is evidence of the telling force of the Gospel of our Lord Jesus Christ at work in and through a human instrumentality. His boyhood days were colored by the impact of the Gospel message. Religious services held by itinerant preachers in the Houghton Creek school house resulted in his conversion at the age of thirteen. However, the temptations of youth overwhelmed him and he lost his spiritual foothold. It was in the winter of 1851, when a young farmer of twenty-five years of age, that Willard Houghton came to know God as a transforming and compelling force in his life. Though untrained, the spirit-filled and God-possessed man set out on forty-five years of far-reaching service for the Lord.

Almost immediately he identified himself with the Lord's work by joining the small Wesleyan Methodist group of the Houghton Creek circuit in 1852. He continued his membership with this church throughout his life and contributed effectively to the development of the church. Until 1876 the services of this group were held in the Caneadea District #6 school house. However, through his personal canvass of the Houghton Creek neighborhood, Willard J. Houghton secured pledges of work, lumber, and standing timber which resulted in the building of the first church edifice in Houghton. This building, now the West portion of the college recreation hall [demolished in May 1989], was dedicated in December of 1876.

His spiritual awakening in 1851 started Willard J. Houghton on a life of service which is remarkable to behold. He was possessed by a burning zeal for the spiritual welfare of children and young people. This zeal was manifested at first by work in the founding and building of Sunday Schools. This Sunday School activity absorbed all the time he could spare from the farm. By 1868, he had organized twelve Sunday Schools within a radius of about twenty miles of Houghton.

One of the hallmarks of Willard J. Houghton's Sunday School work was the attractively decorated scripture text cards. Thousands of these cards were distributed to children who cherished them and read them and through memorization wrote these choice portions of the Word of God on the tablets of their hearts. Wherever Willard Houghton went in his Sunday School and revival work, children eagerly anticipated these colorful scripture text cards.

The technique which Willard J. Houghton used in forming a Sunday School in an unchurched area reveals some basic reasons for his success. He would visit from house to house urging people to come and bring their children to Sunday School. Very tactfully and kindly he tried to disarm people of prejudice against the Sunday School and to fill them with concern over the welfare of their children. In one case a reporter sent to the *Wesleyan Methodist* the following statement: "The honest hearty manner in which his invitation was given brought nearly the whole neighborhood out at the appointed time and a large Sunday School was organized." Not infrequently some very poor people could not send their children to Sunday School in cold weather for lack of shoes. Willard Houghton would somehow get shoes for the children, and another family became regular attendants.

Willard Houghton possessed a compassionate sympathy for children and youth. This endeared him to them and resulted in many conversions. In fact the main focus of his Sunday School effort was on the personal salvation of the children and youth. His emphasis in exhorting older people to join him in Sunday School work was on the importance of keeping the Gospel message simple and clear so children could understand and believe. The point was aptly expressed in his own words: "We don't want to get the feed too high on the rack for the lambs."

Illustrative of the interest which Mr. Houghton had in children is the following incident related by a pastor serving his first appointment:

> [We] were driving along a public road. The horse was traveling at a good pace when Brother Houghton suddenly and imperatively called out, 'Whoa.' The animal stopped and he sprang out, and running around to the opposite side of the roadway, climbed the bank where a couple of little children were standing. He placed in their hands some pretty (scripture text) cards, (offered prayer over them), and returned to the carriage.

The ever widening circle of Willard Houghton's ministry as a Christian layman took him out of the confines of his community to other counties and other states. By the late 1870s he was receiving many calls to help with Sunday School projects and church revival efforts. In 1883, Mr. Houghton felt God's call to give up farming and to give full-time to the work of the Lord. For the next eleven years his labor was primarily concerned with promoting the work of Houghton Seminary. However, his Sunday School and revival efforts continued in importance as revealed by the numerous reports published in the *Wesleyan Methodist*.

Though broken in health, Willard Houghton spent the last months of his life in vigorous revival efforts. His zeal for the work of the Lord, his compassionate interest in children and youth drove him to forty weeks of meetings during his last year on earth. Seven days before he died, he wrote to a friend as follows: "The time will soon come that I shall have to stop . . . but wherever I go I expect to keep at work as there will be plenty of time to rest when we reach the land of perpetual youth."

Willard J. Houghton's expectation of keeping at work till the end was realized. On the last day (Sunday) before the stroke which took his life, he attended morning church service, the Sunday School at which he talked to the children, a 4:00 p.m. holiness rally at which he gave a message, the evening church service where he gave a short impromptu exhortation, and a conference meeting following the service. With the close of this busy day spent in service glorifying to this Lord, the beloved Sunday School man, the lay evangelist of the hill country, the founder of Houghton College had completed his labors and was called to his abundant heavenly reward.[3]

In 1846 Willard married Harriet Wilson and to them were born four daughters (Emily, Jeanette, Ella, and Blanche) and one son, Leonard F. Houghton. Leonard was described as "a Methodist local preacher and a man of excellent business ability," and in 1880 he owned a national bank in Illinois.[4] Upon Willard's death, Leonard received as a bequest much of the land where the current Houghton College campus stands. His daughter, Jennie Cudworth, was a major funder of the college library, named for her father.[5]

Willard's dedication to serving the youth of the area, both through Sunday schools and through the good secondary education that his seminary could and did offer, fired him with a consuming zeal. In a letter written in 1878, he said, "It is hard to bend the old oaks but the tender twigs may be straightened. . . . This is the only hope of the future of our country."[6] Toward this end, he solicited and collected funds for Sunday school work and later for Houghton Wesleyan Methodist Seminary. In a thank-you letter to one faithful supporter, he said, "May God reward you abundantly for your liberal help in this great work of reforming the world."[7] And he knew that church building and seminary building required a strong team effort: "We told them if all would pull together we thought they might arise and build and honor God and themselves and leave a blessing for generations to come."[8]

Willard Houghton's conversion in the community's little schoolhouse also slowly produced a significant change in the area as his influence spread. The wild and wooly Houghton of the old canal days first began to improve after the railroad supplanted the canal and the rowdier elements no longer stayed for extended periods in Houghton. By example and precept, Willard Houghton and his fellow worshipers in the tiny Wesleyan Methodist Church helped change that atmosphere to one of peace and godliness. The area Sunday School Concerts that he organized, events in which the children were the sole participants, attracted families for miles around.[9]

Feeling that he was definitely called to the ministry, Willard accepted a pastorate at Phillips Creek (between Belmont and Alfred) and later one at Short Tract, the childhood home of the man who would later become President J. S. Luckey. The effect of Mr. Houghton's work was received with such warm regard that eventually he was called to serve as an itinerant preacher, and in his travels he organized many Sunday Schools.[10]

One of Willard's great concerns around 1880 was the nearly defunct congregation and decrepit building of the Short Tract Wesleyan Methodist Church. His ardent engagement of the situation, including fund-raising and flock-developing, led to a new church building and a reinvigorated congregation. To celebrate the turnaround, a rededication was planned, and the Reverend Dennison S. Kinney was called to preach the dedicatory sermon. This service turned out to be of special significance for the future Houghton Wesleyan Methodist Seminary, for Rev. Kinney took Willard aside and laid on his heart a special project.

(It is an interesting sidenote that Rev. D. S. Kinney had labored for a number of years in the arch-conservative Allegheny Conference before assuming the post of Connectional Agent. One might presume that he favored a strictly-controlled school with little potential of service to students from other, more liberal denominations.)

In a letter to his friend Orrin T. Higgins, Willard reported the discussion that led to the establishing of Houghton Wesleyan Seminary:

At the dedication of the new church [building] at Short Tract last December 5, 1882, the Rev. D. S. Kinney of Syracuse who is Connectional Agent and also Treasurer of the Wesleyan Educational Society of the Connection, said to me that the Society was about to plant a first-class seminary in these parts to accommodate the children of our people, especially for Western New York and Northern Pennsylvania and that he had already in his hands a partial endowment for such a school and that they wished to put it by the side of the railroad, easy to get to and from. Said the school must be run on strict moral and reformatory principles, taking the Bible for the standard.[11]

Though modern Houghton students may regard Houghton ironically as a "reformatory school" (in terms of the expectations for embracing the constraints of pious behavior), in that era the word implied an institution that would be a factor in reforming mankind and uplifting the nation. Willard was among those who believed that if all men could make an indwelling love of God the basis of their daily existence, the world would have to be a better place.[12]

He expressed this conviction early in his Christian life, saying in an 1865 letter to a friend: "What a blessed world we would have if all men were Bible Christians and had the great principles of supreme love to God and love to their fellow men established in their soul [as] the fountain of moral actions."[13] He reiterated the thought in another letter in 1881: "We Wesleyans as a reform church are letting our lights shine very clearly on the dangerous places, exposing the rocks and sandbars that the masses are striking."[14]

The hamlet of Houghton Creek offered very little in the way of business or accommodations. According to the local pastor, "The village in 1884 was composed of about a score of buildings: a store where no tobacco was sold, a temperance hotel, a church, a cheese factory, a blacksmith shop, and fourteen dwelling houses."[15] That meant that the new seminary would require a new and rather large building.

The original building proposal involved a structure that would hold 200 students, but in a letter written a month before the charter application was submitted, Willard mentioned a capacity of 250. He (and perhaps others) had originally envisioned a wooden structure, but conference pastors who were asked to take a hand in the effort said that it would not be easy to endow a wooden building. One constraint probably was apprehension regarding the number of wooden structures being destroyed by fire. Consequently, the decision was to use brick, and there was clay of sufficient quality near the site so bricks could be made locally. A brick maker was brought in from Syracuse, and the report from the construction crew indicated that the bricks he produced were of a quality equal to any in New York State.[16]

Willard described the main structure as to be "about sixty by seventy feet, with some basement eight feet deep and two story of bricks above," with interior ceiling heights of fourteen feet.[17] Old photos of the seminary building show a roughly square structure with projections of about eight feet in the middle of each side and a modest tower on the front. This design probably helped strengthen the foundation as well as allow more light in middle rooms. The builder's hope was to have the structure enclosed by the time snow flew and to continue interior work as temperatures and finances permitted. Though the building was not completely finished by September 1884, work was far enough along to allow the first students to begin classes in a bare-bones environment.

When the seminary opened for business in 1884, Willard's name appeared on the letterhead as the school's agent or fund-raiser. But his efforts went well beyond seeking money: he also worked aggressively to draw students to the new seminary, and he labored equally hard to attract new residents, believing that a growing community of believers would inspire village and seminary in a positive way.

The Rev. James E. Tiffany was pastor of the local Wesleyan Methodist church in the 1880s. Of Willard Houghton, Tiffany wrote, "I found him full of enthusiasm and zeal for the success of the Seminary and exceedingly optimistic as to its success. He related how the Lord had given him a vision of it in a dream, and told him what to do to secure the success of the undertaking."[18]

Roberta Molyneaux Grange (a 1929 alumna and author of a six-volume journal[19]) told of her mother's difficult days as a young student at Houghton Seminary and how her father moved to a farm south of town to place his brood closer to a good education. The Molyneaux family, which arrived after Willard's death, had its relocation memorialized on a local sandstone monument:

J. Robert Molyneaux and Pearl Ingersoll Molyneaux . . . moved to Houghton, New York, from Sullivan County, Pennsylvania, in the year 1912 to provide an education for their six children, all of whom attended Houghton Seminary and Houghton College between the years 1912 and 1936.[20]

One contemporary expression of a later era was "It's better to wear out than to rust out." Willard Houghton in no way rusted out. He spent his later years in a vigorous, health-battering effort to bring the seminary into existence and to put it on a solid financial foundation. His good friend Arthur T. Jennings, editor of *The Wesleyan Methodist*, characterized the Houghton seminary's founder thus at his funeral:

> [Willard's] spirit of devotion to God and the good of men, his irreproachable purity and sincerity, his cheerful and utter self-denial, his perfect consecration, his holy boldness, his faithfulness to the word . . . these spiritual qualities made him a man of power and gave him success in his high calling.[21]

Willard retired from service to the seminary in 1894 due to exhaustion and declining health, but he kept active in church work. His biographer reports that he conducted forty weeks of meetings in his final year, and, as Willard Smith reported, he spent even his last earthly day in church work. Willard J. Houghton died April 21, 1896.

At Houghton's centennial, author Kenneth Wilson said, "The man no one could have imagined to be a college founder, produced by a village no one would have thought to be a college town, carried through."[22] In terms of vision, spirituality, and dogged effort, Willard Houghton cast himself as the footer upon which his "moral lighthouse" was erected.

The Early Days

1883–1908

The bulk of this chapter is drawn directly from the unpublished doctoral dissertation of Willard G. Smith, The History of Church-Controlled Colleges in the Wesleyan Methodist Church *(New York University, 1951), pages 98–116, and the endnotes include all of his original footnotes. This excerpt is used with the author's permission. Tables cited in the text are appended to this chapter.*

Houghton College, Houghton, New York

The school at Houghton was established largely through the interest and labors of a humble, uneducated layman, Willard J. Houghton. Because of his intense activity in the establishing of Sunday Schools in the rural area within a radius of about twenty miles of the hamlet of Houghton, he had acquired the affectionate title of "the Sunday School man." Also, he took particular delight in giving new life to run-down churches. [As mentioned in chapter 3] it was at a rededication of such a church at Short Tract, New York, a community near his home at Houghton, that the idea of a school began to take form.

The officiating clergyman at this dedication service, on December 5, 1882,[1] was the Rev. D. S. Kinney, the publishing agent of the Wesleyan Methodist Church and the treasurer of the Wesleyan Educational Society. It was during the night following this service that Willard J. Houghton and D. S. Kinney, who were rooming together, began the deliberations which resulted in the founding of Houghton Seminary. The gist of their discussion was recorded by Willard J. Houghton:

> [Rev. D. S. Kinney] stated to me that we as a denomination very much needed a school in Western N. Y. as it would be a central place whare [sic] we as a church could school our children away from the environments of the large towns and cities. Also said that Houghton would be a good place as it was free from the evils of the larger towns and cities. Also said that if I would take hold of the work he would do all that he could to put an endowment on it. So as to make it easey [sic] for the poor and an object for our people to send there [sic] children from a distance to their own Christian school.[2]

Kinney's interest in developing a school in western New York may have been grounded in his own experience as a faculty member at coeducational Michigan Union College (Leoni) in the 1880s.[3] This experience affirmed the importance and benefits of advanced education for Christian youth. Another dimension of his relation to the new institution was that he had served as president of the Allegheny Conference, which, though growing ever more conservative, was interested in educational matters.

In the weeks following this initial discussion, there was "much prayer and consultation"[4] with the officials of the denomination and others. In an effort to crystallize the proposals, Willard J. Houghton wrote to every preacher in the Lockport Conference, within the bounds of which Houghton, N. Y. was located, inviting them "to meet at the Houghton Creek Church Feb. 1, 1883 to consider this matter."[5] The group which assembled "agreed to stand by and help on the work"[6] and asked Willard J. Houghton to begin a canvass of funds in the vicinity of Houghton, with the understanding that a school would be located there if interest was expressed by sufficient contributions.

Organization and Opening

On February 3, 1883, the "first subscription was taken in the Houghton Church."[7] After about a month of effort within a radius of five miles of Houghton, the subscriptions totalled about one thousand dollars.[8] The executive board of the Wesleyan Educational Society met on February 15, 1883 and considered the proposal for this school. They took action appointing their president and treasurer to "aid in the organization of the board of trustees . . . (and) see to it that the land is properly deeded so that it cannot be alienated from our connection."[9] In a personal letter on March 5, 1883, Willard J. Houghton reported that the subscription totaled $6,600, *including* the eleven acres of land which had been donated as a building site.[10] The official existence of Houghton Wesleyan Methodist Seminary started with the completion of incorporation papers in April, 1883.[11] The charter document was signed April 21, 1883 and approved May 7, 1883.[12]

Building operations were started in April of the same year. The structure was a two-story building with full basement, which was intended to provide instructional facilities for about two hundred students. There was a crop failure in the summer of 1883. Since most of the people who had pledged to the support of the school project at Houghton were farmers, this failure was a serious threat to the building fund. But the General Conference of the Wesleyan Methodist Church, which met in October, "lifted the cloud" by a cash subscription of more than eight hundred dollars.[13] On August 20, 1883 the building was dedicated "to God and the cause of sanctified education."[14] Up to that time there had been twelve thousand dollars expended on the building.

Even though the building was not fully completed, school opened on September 15, 1884,[15] with a staff including a principal and three teachers[16] and with "from seventy to eighty scholars."[17] Instruction was offered on both high school and elementary levels. Definite assurance was given to the Wesleyan constituency that instruction at Houghton Seminary would "combine moral and mental culture."[18]

In summing up the struggles and hard work which made possible the opening of the school at Houghton, Willard J. Houghton stated: "Time would fail to speak of the many interesting Providences connected in the planting of this school. Heaven seemed to smil [*sic*] upon it from the begining [*sic*]."[19] The instances of Willard J. Houghton's devotion to the school project is suggested in an excerpt from one of his letters written December 16, 1884:

I have lifted and lifted, runn [*sic*] and runn [*sic*] night and day untill [*sic*] it seems to me that I shall die. . . . Please remember me in your prayers. And pray especialy [*sic*] for our school work. I had rather die than to have that stop. For this will go on benefiting [*sic*] the world after we have all gon [*sic*] to the Fathers.[20]

When Houghton Seminary began its corporate existence, the trustees appointed Willard J. Houghton, agent. During the period from April 12, 1883 to June 15, 1887,[21] he collected $11,822.22 in cash.[22] Although the trustees agreed to pay him five hundred dollars a year, Mr. Houghton took almost no pay, having contributed $2,510 to the school in services and expenses during the four years, which sum was not included in the above total.[23]

The First Twenty-Four Years, 1884–1908

For several years after the opening of the Seminary in 1884, the work was handicapped because the facilities were not completed. A year after the dedication, the basement and upper story of the building were still unfinished.[24] A furnace was not installed until 1891,[25] and the first blackboards were placed in the classrooms in 1898.[26] The work in science was carried on with practically no equipment until 1899. At that time, Leonard F. Houghton, a son of the founder of the school, gave sufficient money to equip a "chemical room."[27] In the same year, the principal, A. R. Dodd, sent out a general appeal for contributions to an "apparatus fund."[28] The contributions received were sufficient in 1906 to purchase surveying instruments and five new microscopes "in addition to the one we already have."[29]

The library of the Seminary was inadequate. In 1900, it was described as a small collection with few books "really necessary to a high school or college library."[30] As a means of organized cooperation in the improvement of the library, the Willard Houghton Memorial Library Association was formed in June, 1900.[31] Meetings of the association were held annually and its membership included individuals who contributed each year to the library fund. The treasurer's book recorded contributions totaling $1,098.35 from June, 1900 through June 1908.[32]

So much of the eleven acres of land in the original building site was in the hill side at the edge of the small plateau that there was not sufficient space for the addition of any major buildings. Therefore when the need arose for additional buildings, the Wesleyan Educational Society voted in 1902 "to purchase new grounds at Houghton and to proceed at once to the erection of a new building for the school as well as for the girls dormitory."[33] The land in and around a new fifteen-acre campus site was carefully laid out in lots and streets.

By May, 1903, "sheds for the new brick making plant" were up and work was "moving along slowly" in the manufacture of bricks from the clay soil at the rear of the new campus area.[34] There was considerable difficulty with the brick-making project, which resulted in the resignation of the first superintendent of the job in August, 1903.[35] Although the original plans had been to begin building at once, it was not until the spring of 1905 that "ground was broken for the new college building" (Jennings Hall, also known as Old Admin and now the re-sited Fancher Hall.)[36] Construction progressed sufficiently to hold the Commencement exercises of June, 1906 in the third floor auditorium. In the spring of 1906, construction began on a ladies' dormitory and as when this was completed a president's home was built.[37]

An examination of the catalogs of Houghton Seminary from 1893 (the first one available) through 1908 revealed that the school was primarily a private academy or high school. From 1886 through 1899, there were three basic curricula in the academic department: the "Classical Preparatory," including both Latin and Greek; the "Latin Scientific," replacing Greek with certain science courses; and the "English Course," a two-year sequence for individuals not prepared to enter the other courses. From 1886 through 1895, there was a "Commercial and Business Course." This was again introduced in 1905–1906. A two-year elementary teachers' training course was listed from 1893 through 1903. Regular instruction in music was not introduced until the school year 1906–1907.

Action was taken in June 1899 by the church board "to raise Houghton Seminary to the grade of the college as soon as the conditions of the Seminary will warrant such action."[38] The first college course was listed in the catalog announcements for the school year 1899–1900. This four-year course leading to a diploma continued to appear in subsequent catalogs during the remainder of this period (through 1908).

A "Bible Training Class" was started in September, 1888,[39] although formal action of the Wesleyan Educational Society was not secured until June, 1890.[40] The "Historical Notes" in the front of the record book of this department gave the facts about the founding of this program:

> The Houghton Wesleyan Methodist Seminary, having called together a number of students who wished to pursue theological studies, Rev. W. J. Houghton, then agent of the Seminary, devised

a plan for the opening for such students of a Bible Training Class, securing the funds for their tuition in Seminary studies, and engaged Rev. B. S. Laughlin, pastor of Houghton Church as the teacher of this class, who performed this double work for a number of years, until the work having developed on his hands, a demand arose for a more extended provision for this class of students, when Houghton Seminary Board of trustees petitioned the Wesleyan Educational Society to take the matter in hand and provide for this growing necessity. This call following as it did the discontinuance of Wheaton Theological Seminary, led the Educational Society in its annual meeting of its Board of Trustees, June 27, 1890 to found Houghton Bible Training School. . . .[41]

By action of the Wesleyan Educational Society in 1895, the official name of the "Bible training" part of the Seminary was changed to "the Bible Training Department."[42] Four years were required to complete the course of study until the school year 1895–1896, when the English Bible course was shortened to three years. The entire course of study for the school year 1899–1900 was shortened to three years. The catalog announcements for 1904–1905 introduced a three-year elementary theological course for individuals not qualified to pursue the advanced work. Students training for the ministry received free tuition and signed a pledge promising "in case they fail to devote their lives to the Christian ministry . . . to pay the full amount of tuition."[43]

The chief administrative officer of Houghton Seminary was a principal until June, 1894, when the title was changed to "president."[44] The principals and presidents carried regular teaching loads along with their administrative duties, with the exception of Silas W. Bond, who during his last year in office, was "in the field nearly all of the time."[45] With the exception of the shift in administrative officers at the end of the Rev. E. W. Bruce's principalship, the change took place during the summer months. At the executive committee meeting of the trustees of the Seminary on December 4, 1893, action was taken offering the "Rev. J. R. Hodges the principalship of the school the remainder of the year at the rate of $600 a year and the use of the house and garden additional."[46] After serving "only a few days,"[47] he presented his resignation, which was accepted by the executive committee of the trustees, who voted to pay him thirty-one dollars for his "services while principal." At the same meeting on January 3, 1894, action was taken "that J. S. Luckey be requested to act as principal of the school the remainder of the present term

at his present salary of $400 per year."[48] J. R. Hodges had accepted appoint-
ment in response to considerable personal solicitation and pressure.
However, after some reflection, he concluded that as a matter of conscience
he could not give up the ministry.[49] Silas W. Bond, who followed James S.
Luckey as president, resigned in 1908 to become educational secretary of
the Wesleyan Methodist Church.[50] (The administrative officers of Houghton
Seminary and their terms of service are presented in Table 1.)

During the time from 1884 through June, 1908, forty-eight different
individuals served on the instructional staff of the Seminary. Of this number, nineteen were men and twenty-nine, women. Nine of the teachers
were ordained ministers. The size of the staff averaged between six and
seven members, the smallest being four members in 1884–1885 and the
largest, eleven in 1907–1908. The academic preparation of the staff is
suggested by the following: only eight members held degrees, six having
Master of Arts and two Bachelor of Arts; fifteen members of the staff
were Houghton Seminary graduates, who were retained as teachers. There
was a frequent turn-over in staff. The average term of service of teachers
was only three years. (The distribution of terms of service are presented
in Table 2.)

Complete records could not be found on the salaries paid to the
Houghton Seminary teachers during the beginning period of the school's
history (1884–1908). In 1887, the executive committee of the trustees voted
salaries which included $800 for the principal and from $275 to $500 per
school year for the teachers.[51] These salaries were in line with the other
offers recorded until 1908. However, the scarcity of funds resulted in the
failure to pay the projected salaries. (The distribution of salaries offered to
teachers is presented in Table 3. The average annual payments to teachers
are presented in Table 4).

John S. Willett, first graduate of the college department of Houghton
Seminary and later editor of the *Wesleyan Methodist* and agent for the
Wesleyan Methodist Church, wrote a letter in 1904 in which he pointed out
the sacrificial service of the Houghton teachers.

> Possibly the church at large does not realize the sacrifice which our
> little band of teachers is making. But we who know them know that
> men connected with the public schools, no better qualified than they
> and doing no more work, are receiving three or four times the salary.
> Yet they make this sacrifice willingly for the church they love.[52]

A significant event in the early years of the school's history was the death of Willard J. Houghton on April 21, 1896.[53]

Single handed and alone our dear lamented brother traveled from conference to conference, from church to church in the west and in the east, securing cheap conveyance, and refusing to take a sleeper because of the expense; he would rather forego the comfort of the needed rest than spend the hard earned trifle to secure his own ease, in order to obtain the means with which to build the seminary; and for eleven years he kept up this strain upon his constitution in the interests of the school . . . There would never have been any Houghton Seminary had it not been for the self-sacrificing devotion of our departed brother. He was the financial agent for years, and secured upwards of $20,000 in sums from a nickel up to $100.[54]

The student body of the Seminary doubled in the first twenty-four years. Because of the changes in the division of the school year, the registration statistics are not in the same form for the entire period. From the beginning through the school year 1894–1895, the year was divided into three twelve-week terms; from the school year 1895–1896 through 1898–1899, four nine-week terms; from the school year 1899–1900 through 1905–1906, three twelve-week terms again; for the school years 1906–1907 and 1907–1908, two twenty-week terms. (The registration figures are presented in Table 5.)

Although it was impossible to determine what provision was made for the proper handling of the instruction of the college department in the beginning days of this work there were students listed in such courses. (The total number and distribution of college students are given in Table 6.)

Houghton Seminary during this period of its history became a church-wide-institution in its service as indicated by the geographical origin of its student body. The reports of five different years were found, which showed that students from states other than New York constituted 35 to 71 percent of the total student body. (Details of the geographical distribution are given in Table 7.)

Religious activities predominated in the campus life of Houghton Seminary. Two chapel services were held on each school day, "at which all of the students are expected to be present."[55] A students' prayer meeting was scheduled on Tuesday evening of each week.[56] This service became a regular weekly event on the campus.[57] A report in 1899, referred to the "noon prayer meetings . . . [as being] well attended."[58] Reports in the church paper indicated that once or twice a year a series of revival services were conducted for the benefit of the students. "The Young Peoples' Foreign Missionary Society of Houghton Seminary" was formed in June, 1900.[59] It became the custom on Sunday evening of the annual commencement week for this society to sponsor a missionary service, when an offering and pledges were taken for the support of foreign missionary work.

There were a few organized activities for the students. The Neosophic (literary) Society was founded during the first term of the school's operation. The purpose of the society as stated in the preamble of its constitution was "for mutual improvement in elocution, composition, and debate, and for enlarging our fund of general knowledge and intelligence."[60] The reports and minutes of this organization indicated that about one-half of the student body were active members. In 1898, an athletic club was organized[61] and in 1906 a gymnasium room was set aside for the boys to exercise in.[62] Oratorical competition among the students was given impetus by the oratorical contest at commencement time. Cash prizes of ten and five dollars were furnished by Leonard F. Houghton for the first time in 1902.[63] The alumni of the Seminary organized in June 16, 1897 as the "associated Alumni of Houghton Seminary."[64] The object of the organization was stated as "social intercourse and mutual improvement in annual meetings: to be held during commencement week."[65]

Financial Aspects

In carrying on the school at Houghton, the board of trustees decided in the beginning on "a pay as you go" policy.[66] Willard J. Houghton strongly affirmed that while he was agent for the school "we will not plunge headlong in debt."[67] Another definitely stated policy was low tuition and fees in order to attract students "from a distance to come to their own school, and also benefit the poor."[68]

The no-debt policy of the trustees was quite consistently applied in plant and equipment improvement, until the time of completing the first buildings on the second campus site. However in current operation, the school was almost continually embarrassed. The teachers seemed to be the greatest sufferers, because teachers' pay was the first item to be held back in the case of current fund shortage.[69] In total dollar value the current indebtedness was not great, but in terms of the amount required annually to meet expenses it was a significant percentage. In December, 1886, Willard J.

Houghton stated that "about $900 last year over tuition to run our school" was the cost of operation.[70] In 1894, B. S. Laughlin, the agent of the school, reported that $1,000 beyond tuition income was required to pay the costs of operation.[71] Current indebtedness ranged from $1,500 in May, 1885[72] to $150 in December, 1893.[73] Only in August, 1899[74] and in June, 1906[75] were announcements made that there was "not a dollar of indebtedness" and "all bills are paid up to date." When the school was moved to the new site and new buildings were constructed, income producing endowment money was put into the plant with the result that income from interest was cut off. This created "trying financial conditions" which caused the trustees in 1907–1908 to send the president into the field for a whole year soliciting students and funds.[76] Another source of financial difficulty was the fact that the buildings on the new campus site were larger than at first contemplated and the costs of construction materials increased after building was started. This made necessary the borrowing of money.[77]

Several attempts were made to meet some special needs of the school through specific appeals for designated funds. These appeals were only partially successful. There was an apparatus fund which was started by Principal A. R. Dodd in 1889.[78] In the spring of 1890 a fund was started with a goal of one thousand dollars. The solicitation was carried on through appeals in the church paper. After about two years, the total received was only $529.52.[79] In an attempt to finance the installation of furnaces in the first seminary building, an appeal was made to contribute to a furnace fund. This bought in $259.36 of the four hundred dollars requested.[80] There was also a "Two Hundred Names Fund" started in September, 1892.[81] The result of this project, reported in July 1893, was $917.75.[82] In 1906, seminary president Silas W. Bond started a plan of support in the form of food supplied by the various church missionary societies.[83]

The support which the church gave to Houghton Seminary was obtained through frequent appeals in the columns of the church paper and the personal solicitation of agents. The major portion of the funds raised were produced by the labors of the agents, who visited churches and the annual conference sessions. The work of Willard J. Houghton raised more than seventeen thousand dollars for the building and operation of the Seminary[84] and in addition to this a few thousand in support of the Bible Training Class project. Through the labors of another agent, the Rev. J. L. Benton, $11,704.07 was raised.[85] The agents were paid on an annual salary basis. On June 28, 1887, a resolution of the executive committee of the trustees fixed the salary of agents at "$500 per annum for time employed and expenses."[86] One of the problems in the work of these agents was delinquency in payment of pledges and endowment notes. The endowment notes were promises to pay principal at a certain rate per year and interest on the unpaid balance. The payment record on the endowment notes was particularly bad. In 1908, out of a list of more than "one thousand names of those who have given endowment notes for the educational work, scarcely one in twenty-five have paid their interest that was due in 1907 or 1906."[87]

Shortly after the start of the twentieth century, the already tight financing of the schools was exacerbated by financial irregularities in the office of the connectional agent.[88] The fiscal records of Alvin W. Hall were carefully investigated and in most cases the study team determined that the agent had not diverted funds for his own use. Nevertheless, several details remained cloudy and Hall resigned, to be replaced by his assistant, James Bowen.

The problem was addressed gently in *Conscience and Commitment*: "The connectional agent's office became involved in difficulties during the 1903–1907 quadrennium that resulted on March 16, 1907, in the resignation of Rev. A. W. Hall after seventeen years' service in this capacity."[89] "Mr. Hall thought it was within the privileges of his office to take over from one corporation [the several Wesleyan societies, all with a common board] to another any funds that might be found available for a pressing obligation, without asking permission from the trustees of that fund, and, as a rule, without their knowledge."[90]

One major problem concerned the funds tendered the denomination by Rev. Henry T. Besse. His statement indicated that a sum of over $91,000 had been loaned to the Connection, and that he was to have been paid an annuity equal to 5 percent interest (somewhat in excess of $4,000 per year). The original corpus included both cash and real estate, and it appears that the real estate had been very optimistically appraised at the time the agreement was created. At the time of reckoning, certain funds had been applied to denominational needs and the corpus had been reduced to $40,000, far below the level needed to pay the annuity and operating costs of the fund. Of this sum, $15,000 had been apportioned to building the women's dormitory (originally named Besse Hall) at Houghton Seminary. After several days of negotiations, this expenditure and one other major use were approved as a grant from Rev. Besse, but the balance of the funds were to be returned. This put severe stress on the Wesleyan Methodist treasury.[91]

Tables from Willard Smith's Dissertation

TABLE 1	Chief Administrative Officers, Houghton Seminary, 1884-1908		
Term of Service	**Name**	**Title**	**Years in Office**
1884-1886	Rev. W.H. Kennedy	Principal	2
1886-1892	Rev. A. R. Dodd	Principal	6
1892-1893	Rev. E. W. Bruce	Principal	1
1893	Rev. J. R. Hodges	Principal	a few days
1894-1896	James S. Luckey	Principal, President	2
1896-1908	Rev. Silas W. Bond	President	12

Data on the administrative officers of Houghton Seminary were gathered from catalogs of the school, the Seminary Tuition Book, various issues of the *Wesleyan Methodist*, and Subscription and Constitution Book of Willard J. Houghton.

TABLE 2	Length of Service, Houghton Seminary Teachers, 1884–1908		
Length of Service	**Number of Teachers**	**Length of Service**	**Number of Teachers**
Part year	4	7 years	4
1 year	13	8 years	1
2 years	10	9 years	1
3 years	8	10 years	1
5 years	2	12 years	1
6 years	3	Total Number of Teachers	48

These data were collected from the catalogs of the school, minutes of the Wesleyan Educational Society, the Executive Board of Trustees, and financial and academic records.

	Distribution of Salaries Offered,
TABLE 3	Houghton Seminary, 1887–1895

Annual Salary	Number of Men	Number of Women	Total Number of Teachers
$800	1	—	1
$500	2	—	2
$400	1	1	2
$325	—	1	1
$300	1	—	1
$275	1	1	2

These data were collected from minutes and financial records of the school.

	Average Annual Salary Payments,
TABLE 4	Houghton Seminary, 1889–1908

Teacher's Name	Number of Years Included	Average Annual Salary
Silas W. Bond, Prin.	8	$477.14
H. Clark Bedford	7	$171.72
Hanna Greenberg	7	$352.91
Howard W. McDowell	4	$281.13
Hattie W. Bond	3	$125.64
Florence Yorton	3	$251.93
Jennie Ried Clawson	2	$292.25
William Greenberg	2	$245.00

These data were processed from the Houghton Seminary Tuition Book containing records of pledges, gifts, tuition charges, receipts, and expenditures, 1889–1900.

TABLE 5				Houghton Seminary, Student Registration, 1884–1908			
School Year	Full Term	Winter Term	2nd Winter Term	Spring Term	School Year	Bible Training Class
1884–1885*	70–80	—	—	—	—	—
1885–1886**	—	113	—	—	—	—
1886–1887	84	95	—	44	—	—
1887–1888	83	106	—	41	—	—
1888–1889	62	100	—	43	—	20
1889–1890	64	85	—	42	—	15
1890–1891	58	25***	—	35	—	15
1891–1892	72	98	—	44	—	23
1892–1893	55	66	—	45	—	23
1893–1894	52	58	—	39	—	30
1894–1895	63	92	—	54	—	33
1895–1896	40	65	54	26	—	16
1896–1897	32	52	46	36	—	16
1897–1898	51	63	59	34	—	11
1898–1899	53	67	55	37	—	16
1899–1900	68	90	—	57	—	29
1900–1901	65	77	—	60	—	32
1901–1902	82	98	—	87	—	43
1902–1903	105	121	—	89	—	43
1903–1904	113	120	—	89	—	30
1904–1905	100	104	—	83	—	12
1905–1906	108	122	—	110	—	25
1906–1907	—	—	—	—	153	25
1907–1908	—	—	—	—	183	26

*A letter written by Willard J. Houghton, December 16, 1884.

**Wesleyan Methodist*, Vol XLIV, Mar. 24, 1886, pp. 4–5.

***A page or pages are missing from Book I for winter term of 1890–1891.

These data were secured from the following sources: the Bible Training Class from the student roster in the various annual catalogs of the Seminary; from the counting of names listed in the student record books of the Seminary (Book I, 1886–1891; Book II, 1891–1906), and the student register book, 1896–1923.

TABLE 6	Registration in College Department, Houghton Seminary, 1899–1908				
School Year	Freshmen	Sophomores	Juniors	Seniors	Total
1899–1900	1	1	4	—	6
1900–1901	4	1	1	1	7
1901–1902	4	4	1	2	11
1902–1903	2	5	4	—	11
1903–1904	4	3	4	4	15
1904–1905	2	3	2	1	8
1905–1906	—	—	1	—	1
1906–1907	10	2	—	1	13
1907–1908	2	11	1	—	14

Data obtained by counting the names in the student rosters in the catalogs.

TABLE 7	Geographical Distribution of Houghton Seminary Students, 1900–1905				
State or Country	**1900**	**1901**	**1902**	**1904**	**1905**
New York	63	35	30	44	57
Canada	2	—	1	—	—
Colorado	—	1	1	—	—
Georgia	—	1	1	5	1
Illinois	2	—	3	3	2
Indiana	4	8	8	6	1
Iowa	3	4	11	12	6
Kansas	4	12	8	3	15
England	—	—	—	—	1
Michigan	10	6	6	10	8
North Carolina	—	2	2	—	2
Ohio	1	2	2	4	2
Oklahoma	—	—	—	—	1
Pennsylvania	7	8	14	15	14
South Carolina	—	—	—	1	—
South Dakota	1	1	7	8	5
Vermont	—	—	—	2	2
West Virginia	—	1	3	3	1
Wisconsin	—	—	8	4	2
TOTALS	97	81	105	120	120*
From New York State	65%	49%	29%	37%	48%
From other states/countries	35%	57%	71%	63%	52%

* These registration totals do not agree with those in Table VII. They were probably drawn up at different times during the school year.

Sources of data in this table were as follows:
1900   Silas W. Bond, a news item, *Wesleyan Methodist,* Vol. LVII, Mar. 21, 1900, p. 12.
1901   *Wesleyan Methodist,* Vol. LVIII, Nov. 13, 1901, p. 5.
1902   Ibid., Vol. LIX, Nov. 26, 1902, p. 4.
1904   Ibid., Vol. LXI, Mar. 30, 1904, p. 4
1905   Ibid., Vol. LXII, Dec. 27, 1905, p. 4.

FIVE

Toward Being a College

1899–1923

D uring the latter third of the nineteenth century, the movement to establish public secondary schools was sweeping across America. To have local access to a higher level of education was greeted with enthusiasm by most citizens, but within evangelical denominations there was an urge to go a step farther and offer such schooling in a clearly sectarian setting. In 1883, a strong desire among Wesleyan Methodists to offer their own affordable Christian schooling gave the primary spark to create Houghton Seminary. Though several earlier attempts at establishing denominational schools under annual conference sponsorship had failed for a variety of reasons, the time now appeared ripe to establish a private, Christian secondary school to provide a quality education for local students.

A few years later, while Silas Bond was seminary president, the leaders of the denomination became aware of the rapid growth in numbers of church-supported or -related colleges and apparently felt apprehensive about being left behind. Although founder Willard Houghton in all probability did not envision the seminary expanding its offerings to become a college, the Wesleyan Methodist leadership definitely did. Consequently, the Wesleyan Methodist Educational Society (which had been established under the Book

Committee but with identical membership) directed Houghton Wesleyan Seminary in 1898 to begin offering collegiate work.[1]

Collegiate Curriculum

In response to that request, the seminary listed college-level course work as early as 1899, in a component labelled the College Department. The cover of the catalog for 1898–1899 contains these words: "Fifteenth Annual Catalogue of the Houghton Seminary and Announcement of Houghton College, Houghton, N.Y." Inside, under the heading of College Department, the catalog says: "A thorough course of study is provided for those who wish to enter upon a regular curriculum of college training."

The proposed collegiate course of instruction is presented in the following table. That this was a rather imaginative package may be deduced from the fact that only five faculty were identified to teach in the program.

TABLE 8	Collegiate Academic Program for the Proposed Houghton College, 1898[2]	
FRESHMAN YEAR		
Fall Term	**Winter Term**	**Spring Term**
Memorabilia	Antigone	Plato
German	German	German
Rhetoric	English Literature	American Literature
Bible	Bible	Bible
History of England	History	History
Delivery	Delivery	Delivery

SOPHOMORE YEAR		
Fall Term	**Winter Term**	**Spring Term**
Horace	Tacitus	Tertullian
German	German	German
Chemistry	Chemistry	Trigonometry
Bible	Bible	Bible
History of France	French Revolution	Fifteen Decisive Battles
Essays	Essays	Essays

JUNIOR YEAR		
Fall Term	**Winter Term**	**Spring Term**
Greek Testament	Greek Orators	Livy
Physics	Biology	Physics
Astronomy	English Criticism	Astronomy
Bible	Bible	Bible
History of Germany	History	History
Orations	Orations	Orations

SENIOR YEAR		
Fall Term	**Winter Term**	**Spring Term**
Mental Philosophy	Philosophy of Religion	Moral Philosophy
Political Science	Evidences of Christianity	Political Economy
Geology	Sociology	Logic
Bible	Bible	Bible
American History	History	History
Senior Essays	Senior Essays	Senior Essays

The catalog for 1899–1900 listed the following students in the College Department.

Junior class: Clark Bedford, Dean Bedford, Charles Wiles, and John Willett.

Sophomore class: Florence Yorton

Freshman class: Gertrude Preston.

All except Wiles had been listed in the previous catalog as members of the junior class of the seminary's Academic Department.[3]

In 1905 the academic schedule was rearranged into two twenty-week semesters per year. The revised course of study, as listed in the catalog for 1907–08, was as follows:

TABLE 9	College Department Course of Study, 1907–1908[a]

FRESHMAN YEAR	
First Semester	**Second Semester**
Memorabilia and Plato	Sophocles and Aeschylus
Advanced Algebra	Advanced Algebra
Trigonometry	Trigonometry
Rhetoric	Rhetoric
English Literature	English Literature
Biology	Geology
Botany	Botany

SOPHOMORE YEAR	
First Semester	**Second Semester**
Horace and Tacitus	Livy and Tertullian
American Literature	American Literature
Astronomy	Surveying
Bible	Bible

JUNIOR YEAR	
First Semester	**Second Semester**
Zoology	Zoology
Demosthenes and Lysais	Aristophanes
Greek Testament	Greek Testament
Chemistry	Chemistry
Physics	Physics
English History	History of France and Germany
English Criticism	English Criticism

SENIOR YEAR	
First Semester	**Second Semester**
Zoology	Zoology
Psychology	Evidences of Christianity
Moral Philosophy	Plan of Salvation
Political Science	Logic
American History	Sociology
	Political Economy

Obviously, when J. S. Luckey returned in 1908, he had his own ideas about curriculum, and he no doubt had been influenced by the concept of elective coursework that had been permeating American higher education for the preceding four decades. Charles William Eliot, president of Harvard from 1869 to 1909, forcibly shifted that college from its highly prescriptive, classical curriculum to a program of elective choices. Said Eliot:

> The elective system fosters scholarship, because it gives free play to natural preferences and inborn aptitudes, makes possible enthusiasm for a chosen work, relieves the professor and the ardent [student] . . . of the presence of a body of students who are compelled to an unwelcome task, and enlarges instruction by substituting many and various lessons given to small lively classes, for a few lessons many times repeated to different sections of a numerous class.[5]

Eliot's approach is also credited with fostering depth of study and encouraging graduate work, and with lifting Harvard from a college to a major university. Historian Frederick Rudolph described the elective principle as "a device for bringing science and the other new disciplines into equality with the old subjects."[6] "Election permitted the professor to indulge his interests and the students to follow theirs; it encouraged the accumulation of knowledge and welcomed into the world of learning subjects that had been forbidden through an ill-considered belief that the ancients knew everything worth knowing."[7] One aspect of this system, in the words of the 1890s president of DePauw University, was that "The Old Education ascribed the virtue to the subject, the New Education ascribed it to the process. If the virtue be chiefly in the process rather than the subject, then . . . the choice of that subject should depend largely on the tastes and probable future vocation of the student."[8]

Given his background with Harvard's elective system, it is logical that President Luckey would have a dream of shaping his institution to this "Harvard ideal." Under his leadership, the curriculum was changed drastically the very next year to the arrangement discussed below for 1923, the year when Houghton received its provisional charter and students could pursue their bachelors' degrees locally. Starting in 1909, sophomores could take half of their normal semester load as electives, juniors could take three-quarters, and for seniors the entire expectation was for electives.[9]

Although Houghton rapidly became ready to educate students up to the bachelor's level, the New York Department of Education would not permit the awarding of baccalaureate degrees by a mere seminary (meaning, in the language of the era, a private secondary school)—and demanded that Houghton rename its College Department, which soon became the Academic Department. But Luckey had great confidence in the true collegiate level of the coursework, and he devised an interim plan to prove that fact.

In the spring of '09, President Luckey left for Oberlin to negotiate with administrators of that institution to the end that students of Houghton's Advanced Department might enter Oberlin with three years' recognized credit. Provided the probationers did well, they were to be graduated with an A.B. degree after one year at Oberlin. If they failed to make the grade, no credit was to be given. The proposition was accepted—doubtless because the work [at Oberlin] of the interviewer [Luckey] was recalled as having been highly satisfactory.[10]

The record shows that Oberlin awarded A.B. degrees in 1910 to William F. Frazier, Ralph Rindfusz, H. Clark Bedford, and Leland Boardman; to Herbert LeRoy Fancher and Stanley W. Wright in 1911; and to Frank H. Wright, Harold H. Hester, Paul H. Fall, Jesse Frazier, and Willard LaVay Fancher in 1914. (Of these, all but Jesse Frazier returned to Houghton to teach, and three of the men—Boardman, Fall, and LaVay Fancher—are known to have received doctorates.[11]) Similar advanced placements were achieved at Ohio Wesleyan University, the University of Nebraska, and the University of Michigan.[12]

While the degree-completion program at Oberlin and other colleges clearly established the quality of college coursework offered at Houghton, a student's transfer to an accredited institution with different academic standards and theological environment was somewhat of a mixed blessing. Alumna and one-time faculty member Roberta Grange shares her impressions:

[My brothers] Max and Glenn [Molyneaux] each spent the last two years of their college years at Oberlin College. Houghton was not [then] accredited to grant degrees although she offered college courses for many years. It was customary for young people of moderate circumstances generally to take two or three years at Houghton and then transfer to some other college to finish up and get a degree. There were a number of colleges with whom Houghton had arrangements for such transfers. One of the reasons the Wesleyans wanted to have Houghton accredited was so that these young people might finish at Houghton and thus be more likely to stay in the church. Those who went to other colleges often took on so much of the coloration of those new environments they were no longer able to return and so were lost to the church and their home communities.[13]

Physical Plant

While the work offered in the academic department was demonstrably of college caliber, the physical plant of the college-to-be was definitely not. The year J. S. Luckey returned, the campus boasted but one academic building and one dormitory, and the lion's share of the academic space was used by seminary students. For the year ending in 1908, the seminary reported 183 students, far outnumbering the fourteen who were enrolled in the Academic Department.[14]

One of the challenges of campus upgrading that faced J. S. Luckey and his co-workers was to improve utilities for the campus. One effort involved providing a new form of energy for building lighting. The original power, acetylene, was produced on-campus: behind the women's dorm stood a building that held the acetylene generator, where calcium carbide and water were combined to provide the highly flammable gas (which also was used in early automobile headlights). In 1920, Rochester Gas and Electric brought electrical power to the campus,[15] and what was known as a knob-and-tube wiring system was used to install lines in the campus buildings to transmit power for electric light bulbs.

According to a 1931 alumnus, telephone service had reached Houghton village in 1910, and the seminary eventually rented one of the party-line, hand-crank phones.[16] (Another alumnus reported that hand-cranked phones were still in use as late as 1957.[17]) Later, in 1918, the Advisory Board opted to provide half the fee to rent a telephone for the college farm.[18]

Providing the other major utility, water, turned out to be a far more complex project. The new houses built adjacent to the campus depended on wells and rain water collected in cisterns. However, when the two original buildings on the current campus, Jennings Hall and Besse dormitory, were opened in 1906, the drinking water supply came from a spring below the hillside, pumped to the level of the new buildings by a one-cylinder gasoline engine.[19] H. Clark Bedford, in addition to his teaching duties, spent many hours keeping the gasoline engine running to power the pump. And, in an era when faculty earned about twenty dollars per week, certain individuals were hired to tend to pumping matters for $3.50 per week.[20]

That first supply of drinking water soon proved inadequate, and in 1912 J. S. Luckey and Clark Bedford began their search for a better source. They found a good spring about a half-mile to the west of the campus and at a considerably higher elevation, and according to the seminary advisory board minutes for September 17, 1908, "Prof. Bedford was authorized to take such steps as he might deem wise to get the water [now] going to waste from the springs."[21] President Luckey called for volunteers from the student body to dig a trench for a pipe line to connect the spring to the seminary. Before long water flowed into a new reservoir built at an elevation of seventy feet above the campus. Now there was a good gravity-fed water supply into the two campus buildings.[22] Then, in 1915, the Advisory Board named President Luckey as chair of a committee (the other two members were John Coleman and G. Tremaine McDowell) to put in a water line to the new gymnasium, including securing the pipe and looking after any other details.[23]

Access to this water system was evidently granted to homes adjoining the college, for the advisory board minutes for January 13, 1913, show annual water rates of seven dollars for a house without a water closet, eleven dollars for a house with a water closet, and an extra three dollars for a stable with one horse or cow.[24]

Because the seminary was the property of the Wesleyan Methodist Educational Society, this water system belonged to that agency also. Subsequently, in April 1913 the advisory board voted to ask the educational society to extend the water line through the village of Houghton.

To provide water service to all village residents apparently established a need for a more formal contracting system to control and prevent problems, and the advisory board on May 14, 1916, approved a motion that "we have a committee to decide on rates, regulations, and contracts for the water supply."[25] The committee's report consumed six pages in the record book and addressed such matters as controlling leaks, prevention of freezing, and special permissions for multiple family use, lawn sprinkling, and timely payments. Annual water rates were set at six dollars for the first faucet in a kitchen, plus one dollar for each additional faucet, two dollars for a bathtub, and three dollars for a "water closet." A package price of ten dollars was offered for "one kitchen faucet, a hot water boiler, one bathtub, one closet, and one wash basin."[26]

One other "utility" involved the matter of sanitation. A brick outhouse, as noted, had been built, apparently in 1905 or 1906, to serve the new women's doritory. In 1912, the Educational society approved the installation of "two [water] closets in the ladies dormitory and two closets in the girls cloak room of the Seminary."[27] In 1913, the advisory board minutes reported that "In view of the fact that there is a delay in installing the men's toilets, a motion was made and carried that the money contributed by the men for the expense of putting in toilets be returned if desired."[28] While there is no further record of this matter, a later source reported that the eventual accommodations included back-to-back facilities for both sexes.

While records are sparse (most likely due to a sense of delicacy), it appears the regime of Houghton's great brick privy and the concomitant dormitory chamber pots persevered until the early '20s, when an adequate number of indoor toilets were installed. The Advisory Board minutes for August 1922 report that the board "voted to build a septic tank for the Ladies dorm," the first step toward large numbers of flush toilets.[29] Later, in the 1930s, the sanitary engineer for Allegany County insisted on a central sewer line for the campus, replacing the individual cess pools and septic tanks, and this work was accomplished with the assistance of the Works Project Administration. But no central sewage disposal was yet provided, and the sewer system effluent was allowed to drain to the surface on the hillside east of the present Campus Center.[30]

Regarding the need for larger buildings, there were some very real constraints on enlarging the physical plant. The most obvious was finances: according to the seminary catalog of 1888–1889, "It is the aim of the institution to afford those of limited means an opportunity to obtain an education."[31] The rates, which had begun at four dollars for a term of English education, had increased only a little. In 1916, according to the Advisory Board minutes, "The Elementary tuition shall be $10 per semester; the High School tuition shall be $15 per semester; the College tuition shall be $20 per semester."[32] By 1923, the college tuition charge had increased to fifty dollars per semester, with additional fees for laboratories (two to six dollars), library (one dollar), gymnasium (one dollar), and graduation (one dollar).[33] In 1927, a student medical fee of one dollar per semester was levied.[34] Even as late as 1927, according to the catalog, "Tuition rates are so low that they pay but little more than fifty percent of the college's current expenses."[35] Yes, there was denominational support, though not in robust amounts, and the gap in the budget had to be filled by gifts from alumni and friends. Capital construction funding had to be provided through special giving, and raising money for bricks and mortar was never easy.[36]

(It is interesting to note here three items of campus economics. While in 1912 most male faculty were paid $800 per year, the female seminary teacher was paid $550 and Philinda Bowen, who handled all the elementary duties, was paid $500.[37] That same year, it was approved to pay the library attendant fifteen cents per hour but the board decided "to pay twenty-five cents per hour to men to clean out the cess pool."[38] In 1916, meal charges of seventeen cents per meal were adjusted to allow extra eggs for breakfast at four cents each and extra toast [unbuttered] at three cents for two slices.[39])

One of the first felt non-academic needs of the burgeoning institution was for gymnasium space. Prof. H. Clark Bedford took a special interest in this need, and enough funds were on hand in 1914 to begin construction.

Two years later, the catalog reported that "a splendid gymnasium is being erected"[40] and expressed hope that the building would be in use in 1917. The same statement was repeated the next year, with occupancy predicted for 1918. The gymnasium did open in 1918, though the catalog for that year reported that the basement area, which was to offer lockers and showers, was not finished. The tiny swimming pool, fifteen by forty-five feet, wasn't opened until 1926.

Additional dormitory space was obtained in 1920 when the deed for the former Waldorf Temperance Hotel was acquired in exchange for an annuity to the owner and his daughters. More washbasins, two bathroom mirrors, and a shower-bath were soon added to Waldorf; however, cooking in this new dormitory was prohibited.[41]

The next academic building, originally named Bowen Hall (and later Old Science and then Woolsey) opened in 1923, the year the provisional charter was granted by New York. These two sorely-needed structures, Bedford Gym and Bowen Science, completed the pre-charter growth even as they strained Houghton's available fiscal resources.

One other effect of the very tight funding was an inability to hire outside help for a number of campus needs. Therefore, J. S. Luckey decided to address the situation in true missionary-service fashion by establishing a series of faculty committees to attend to these matters. These were first listed in the catalog for 1908–1909. Two dealt with physical plant: Buildings and Grounds, chaired by William Greenberg, and Heating, Lighting, and Waterworks, chaired by Rev. E. W Bruce. But a host of other committees dealt with more routine academic matters: Additional Work, Athletics, Catalogue, Chapel Seating, Commencement, Lectures and Entertainments, Library, Literary Societies, Music, Petitions and Requests from Students, Reading Table, Regents' Supplies, Religious Work, Students' Publications, and Oratorical Contest. Most had a membership of three, though some with narrowly defined duties had but one.[42]

Library resources were extremely modest at best. While the catalog for 1888–1889 reported that "a large number of books have been . . . added to the library during the past year,"[43] in 1904 the library was reported as holding a mere 1500 volumes[44] That number slowly grew to 2000 volumes in 1908, 3000 volumes in 1912, 4000 volumes in 1920, and more than 5000 volumes in 1923, the year the college was granted a provisional charter.[45] In comparison, there are several contemporary faculty members whose personal libraries approximate this latter number.

Alan Graffam reviewed the student publications of the early college days and wrote this summary of the apparent effects of one of the early twentieth century's major social upheavals, World War I:

> The impact of World War I came to the campus only as students and faculty left for military service. *The Houghton Star* printed general editorials about "The European War" and "Patriotism" as early as 1915 but did not print specific news of the War until 1917. In 1918 *The Star* gave its most complete coverage of war-related incidents in reports of the casualties among former students. A column entitled "Khaki News" provided information regarding Houghton students' involvement in the War continued for many months after armistice.
>
> Other than stories about individuals, the only account of school-wide action reported in *The Star* described the extension of the Christmas holidays of 1917 to conserve material useful for the war effort. *The Star* regularly buttressed editorial comment with discussion of patriotism; it contained no dissention concerning the war and supported involvement and cheered heroes. There was no mention of the war in faculty minutes or other official sources; school was business as usual. In fact, *The Star* reported that the college remained financially stable through the period with all bills paid and a minimal decrease in enrollment.
>
> Except for a few battlefield reminiscences by returning soldiers, the subject of World War I dropped from view quickly. The school was on the verge of receiving a State charter and excitement was high. The mood was optimistic, and few were prepared to look back at the unpleasantness of the conflict.[46]

A number of Houghton alumni served in the U.S. forces during that war, and three lost their lives: William Russell, Harry Meeker, and Curtis Rogers. Their memory was honored by the planting of three evergreens on the hillside in front of Gaoyadeo dormitory, near where the relocated Fancher Hall stands today.

Alumna Roberta Molyneaux was in sixth grade in 1918, but she recalled the departure of her brother Glenn and three others for an officer training program at Oberlin:

> It was a program by the government in the colleges to train college-caliber students as officers. They were allowed to take some college

work along with their military training. Glenn and three other boys from Houghton (Pete Lapham, Harold Luckey, and Ira Bowen) left on the morning train on September 14, 1918, for Oberlin College in Oberlin, Ohio. . . . It was a heart wrenching time for Mother and Father. There were heavy casualties on the "Western Front" and heavy casualties in our training camps. Disease ravaged them. Influenza was especially virulent, and there were no methods such as vaccines for controlling it.[47]

When the war ended on November 11, 1918, before Glenn and the others could be sent overseas, excitement struck Houghton:

Wild rejoicing broke forth everywhere. People went crazy with joy. There was shouting and laughter. The bells were rung. People rushed into the streets. They wanted to rejoice together. Impromptu parades appeared. . . . Many people from our village and the seminary walked the four miles to Fillmore, just to be with other people and rejoice.[48]

Provisional College Charter

By 1919 the track record of Houghton students who pursued degree-completion at the other colleges was well established, and it was time to take the next step: to petition New York State to grant Houghton a college charter. According to Kenneth Wilson, "Houghton could qualify [for a state charter] if the president could get [an endowment of] $100,000 and the promise of $15,000 annually from the church. The Wesleyan Methodist Board in Syracuse, N.Y., voted to let him try."[49] On February 16, 1920, a special public service was held in the seminary chapel to begin the drive to raise the $100,000 endowment.[50] Underlying these concerns was the simple fact that the vast majority of colleges chartered in the nineteenth century did not survive to see 1901, and the biggest single reason was the lack of adequate finances. To paraphrase an old folk saying, the road to a defunct college could easily be paved with good intentions. College status would need to be based on clear mission, adequate manpower, and enough money. And then the denomination's headquarters would have to approve the petition request.

Official permission to pursue the charter came from the Educational Society on February 8, 1923: "Voted to consider the recommendation from President Luckey to apply for a college charter." On February 12, 1923, the recommendation was finally approved.[51]

In a 1922 letter to President Luckey, New York's Assistant Commissioner for Higher Education Augustus S. Downing spelled out the state's requirements.

First, there must be an assured minimum productive endowment of not less that $500,000. . . . Part of this might be shown as cash invested and part of it might be shown as a guaranteed annual income from the authorities of your church. Such guaranteed income plus the interest from the invested funds would need to be in the amount 4 percent of $500,000 [$20,000].

Second, there must be . . . the eight distinct departments . . . and the heads of such departments must be, in majority at least, men and women thoroughly trained and having a degree equal to that of master, or doctor of philosophy.[52]

The letter went on express a special concern of the Education Department that adequate salaries be offered to professors and instructors.[53] The figures cited were a minimum of $5,000 for the head of the institution, $1,800 to $2,500 for department heads, and $900 to $1,500 for instructors.[54] Said Downing:

Although certain men and women at the time being might be perfectly willing from purely altruistic motives to give their time and their life energy to an institution for a bare competence, there must always be had in mind the possibility that such altruistic individual be taken away by death, or become incapacitated by illness, and then the institution must go into the open market for someone to fill such person's place.[55]

According to data tabulated by Willard Smith, the average Houghton faculty salary that year was $1,165, ranging from the president's $1,680 to $600.[56]

The fund drive, spearheaded by President Luckey, involved seeking gifts from faculty, students, community, and church. Enough progress was made over the next two years that the Wesleyan Methodist Educational Society approved the college charter drive. But the society's approval sounded somewhat grudging: it was resolved " . . . that Houghton Seminary be permitted to reach the chartered state as soon and as fast as its supporters are willing to meet the bills."[57] Any intention of denominational financial support seemed to be tentative at best.

A year later, with adequate funding apparently identified, the Educational Society voted to make application for a college charter at the next session of the

New York Board of Regents. President Luckey attended the Regents' session in April 1923 to answer questions, and he was overjoyed when the provisional charter was granted.[58] Now, as soon as a fully coherent curriculum (including an on-premises senior year) could be established and the required $500,000 in productive assets acquired, Houghton would be able to grant baccalaureate degrees.

According to the catalog for 1923–1924, the college curriculum had been revised to require a number of basic courses, a major study field, and enough electives to amass 120 credit hours. Majors were available in foreign language; English; mathematics; biological science; physical science; economics, political science and history; philosophy, psychology and history; and history. The degree of bachelor of arts would be conferred on those who successfully completed all required work plus enough electives to make a total of at least 120 hours. A bachelor of science degree could be earned by those who completed eighteen hours of mathematics and thirty-six hours of laboratory science and aggregated at least 120 hours.[59]

Freshmen were to take College Rhetoric, Freshman Bible, Ancient Languages or Mathematics plus seven hours of electives each semester. Sophomores were to enroll in Sophomore English each semester plus enough major courses and electives to total fifteen credits. Sophomores were also expected to include at least six credit hours of history and six of laboratory science. Juniors had Psychology one semester and Ethics the next, plus the major and elective courses. Seniors merely were tasked to complete major requirements and the balance of their electives.[60]

It is interesting to note that there was practically no change in faculty numbers from 1908 to 1923. According to data collected by Willard Smith, during those years the seminary had ten or eleven faculty in all but 1913 and 1921, when twelve were counted.[61]

Houghton was now officially (if provisionally) a college, at least for five years. But significant work lay ahead before the next goal, the granting of a permanent charter, could be achieved.

God's Man for
a Christian College

James Seymour Luckey

Although Houghton's existence as an institution extends back into the late nineteenth century, in one sense it is still but a two-generation school. James S. Luckey's Houghton connection began in 1884, while founder Willard J. Houghton was still the seminary's agent for fund-raising, and Luckey's son Robert, a long-time Houghton College faculty member, in 2004 lived as a retiree in the community.

Only a handful of individuals spent all or almost all of their lives in the Houghton educational circle. Of these few, the most significant was Houghton's first president, James S. Luckey.

Early Days

James Seymour Luckey was born on the first day of August in 1867 to James Luckey and the former Pollyanne Davis, on a farm near the hamlet of Short Tract, New York, perhaps ten miles northeast of the little community at Houghton Creek. Young James apparently possessed little interest for the severe manual labor demanded by mid-nineteenth-century farming, holding instead a craving for books and the treasures they offered. His special interest was the structured and precise world of mathematics.

When Luckey was seventeen, he enrolled in the new seminary at Houghton Creek. His biographer, Erma Anderson Thomas, reported young James's initial Houghton days:

> The chilly December of 1884 found him entering Houghton Seminary. (When the Seminary first opened, there were three terms of thirteen weeks each. He entered for the second term of the first year.) In actual currency that term cost him thirteen dollars, which sum included board, room and tuition. He did not receive over ten dollars in cash from his parents for the expense of his entire schooling, but they did send him from home such supplies as food and fuel.[1]

The need for finances interrupted his schooling the very next year, when he took a teaching post in a district school in Weaver's Settlement. His salary was six dollars a week, less two dollars for board. Then in 1886 he returned to the seminary, where he augmented his teacher's savings by working for book-money as a janitor.[2]

In January of 1887, influenced by a sermon by Rev. James E. Tiffany, James Luckey surrendered to a call to serve a consecrated life. He at first believed it was a call to the ministry, but he subsequently felt that God's specific instruction to him was to become an educator.[3]

Following his graduation from Houghton Seminary in 1889, James spent a year as master of a district school in Rockville, then he was called back to Houghton Seminary to teach. His coursework included shorthand, typing, Greek, and mathematics. In 1894 he was asked to serve as principal of the seminary, and that same year he married one of his former students, Edith Bedell Curtis, from Mexico, New York. The following year, his Houghton Seminary title was changed to president.[4]

James interrupted his teaching career to pursue official teaching credentials through Albany Normal College, receiving his PdM (master of pedagogy) certificate in 1898. Then, for four years, he worked as principal of the high school in Millerton. During those years, his elder son, Harold James, was born on May 17, 1899, followed by his daughter, Ruth Evangeline on March 11, 1901. His second son, Robert Ruel Raphael, arrived some sixteen years later on November 11, 1917.

Early in his teaching career, James was forced to encounter and resolve for himself an issue of attire as addressed in edicts from officials of the Wesleyan Methodist Church. Thomas reports some details:

In the early days of Houghton Seminary our leaders sometimes had not altogether necessary nor scriptural views. When certain teachers and pastors advocated that the necktie was a needless article of attire, Mr. Luckey was not seen wearing one for many a year. After he had gone to Albany Normal College for teacher training and was about to enter work in one of the high schools, President William Milne one day called him aside and asked him if he went without his necktie for religious reasons, adding if he did so, he had nothing to say, but that if no principles were involved, he thought his appearance would be neater and his general influence upon the young men better if he wore one. Mr. Luckey responded that it was a matter of religious conviction and continued without a tie. Notwithstanding this handicap, he was one of the first to secure a position and began teaching as the principal of the union school at Millerton, New York. While teaching there he received an anonymous gift of a necktie, and he decided to investigate more thoroughly the reasons for omitting this article of apparel. Upon studying the phrase in 1 Timothy 2:9 "in modest apparel," he found that *modest* is also translated *well-ordered* and *becoming*. He decided then that if his dress was to be becoming, he should wear his tie, and the question was settled once and for all.[5]

(Another aspect of this issue of ultra-conservative attire was to raise its head in the 1950s and '60s, with highly disruptive effects on the college. A discussion of this problem is among the several contentious issues addressed in chapter 15.)

From Millerton, Luckey's path led to Oberlin College in Ohio, where his academic labors were later reported by Professor W. D. Cairns:

President Luckey spent the two academic years 1902–1904 in completing his course for the A.B. in Oberlin College, with a major in mathematics. . . . He was a teacher of mathematics and assistant in physics the next year and along with this took his A.M. degree with very high grades in mathematics and physics. He taught [at Oberlin] as an instructor in mathematics and physics for the next three years.[6]

Luckey's innate brilliance and his accomplishments in mathematics were recognized by at least one of the great Ivy League institutions, as Harvard extended to him a scholarship offer that would allow him to earn a master's degree. He had barely finished that course and was contemplating another year's study there, as a first step toward a doctorate, when the trustees of Houghton Seminary re-elected him to the post of president of the growing institution. Professor Ray Hazlett, then a young lad, described Luckey's return as having ." . . no fanfare, no elaborate ceremonies and inaugural speeches." In his words, President Luckey was "a slender, soft-spoken, bespectacled, youngish-old man with just a trace of the asceticism of the scholar in his face and manner."[7]

Presidency

The post-Harvard J. S. Luckey was the first real educator to head the seminary. The other men had been church men, and they took the principal's post just as they would have taken any other assigned position in the denomination. One of the concomitant problems with this arrangement was that the first allegiance of each of these men was to the conference in which he held membership. As "stationed pastors," they perforce had limited vision of what the seminary might become. But James Seymour Luckey had much longer-range eyes: "His Harvard ideal was a driving factor in the back of his mind . . . . Everything he did was to move Houghton toward that academic classic goal."[8]

The effect of Luckey's return to lead the growing institution was reported by one of the seminary's students: "After President Luckey came to Houghton things began to change somewhat. He brought an atmosphere of education to the school it didn't have before. . . . When I went there in 1907 it was completely isolated, no contact with any other school and no organizations except the church."[9]

In 1898, the fourteenth year of the seminary's existence, the Wesleyan Methodist Educational Society directed the young institution to begin offering college-level work. The seminary responded with grand plans: the 1899 catalogue showed a great array of proposed coursework, as presented in the last chapter. Only a handful of faculty, however, were initially available to offer these courses. These included Silas Bond, Rev. J. N. Bedford, Hattie Bond, Ralph Davey, and Mary Lane.[10] But courses were offered, students enrolled, and dreams of becoming a real college grew.

In 1908, Silas Bond left Houghton to become educational secretary for the Wesleyan Methodist Church, then was elected to serve as founding president of Miltonvale College in Kansas. The Book Committee selected Rev. Howard W. McDowell to be his replacement, but McDowell declined since he believed he was not suited for administration, recommending in his stead former principal and president J. S. Luckey. Later, however, following Silas Bond's retirement from Miltonvale College, McDowell took the Miltonvale presidency from 1912 to 1924, where he "was considered a good educator, administrator, orator and gentleman."[11]

When J. S. Luckey returned in 1908 to head Houghton Seminary, the faculty had been enlarged but not hugely so. Listed in the catalog for 1908–1909 were Luckey himself, Howard W. McDowell, H. Clark Bedford, William and Hannah Greenberg, Henry R. Smith Jr., Elizabeth H. Dow, Rev. Erwin W. Bruce, Vera M. Jennings, Philinda S. Bowen, Bessie V. Farnsworth, Laura A. Whitney, W. LaVay Fancher, and Harry J. Ostlund.[12] Several of these fourteen also bore the responsibility of teaching at below college level in the seminary, and all had other demanding duties within the institution. Luckey had a vision, but the available resources were slim: a program that was slowly growing from paper to practice, a minuscule faculty, and a campus that featured but three buildings—these were what J. S. Luckey had to work with.

Much as the academic program had already entered a period of growth and expansion, the physical plant needed to be enlarged. The three buildings on the new campus, all constructed of brick, were Jennings Hall (later called Old Administration), the sole academic building; Besse Hall (later Gaoyadeo), the women's dormitory; and behind Besse a sturdy "necessary" (outhouse) offering five seats per gender. Luckey's desire was to add a facility for physical education and intramural sports, and Professor H. Clark Bedford took responsibility for planning and erecting such a structure. At the alumni banquet in 1913, Bedford outlined the need and issued a challenge, and at Arbor Day the next spring ground was broken by a "team" of eighty men pulling a single moldboard plow. Much of the timber and brick used in the project was salvaged from the old seminary building.[13]

Building the gymnasium proved to be a lengthy project, delayed mostly by a shortage of funds. It took two years before the windows were installed and a concrete floor was poured in the basement, and the dedicatory chapel service took place in 1916. It was yet another year before the gymnasium floor was completed, and the tiny swimming pool was not opened until 1926.[14]

Campus utilities of that early era were at best rough. Luckey and Bedford spent time in 1912 laying out a gravity water line to the campus from springs farther up the hill, and in 1920 electricity finally replaced the original illumination systems of gas lights, hand-carried lanterns, and candles.[15] And, while definitive dates are lacking, it appears that it was another five or six years before flush toilets were installed throughout the seminary's dorm and in the gymnasium, and classroom buildings, and the old brick outhouse was demolished.

One of Luckey's greatest challenges was to assert the need for Houghton to develop as an academic institution and not as a Bible college, which would have been more to the liking of the denominational authorities and of some faculty members. As with most hot issues that appeared to defy church authority, limited material on this controversy is available in denominational resources.

One alumna, a life-long Wesleyan Methodist and a student at the seminary as well as the college, described the challenges faced by J. S. Luckey, and his tenacity:

> The president of the seminary . . . had turned away from some excellent offers to come to Houghton. He was to spend many years slowly building up this school to become a college. This was an undertaking that required all he had to give, a lifetime. Not only did he have to build up the school but he had to prepare the church, the community, and the student body for the idea that this should be a college. This was a task that would require years of constant planning, living, thinking, talking.
>
> Our church did not accept readily the idea that we should have a fully accredited college. Many were suspicious of education. There was much fear of "modernism" in thinking, in religion. . . . The laity were poor people, mostly rural, and while they wanted their children to have a better education than they had, they feared that higher learning meant alienation from God, from all they had been taught, and from themselves.
>
> Our president worked for years to educate the laity and ministers of the church as well as the local community to the value and importance of this little "school on the hill." A lesser man would have "shaken the dust off his feet" . . . or refused to work with people of such narrow vision. But he kept the vision of a fully accredited college here in this small community always in sight. He built

patiently year after year, holding always before the student body a high ideal of excellence, both mental and spiritual.[16]

Even as Luckey strove to move Houghton from Bible-based secondary school to Christian college, he never pursued the idea of developing Houghton into the sort of grand secular university that other schools with religious roots had become: Syracuse, Yale, Princeton and even his educational ideal, Harvard. His vision was for an institution that held to the unity of scriptural fealty and academic vigor, and this view has been sustained and nurtured by his successors.

Recollections

Of the more than one hundred individuals interviewed for this volume, nearly twenty had clear recollections of President Luckey. One man, whose Houghton residency and service includes the years from his birth here in 1911 to his retirement in 1972, reported:

> [There was] tension during J. S. Luckey's administration between the church's concept of education and the Harvard ideal of higher education, and the church—many of the church leaders—felt that excellent liberal arts education was suspect and not compatible with spiritual and biblical and theological accuracy and integrity. However, J. S. Luckey felt that the ideal was the wedding of liberal arts excellence and biblical and theological excellence.[17] . . . They were just sure that the purest people were the people who hadn't been in college or university. To be a pure, excellent, Wesleyan, Arminian believer you couldn't be that and have gone to college much less university and certainly not if you got a doctoral degree.[18]

Though his administrative and other duties consumed a huge amount of time, President Luckey remained a teacher in what time he could spare, and there is convincing evidence that he was a strong instructor. One former student reported that "In his teaching, he was a superb teacher, and his requirements in his math courses were tops. In his presentations or debates with people his stuff really lined up."[19] Another added these words:

> President Luckey came in [to class] the first day. He made an assignment, so many problems to do. We took it and not one of us

could work the problem. The next day he came and said, "Any questions?" Well, we didn't ask any questions because we thought he would demonstrate on the board, so we just kept still. "All right," he said and gave us the next assignment. The third day we were swamped. We admitted that we couldn't do the problem. He went to the board, put on a long equation, stood back and took a look at it and said, "Isn't that beautiful? That's as good as it'll run." Then he proceeded to solve it, talking out loud every move he made so we knew why he was doing it. I think he did it purposely; he made two or three wrong moves to show us how, if we made a wrong move, how to go back and pick up. . . . I always remember him as a strong math teacher.[20]

J. S. Luckey was notably frugal, and one anecdote about his thriftiness came from a Houghton veteran, at that time a young lad, who worked for him. The college had been digging for a building foundation and dumping the excavated dirt at the edge of the ravine in front of what today is Lambein dormitory. The boy was being paid a dime a load to shovel the dirt into the ravine. One night, when he was worn to a frazzle after moving six loads and suffering an encounter with a nest of yellow jackets, his dad (the campus janitor) gave him a hand with the last load. When Luckey asked the boy if he had had help, he said yes, so Luckey refused to pay him for the load.[21]

A '30s-era alumna, when asked to describe J. S. Luckey, used these words:

Oh, he was a benign despot. He was a wonderful man. He was a leader among leaders. I had him for freshman math, and I was hopelessly terrible in mathematics. That was an anathema to me, but he was still teaching while he was president; he couldn't leave it alone. He would put this problem on the board and he would just say, "Young people, isn't that beautiful? Can't you see God's hand in that?" To him, God was in everything. His specialty was in the field of mathematics.[22]

Another Houghton alumnus and son of a long-time faculty member, a boy who shoveled sidewalks for J. S. Luckey in the early '30s, described him as a very kindly gentleman who "was what you would now call a micromanager. He was responsible, and therefore he was in charge. . . . Dad said that when a chicken wanted to lay an egg up on the farm it had to check with President Luckey first."[23]

One former faculty member who lived in Houghton during the later Luckey years described him as "Tall, as I recall, quite thin. Somewhat of a princely kind of appearance . . . A person who, I think, appreciated and enjoyed a little adulation. He was always a humble man but didn't mind being applauded."[24]

A former president of the Houghton alumni association commented on some aspects of the education he received when J. S. Luckey was at the helm:

> I think of the things that Houghton taught. They taught you not to smoke; it was bad for you. They taught you not to drink; it was bad for you. They taught you that the color green was God's color. Everything was green at Houghton because President Luckey thought it could be any color you wanted as long at it was green. . . . The chapel was always painted green. He said if you're going to paint something, paint it green. . . . Like Henry Ford's [favorite color] was black, his was green.[25]

Helen Paul Paine, alumna and widow of Stephen W. Paine, described J. S. Luckey as being "greatly admired by students and faculty . . . he had a beautiful spirit. . . . He was a very kindly person." She went on to report another aspect of his character: "One thing I remember is watching him go to sleep in church. I never saw anyone sleep so gracefully in church as he did. His head wouldn't bob down; he would just sit there."[26]

J. S. Luckey is also remembered as less than orderly in the maintenance of his work space. Biographer Thomas offers a glimpse of his administrative habits:

> His office was typically that of a genius. An amazing pile of letters, unfinished documents, pamphlets, catalogues, file trays, books and pencils usually adorned its polished top. . . . Strangely enough, *he* could always locate the desired epistle. One curious streak of neatness pervaded the whole: he always placed a letter back in its envelope after it was read.[27]

Others have described Luckey as stern, dogged in his determination, and congenial but essentially reserved. One early alumnus reported two incidents, both involving mishaps to the president, where his ability to restrain his temper was demonstrated. The first occurred during one

Christmas vacation, when a small fire broke out in the seminary's heating plant, built into the hillside behind the women's dormitory. Smoke poured from the nearly-underground building, and gangs of men quickly formed a bucket brigade to extinguish the blaze. When the fire appeared to be under control, President Luckey took a lantern and entered the building to investigate. Two men students went with him. Then someone saw the light from the lantern through the smoke and shouted, "There's the fire!" whereupon the three investigators were doused with water. The temperature that night was ten degrees below zero, so the wet clothing quickly froze. President Luckey remained calm but it was obvious that he was not amused.[28]

In another incident, several of the boys had cobbled up a bobsled. They built metal shoes for the sled's wooden runners using tines taken from an old hay rake, and this allowed them to achieve great speed on the packed track they had established down the steep hill in front of the girls' dorm. Standard practice was to shout "Track! Track!" just before commencing a run to make sure the track was clear.

One Saturday, President Luckey was returning from the post office and walking up the hill, right in the track. He had no idea what the call of "Track! Track!" meant, until he looked up and saw the bobsled rushing at him. The driver wrenched the sled out of the track and dumped his passengers in the road, while President Luckey jumped aside over the bank and lost the package he was carrying (a box of Regents exams) down the slope and almost into Houghton Creek. The president wasn't very happy about the incident and threatened to bar students from sliding on the roadway.[29]

According to one former student, J. S. Luckey on one occasion expressed a view that may not have been wholly congruent with the dogma of his parent church.

> I remember President Luckey one day saying (and I think this must have been in Sunday school because I know he was saying it in front of a small group, not in front of the whole college group), he said he had no quarrel with the beliefs of the Catholic church with the exception of the elements which he said they represented as the body and blood of Jesus Christ. He said other than that he couldn't quarrel with them. He said he could understand the church having a head of the church, and he felt that all of us have a divine inspiration of some sort and have a responsibility for leadership, and maybe the Pope's leadership was of a higher level than ours but it was a leadership of a Christian community. He was very tolerant of that.[30]

Even as J. S. Luckey was passing seminary graduates to Oberlin and other colleges for "finishing" and awarding of degrees, he constantly pursued a state charter and eventual national accreditation for Houghton College. One supporter at the state level was Herman Cooper, then assistant commissioner of education for the State of New York, whom Houghton College recognized as one of its first three honorary degree recipients (see appendix J). Another friend was the commissioner himself, Dr. Augustus S. Downing. When Luckey in 1922 presented evidence that the seminary had achieved enough funding and added testimonials from key individuals at institutions that had worked with Houghton's advanced graduates, Downing hinted that Houghton might be able to secure a charter. In February 1923 the Wesleyan Methodist trustees approved presenting a charter petition to the state, and in April the petition was approved.[31] The text of the provisional charter is in appendix G.

The effort to offer college-level courses and achieve both a state charter and regional accreditation will be discussed in more detail in the following chapter.

Final Decade

As if he did not have enough to do, J. S. Luckey was asked in 1929 by the denomination to act as temporary president of struggling sister-institution Marion College (founded in 1919), taking charge of its academic and business affairs while its trustees sought a new president. During Marion's ten years of existence, financial stresses and conflicts involving the administration, faculty, students, and the conference led to the departure of two presidents. The second president was forced to resign by the Book Committee due to his spending proclivities and his resistance to close supervision of this midwestern school by the "Eastern Board." His turbulent five-year tenure and departure followed the troubled three years of the first president, the orthodoxy of whose theology was called into question. A third, interim president was appointed, but this man's advancing age and status as a non-Wesleyan limited his service to two years. Then Luckey was called in.[32] This additional duty required a number of train trips, one day and five hundred miles each way, adding strain to his sixty-two-year-old body.[33]

President Luckey's great efforts in behalf of Houghton College, Marion College, and the Wesleyan Methodist denomination were formally recognized in 1932 when Wheaton College awarded to him a doctor of laws

(LLD) degree. At long last, the dedicated teacher and scholar of mathematics who elected to leave Harvard before his terminal-degree work could be completed would be known as "Doctor Luckey."

Two years later, Houghton College suffered a major loss in its faculty ranks when Dean W. LaVay Fancher died by his own hand. According to several acquainted with the matter, Dr. Fancher, weakened by overwork, suffered a major tooth infection which apparently poisoned his entire system, clouding his judgment and causing him to seek drastic relief. Some thirty years younger than J. S. Luckey, holder of a doctorate from Cornell, and highly regarded on campus and in Wesleyan circles, it appears he would have been a logical successor to Luckey upon the latter's retirement. But this was not to be.

Then, less than six months after the college was accredited by the Middle States Association, J. S. Luckey suffered another emotional blow on April 17, 1936, when Edith Curtis Luckey died. She had always shared his vision and had been a major moral support. Her role was described by Professor Ray Hazlett:

> [At events honoring her husband] I can see Mrs. Luckey in the background, proudly self-effacing and beaming her . . . approval of the students, the pounding of the bass drum and the blatting of a hastily organized band, the noise and the speeches, and in short everything and everybody connected with Houghton and her husband. Her faith in both may have been childlike in a sense, but it was sublime."[34]

She would be sorely missed, and her loss would shorten J. S. Luckey's own days. His health had been deteriorating for some time; one person who had been a student in the middle '30s felt that President Luckey was "over the hill in some respects before he died."[35] On a tour in October with the A Capella Choir, Luckey was seriously stricken and endured two surgeries in Plattsburgh, New York. He was able to return to Houghton, and he rallied enough to award Houghton's first three honorary doctorates at the Founder's Day convocation in late November. But he continued to weaken, and on April 7, 1937, the cancer which had laid him low claimed his life at age sixty-nine.

The former president of the University of the State of New York and Commissioner of Education offered these words of eulogy:

It is my opinion that the present prosperity of Houghton College is largely due to the leadership and devoted work of Doctor Luckey. As a result of the improved standing of the institution, the Board of Regents felt justified in 1923 in granting a provisional charter to Houghton College and extending this into an absolute charter four years later. The record of Houghton College from the date of the original charter shows steady improvement, both in material resources and in educational standing. . . . A large share of the credit for this fine showing, through a period when many colleges were closing their doors or proceeding on reduced scales, should go to Doctor Luckey.[36]

According to one alumnus of Houghton Seminary, J. S. Luckey felt tension from the more conservative elements of the denomination. "I got the impression from [President Luckey's] attitude that he was not always in accord with the strict rules he had to enforce."[37] He also offered this succinct thought: "He was really a remarkable man, a great educator, who was trying to bring a lot of various forces into line so Houghton could become a recognized college with a charter from the New York State Department of Education, allowing it to grant degrees."[38]

Serious students of Houghton College history who carefully examine the strivings of J. S. Luckey and the changes he helped to bring about from 1908 to 1937 will reach the conclusion that here truly was a dedicated and fearless Christian educator. He was a servant-scholar-soldier who faced and fought the dragons of tradition, denominational anti-intellectualism, weak financial support, severely limited campus resources, faculty and staff overloads, and a host of other academic hindrances. Such thoughtful scrutiny will lead them to agree with this summary offered by denominational historians McLeister and Nicholson:

The outstanding personality of Houghton Seminary, and later of Houghton College, was James Seymour Luckey, whose two-year term as principal [1894–1896] was followed by almost thirty years [1908–1937] as president. . . . When he took [the presidential] office in 1908, Houghton College [sic] had 202 students with 12 enrolled in the collegiate department. Before his death [in 1937] the school was a fully accredited college with 460 students, of whom 394 were registered in the college.[39]

There can be no question that James Seymour Luckey was the right man for the job of moving the institution at Houghton from its status in 1908 as a small, local, denominational secondary institution with hopes of becoming something greater, through years of turmoil and strain to become a chartered and fully-accredited Christian college of liberal arts and sciences.

Chartered and Accredited

1923–1937

The extended and strenuous efforts of faculty, administration, and trustees paid off in 1923 when Houghton's provisional college charter was granted by the Regents of the University of the State of New York (see appendix G for the text). But that achievement, so thrilling to all at Houghton, was merely the first of three giant steps to be taken by the college to achieve regional and national stature. The next was to qualify for a permanent charter, and before that could be done the Regents mandated certain requirements to be met. Prior to the expiration of the provisional charter in five years, the college library must be increased, the music program needed to grow, courses for pre-medical work needed to be developed, and a system of leaves of absence had to be implemented to allow faculty members to pursue higher degrees. According to Willard Smith, the New York State Department of Education stipulated that the college needed an income from gifts and endowment of at least $20,000 annually.[1] Concurrently, one of the largest requirements was that the college must achieve a net worth (including buildings, property, and endowment) equivalent to $500,000.[2] And how immense was that challenge? Expressed in 2004 dollars, that figure would equal about $10 million.

A special 1923 document called the *Bulletin of General Information*, prepared and published as part of the application for a provisional charter, reported the status of Houghton's physical plant:

Buildings:

Jennings Hall [later Fancher Hall]: This is the main recitation building for the college work, and also contains the library, and the chapel which seats four hundred in the main room, with additional space for one hundred in rooms opening from it.

Bowen Hall [later Woolsey Hall]: This is a fine new brick building in the process of erection. It is now enclosed and nearly plastered, therefore it is expected that it will be completed, equipped, and ready for use next September [1923]. This building is to contain the college laboratories and the recitation rooms of the preparatory department.

Bedford Gymnasium: This gymnasium for men and women was made possible largely through the efforts of Professor H. C. Bedford. It is a fine brick building, with a splendid gymnasium floor and a gallery. The basement is to be used for lockers and shower baths, but these are not yet installed.

Besse Hall [later Gaoyadeo dormitory]: Besse Hall was named in honor of Rev. H. T. Besse of San Jose, California who furnished the funds for its construction. It is a fine brick building used as a dormitory for women, and accommodates fifty. It receives fifty men for table board.

Laboratories: One half of Bowen Hall is to be used for the teaching of science, and three new laboratories each connected to its own recitation room will be devoted to college work. One laboratory and recitation will be devoted to Chemistry, one to Physics, and one to the biological sciences.

Jennings Hall: 76 by 57, basement and two stories.

Bowen Hall: 80 by 56, basement and two stories

Bedford Gymnasium: 40 by 80, two stories

Heating plant: small brick building with tubular boiler.[3]

But even as the college was preparing to apply for a permanent charter and beginning to move towards its future as a nationally-recognized Christian institution of the liberal arts and sciences, the denomination was looking somewhat askance at the risks of such pursuit of truth. During the

Twenty-First General Conference of the Wesleyan Methodist Church, held in June 1923, the Committee on Education, chaired by Houghton alumnus Rev. Francis R. Eddy, proposed and saw adopted by the conference these standards to which the schools of the denomination would be required to conform.

> We are aware that most great moves away from the simplicity of the gospel and away from the fundamentals of the faith in the various churches have had their beginnings in the school systems, and we believe that it must be insisted upon that all our schools should function to produce trained Christian workers for her ranks. General education should be a secondary matter not the primary object of the church. No school under church patronage and support shall be allowed to call in question, much less deny, the position of the church on any point of doctrine or church polity. The province of the Church is to declare doctrine and of the school to teach what the Church declares. . . .
>
> . . . To the accomplishment of this end the Book Committee shall be in general control and supervision of all the educational institutions of the Church no matter what their organization, and be able thereby to formulate and effect a unified procedure in the teaching and promulgation of the ideals and the doctrines of the Church.[4]

As mentioned in chapter 6, President Luckey must have felt a bit of frustration over the church's overt posture relative to his efforts to continue developing a Christian college of liberal arts rather than a sectarian Bible school. But, even as he sought a peaceful continuance of church-college relations, he (like his successor, Stephen Paine) worked to promote and achieve academic excellence. His efforts are reflected in an oft-chanted campus ditty:

> Head full of brains,
> Brains full of knowledge.
> Rather be in Luckey's school
> Than any other college.[5]

First Graduation

It was a truly gusset-busting day in June 1925 when Houghton College held its first collegiate graduation convocation and awarded degrees to twenty beaming scholars:

Allen M. Baker	Esther Haynes
Laura Baker	Herbert Lennox
Fred L. Bedford	Josephine Rickard
Mark Bedford	Pearl Russell
Arthur Bernhoft	Clarice Spencer
Mary Anna Churchill	Helen Davison Stark
Rachel Davison (Fee)	Laura Steese
Keith Farner	Earl Tierney
Kenneth Gibbin	Edward Williams
Alice Hampe (McMillan)	Mary Williams

Two of the names should be very familiar to students of Houghton history: Rachel Davison Fee served Houghton for thirty-four years as a mathematics teacher and registrar, and Josephine ("Doc Jo") Rickard devoted forty-three years to the fields of writing and English. Three others from the class of '25 also returned to work for their alma mater: Allen M. Baker taught French for nine years (during which time he surveyed the old alumni field, today the tennis courts and parking area); Alice Hampe McMillan, who had served as dean of women for three years prior to her graduation, later came back for thirteen years as a Bible teacher; and Helen Davison Stark spent three years as dean of women and two more as faculty.

As the first graduates departed the campus in 1925, Houghton was not yet in a position to require all teachers to have an advanced degree, although the college was moving rapidly toward that time. Historically, the institution first sought teachers of ability who could "fit in" at Houghton and then encouraged them to work on advanced degrees.[6] As we shall see in later discussions, however, pressures in higher education caused Houghton to shift its emphasis, seeking first as faculty individuals who were holders of doctoral degrees and then encouraging those selected to conform to Houghton's academic and theological milieu. But not everyone welcomed these pressures from outside agencies. One Houghton historian noted: "Some members of the Wesleyan Methodist Board, based in Syracuse, were fearful that academic standardization might result in lessened spiritual effectiveness."[7] Others later reported that they saw a negative change on campus in terms of increased personal commitment to the specific academic disciplines and lessened dedication to Houghton College as a collegial institution.

The 1926 Revival

Houghton over the years has been blessed with several great revivals, and the earliest to be identified occurred in February 1926. The Rev. Charles V. Fairbairn, a bishop in the Canadian Methodist Church, served as evangelist, and he reported on the experience in a magazine article (publication and date unknown) by quoting two letters. In the first letter, dated February 22, 1926, Houghton pastor Rev. Joseph R. Pitt said:

God has given us the mightiest revival in the history of Houghton. . . . Never before have we faced such a crisis as we did this year, owing to the fact that Houghton had become a chartered college and . . . needed a corresponding advancement in spiritual life. After months of agonizing prayer, God has fulfilled the petition of his people. . . .[8]"

The second letter, written during the revival week from Fairbairn to his wife, said:

When I tell you that 259 seekers have been to the mourners' bench, you will see that Almighty God has undertaken as I have not seen him undertake in several years. Not only are they seeking at the altar, but conviction has spread until the professors are having prayer services in their classrooms instead of lessons. . . . Yesterday the vocal teacher broke down and prayed through. Classes were broken up, and for hours the students prayed for salvation and victory. . . .
   . . . We do not know what turn these services will take, but the Lord has things in hand.[9]

A close reading of the first letter's text hints that there was some concern about a possible drifting away from the pious dimensions believed to be found in a school with a strong biblical foundation toward being a liberal arts college with an as-yet undetermined spirituality. The success of the revival seemed to assure those most concerned that God still had his hand in the endeavor.

Growth under the Charter

Although its administrative records from the 1920s are not extensive, Houghton managed to meet the stipulations of the New York Regents within four years,[10] and the college's permanent charter was granted on June 30, 1927 (see appendix G). Then, once the financial footing had been solidified and the permanent charter was in hand, the next need was to achieve accreditation by the Middle States Association of Colleges and Secondary Schools. To be thus recognized would give Houghton College official status on the national academic scene, allow credits earned by its students to be readily accepted by other accredited colleges, and greatly enhance its image in the eyes of its constituency—and of the Wesleyan Methodist Church. But this too would require moving beyond the Houghton of 1923 and 1927, and work soon began or continued on a variety of projects.

In 1923, faculty and students had joined in connecting the gravity water line installed in 1912 to two additional springs. In 1928 a small reservoir was built at an elevation above the campus and a new line was laid to feed water to it from the springs.[11] That same year, a fund drive was established to provide some sort of medical facility for the college. The brick residence of George Hussey (the former home of J. N. Bedford), standing on the lip of the hill on the southeast edge of the campus, was remodeled into an infirmary with four private rooms plus a physician's office and a sunroom. Later called McDowell Cottage, it was eventually renamed Bedford Infirmary. Two nurses were hired to work part-time to attend to student needs.

In October 1929, the crash of the stock market threw America into the Great Depression, and once again a national economic disaster (as in the Panic of 1893) adversely affected Houghton. Though the Wesleyan Methodist Church had pledged to the college $15,000 annually starting in 1927, giving never reached that level until 1938. The annual report for 1932 showed total college income that year to be $106,888.53 (including $11,177.15 from borrowing).[12] Total disbursements were $102,014.68, with cash on hand on December 31 of $6,172.57. The years immediately earlier and later were not much different, and President Luckey identified two prime effects of the Depression on the college: decreased enrollment and reduced church giving. The president also reported net assets of the college on December 31, 1932, as $399,018.29.[13]

The lean economic times and the lack of construction funds hampered significant expansion of the physical plant but did not stop it entirely. In 1932, a solid, three-story brick building was erected to hold the music program.

Called simply the Music Building (though later nicknamed "Cacophony Hall" for the din from the incessant practice sessions, especially in seasons when windows were opened), it stood and served for over sixty years, far beyond the tenure of both J. S. Luckey and Stephen W. Paine. Then in 1934, a new village church (funded by sacrificial giving plus many promissory notes) was completed and dedicated, allowing larger congregations to assemble than had been possible on the second floor of Old Admin.[14]

The music program, which had been active earlier, grew significantly in the 1930s. According to essayist Kenneth Wilson, Houghton's touring musical groups were of prime significance in spreading awareness of the college throughout the evangelical community in the Northeast.

> The A Capella Choir was probably the biggest factor in putting Houghton in the public eye and ear. Merging the existing glee clubs when he came in 1931, Wilfred Bain made the choir the most select organization on campus. Members were chosen by competitive audition. Their training to near perfection under a severe regimen of constant practice and strict discipline became legendary. Traveling from Boston to Chicago and from Toronto to Washington, the A Capella presented concerts in churches of many denominations, sang in local and network broadcasts. . . .[15]

Many of the individuals interviewed for this book cited their opportunity to hear a Houghton musical group as being a prime factor in their decision to apply for admission to the college.

Data assembled by Willard Smith show that enrollment in Houghton College expanded by nearly 300 percent from 1923 to 1937 (see table 10). In 1923, 54 men and 51 women were enrolled (total of 105), and by 1927 there were 159. Men held a slight numerical edge until 1928, when women first outnumbered them, 87 to 95, a situation that was reversed only in 1934. The year 1930 saw 268 on board, and by 1937 total enrollment reached 394. Of this latter number, 184 were men and 210 were women.[16]

Alan Graffam, after reviewing student publications, wrote this summary of the apparent effects of the Depression:

> While different in kind, the impact of the Depression on campus life did not change significantly from that of the first World War. *The Star* conveyed the impression that student life was relatively unchanged, editorially mentioning the problem of complaints concerning the

country's leadership during the Depression, but otherwise representing student life as quite normal. Reports emphasized the debate team's success and performers in the concert series. The problems created by the Depression were not high on the students' priority list; other events carried greater importance at the time.[18]

One of these, of course, was the hope for accreditation by Middle States, bringing with it with the ready portability of Houghton College academic credits.

TABLE 10		Enrollment at Houghton College, 1923–1936[17]	
Year	Men	Women	Total
1923–24	54	51	105
1924–25	65	65	130
1925–26	76	66	142
1926–27	82	77	159
1927–28	87	95	182
1928–29	91	132	223
1929–30	93	141	234
1930–31	111	157	268
1931–32	138	153	291
1932–33	123	133	256
1933–34	140	138	278
1934–35	132	155	287
1935–36	171	184	355

Accreditation in 1935

In the years from 1930 to 1935, Houghton College worked hard to gain accreditation by the Middle States Association. Although Houghton held an absolute charter from the New York State Regents as a degree-granting institution, for it to achieve regional recognition depended on being granted accreditation. However, the Middle States committee did not feel that Houghton was ready.

In his commemorative publication, *Consider the Years*, Dr. Kenneth L. Wilson described the slow progress toward accreditation. "When the college applied for admission to the [Middle States] Association in 1930 and again in 1933, the inspecting commission pointed out that certain improvements would be necessary before approval: building alterations, administrative changes, library expansion, faculty salary increases."[19]

Interestingly, Houghton's several applications for accreditation by the Middle States Association of Colleges and Secondary Schools do not appear to have survived. The first application (most probably in 1930) led to a site visit by a team representing the Middle States Commission on Institutions of Higher Education. It resulted in a letter of postponement, dated November 29, 1930. Among the subjective points cited were these:

- Insufficient funds for the proper maintenance of a fully efficient college.

- Insufficient graduate training completed by members of the faculty.

- Inadequate salaries to sustain well-trained scholars with any degree of permanence.

- Loose administration of admission of students.[20]

In 1931, the Middle States Association of Colleges and Secondary Schools published its standards for accreditation. Houghton's next application, in 1933, was measured against these standards. An extract from these standards follows, accompanied by appropriate data from Houghton records.

Middle States' Principles and Standards for Accrediting Colleges, November 1931
From item 3:
For a college of approximately 100 students in a single curriculum, the faculty should consist of at least eight heads of departments devoting full time to college work *[Ed note: that suggests a student to faculty ratio of 12.5:1.]*. With the growth of the student body the number of full-time teachers should be correspondingly increased. . . .

[In 1933, the year of its second application, Houghton had 24 full-time faculty and 256 students, a student to faculty ratio of 10.7 to 1.][21]

The training of the members of the faculty of professorial rank should include at least two years of study in their respective fields of teaching in a recognized graduate school. It is desirable that the training of the head of a department should be equivalent to that required for the doctor's degree or should represent a corresponding professional or technical training.

[Of the 24 faculty, 21 percent [5] held doctoral-level degrees, 54 percent [13] held master's degrees, and 21 percent [5] held bachelor's degrees, though four of these had the BMus as a second degree. One teacher had a conservatory certificate.][22]

4. The minimum annual operating income for an accredited college, exclusive of payment of interest, annuities, etc., should be $50,000, of which not less than $25,000 should be derived from stable sources, other than students, preferably from permanent endowments. Increase in faculty, student body and scope of instruction should be accompanied by increase in income from endowment. . . .

[The 1932 annual report showed income from students at $51,380.67, income from investments at $9,273.71, and income from gifts at $8,345.43 [of which $6,060.98 was from the Wesleyan Methodist Church budget].][23]

5. The material, equipment and upkeep of a college, including its buildings, lands, laboratories, apparatus, and libraries, and their efficient operation in relation to its educational progress, should also be considered. . . .

[As mentioned earlier, the net assets of the college were reported as nearly $400,000.]

A college should have a live, well-distributed, professionally administered library of at least 8,000 volumes, exclusive of public documents, . . . with definite annual appropriation for the purchase of new books.

[According to the Catalogue for 1933–1934, the library's holdings totalled 10,000 volumes. Also, the library had received its own NYS charter in 1931, for "attaining the standard of efficiency."][24]

6. A college should not maintain a preparatory school as part of its college organization. . . .

[Though Houghton Seminary was operating under its original 1883 incorporation document and Houghton College under its 1927 absolute charter, both were under a common board of trustees, and the seminary was identified as the preparatory school for the college. Of the eight persons named as seminary faculty, four were primarily college faculty.][25]

7. In determining the standing of a college, emphasis should be placed upon the character of the curriculum, the efficiency of instruction, the standard for regular degrees, the conservatism in granting honorary degrees, the tone of the institution and its success in stimulating and preparing students to do satisfactory work in recognized graduate, professional, or research institutions.

[Houghton alumni were achieving success in graduate programs, though no detailed data have been kept. Honorary degrees were not granted until 1936.]

The paper trail of Houghton's accreditation events is very limited, but this paragraph was located in the records of the Middle States Association concerning the Houghton application in 1933:

The Commission voted to defer action on the application of Houghton College. This action was taken in view of the following facts among others: the financial resources which seemed not yet to be entirely adequate, the maintenance of separate schools of theology and music in the organization of the institution whereas these are in effect no more than departments of the college, the fact that the scholastic index of the college as shown by the College Entrance Inquiry made under the direction of Dr. Philip Cowen of the New York State Education Department in 1932 was distinctly low. The Commission would suggest also the modification in the direction of greater simplicity and dignity of certain of the statements in the catalogue regarding certain prohibitions[26]

In the summer of 1935, President Luckey undertook another attempt to convince Middle States of Houghton's improvements and qualifications. Dean Stephen Paine accompanied him on his trip to Hamilton College to call on the Middle States committee chairman, Dr. Frederick Ferry, and the visit was described in the Paine diary:

> President Luckey made a wonderful and well-substantiated appeal that this was the year that Houghton should be admitted. Dr. Ferry was very courteous, and you could see that he admired Dr. Luckey very much. . . . [But Ferry still felt that Houghton needed to improve in several areas] . . . We went out of that meeting rather discouraged. . . . [27]

From there Luckey and Paine drove on to Albany to see Dr. Harlan Horner, Associate Commissioner for Higher Education in the state Department of Education. According to the Paine diary:

> President Luckey gave the same speech he had given to Ferry. I was waiting for the same reaction, but instead of that, this man leaned back in his chair and looked at President Luckey and said, 'You will remember that a year ago I talked with you about this matter and told you at that time that I didn't think that Houghton was quite ready to be accredited as a full four year liberal arts college. I want to tell you how I look at it today. I think you have been very conscientious and have made some of the improvements that were suggested. I think that you are ready and I'll recommend you.'[28]

After a third application, the news received from Middle States was much better. Again, an excerpt from the commission's minutes, this time from November 13, 1935: "President Ferry presented his report on Houghton College which was represented before the Commission by President Luckey. It was voted to include the college in the accepted list of the Association."[29] Tradition has it that the message of success was relayed over an open phone line to the college community assembled in the chapel on the top floor of the administration building, and President Luckey reported from Baltimore that he could hear the loud ringing of the college bell.

With that last milestone reached and with economic times slowly improving, the college was poised for expansion and growth. An amendment to the state charter in 1936 allowed the awarding of honorary degrees,[30] and three individuals who had played a major role in the chartering and accreditation of Houghton College were selected to be the first recipients: Ira F. McLeister, president of the Book Committee and president of Houghton's board of trustees; Herman Cooper, Assistant Commissioner of Education for New York; and James O. Buswell, president of Wheaton College during Stephen Paine's undergraduate days.

But a dark cloud soon shadowed the campus with the death of James S. Luckey in April 1937. His successor, Stephen W. Paine, took office on July 1. In bidding farewell to his predecessor and mentor, Dr. Paine said:

> During the past few years it has been my rare privilege to be, in some measure, his fellow-traveler and co-worker. I have thoroughly enjoyed his genial sense of humor, have loved him for his kindly interest in the lives of friends and associates, have marvelled at his untiring energy, and have coveted his mountain-removing faith. Humanly speaking, I cannot think of anyone under whose direction I'd rather serve.[31]

The college that Stephen Paine received was well begun, but the physical plant was already groaning from pressures of student enrollment, Middle States had made clear that great improvements in faculty credentials and salary were expected, financing continued to be tenuous, and the Wesleyan Methodist Church would be watching carefully this very young man from one of its more "liberal" districts. The road ahead would be challenging, uphill, and quite bumpy.

The Youngest President

Stephen W. Paine

Stephen W. Paine looms large in the memories of thousands of Houghton alumni, especially the five thousand or so who graduated while he was a faculty member or president. And because most of the twenty years of his retirement were spent in the Houghton community, another four or five thousand were allowed to at least glimpse the man they had heard so much about. While the story of his life is presented in great detail in his daughter Miriam's book, *Deo Volente, a Biography of Stephen W. Paine*, some essential details need to be covered here.

Early Days

Like his predecessor in the president's office, Stephen Paine was a life-long Wesleyan Methodist. But, while J. S. Luckey was a local lad, Stephen William Paine was a Michigander who took his higher education in Illinois. He was born on October 20, 1908, in Grand Rapids, Michigan, to Stephen Hugh Paine (1862–1953) and the former Mary Wilfrieda Fischer (1883–1969), as the eldest of ten children. His paternal great-grandfather, George Lansing Paine, had been a charter member of the Wesleyan

Methodist Connection in 1843 and founded the Wesleyan Methodist church in Berrytown, Pennsylvania, in 1860. And his mother's maternal grandfather, Jonathan Blanchard, was the first president of Wheaton College. According to the Wheaton College Web site, "In 1859 Jonathan Blanchard left his position as president of Knox College in Galesburg, Illinois, to lead the struggling Illinois Institute, founded in Wheaton, Illinois, by the Wesleyans in 1854. This able administrator was known widely as a staunch abolitionist and crusader for social reform."[1]

Stephen Paine credited his interest in becoming college faculty to the influence of his great-uncle, Charles A. Blanchard (brother of Jonathan), who was president of Wheaton when Stephen was growing up and during his first semester of attendance at that college.[2] Yet Stephen was not dogmatic about his career plans: asked on the Wheaton application to state his life's goal, he wrote, "My goal is to do the will of God."[3] A dozen years after his retirement, Stephen Paine added this thought: "How little I realized the implications [of that statement]. . . . The intervening years have brought the ever-thrilling discovery of the great affirmative answers to [my] questions."[4]

It is fascinating at this point to note the similarities between James S. Luckey and Stephen W. Paine. Both were stalwart, assertive personalities, both were well-focused on what they believed to be their calling from God, and both were brilliant. Luckey's mental acumen may be presumed from his acceptance into Harvard's doctoral program in mathematics; Paine's great intellect is attested by the fact that he was the top student in his class all four years at Wheaton College, receiving a full-tuition scholarship each year for his achievement.[5] Both were competitive: Luckey wanted the best Christian liberal-arts school possible and was willing to battle the Wesleyan Methodist hierarchy to achieve that goal; Paine was active in athletics (baseball, cross-country, and tennis) and in debate (much like his spiritual ancestor, John Wesley[6]), and he eventually donned Luckey's mantle in the liberal arts–Bible school fray. Stephen's interest in the sport of forensic disputation displayed on one hand his competitive nature and on the other his belief in the benefits of such a rigorous activity. He obviously subscribed to Wheaton College's assertion that "One who can express himself, winning adherents to his cause, shows mental preparation and experience essential to the well-trained man or woman."[7]

After earning his bachelor's degree from Wheaton, young Steve Paine enrolled in graduate school at the University of Illinois in Champaign-Urbana. There he met the youthful Helen Lucile Paul, then sixteen years old. Here's the story in her words:

I met [Steve] when he came to the University of Illinois. That's how we got acquainted, in a little independent church [Champaign Gospel Tabernacle] that was there. . . . He said the first time he ever saw me, I walked out of the church carrying a baby—that was my little nephew. Our house was just near the university . . . and my mom was good to have people over for dinner. So that's how we got acquainted.[8]

They were married on August 17, 1934, a year after Steve Paine completed his doctorate in classics and accepted a teaching position at Houghton College. Five children were born to this union: Marjorie Helen (1935; deceased from complications of poliomyelitis in 1955), Carolyn Esther (1938), Miriam Ruth (1942), Stephen William Jr. (1953), and Kathryn Elizabeth (1956).[9] A sidenote is that the eldest three were all born in the little Fillmore (New York) hospital, now long gone.

Teaching at Houghton

According to Helen Paine, President Luckey wanted Houghton to be an outstanding educational school and to this end sought to add doctorate-holders to the faculty. "When he heard Steve was getting a PhD from Illinois, he came out to Champaign to see him and wanted him to come to Houghton. . . . He said, 'We'll *make* a job for you,' and he did."[10] The board promptly approved Luckey's request to offer Stephen Paine a position as an instructor in the classics at a starting salary of $800 per year plus room and board.[11]

Edward Willett, class of 1939 and a long-time Houghton faculty member, reported that his father, Wesleyan Methodist publishing agent John S. Willett, was the one who recruited Stephen Paine.

My father had to go out to the Michigan Conference as denominational representative, and when he was ready to come back to Syracuse somebody had to take him to Kalamazoo to the train, and Stephen Paine was elected. He'd just finished his PhD at Illinois. On the way down, Dad asked him what he was thinking of doing with his PhD, and Steve said, "Well, I've been thinking I'd like to teach." Dad said, "You wouldn't consider a contract at Houghton College, would you?" He said, "Well, I might very well." So when Dad got home he apparently consulted with President Luckey and the next thing Steve wrote he had a letter which he showed me—he kept it all these years—where my father had sent his first teaching contract.[12]

It is obvious that Houghton's administration and trustees alike felt a need to enlist Steve Paine and his new doctorate to labor at Houghton. The quest for Middle States accreditation also added some pressure to recruit for faculty service individuals who held doctorates; when Doctor Paine came aboard, he became doctorate-holder number four. An alumnus from 1935 reported on Stephen Paine's arrival in 1933:

> When he came to Houghton as a young man, many of us smiled at his quiet movement on the campus because he was so humble he didn't identify himself. He would be in the dining hall and students would say, "What class are you?" and he'd play along with them . . . "I'm just new here. I'm a freshman on campus."[13]

S. W. Paine brought to his classroom his superb mastery of Greek and a certain intensity. Arthur Lynip, class of 1938 and later dean of the college for sixteen years, described his teaching style: "His classes were fairly exacting. One was a little afraid of him. . . . He had a succinct way of saying things were wrong that made a person uneasy. I can think of just plain fear enveloping us that we would be caught not knowing, because it was clear that knowing was the name of the game."[14]

Eugene Lemcio '64, who later married Miriam Paine, described Stephen Paine's chapel exploration of the authorship of the Pentateuch: "Dr. Paine tackled the most damaging critique and the ablest defense of the Mosaic authorship of Genesis through Deuteronomy. . . . Those talks, not always comprehensible and hardly ever boring, were the sort of thing that one might expect to hear in college. Our intelligence was being given the benefit of the doubt."[15]

Near the end of Stephen Paine's first year of teaching at Houghton, he was contacted by President J. Oliver Buswell of Wheaton and offered a professorship there, at about three times his Houghton salary. The offer was presented just a few weeks before the day he received a half-month paycheck for $12.44 from cash-strapped Houghton—and five dollars of that was needed to send his Houghton-student sister Mary on the spring choir tour. The offer of more money was attractive, and there were other pressures leading him to consider Wheaton: its proximity to libraries in Chicago, its nearness to his family's home in Michigan, and—more importantly—its proximity to fiancee Helen Paul's home in Champaign. Helen's father had died suddenly in March 1934, and Steve knew it would be hard for her to move away following their planned August wedding.[16]

Then another factor intervened: in May 1934, after academic dean LaVay Fancher died by his own hand, Dr. Luckey offered Steve the acting deanship at a more-than-doubled salary. (Former history department chair Frieda Gillette commented many years later, "The way he [LaVay] went was traumatic, indeed, but perhaps the Lord was in it."[17]) When the Wesleyan Methodist board unanimously confirmed his permanent appointment, recommended by the faculty, Steve felt his prayers had been answered concerning his serving where he was most needed, and he accepted the Houghton post. Though Dr. Buswell said he would hold the Wheaton teaching position available for a year, the split duties of teaching and administration at Houghton seemed to be a fit. Paine had not yet turned twenty-six when he moved into the dean's position, but he quickly took to the responsibilities of the office even as he continued to instruct.

Dr. Paine began his Houghton service as a teacher of Greek (and simultaneously of Latin, French, and Argumentation), and for twenty years he painstakingly prepared and refined his Greek class notes and teaching materials. Eventually he became dissatisfied with the traditional "disciplinarian" method of teaching Greek, which depended largely on memorization work, and in 1953 he began to develop his own textbook. He commented, "The inductive system has taken over the field of modern language study but has not been applied to the classics."

Over the next five years, he used his unpublished text in his beginning Greek classes and revised it in light of the experience of students and teacher alike. His text included a vocabulary of 1400 words instead of the usual 400, and it included a larger range of literature. In 1958, he began to prepare the text for publication, and in 1961, Oxford Press released his book as *A Functional Approach to Beginning Greek*.[18]

Presidency

As Dr. Paine was beginning his third year as dean, Dr. Luckey's health began to fail rapidly. He rallied briefly to present the first three honorary degrees in November 1936, then grew worse, and vice president H. LeRoy Fancher and dean Stephen Paine picked up an ever-increasing part of the presidential workload. Then, in April 1937, Dr. Luckey died, and vice president Fancher moved in as acting president until the board could select a replacement.[19] In June 1937 the trustees named Stephen Paine as Luckey's successor,[20] and he began his service as college president on July 1, 1937. He would not turn twenty-nine until October. Helen Paul Paine, the college's new first lady, was but twenty-three.

While Paine was a most logical successor to Luckey, there were those on the board who had held reservations about this obviously young man from a Wesleyan Methodist conference known to be on the liberal side. Professor Edward Willett's interview with Roy Nicholson offered some details:

> Dr. Luckey's name was a charmed name in Wesleyan education, and when he died there was a great vacuum and the question was, who will take his place? . . . Here was this young PhD, not many of [the board members] knew him and, very frankly, a lot of times the younger man with a high degree would be suspect as to his loyalty [to the denomination]. . . . When the name of Dr. Stephen Paine came up [before the board], somebody immediately raised the youth question, but they also raised the question of whether or not he was committed to the doctrines of the church. . . . I knew that some of them were going to publicly raise the issue. . . . So when the nomination was made, with great fear and trembling but before God and in all sincerity and honesty, I wrote out a question and . . . asked if the nominee would say right there and answer affirmatively in reference to a certain paragraph in the Discipline. . . . Dr. Paine rose very graciously and very kindly said, "I can answer in the affirmative." When he said that it eased everybody's mind.[21]

With characteristic modesty, the new young president requested that the trustees not hold a formal inauguration ceremony, and he quietly moved his professional possessions from the dean's space into the presidential office.

There were those in the community who had feared that the board would make an unwise presidential selection in a different direction. Willard Smith, county judge Ward Hopkins, and *Perry Herald* editor Guy Comfort were chatting in front of the Houghton church after Luckey's funeral. According to Smith, the other two expressed their concern that "the school would go to the dogs because the church would put some tactless preacher in for president. I most emphatically assured them that we (the faculty and staff) felt no such folly would occur."[22]

Edward Willett related an incident from Dr. Paine's early days as president that illustrates his focus on achievement:

He was in the old tabernacle on the [Wesleyan Methodist] camp-ground, inside after the service. He was standing near one of the sliding windows that was open because of the temperature, and . . . some people [whom he could not see] were talking outside about him in a very, very favorable light. He said, "Ed, I made up my mind then I had to live up to it."[23]

That Stephen Paine settled into the new office with an awareness of Wesleyan Methodist and college expectations and with great determination was affirmed by Silas Molyneaux, class of 1935. Silas told how the perceived requirements of his new office affected Dr. Paine:

[Steve] was only twenty-eight years old or something at the time [when he became president]. His reputation as being very rigid [and] formalistic in his approach came from that period when he was a little apprehensive, and he wanted to set a standard [for the college]. He changed in his later years and became less rigid in his approach to things and became a very good friend of mine.[24]

One of the standards that Stephen Paine set for the college was quite high. In an interview published in the Rochester *Democrat & Chronicle*, the reporter quoted Dr. Paine as saying he was out to make his Wesleyan Methodist institution "the outstanding Christian College in the East."[25] The college's progress toward that goal is reported in subsequent chapters.

Arthur Lynip offered another observation, perhaps a bit tongue-in-cheek, that gives a glimpse of the high regard in which Stephen Paine was held by Houghton students:

I'll tell you who the young President Paine was. He was the recent groom who, on a business trip alone to New York City brought back a dress for Helen, his equally recent bride. Who'd dare do that today? But *then*, because we students thought he did everything right, we all went out and got wives . . . WE would go on a trip and come back with a dress.[26]

Both S. W. Paine and J. S. Luckey were prayerfully humble, relying on God to provide for personal and collegiate needs and to achieve great things. Their biographies are rich with examples of prayers of praise and of supplication, of intercession and of importunity. Neither actively sought the high office of president nor exulted in it, though each accepted it and distinguished himself in that position. Both believed that "blessed are the peacemakers": Luckey carefully worked with the conservative members of the denominational Book Committee and secular representatives of the Regents to achieve the state charters, while Paine devoted great efforts to what proved to be a futile attempt to placate the arch-conservatives in the church and sustain good denominational relationships.

Not all the battles regarding liberal arts education and academic excellence had been fought and won during the Luckey regime. As an alumnus from the early Paine years reports, "Academic proficiency was in [1937] a highly suspect guest in the house of holiness. He, as have few other Christian college presidents, made academic disciplines acceptable to cautious religious conservatives."[27]

One of Paine's long-time key associates offered these words:

> I deeply respected Stephen Paine because he did what he did not from how it would appear politically but from very deep-seated conviction. Everything he did [was done] because he was convinced it was what he ought to do or because it had to be done. . . . He didn't care two hoots who got [credit for] the results as long as he got the job done.
>
> In fact, his humility bothered me. It was a humility which became embarrassing when the institution needed to be represented aggressively. "I'll take the back seat; I'm the president of Houghton College" when he should have been up front shaking hands with the significant people. . . . We had to goad him, "Steve, get up there! You're important, you're on deck, you're the top man."[28]

This same associate, later quoted by Edward Willett, also commented on the benevolently autocratic style of Stephen Paine regarding his administrative associates.

> I do remember [Willard] saying to me one time that working for Stephen Paine was not the easiest thing to do. He said this quietly, looking at [the president's] inner office door, "There's at least one time when every one of us junior administrators almost literally crawled out under that door." In other words, Steve was the boss and if they got too feisty, he let them know it. But he always did it nicely, except that when you got those bushy eyebrows and those

dark eyes fastened on you and no smile. . . . On the campus [Dr. Paine] felt that it was a role [disciplinarian] that he had to play as a last resort, and he played it, though I think it was very hard on him.[29]

Those who knew and worked with Stephen Paine depicted him as larger than life, for many intents a Wesleyan saint. Without question he was a very special man, a conscientiously godly man. But Stephen Paine was quite human, and he felt distress and pressure and frustration like other humans. The death of his first-born in 1955, due to complications from polio, sorely tried his soul then and thereafter. Sadly, that loss occurred just three months before the quadrennial conference (meeting at Houghton) rebuffed the long-term efforts of S. W. Paine and others to achieve union with the Free Methodist Church and rejected the motion for union by a notable margin (ninety-six to sixty-two). The proposed union would have strengthened the evangelical outreach of both churches, provided the stronger voice that would come from the larger membership, promoted administrative efficiency, and spurred growth in both of the joining bodies, but it was not to be. (Further discussion of the union problems may be found in chapter 15, "Issues of Contention.")

And there were frustrations in college administration. Never having adequate finances to achieve many of the goals he believed needed to be accomplished weighed heavily, and though he felt blessed to have for many years on his inner administrative team three great and brilliant Christian academic soldiers, the three—Bob Luckey, Willard Smith, and Art Lynip— were almost equally strong-willed. Keeping the peace often meant not speaking his piece. As he remarked to one daughter, "An administrator never has the luxury of saying exactly what he thinks."[30]

Physical distress also crept into Stephen Paine's life. Later in his presidency, he began to suffer back discomfort, and it reached a point where it altered his capacity for work. Often, he was forced to work from his bed at home while waiting for the growing discomfort to recede. And a small accommodation was made in his office, where a lectern-style stand-up desk became an essential piece of furniture. Eventually, in 1970 he was hospitalized for diagnosis and treatment, and surgery was required.[31] In August 1970 a spinal disc was removed and over the following months his back improved.

Probably the most devastating ailment was the onset of Parkinson's disease, a chronic, progressive disease of the nervous system that is marked by tremors and physical weakness. This was discovered less than a year after his successful back surgery. Dr. Paine felt that this was the signal for him to bring his presidency to a close, and he notified his administrative team that he would retire following the 1971–1972 academic year.[32] He was sixty-four when he stepped down.

Stephen Paine and the New International Version

Stephen Paine helped found the National Association of Evangelicals (NAE) in 1941, and Houghton College applied for membership in the NAE in 1943.[33] During the annual meeting of the NAE in Buffalo in 1957, Stephen Paine was given what he called a "very nominal assignment"[34] to be among those evaluating the host of new translations then coming out. The assignment began because NAE felt that no one was paying any official attention to the new translations and that many of them contained passages that had been poorly translated. According to Dr. Paine, the newly-available Revised Standard Version (RSV) was adjudged as having the best chance of supplanting the traditional King James version, but NAE members had strong concerns about the Biblical exactness of the RSV. Because Dr. Paine had been one of the organizers of NAE and in 1941 had helped to write its doctrinal statements, he was among those asked to make a careful critical study of the RSV. Underlying the NAE request was a desire of the Christian Reformed Church to enlist like-minded conservative churches to unite in an effort to sponsor or facilitate "a faithful translation of the Scriptures in the common language of the American people."[35] The language of the King James, which had been translated originally in the seventeenth century to present the scriptures in the language of the English people, was felt to be now rather archaic, and a new version, casting the text in contemporary language while avoiding the perceived faults of other contemporary versions, was needed.

Concerning the King James version, Dr. Paine commented:

> The King James Bible did not become popular until about fifty years after it was written, and I myself think the strength of the King James was [that it was] an honest, straightforward type of translation (given the outmoded diction), but nevertheless the doctrines were straight and largely unselfconscious. Whereas in all the present translations . . . there's more self-consciousness.[36]

Steps to organize the work progressed very slowly, since limited funding restricted meetings of the committee to the annual NAE conference.

While the original intent had been to work with the authors of the RSV to amend what were felt to be unscholarly translations, the conviction quickly grew that a complete new rendering was in order. Consequently, at a multi-denominational conference on Bible translation in Palos Heights, California, in 1965, a formal statement was issued that established the need for a contemporary translation of the Bible. The "Committee of Fifteen" soon was organized.

Three years later, Stephen Paine spoke to the assembled translation team, now renamed the Committee on Bible Translation, and reviewed the genesis of the group and its task. He emphasized that the goal assigned to the committee was to produce "a good and fair translation which will permit the Bible to speak as it wants to speak,"[37] and that the translators must be "scholars of known evangelical commitment." Essential to this translation effort was this statement:

> In harmony with the expressed objectives of the program of the translation, it seems desirable that each person engaged in the work of translation should be clearly on record as to his beliefs. Everyone is to subscribe to the following doctrinal statement (or to a similar statement expressing an equally high view of Scripture): "The Bible alone, and the Bible in its entirety, is the Word of God written, and is therefore inerrant in the autographs."[38]

Asked how he found time to work on the translation while he was serving as Houghton's president, Dr. Paine replied that he wasn't one of the main resources, that others actually did the bulk of the translating. Because of the limited time available, he said, "I limited my activities to the editorial work of the committee."[39] But his office as chairman of the translating committee put him in a position to lead, encourage, and steer the work, and the final product included many thousands of his hours.

The physical and emotional stress of the years of attempted peacekeeping with factions of the Wesleyan Methodist church, plus the pressures of leading in the campus expansion of the late '50s and early '60s, were wearing on the no-longer youthful Stephen Paine, plagued with back problems and a growing measure of fatigue. In June 1967, a year after the secession of the Allegheny and Tennessee conferences, the board of trustees granted him a nine-month, half-pay sabbatical. During Homecoming Weekend the previous fall, the alumni association had presented the Paines with a check for over $8,000, specifying that it was to be used for personal study and travel abroad. Dr. Robert Luckey was named to be acting president, and the Paines' first substantial release from college rigors was soon planned.[40]

During the fall semester, the Paines (accompanied by their two youngest children, fourteen-year-old Stephen and one-year-old Kathryn) rented a house in Wilmore, Kentucky, near daughter Miriam and her husband, Eugene Lemcio, and Dr. Paine began an immersion study of Hebrew. Then, in the spring semester, the Paines traveled by train to the west coast and embarked by ship for Yokohama, then Hong Kong and Saigon, to visit daughter Carolyn and her husband, John Miller, who were Wycliffe missionaries to the Bru people near the Cambodian border of Vietnam. They arrived shortly after the bloody Tet offensive of 1968, which had forced the Millers to evacuate from Khe Sanh to Nha Trang. After six weeks in Vietnam, the Paines' journey continued to Bangkok, New Delhi, Tel Aviv, Thessalonika, Athens, Rome, Florence, Venice, Zurich, Frankfurt, Paris and London, plus stops in Scotland and Ireland. Back in America, refreshed and recharged, Stephen Paine resumed his presidential duties.[41]

Following his retirement in 1972, Dr. Paine was able to devote significantly more time to NIV translation efforts, including an extended stay in Greece. This took place in 1975 during the months while his daughter and son-in-law, missionaries Carolyn and John Miller, and their youngest daughter, LuAnne, were being held captive in Vietnam. Not only did the work in Athens partially divert his attention from the captivity, his contacts in Greece helped him reach North Vietnam officials living near Paris who might help effect a release. (Carolyn and John were freed in October 1975.)

Asked to state what was the most meaningful part of this NIV experience, Stephen Paine said, "I think the biggest basic satisfaction was [that] . . . we all agreed on . . . the inerrancy of Scripture."[42] Beyond that, he felt the most important aspect for him personally was to become acquainted with some of the greatest Hebrew and Greek scholars in the world and to hear their explanations and analyses.

Leave it to a wife to put things in perspective: during an interview in 1996, some four years after her husband's death, Helen Paine quoted Stephen as having said, "Maybe this [the NIV work] is the most important thing I've done in my life." But she disagreed, saying, "I think his influence on the students through all those years . . . would be more important to the Lord."[43]

Among the many aspects of Dr. Paine's dedicated Christian service are the long presidency of Houghton, a founder of the National Association of Evangelicals, a founder of Empire State Foundation of Independent Liberal Arts Colleges, a Greek textbook published by Oxford University, and extensive work on the New International Bible as a member and chair of the translation committee.

Characterizations

But a recitation of facts doesn't let anyone meet the living—and lively— Steve Paine. Consider these observations from those who knew him.

Dr. Kenneth Wilson '41 recalls the classroom teacher: "Dr. Paine had special expectations about faith and works. That is, whatever praying you might have been doing, you had better have done your homework. . . . To Doc, faith was something to help you get your job done, not an excuse for not doing it."[44]

Dr. Lee M. Haines, a former Wesleyan general superintendent and peer of Dr. Paine at the highest church levels, described him thus:

Oh, he was a delightful brother, so tremendously capable and yet so tremendously humble. Just very sweet-spirited, deliberate in his approach to making decisions, a wonderful counselor on the boards—we sat together on the General Board, he and I did. I was always just delighted to be around him. . . . We had a wonderful friendly relationship.[45]

Former vice president for development Robert R. Luckey '37 had these words about his long-time friend and boss.

Steve was a tremendous educator and a tremendous leader. We knew if we could get Steve on our side in something it would go because he had pretty much the mind not only of the faculty but of the church. . . . He functioned not only as a college president but he was on all the boards of the church.[46]

Dr. Paine was an easy leader to follow. He allowed his junior administrators room for creative development and gave them as much responsibility as they were willing to handle. Many is the time Steve said, facetiously, that he was working for me. This was his way of saying we worked together in the development of the institution. His dependence on God in every aspect of the collegiate scene, I will never forget.[47]

Said former academic dean Arthur Lynip '38, "Characteristic was his slipping into a deliberative mode when the pressure was on. He was always open to any opinions and weighed all carefully. . . . But without fail he tried to find the Lord's will in every impasse."[48]

Both J. S. Luckey and Stephen Paine were brilliant scholars and strong leaders. Both demonstrated a life-long dedication to accomplishing the mission of Houghton College. But in at least one respect they differed: desk management. Dr. Paine's daughter Miriam tells us more:

> The desk top was always neat with a dark walnut "In-Out" basket; a pile of typed letters awaiting a signature; another of correspondence opened and ready for his perusal. The desk had virtually no clues of the man who worked behind it. I regularly checked the desk drawers: pens and pencils lined up, letter opener and glass dish of paper clips, scissors in a brass case. I can still picture Dad sitting there, desk drawer slightly ajar, methodically processing the piles of material before him . . . and always leaving the desk in order.[49]

Many others shared a few words of description. Bruce Gallup '72, speaking at the May 16, 1972, chapel honoring Dr. Paine:

> At approximately 8:00 a.m. Monday, Wednesday and Friday, he would walk into the classroom, remove his cap, and place his briefcase on the table. Sometime he paused to chat briefly with a student in the front of the room. Sometimes he just opened with prayer. After this he might hum a few notes to start the morning hymn, punctuating it with background remarks about the life of the hymn writer and about the hymn itself. Or he might exhort the class to "chop right to the white meat of the coconut" or remind the students that "it is time to get the train on the tracks." That meant that all books were to be closed and all papers put away for the morning quiz.[50]

Willard Smith, speaking of Stephen Paine as a campus builder: "In 1937, Dr. Stephen W. Paine presided over a campus of five major buildings with 79,000 feet of floor space. In 1972, he presides over a campus with sixteen major buildings and 471,000 square feet of floor space."[51]

Silas Molyneaux '36 and former Houghton alumni president: "Steve was a good teacher. . . . He was tough but I learned a lot from him.[52]

Robert Luckey, answering a question about presidential counselling of students:

[Steve was the] students' friend. Open door policy to students. He would consciously study the Boulder pictures so that he could speak to students by first name. He probably did a lot of unofficial counselling by having students up to his house, and if a student was in trouble (say a *Star* editor) . . . he would be called into the president's office. He did an awful lot of unofficial, friendly counsel because of his knowledge of the students.[53]

Richard Alderman '52 wrote:

I never missed his chapels. . . . Brilliant mind, had a way to get to the critical points in the decision-making process—what really mattered and what the consequence would be. His wit and his ability to express a profound idea in the language of a layman have been a delight to us all. Greatest to me, however, is the humility of the great man of God as he continued to serve day by day.

I knew him both as the president (I never had a class from him) then when I came back on as faculty, I was with him one year as administrator. I admired him greatly. . . . I feel he brought Houghton to the academic excellence that was here even when I arrived on campus.[54]

Paine's wife, Helen Paul Paine '37, wrote:

I think he reached most of the goals that he had for the college. . . . He wanted to keep the school true to the Lord and true to The Wesleyan Church. . . . He took quite a bit of criticism because . . . he saw the viewpoint of some of the more strict conferences. . . . He felt very strongly that we should be willing to give up a little bit in order to keep those conferences working with us.[55]

Shortly before Steve's death, one of his grandsons said, "You know, Grandpa doesn't think he does very much, and he doesn't think he's done very well, but when I think of what it means to be a godly person, I think of Grandpa."[56]

Virgil A. Mitchell, a general superintendent of The Wesleyan Methodist Church, said this about President Paine:

Stephen W. Paine has been in the vanguard for spiritual advance at Houghton, in the Wesleyan Methodist Church, and in the National Association of Evangelicals. He has faith in God, in people, and in his work.

He recognizes that there is always room for legitimate difference of opinion in church, school, and administrative matters. He respects the honesty and intellectual integrity of other men.

He has a trained mind, a disciplined body, a sympathetic ear, and a Spirit-filled heart. He listens, he teaches, he counsels. He does not run from a difficult task.

He fights to win but does not gloat in victory. He is kind and thoughtful. He is a man of faith, conviction, and ability. He is wise, conservative, and spiritual. He is magnanimous in spirit, humble in attitude, and courageous in action. He is God-fearing, unselfish and thorough.[57]

Toward the end of his life, Dr. Paine attended a Sunday evening service in which he was praised for his accomplishments by a co-worker of many years. With characteristic modesty, Stephen rose to his feet and said, "All I have done has been done by the grace of God. All the glory belongs to him."[58]

Like both of his significant predecessors, Willard J. Houghton and James S. Luckey, Stephen W. Paine was God's man for God's job in God's good time. As he had promised upon entering Wheaton College in 1926, he lived his life in a manner to achieve his goal: to do the will of God.

Stephen William Paine died February 9, 1992.

NINE

Houghton and the World War II Years

1937–1946

I magine yourself as young Dr. Stephen Paine, new president of Wesleyan Methodism's bellwether college at Houghton. Working with you are thirty-one faculty members,[1] and college enrollment in September 1937 is 406 (198 male, 208 female) plus fifty-two seminary (high school) students.[2] The college's physical plant consists of five buildings, lying pretty much in a northeast-southwest row near the edge of the campus bench. Just above the hillside road ascending from the village is Gaoyadeo Women's Dormitory. Then comes the Administration Building, called "Old Admin" until renamed in honor of the many Fanchers who served the college. Next in line is the Science Building, later renamed to honor Houghton's Woolsey clan. The smallest structure (not counting the heating plant behind Gaoyadeo) is the Bedford Gymnasium. Standing on the northern end of what will eventually become the main quadrangle is the newest structure, the Music Building, dedicated in late 1932. The budget is tight, the Great Depression has yet to run its course, the academic buildings are beginning to bulge at the corners, and you personally have amassed all of four years of collegiate teaching and administrative experience.

That surely was a daunting commitment for a young man, but Stephen Paine knew he was not facing these great responsibilities alone. On one hand, he was supported by a faculty and staff that willingly would continue to serve above and beyond. On the other, he had his stalwart faith in God, and he spent many an hour in focused and fervent prayer as his new life opened up.

But Dr. Paine never could have guessed what the future soon would offer: the trauma of World War II, the draft-influenced decline in enrollment, the dearth of funds and scarcity of materials for new buildings, the post-war deluge of veterans, and some other irksome problems. Symbolic of the great changes to come was the departure in 1937 of the final passenger train from the Houghton station.

The Last Few Years of "Peace"

In the first four years of Stephen Paine's service at Houghton [1933–1937], student enrollment had expanded by 50 percent, with little or no increase in classroom or office or dormitory or food-service space. Having a New York State charter helped produce a doubling of enrollment in just five years after 1923; would the 1935 accreditation by Middle States now do the same? Enrollment trends indicated this might be possible, but in the twilight of the Great Depression, where would funds be found for the needed plant improvements?

In the spring of 1931, an addition to the east end of Gaoyadeo Hall had appended sorely-needed dining room space on the ground floor and twenty-one sleeping rooms on the floors above, and in 1936 another addition on the west end provided laundry space and some additional food service area on the ground floor and thirty-eight student rooms above. Then, shortly before Stephen Paine began his presidency in the summer of 1937, a two-story addition (called the Arcade) linked Science and Old Admin. This housed classrooms, the college library, and the college printing plant.[3] Later, in 1939, the attic space in the Science Building was developed for use as an art studio and classrooms.

A fund drive begun in 1935 to raise $250,000 in endowment, as requested by Middle States, topped out at $29,866—and expenditures to produce that total were recorded as being $14,888, for a net of just under $15,000.[4] Money was scarce, and Houghton alumni—many of whom were preachers and public school teachers—typically did not have the resources for major gifts.[5]

One of the great needs was for a single building to house the president and his administrative team, including the treasurer, academic dean, registrar, and financial staff. In April 1941 ground was broken for what would be the Luckey Memorial Building, the first structure in a new campus quadrangle layout. Building supervisor Chester York devised several strategies to save money; one of the most notable was to face the building with flat stones taken from a nearby creek rather than expensive brick. He also made extensive use of student labor, which minimized the effects of booming wartime wages. As a result of his efforts, a building that had been estimated to cost $75,000 was finished for $39,000.[6] Part of the funds came from the Jenny Houghton Cudworth estate, and part from sacrificial alumni giving.

But all was not sunshine and light concerning the erecting of the new administration building. One college-student prank on the night after the ground-breaking for the Luckey Memorial Building left the dean of men, Stanley Wright, with near apoplexy. That day, the final intramural baseball game had been played on the athletic field facing Old Bedford gym. Once the game was over, an official committee opened the ground, with young Bob Luckey '37 honored to dig the token hole. That night, a small group of students filched a local outhouse, relocated it over the hole at the building site, and put on it a sign, "Luckey Memorial Building." The dean was aghast that such disrespect had been shown for the memory of this grand old man, and the aromatic shanty was quickly removed.[7]

While the building of Luckey Memorial was in progress, America entered World War II, and certain supplies began to be scarce. Former vice president Robert Luckey commented on the difficulty in finding framing steel and lumber:

> You couldn't get steel during the war, and he [Chester York] found some steel in . . . a wrecking company in Buffalo. He bought that steel, took it to a fabricator and had it re-fabricated, and it became the steel in that [Luckey] building. And of course when they built, they cut their own oak [and pine] . . . a bunch of that oak was on college property, and the only way they could get it was to have their own sawmill and they sawed it up themselves.[8]

Stephen Paine wrote a widely-distributed short report describing this economic miracle. In it, he said: "Any person attempting to account for the presence of our buildings in Houghton would, I feel, be unable to produce an adequate cause unless he should mention as the greatest factor the providence and power of God."[9]

Students too became scarce (see table 11), and for an institution so heavily dependent on tuition income, that meant serious fiscal problems.

Programs were curtailed or temporarily discontinued, faculty were released, and the additional duties of remaining faculty were doubled. While the national mood in January 1942 was for young men to enlist, most at Houghton elected to finish that academic year. Then the numbers began to drop. In the fall of 1941, 196 men and 236 women had registered, and in September 1942 the numbers were down to 177 men and 215 women. The biggest drop occurred the next fall, when only 93 men and 199 women registered. September 1944 saw a similar headcount, with 95 men and 238 women. The upward trend in enrollment began in 1945, with 139 men and 331 women on hand. One reason the numbers did not jump more rapidly that year is that military commitments were for "the duration plus six months," and many veterans were not released from active duty until long after college classes had begun. Consequently, the greatest number bulge came in 1946, when 354 men and 366 women signed in. The following year enrollment was up again, and in 1947 men outnumbered women (395 to 367) for the first time since 1938.[10] (Note: enrollment figures for subsequent years may be found in table 12 in the next chapter.)

TABLE 11	Fall Semester Enrollment at Houghton College, 1937–1945[11]		
Year	Men	Women	Total
1937–38	198	208	406
1938–39	222	204	426
1939–40	226	243	469
1940–41	234	248	482
1941–42	196	236	432
1942–43	177	215	392
1943–44	93	199	292
1944–45	95	238	333
1945–46	139	331	470

As the war years were about to begin, the advisory board began to feel that the number of tasks assigned to the president was beginning to exceed his physical limits, and it was decided to hire a business manager to help supervise the college farm and attend to other college business matters. Unfortunately, the first man selected was not up to the job, though achieving his dismissal was a slow and difficult process.[12] Several months later, Willard Smith was named as business manager; eventually the treasurer's responsibilities were added, and Dr. Smith held this position until his retirement in 1972.

Wartime exigencies dictated that Houghton practice old-time Yankee frugality, as suggested in this short verse:

> Use it up,
> Wear it out,
> Make it do,
> Or do without.

This thought was at the root of many transactions during those tight years, and it even showed up in hiring practices, as the war brought some unexpected personnel difficulties to the college.[13] Wages in defense industries were much higher than Houghton could afford to pay, and the college's blue-collar workers were of two categories: those who felt called to serve in this mission field (which included the vast majority of the faculty) and those who were merely willing to accept the tiny stipends. According to Willard Smith, one problem was "the maintenance and operational crew. Most often they had been selected on the basis of willingness to work for Houghton's low wages rather than on qualifications for a particular job. Therefore it was difficult to get professional performance out of some of these workers."[14] He went on to report the case of a custodian who was hired to work the then-standard fifty-hour week and was logging that amount but was found to be putting in only thirty-five hours on the job. The man's rationale? "I work much faster than most people and can do ten hours' work in seven."

World War II

One Houghton student from 1939 to 1943 was Katherine L. Walberger, who later married Kenneth Lindley and returned to the college as a long-serving professor of history. In a special Houghton Heritage chapel message to the student body in 1996, Dr. Kay Lindley reported on her experiences as the war began:

> Adolf Hitler invaded Poland and I enrolled as a freshman at Houghton College in the same week in September of 1939. Now, I don't suppose that historical fact made much impression on Hitler but, as a matter of fact, it made a tremendous impact upon my life.
>
> My parents paid my tuition, the entire sum of $400 for the year. I hate to tell you but that also included board and room in Gaoyadeo dorm and actually was supposed to cover the cost of our books as well.
>
> In 1939 I was one of 469 students on this campus. That was the total, about equally divided at that time between men and women. Four years later in 1943 when I graduated there were 292 students of which 93 were men.
>
> The first two years of the war [1939–1941] had little impact on our lives. U.S. policies of non-involvement and neutrality seemed good to us. . . . When in September of 1940 Congress passed the first peacetime draft in our history, we were forced to take note, but it all seemed very far removed from Allegany County until December 7, 1941. On that Sunday evening most of us were attending a Christmas vespers service in the village church. The sanctuary was dark except for the dimmed lights around the organ when Pastor Black stood up, walked to the podium, interrupted the music, and read to us the announcement that Pearl Harbor had been attacked, and our nation would be at war.
>
> Even the next day several of the fellows left to enlist, and all around campus we talked about draft status, the possibilities of exemptions from the draft, whether changing majors might keep one out of the draft. A few students even argued that, with such an uncertain future before us, we ought to abandon all study. . . .
>
> Women students began talking of leaving college to work at defense jobs. . . . The temptation of jobs with what seemed astronomical wages was very great. You could convince yourself, especially at one of those times when papers were due and test times loomed, that working at a defense factory was really your patriotic duty. And, indeed, there was a critical shortage of labor. The Army and the Navy and the Air Force began planning the lives of many of

the fellows on campus. One by one many left. Some would return several years later to complete their degrees. Pre-med students were sent to medical school before completing their B.S. degree.

Those of us who remained on campus carried on, although with increasing war-time restrictions. After debating whether to cancel all extra-curricular activities in light of the serious situation, we turned our efforts to contributing to the war effort. Sometimes we planned refugee dinners . . . . there was a lot of rice in them. But we sent the savings from those refugee dinners to the Red Cross. We rolled a lot of bandages, we gave blood, we wrote a lot of letters, we bought war stamps—stamps because most of us couldn't afford a $25 [savings] bond. The going wage on campus was 20 cents an hour. If you collected enough stamps you could exchange them for a bond. Instead of corsages, fellows bought their dates "warsages" made of stamps wrapped in cellophane strips. And if you had been here you probably would have received a "warsage" for a Valentine. It was kind of nice. You could exchange those stamps later toward the bond. You see, it was worth something—[and it] lasted longer. As the enrollment went down some faculty had to find other work, and the academic programs had to be cut. Only later did I understand the great sacrifices that many of these servants of God made. Mrs. [Marjorie] Stockin reminded me a few days ago that the fledgling art program was the first academic program to be cut. She managed to keep an art appreciation course in the curriculum by teaching without salary. The ratio between women and men was deplorable. Women came to outnumber men three and four to one. The rules of the annual Sadie Hawkins Day[15] were changed to allow three girls to date one guy. But women discovered that they could handle positions traditionally reserved for men in publications, government, and clubs, and they did a good job. Inter-collegiate debate was terminated, the A Capella touring choir soon became an all-women's choir, and they took shorter and shorter tours. Gas rationing and shortage of rubber for tires meant there were few cars on campus, and getting off campus was a real treat. To date a man with both a car and the gasoline to run it was an achievement worth writing home about. To be sure, any man that remained on campus by 1944 was probably a theolog (that is a ministerial major) or he'd flunked his Army physical.

Air raids [drills] added a little spice to our lives. They often came at night when we were trying to study, but most of us in Gao dorm had already learned the art of studying under a blanket with the help of a flashlight. You see, we had lots of rules in those days and one of those was a 10 o'clock curfew, and so we had learned how to study under a blanket with a flashlight. But why would we have air raids in this out-of-the way place? Well, the answer was really quite easy. Buffalo had several wartime industries which the enemy might bomb if they were ever able to launch planes or rockets from some point on the East Coast, and we didn't know but what that was quite possible. Since Houghton was on the direct route from New York to Buffalo the whole town was often blacked out, and a German pilot seeing Gao dorm with its many lighted windows might easily drop a bomb on what he thought was a factory.

At that time the idea wasn't quite as remote as it seems to you now, I think. Even as our graduation ceremony in 1943 was coming to an end, the air raid sirens went off. And you thought we never had excitement here at Houghton.

It was a stressful period for all of us, but in the midst of it we saw God at work. In February 1942 we experienced revival on campus; times of confession, repentance, and prayer replaced our classes. Many of our lives were changed forever. We saw God at work, too, as Luckey Building took shape in this period despite impossible war shortages, restrictions, and the mounting cost of labor. The first building on the quad, Luckey Building, was occupied in 1942 free of debt, a miracle which I believe has never been repeated.

Within a year of Pearl Harbor the death of the first of the ten Houghton alumni killed in the war was reported, J. Merton McMahon, lost at sea in a submarine accident. Carl Wagner, who sat beside me in Modern European History class, was called to active duty in the spring of 1943. He died nine months later when his plane crashed. In June of 1942 Richard Bennett said goodbye to his fiancee, Ruth Brooks. Dick and Ruth had just completed their sophomore years on campus. Two years later, after earning several medals, he was killed when his plane went out of control. Henry Samuels, the brother of Sammy Ries, registered first as a conscientious objector but came to feel he must share in the suffering of the war. A little over a year later he was buried in St. Arvold Military Cemetery in France.

These were our friends, our classmates. We mourned. When you walk back to the campus center this morning look at the beautiful oak trees along the quad. There are ten. One for each of our friends who gave his life in World War II. Their names are listed on a plaque in the foyer of Fancher Hall.

We also rejoiced with those of our classmates and alumni who returned safely from the war. Some of you know the names of alumni veterans who still live here in Houghton. They are Smith and Ries and Prinsell and Woolsey and Cummings and Coddington, among others. But did you know that shortly after the war many of these Houghton alumni veterans, along with a whole host of others, returned overseas to Asia and Africa and around the world as missionaries of the Gospel of Jesus Christ? World War II was followed by one of the greatest missionary movements of all times, and many I have named were a part of that.[16]

Ben Armstrong '45, who later spent over fifty years in the ministry, was a freshman at Houghton when the Japanese attacked the U. S. naval base on Oahu. He stated:

Everyone knows where they were on December 7, 1941. . . . When the attack on Pearl Harbor happened I was a first year student at Houghton. I was listening to a radio program when I heard the news.

Dr. C. I. Armstrong [a distant relative], pastor of the Houghton Wesleyan Church, called a prayer meeting for the entire student body the next day.

President Roosevelt (FDR) declared war, and our fellow students responded quickly to serve the country. Many died. Warren Dayton was shot down in Germany as a tail gunner in the US Air Force. My buddy, James Stuart Campbell '44, had the exceedingly difficult task of visiting Warren's mother on Long Island and telling her about her son. Others went into the service and did not return. While at Houghton College in the early forties my draft board in Buffalo deferred me as a theological student, a 4D classification. My fellow girl students complained that they were left only with boys with a 4D or a 4F (deferment.)[17]

The 1942 Revival

Shortly after America was drawn into World War II, a major spiritual revival washed over the campus during the two weeks of special meetings that started on Tuesday, February 4. Prior to the meetings, a group of dedicated women met at the village church each morning at eight to pray for a revival. Then, as the meetings began,—just two months after the start of World War II—the spiritual concern of village and campus alike was heightened by two deaths in the community. One of Houghton's "old saints," Rose Tarey, passed away, and a child, Robert Ingersoll, vanished through the ice on the Genesee River.[18]

The revival itself started on Sunday afternoon, February 8, 1942, when the drowned boy's funeral was held. According to Kenneth Wilson, "It was a solemn prelude to the evening service at which the sermon was preached from the text, 'So, then, every one of us shall give an account of himself to God.' Dozens of young people who sensed that their accounts were in alarming disorder . . ."[19] came forward to proclaim their repentance. The revival grew during the week of special meetings, led by Rev. B. N. (Burdette Newton) Miner. Warren Woolsey, a junior who was not then a Christian but who found new life through the revival, shared his memories of that time:

> The invited evangelist was a Free Methodist by the name of B. N. Miner, who was a professional evangelist . . . The skeptics among us used to take delight in saying we know what's going to happen. Many evangelists have a certain sequence: the first night will be this, the second night will be that, and we used to predict . . . Miner had a nice spirit but there was nothing new, nothing particularly attractive in his preaching. It was just a compelling sense of the Spirit's presence, not manipulated by any skillful personality.[20]

Apparently a concerned group of students, led by Alden Gannett '44 (who went on to head the London Bible Institute in Canada, then served as president of Southeastern Bible College in Birmingham, Alabama, for twenty-five years), had also done a lot of praying before the two weeks of special meetings. Ella Phelps Woolsey reported that the services seemed to touch a number of students who had not been involved spiritually before, though neither of the Woolseys felt that the recentness of the Pearl Harbor attack had much to do with the revival. Said Warren, "It was just a strong feeling God is here and he's calling, and this is the time to respond."[21] The hostilities were little mentioned in the preaching, and most Houghton students in that February felt the war was something that wouldn't affect their lives until after graduation. "We were so naive: you'd go off and fly airplanes; you weren't going to die. At least I don't think many of us thought it was going to happen to us anyway."[22]

Stephen Paine commented on two special attributes of the 1942 revival. Said he, "The meetings were characterized by a forgetting of denominational fences. . . . Denominational placards will not be found in heaven . . . and here on earth we [should] be able to enjoy the company of all God's children." And there was an excitement to share the blessings of the revival with friends and family beyond the campus circle. "Long distance wires were kept hot with messages to parents announcing God's coming into the lives of various students. Letters were burdened with messages concerning the revival . . . and hitchhiking students were able to win souls for Christ."[23]

Campus Attitudes

For his dissertation exploring denominational persistence at four Christian colleges, Alan Graffam carefully reviewed T*he Houghton Star*, the campus paper published at intervals varying from weekly to monthly. His summary states:

> The attitude on campus was significantly different for World War II than that concerning World War I. One major factor in this was the collegiate age of the World War II era students while the Houghton Seminary students of the first World War were predominantly of high school age. The 1940s faculty developed academic policies for those affected by the war, deciding such questions as credit for students who were drafted before the end of a semester, credit for defense training classes in technical skills such as electricity, radio and drafting offered on campus, and credit for skills learned in the service. They also discussed the manner in which campus clubs and organizations could best serve the war effort.
>
> *The Star* reported student opinion. In 1938 a straw poll among students supported the coming war; by 1939 there was also a discussion of a "peace movement," and editorials chastised students for a callous attitude toward "a world ablaze." Articles regarding the War in Europe appeared regularly. Throughout the conflict letters from Houghton service men were printed, and news of those entering the service was featured regularly. The students were much more aware of and concerned about this war than they were during World War I. They established a blood bank and sought courses which dealt with war issues.[24]

Wars and Women

Our national history tells us that the American Civil War forced women out of their domestic sphere to labor in farm fields and businesses abandoned by their gone-for-a-soldier husbands and sons. The alternative was starvation, and women handled the challenges in ways that surprised themselves and their menfolk. In World War I, women greatly expanded their horizons as they took on many roles outside the home—factory work, munitions work, street car conducting, delivering messages for telegraph companies, and serving as civilian clerks and stenographers for the military. One result was a big surge in support for the suffrage movement. They logically asked, "If we can work and sacrifice for the war, why can't we vote?" and they demanded that right.

In a parallel vein, World War II lifted women another step toward equality as they routinely replaced men in rugged defense industries and joined the military to serve at home and overseas, including work as ferry pilots and as combat-zone nurses. One Houghton alumna reported on her experiences as a World War II citizen-soldier.

Roberta Molyneaux (later Grange) '29 was teaching English and German in a school in Cheektowaga on the east edge of Buffalo when the war began. The day the Japanese attacked, she was visiting the family home on the south edge of Houghton, and she described the state of her mood as "consternation and shock." Her family was concerned about what the war would do to their lives and the lives of their loved ones.[25]

Because her students' interest in studying German vanished once the war was underway, Roberta found herself teaching some science courses, though she felt her efforts were "unsatisfactory."

> The pupils were restless. Too much was happening for them to settle down to study. Many had the attitude, "What's the use? I'll soon have to go to war and maybe be killed. I may as well have a good time!" . . . The manufacturing plants around Buffalo were clamoring for employees. Some [of the older] pupils worked nights and earned more money than their teachers did at teaching.
>
> Evenings we listened on the radio to the news. We were avid for information about what was going on. We could get some very nice music programs, too. . . . In between were ads, of course, and one of them was for a new organization for women volunteers for an

army corps, the WAAC [Women's Auxiliary Army Corps, later the Women's Army Corps]. . . .

. . . I decided to join the WAAC.[26]

Within a month of volunteering, Roberta had orders for basic training near Daytona Beach, followed by business administration school. Then she was off to a year's duty in the personnel office at an Army Air Forces base near Hondo, Texas.[27] In the spring of 1944, she and six hundred other WACs (along with "thousands of men," from whom they were sequestered) sailed on the Queen Elizabeth for England, landing in Glasgow, Scotland, on June 6—D Day.[28] Her eventual assignment was at RAF Burtonwood, an air base near Warrington, between Manchester and Liverpool, where she monitored statistical reports and described the work as "spasmodic and monotonous," and she usually finished her tasks by 10:00 a.m. of her 7:00 a.m. to 5:00 p.m. workday.[29] As recorded in her journal, the highlights of her stay in England were the short trips she was able to arrange to see the countryside and visit London and Edinburgh. "It was the army policy to give as many passes as possible to relieve the tedium that bore down so heavily on the military personnel in the rear, especially toward the end."[30]

Combat Experiences

Many of the male veterans who returned to Houghton reported harrowing service experiences. Robert Cummings '50, who later became a professor of German at Houghton, took part in the Normandy invasion as a bazooka man in an engineering unit. "Outfits were split in half so that if half of you went in first and didn't make it, the other half would come in a couple of hours later and then there'd be a nucleus" for rebuilding the unit.[31] Bob drew a second-shift straw and landed at noon, but the beach was so clogged that his half-unit was ordered back to its ship, where they remained until the next noon. Once ashore, their main task was cleaning up the beach—mainly recovering remains.[32] Later, Bob was in one of the first units to enter Berlin after the war ended.

Dr. Evan Molyneaux '29, a medical officer commanding a field hospital, entered Normandy on the third day and followed Patton's army into Paris. "Of course, we got close to the activity. We had plenty who rolled over too many mines . . . and got fired on some." Later, his unit was in Belgium near the Malmedy Massacre, where one of his lieutenants was captured and executed.[33]

Justus "Jud" Prentice '41 was a naval officer commanding landing craft during the Normandy invasion, and most of the boats in his group were sunk. Jud was one of the very few survivors; he ended up on the beach, where he lay for two days in the shelter of a huge log partially buried in the sand. An army unit discovered him and evacuated him back to England.[34]

Warren Woolsey '43 was commissioned as a bombardier/armament officer on B-24 aircraft and flew twenty-nine missions against Germany from a newly-opened base in southern Italy. The unit's task was to attack German transportation facilities, primarily railroad yards and oil refineries. Though he described most of his missions as "milk runs," several times his aircraft was punctured by German flak.[35]

More than a few felt instances of Divine protection, sometimes even when individuals got themselves in less-than-brilliant predicaments. Consider the dilemma of Lowell Fancher, who later worked for forty-three years in the college printshop. Lowell volunteered for the draft even before he finished high school. His army combat service began in the Philippines, and there on the island of Mindanao he managed to get lost behind enemy lines while on a banana-gathering expedition. He and some others had gone to a nearby river to get cleaned up, and then he wandered into a banana grove to pick some bananas for the company's kitchen. After being chased by a wild boar, he got disoriented and as darkness fell he realized he was lost. He spotted a tiny fire and drew near, only to discover the men were speaking Japanese. As he headed the other way, up and down a small mountain, American artillery fire passed low overhead, giving him a general bearing for his home base. Later, as dawn was nearing, he crept up a slope, unchallenged, between two American machine-gun outposts. At last back in his own camp, he learned that the final slope he'd navigated had been mined.[36]

The names of 371 Houghton alumni were later entered on a Roll of Honor board that was hung in the entry of Fancher Hall. Then, as half a century elapsed and the honoring of veterans passed from vogue, the name board was relocated to the obscurity of the college archives. In contrast, the ten oaks planted to commemorate Houghton's war dead[37] grew to be mighty trees, and their shade continues to grace the campus on hot summer days.

Events of 1945

During the summer of 1945, as it became obvious that a flood of returning veterans and new students would soon engulf the campus, a summer dormitory on the adjacent Wesleyan Methodist camp grounds was leased and "winterized" (though its first forty-eight residents thought this was a charitable description at best). That fall, a barracks-type building was erected to hold another twenty-six students. Then, as the real crowd began to arrive in 1946, work was underway on thirty-eight apartments to hold the families of returning veterans. This cluster of dwellings, erected west of the campus where Houghton Academy now stands, was tagged "Vetville."[38]

Additional classrooms also had to be found or developed before the semester began. Space was rented in the basement of the village church, and the carpenter shop was moved out of the basement of the Music Building so two classrooms could be set up in that space. Also, construction materials were removed from the Luckey Building basement and a classroom prepared there. To equip these rooms, the business manager wangled a few tables and 150 student sidearm chairs from military surplus sources. Classes were also scheduled during normal mealtimes, which made use of then-empty space but caused serving-schedule turmoil.[39]

One other major project in the summer of 1946 was another upgrading of the water system. The old two-inch water supply line had been replaced with a three-inch line in 1939. Then, because of a water shortage in the fall of 1941, a well was dug at the west edge of the campus in the winter of 1942. However, as student numbers began to swell in 1945, the old distribution system and small reservoir became significantly inadequate. The new system involved a 150,000 gallon reservoir, six-inch and eight-inch distribution mains, and a plant for processing the water to assure potability. This new water system was financed through a $65,000 bond issue, and user fees from the community were expected to meet the bond payments and eventually serve as an endowment for the college.[40]

To President Luckey, the question about how large Houghton should become had been strictly theoretical, for college enrolment by 1937 had only risen to 406. He felt it could top out at a thousand. President Paine shared this thousand-student vision, but for him it became a very practical consideration. From 333 students in September 1944, college enrollment jumped to 470 in 1945, 720 in 1946, 762 in 1947 and 816 in 1948.[41] Where the progression might end was a matter of conjecture and concern, because the campus physical plant needed several major additions to keep up. But where would the money come from? The quest for more resources would be neither short nor easy.

Much as the war years were a time of strain and challenge for Houghton College, they also served to begin closing the door to one era in Christian higher education and opening another. Christian-college historian Thomas A. Askew identified three phases that characterized most Christian colleges, primarily in the years before, during, and after World War II.[42] In the first phase, the college was an insular, church-focused institution, and such was Houghton in the late Luckey and early Paine years. Typically, each phase-one college was led by a classic "old-time college president," a man with very strong roots in the church, who was expected to lead faculty, disciple (and discipline) students, raise funds, befriend parents and community members, and administer the entire college. The faculty had a backbone of distinguished, highly loyal veterans, aided by younger men and women who viewed Christian teaching as a missionary endeavor, a special calling for which they were willing to sacrifice. In essence, this described Houghton from its chartering through the end of the war.

At Houghton, as at many other Christian colleges, an aura of separatism was maintained in terms both toward society in general and toward other colleges. The global war, the ongoing revolution in higher education, and the fundamentalist-modernist controversies changed the world around them, and Christian colleges felt the pressures. But they tenaciously "kept the faith" and sustained their existence. In fact, the demands of mere institutional survival during the Great Depression and World War II claimed most of their attention.

Then, with the world war over and as a flood of returning veterans engulfed the campuses, the second phase began: Christian colleges became more aware of their mission, their capabilities, and their need to cooperate with other colleges. This was also an era of increased credentialling for faculty, driven by general expectations in higher education and by specific pressures from regional accrediting agencies. Released from the economic pressures of WW II and imbued with an enlarged vision of their potential to enhance higher education, the accrediting agencies shifted their program from small-team confirmation visits to much larger evaluative efforts, involving detailed pre-visit self-study work by the individual institution. In Askew's words, "There is no impetus like an impending visit from an evaluation team, with the attendant self-study, for clarifying goals, sharpening administrative procedures, and reviewing faculty committees."[43] From such self-examination, however forced, sprang the changes that reshaped Christian higher education. Chapter 10 reports Houghton's evolution into phase two.

Askew's third phase, which includes growing professionalism, an expansion of networks, and burgeoning theoretical-system development, is both more diffuse and more critical to the formation of a clear and enduring educational philosophy for Christian colleges. A characteristic of this phase is the growth of professionalization in non-faculty areas. Administration, student life and counseling, financial aid, and even admissions and enrollment began to demand personnel with appropriate professional degrees. The explosive growth of governmental control and intrusion has increased the need for specially-trained personnel even as it wreaked havoc on college budgets for the areas most affected. This third phase was gaining strength as the Paine years ended (see chapter 11), and it continued to affect Christian higher education past the end of the twentieth century.

TEN

Tripling in Size

1946–1962

I n the fall of 1946, Houghton College faced the full onslaught of the
returning veterans plus a restoration of normal enrollment flow from
high schools. But the college had been stretched even by its scanty wartime
enrollments that averaged under four hundred. When the war ended, there
already was a shortage of classrooms, faculty, housing, finances etc. Now,
to handle an almost immediate doubling in enrollment demanded quick
thinking and great innovation. But Stephen Paine, Willard Smith, and the
entire campus family were willing to confront and attempt to overcome
those grand challenges.

Effects of the GI Bill

In 1944, Congress, anticipating the end of World War II and the need to
re-integrate military veterans into the civilian economy, crafted legislation
that would make advanced schooling readily available for returning GIs.
Officially known as the Servicemen's Readjustment Act, it soon became tagged
as the GI Bill of Rights. For some, this legislation meant unemployment pay or
mortgage assistance or technical schooling or on-the-job training or aviation

instruction. But for many, it meant college study—and for institutions of higher education, it meant a huge surge of potential enrollment; the GI Bill benefits would essentially cover tuition costs. At most colleges, buildings that were under-used during the war now became crammed, and sections had to be added and course offerings expanded. Faculty were in short supply, though some returning vets were qualified teachers or had teacher-wives, and some women who had gone into defense industries were now available.

According to one essayist, "The GI Bill provided educational benefits to 7.8 million veterans between 1944 and 1956, at a cost to taxpayers of $14.5 billion."[1] The law granted each veteran five hundred dollars for up to a year of schooling, plus another year's benefits for each year served. Additional money was provided for living expenses. Though no one in national leadership had any idea how many veterans would pursue college degrees, more than 2.2 million eventually took college work under the bill.

For Houghton, the influx of veterans meant a jump from 333 students in the fall of 1944 to 720 in 1946, an enrollment limit that had been established by the college's administration. (Faculty numbers also increased; the catalog for 1944–1945 listed twenty-four full-time teachers and ten part-timers. The full-time number increased to thirty in 1945, thirty-seven in 1946, forty in 1947, forty-three in 1948 and forty-seven in 1949. Such a doubling in five years put faculty housing in the community at a premium.[2]) Meanwhile, the college physical plant had not changed since the late 1930s, so some swift and radical actions were needed to find classroom and dormitory space.

During the winter of 1944–1945, Willard Smith accompanied Dr. Paine to Albany for a state-wide meeting with Governor Thomas E. Dewey and state education officials, to discuss what "emergency measures" were necessary to address the veterans who would soon inundate the campuses. A key point was establishing conditions for successful cooperation between the colleges and the various state and federal agencies.[3]

One of Houghton's first actions was to lease and refurbish Dow Hall, a summer dormitory on the adjacent Wesleyan Methodist campground, that would hold forty-eight students. Next was to construct a barracks-type building, named Deer Hall, that would house twenty-six single veterans. Because this structure would not be done by September, the college's recreation hall (the old church building on Route 19) was equipped to hold the eventual Deer Hall denizens during the first semester.

Concurrently, work was being done to plan, contract for, lay out, and build what became known as Vetville. The original request to the New York

State Dormitory Authority was for twenty-five apartment units, though the flood of applications to the college registrar's office dictated seeking a higher number. Eventually ten barracks-type buildings were erected, two with three apartments each and the other eight with four apartments each (for a total of 38). Because of paperwork delays, the planned opening of Vetville in September 1946 did not happen, and the young families were temporarily placed in chilly, tiny, and inconvenient summer-use-only camp buildings and travel trailers and in cramped local housing spaces.[4] Consequently, when the Vetville doors finally opened, they eagerly welcomed the new space and the blessings of a coal-fired pot-bellied stove.

Feeding the multitude was also a problem. World food supplies were not yet back to normal, and pressures to supply war refugees and the large armies of occupation meant shortages continued. The college farm was called on to provide more milk and meat and vegetables; while the variety may have been limited, an editorial in *The Star* advised, "Before you complain about dorm food, be glad you have it."[5] To handle the horde of eaters, a second seating was scheduled in the dining hall for most meals. Also, a thousand-square-foot addition for food storage and processing was built on the back of Gaoyadeo Hall.[6]

Classrooms were also at a premium, and classes were held during the evenings and in whatever space could be found in the community. The college received via truck the donated shell of an old mess hall from nearby Sampson Naval Station, reduced to large chunks of wall and roof assemblies, and these were erected on a new foundation to become the Fine Arts Building, which opened in September 1948. This added three classrooms and an art studio plus a studio for what became WJSL radio. The use of creek-stone facing hid the humble origins of the resurrected mess hall and allowed Fine Arts to blend in with Luckey Memorial Building and the plans for the rest of the campus.[7]

Campus radio station WJSL, named to honor James S. Luckey, grew out of a physics class project to build a radio transmitter from surplus materials. Groundwork for the facility was laid by Dr. Robert Luckey, Dr. Floyd Reese, and engineer Everett Gilbert, and broadcasting from the three-watt station began in March 1949.[8]

In a 1948 public appeal seeking financial gifts to the college, President Paine said:

"Where in the world do you put everybody?" is the inevitable surprised report when we tell people how many students the college and high school are serving here in the little village of Houghton

. . . a combined student body of over 800. . . . "Old-timers" . . . can remember when 400 or 500 students was considered a crowd.[9]

Beyond the effects of their numbers, returning veterans constituted a significantly different component of the student body. They were older, they had a much clearer vision of the power of education, many already had family responsibilities, and they were more serious about studying. College rules presented as "because we say so" were often summarily challenged by those who had chafed under military rules and strictures, and the veterans asked for and expected to receive a voice in campus administration.

A professor at a nearby institution made this prediction in mid-1945 to a committee at his college that was contemplating the return and enrollment of the veterans:

I am sure we will find that many veterans will take a more adult, more aggressive interest in promoting constructive procedures in university life and civilian life. As a result of hardheaded experience, they will not be satisfied with a slow-moving, lackadaisical, ivory-tower attitude toward life and toward education. They will be more frank in their criticism of methods, and they will be more loyal in their efforts along progressive lines.[10]

To the question, "How did the return of the veterans change the school?" Josephine Rickard responded, "It raised our intellectual talk, for those military men wanted quality. They were diligent students, no nonsense. . . . They gave us a vision of the world out there and made missions a priority."[11] Veterans led in founding the local chapter of the Foreign Mission Fellowship and in leading in special prayer meetings, and there is some evidence that their prayer efforts were a factor in the great Houghton revival of 1951.

Oddly enough, the arrival of the veterans brought a new restriction to single students: because of Houghton's housing shortage, student marriages were prohibited (mostly, that is; the author knows of several that were achieved under apparently special—and quite moral—circumstances, though at least one student was dismissed six weeks before graduation for defying the edict).[12]

College Constitution

The earliest college constitution found in the Houghton archives is one annotated as being ratified by the trustees on February 18, 1948. In the section entitled "Purpose," this exposition of Houghton's traditional intentions appeared:

[Houghton College's] purpose embraces the aspirations of its founders to establish a school which should be "high in standards, low in expense, and fundamental in belief." This purpose finds institutional expression in the college itself with its staff of scholars and its guiding philosophy of education; and functional expression in the Christian young people it sends forth to serve the Lord Jesus Christ and his Church.

"Fundamental in belief," Houghton College espouses wholeheartedly the evangelical Christian faith and, in particular, the characteristic doctrines of John Wesley and historic Methodism. The school also takes it stand with those Christians raising their voice in protest against civic, social, and personal wickedness and wrong. . . .

"Low in expense," Houghton College avows its purpose to make available its advantage to the church and the nation, without consideration of race or class, at as low a cost as is possible, accepting the conclusion that this can be done only upon the basis of sacrificial service on the part of our faculty and staff and sacrificial giving by the membership of our churches and of our general Christian constituency.

"High in standards," Houghton College declares its conviction that there is complete compatibility between true scholarship and true faith. The school accepts the responsibility of maintaining a collegiate institution whose scholarly standing shall be worthy of recognition by the academic world. It is essentially a college of the liberal arts and sciences, endeavoring to make available to students the refining disciplines of the various branches of human knowledge and culture, always upon basic assumptions in harmony with the historic evangelical view of the Holy Scriptures. Consistent with the foregoing the college recognizes also a responsibility in view of the plans of students for their calling in life, to provide counsel and curricular preparation for this end.[13]

Where once these thoughts existed only in the writings of founder Willard Houghton and intentions of early faculty and administrators, they were now codified in a permanent document that would formally shape the plans and growth of the college.

This constitution also initiated what became a series of adjustments to the administrative and faculty structure of the college. These other aspects of this constitution will be discussed in the chapter on governance and administration.

Houghton's Enlarged Vision

From the college's beginnings through the end of World War II, its leaders had some measure of world-wide vision, starting with an intent to serve the educational needs of the national Wesleyan Methodist Church and other evangelical bodies, and continuing through preparing missionaries to carry the gospel message across the seas. However, there appears to have been a touch of regional myopia: the college often felt itself to be a "holy city," an island of holiness in a regional sea of sin; an "angel factory" (in the words of one local administrator), with a need to maintain a degree of separation from the "world" nearby.

Several of the returning veterans, and at least two continuing administrators, held strong concerns about changing that situation and extending the influence and benefits of the college into the surrounding communities. Social scientist and veteran J. Whitney Shea lead the local movement to achieve some social change in northern Allegany County through cooperative action using the faculty, students, and educational programs of the college. He said:

> When educational-resources people, students, and citizens establish channels of communication, actively work together on local problems, and participate in social research, community blind spots tend to disappear; and when people learn to think and act, in terms of their values and attitudes, their social heritages, their various cultural backgrounds, and the social and economic conditions of the day, they discover solutions to community problems and develop insight and community understanding, which may form a basis for future cooperative efforts.[14]

Professor Shea's concern was partially prompted by the challenges presented in a 1947 report from the President's Commission on Higher

Education, *Higher Education in American Democracy*. This commission's members included twenty-eight distinguished American educators appointed to review America's educational needs and to recommend actions. Shea quoted from the report:

> American colleges and universities must envision a much larger role for higher education in national life. They can no longer consider themselves merely the instrument for producing an intellectual elite; they must become the means by which every citizen, youth and adult, is enabled and encouraged to carry his education, formal and informal, as far as his native capacities permit.[15]

Though the report emphasized that nearly everyone should receive two years of college education at taxpayer's expense, its main effect on Houghton was to help shift the college's attention to the needs and opportunities in the surrounding neighborhoods.

While Shea and his peers and students were extending their educational activities and services into the local communities, at least two Houghton administrators reached out to become members of local business boards and civic organizations, and many others expanded their circles of influence beyond the academic cloister. Houghtonites served on school boards and town and village boards, and were volunteers with fire companies. Spouses taught in local schools, and non-Wesleyans joined nearby local churches of their denominations. Concurrently, some area groups were invited onto the campus for dinners and tours, thus opening the college more widely to the community. No longer were Houghton folks seen as completely isolationist; while barriers remained along church-membership lines, a significant measure of fellowship and participation in community life and leadership was achieved. As a result, community attitudes toward the "hedged island of sanctification" began to warm.

Campus Construction

One of the prime concerns immediately after World War II was for housing, mainly for women. Colleges in that era operated strongly under the doctrine of *in loco parentis*, and Houghton's leaders believed one of their prime responsibilities was to shelter the students—especially the young women—entrusted to the college's care. Houghton's women students were primarily housed in Gaoyadeo Hall plus the winterized Dow

Hall, with others in two local houses reconfigured as small dormitories. Even with doubling-up in already crowded spaces, the overspill into the community reduced the number of rooms available for men, none of whom could live on campus anyway.

TABLE 12	Enrollment at Houghton College, 1945–1962		
Year	Men	Women	Total
1945–46	139	331	470
1946–47	354	366	720
1947–48	395	367	762
1948–49	456	346	816
1949–50	441	346	787[16]
1950–51	439	339	778
1951–52	360	292	652[17]
1952–53	315	310	625
1953–54	302	302	604
1954–55	298	311	609
1955–56	313	316	629
1956–57	303	327	630
1957–58	288	342	630
1958–59	308	355	663
1959–60	334	410	744
1960–61	333	472	805
1961–62	378	530	908[18]

Elizabeth Beck (later Gilbert, later Feller) arrived in 1944 to serve as dean of women, and in the summer of 1945 she returned to the University of Michigan to work on her master's degree. While she was there, she received from President Paine a package of dorm-design materials developed by the college architect, with a request to criticize the plans. This launched her on a quest to examine new dormitories at a number of nearby colleges in Michigan plus one in New York, where she counted and measured rooms and counted showers and tubs and toilets and sinks to establish desirable space dimensions, room layouts, and sanitary facility ratios. Her approach was to first define the needs for the settings and spaces in which Houghton women were to spend the majority of their college hours, including also the social areas, reception area, storage, space for guests, and even the telephone and limited food service facilities, then allow the architect to draw plans. Her academic adviser was quite supportive of her work and encouraged her to develop the project as her master's thesis, a document that was requested by the federal dormitory authority to use in assisting other colleges as they planned. Because of her effort, Houghton's architect redrew the plans for what is now known as East Hall, including the later additions on the ends (Gillette and Rothenbuler).[19]

Fund-raising for the new dormitory facility had been begun in 1946, but it was not until 1950 that enough money was available to begin construction. Three floors of the building were occupied in 1952, and on October 24, 1953, the first section of East Hall women's dormitory was dedicated.

The college business offices became so cramped by 1947 that stress was badly affecting efficiency and the business manager's health. Because of what he termed a "nervous collapse," Willard Smith took an unexpected two-week leave of absence in April from the campus to regroup. (His collapse was but the latest in a series of stress problems; the pressures on campus administrators were enormous. President Luckey in 1911 "found the work and responsibility at Houghton 'more than he could do' and suffered from a nervous breakdown for some time,"[20] and stress fatigue likely played a role in LaVay Fancher's demise. Likewise, Stephen Paine was reportedly drawing close to nervous exhaustion when he was granted a sabbatical in 1967.)

Following Smith's return to the campus, he received word that new offices for the business manager would be developed in the basement of Luckey, allowing his former first-floor space to be used for student billing activities.[21] This work, five years after the opening of Luckey Memorial Building, began the constant parade of remodelings in the Luckey Building that continues to this day.

The growth of Houghton's enrollment and hence of its faculty and staff led to a shortage of living quarters for single professional women. In 1949, business manager Smith remodeled the structure that had been his beekeeper father's honey house (standing just northwest of Luckey Building) into space for three single women. Called the Bee Hive, it continues to serve in 2004 as the home of a member of the mathematics faculty.[22]

Faculty and staff apartments continued to be in very short supply, and during the fall of 1954, Willard Smith arranged private financing to build four two-bedroom apartments on family property along Old Centerville Road. Construction went forward during 1955, and in January 1956 the Campus Heights apartments were opened. Concurrently, business manager Smith developed a plan to make building lots available on the west side of Houghton Creek. The local board authorized the laying out and selling of ten lots from college property. A roadway was build along the creek, electric and water service was extended to the new lots, and within a few years several homes were built in the new Seymour Street area.[23]

Middle States Evaluation, 1953

The Middle States Association of Colleges and Secondary Schools has for many years conducted a reaccreditation program that involves a decennial self-study by the institution, an evaluation visit by a Middle States team, a report of that evaluation, and a response by the college to the recommendations. While Houghton probably was scheduled for its ten-year review in 1945, no data can be found for any years before 1953, perhaps because of the intervention of World War II.[24]

A source at Middle States, who shared some of the history of the self-study program, reported that in the late '40s Middle States was transitioning from a single-person inspection visit to a team visit, done in conjunction with a shift from expecting minimum quantitative standards to measurement against "norms" or standards of excellence. In advance of the Middle States team's visit, each institution was to assemble data for an extensive document based on the Middle States Questionnaire. While the concept of an institutional self-study was first suggested in 1949 and implemented in 1952, it was not officially sanctioned for region-wide use until 1957.[25]

In January 1953, Houghton College submitted a document titled *Data Presented for Consideration of the Commission on Institutions of Higher Education, Middle States Association of Colleges and Secondary Schools*. It contained detailed responses to the extended list of questions provided many months in advance by Middle States. Subsequently, in March 1953, a six-person team from Middle States, augmented by a representative from the New York State Education Department, visited the campus for forty-eight hours.

The college, which had experienced seventy years of make-do existence since its founding and thirty years since its provisional charter, appeared to be ready for a thorough review that would consider where it had been, where it was (especially), and then where it appeared to be going. The members of the visiting team, drawn from institutions of roughly similar size and selected because of their experience and professional backgrounds, reviewed all the materials submitted (including the catalog and other college publications) and investigated carefully on-scene.

These comments appeared in the team's end-of-visit evaluation report:

Although the core curriculum does attempt to insure breadth of knowledge and an introduction to the various subjects, there is a need for some improvement and control in the curriculum. In its present form, the curriculum is too rigid and confining. . . . [Also,] since there is no attempt to correlate all the work taken in a major field through the use of a general comprehensive examination there is a tendency for a student to have a fragmented rather than a unified view of what has been taken in his area of concentration.[26] A subsequent statement added, "Constant effort should be made to develop the students' power of reasoning through creating problem situations which test the student's ability to apply facts learned and knowledge acquired."[27]

Concerning the campus physical plant, the report said, "The buildings and equipment of Houghton College are being utilized to the fullest degree."[28] This observation was reinforced by an earlier comment: "For the size of the institution, the buildings and equipment are adequate for the present enrollment [about 600] and instructional program."[29] This appears to be a most charitable remark, for later in the report the four separate library areas were characterized as being a problem and "immediate planning should be undertaken to provide for a satisfactory library. . . ."[30] Also, "Adequate space for indoor [athletic] activities is not available. The gymnasium is small and does not permit as many activities as the extent of the student participation in athletics would suggest is necessary."[31] Likewise, "The present music building is quite adequate in all respects except for student practice facilities. . . . One of the college maintenance shops is located in the basement of the building, and it is hoped that this can be moved out to alleviate a noise problem."[32] Other recommendations included erecting a maintenance building of some type and planning a dormitory for men students, who at that time were living in perhaps thirty off-campus residences.[33]

On the administrative side, several situations drew comments from the visiting team: "There is no sabbatical plan . . . nor is there a definite tenure plan." (Faculty of the era were employed from year to year on a contract that allowed either party to cancel the agreement upon thirty days' notice.)[34]

"Consideration should be given to the establishment of an effective sabbatical program,[35] and a reduction of the teaching load from fifteen to twelve hours."[36]

And the committee structure drew attention: "The inspection committee is concerned . . . with the added load which so many committee duties impose on the already heavily burdened teaching staff."[37] "An attempt should be made to . . . eliminate much of the present overlapping of duties and responsibilities. Many administrative matters now handled by committees could be referred to various administrative offices. . . ."[38]

Faculty situations also drew comments: "The dedication of the Houghton faculty and staff to their jobs is indicated in part by their continued willingness to work with salaries and wages which are one-half to two-thirds of the wages which they could easily receive elsewhere."[39] And the team recommended one small step to alleviate the discomfort: "The college could ease the financial strain on its music faculty in some cases by allowing faculty members to augment their income by doing a little teaching in the surrounding towns or taking positions as church organists."[40] Divisional budgets also were a concern: "The participation of division heads of the faculty in setting up the budget is recommended."[41] Traditionally all financial matters were under the hand of the president, and only recently had the business manager been granted that authority; division heads had no authority. They were required to clear each purchase with the business office before committing to the buy. This process was professionally demeaning and needlessly time consuming.

One special situation drew several comments. The team was concerned about the financial stress on the college from the preparatory school, Houghton Seminary, and seemed to regard it as an albatross. "The preparatory school is a continual drain on the college finances which they can ill afford. It is recommended that the preparatory school become self-sustaining or be dropped and the funds used for more essential items in the college."[42] "[If it is kept], the college should proceed as quickly as possible . . . to establish the preparatory department as a unit both financially and physically independent from the college."[43]

Overall, the team sounded definitely impressed with the college's sense of purpose, focus, and frugality. It praised the consistency with which the college proclaimed its conviction that[44] "liberal education built on the foundation of a personal faith in God makes life richer, understanding broader, and citizenship more responsible." Of the faculty, the report said, "They believe in what they are doing, know and understand Houghton principles, and are thus dedicated to its obligation to the church and its constituencies."[45]

The college paid serious attention to the findings of the Middle States team.[46] In 1955, Houghton Academy was given an independent constitution, and Dr. J. Walden Tysinger was appointed as principal. In 1956, the same year that the campus enrollment limit was set at 1200, a plan was accepted for a new library and for an open quad. A year later ground was broken for a new chapel/auditorium,[47] with a number of music practice rooms. In 1958, ground was broken for a new Houghton Academy building on the old Vetville site. Work soon began on a new maintenance center, which was dedicated in 1960, and the first men's dormitory, to be known as Shenawana Hall, which was dedicated in 1961.

Other improvement near the end of this period included the installation of a sixty-line college switchboard (which brought the transition to rotary-dial phones) and the addition of the 150-acre Stebbins farm which lay along route 19 to the immediate northeast, allowing the development of athletic fields. Also, 1962 saw natural gas piped into Houghton.

John and Charles Wesley Chapel

The tiny chapel space on the second floor of the old administration building had been long outgrown by the expanding enrollment, and during the 1953–1954 academic year a new committee, the Chapel-Auditorium Building Committee, met frequently to devise and propose a new facility. In June 1954 the general specifications were delivered to the college's Development Committee, but funding was so limited that no approach was made to an architect for another year. Even then, the architect's services were funded only to the point where some promotional drawings were authorized.[48] By March of 1957 enough money was on hand to formalize the architectural contract and allow a ground-breaking ceremony.

In June 1957, the cornerstone for the new John and Charles Wesley Chapel was laid and Dr. Paine offered these words:

The officers, the faculty, the students, and the friends of Houghton College today, June 1, 1957, place in this cornerstone of the chapel-auditorium now under construction token publications pertaining to the life of this institute. We seal these documents with the thought that they may be untouched for as long as the auditorium stands. Speculating on such a span of time, we presume that the next to view these documents may be living at the beginning of the twenty-second century.

The inscription of the cornerstone; "Jesus Christ the Chief Cornerstone" suggests the objective of the founding fathers of Houghton: to establish a school where young people may study in an atmosphere friendly to spiritual values. . . . It is our prayer for future years that this building may be a place where succeeding generations of young people will meet God, where the Holy Scriptures will always be upheld as the source of all truth, all hope, all life, and where the name of the Lord Jesus Christ will be exalted.[49]

On December 4, 1959, the first chapel service was held in John and Charles Wesley Chapel, with President Paine as the speaker. The next night there was a special concert, featuring the National Symphony Orchestra from Washington, D.C., and both orchestra and audience praised the acoustics in the new facility. Later, on April 27, 1962, the 47-stop, 3,153-pipe Holtkamp organ was dedicated, and on May 4 of that year a dedicatory recital was performed by world-famous organist E. Power Biggs.

Divine Intervention

Houghton has always perceived itself to be the beneficiary of Divine miracles, and one of these was reported in conjunction with the construction of the roof on the new chapel building during the winter of 1958. Willard Smith told the story:

The construction of the new chapel-auditorium had proceeded throughout the summer and into the fall of 1957. The goal had been to complete the roof and have it sealed with the hot asphalt coating before snow came. But delays in the delivery of steel meant that the middle of February had arrived and the roof was not completed. The roof planking had been put in place early in January. . . . By the middle of February serious damage to external walls and some inside construction was occurring because of water damage and freezing.

The construction workers along with the college maintenance staff had a prayer meeting every Monday morning before beginning the day's work. One particular Monday morning, Robert

Fiegl, the superintendent of construction, asked the men to share in special prayer for God's intervention in this desperate situation. The group prayed earnestly and longer than usual.

The weather forecast for the week was for continuing snow storms. On Tuesday morning when the group came to work, Mr. Fiegl ordered the men to give the roof a thorough sweeping to remove the snow in the hope that God would answer their prayers. Even though snow was falling all around the Houghton area, there was no snow in Houghton that day. Therefore, the men began to put down the tarred paper base for the hot asphalt coating.

On Wednesday, they continued the roofing work all day. During the day, Ellsworth Decker, who was contributing some supervision to the job, flew his plane in to the Houghton College airstrip. When he arrived at the chapel, he was so overcome he could hardly talk, He stated that two or three miles outside of Houghton he looked down at the landscape and saw what seemed to be a defined line around Houghton within which there was no snow.

By Thursday noon the job was completed, and snow began to fall again in the afternoon.[50]

One more miracle occurred two years later, when stone similar to that used on the chapel's exterior was sought for the new library. The best supply of good stone was in nearby Higgins Mills Creek, and the effective price was two dollars per load, with trucking and labor furnished by the college. Earlier efforts had cleared the creek bed back to the point where the stream came from a narrow gorge. However, the man who owned the gorge area wanted twenty dollars per truckload, which the college could not afford. As usual, the matter was bathed in prayer, seeking leading or intervention as appropriate.

Soon a torrential rain created a huge flood in the stream bed, and great quantities of stone were delivered downstream onto the land of those who earlier had provided the two dollar stone. The result was that the college got all the stone it needed at the original price, and superintendent Bob Fiegl labeled the flood as another miracle.[51]

Faculty Expansion

In 1939–1940 there were twenty-nine faculty members, and five of them (17 percent) held doctorates. By 1949 the faculty count was up to forty-seven, with twelve (25 percent) holding doctorates.[52] Even as all American colleges were expanding and resources for recruiting faculty were tight, Houghton was able to advance the academic credentials of its teachers. In 1944, Frieda Gillette earned her PhD from Cornell, followed by Josephine Rickard and Crystal Rork, both in 1945. Floyd Reese completed a PhD from Purdue in 1947; Claude Ries achieved his ThD from Northern Baptist Theological Seminary in 1945, as did Bert Hall in 1949.[53] Though not originally supported by President Paine in his quest for an advanced degree, business manager and treasurer Willard Smith completed his doctorate at New York University in 1950, and returned veteran J. Whitney Shea received his EdD from Columbia University in 1951.

In 1950, at the strong urging of Willard Smith, fellow new NYU PhD Arthur Lynip '38 was chosen by the board to become academic dean. Lynip's sixteen years in that position, after four good men had held the post over the previous thirteen years, brought both stability and strong academic leadership to the college in the turbulent years of expansion.

One change, perhaps small in effect but large in significance, occurred in 1950 when Frieda Gillette, who had served as acting division chair for seven years, was named chair of the Division of History and Social Science.[54] She was the first woman in Houghton's history to be named a permanent division chair. (Note: Houghton did not have its first female trustee until 1974, when Elizabeth Beck Gilbert [later Feller] was elected to the board.[55])

Another change took place a few years later. Houghton has always been an almost exclusively white school with an all-white faculty, set in a preponderantly white region. In September 1961 Abraham Davis Jr. '55 became the first black faculty member, and later Mary Harris Carey '49 joined the faculty as a librarian. Houghton's efforts to recruit other black or minority faculty have been mostly unsuccessful, and one of the underlying reasons appears to be the lack of black families and fellowship in and around the community.

One notable change occurred in the administrative ranks. Dining hall management became a growing problem in the late '50s, primarily caused by the enlarged numbers of students and the increasingly complex logistics of feeding in double shifts and at two locations. In September 1961, Kenneth Nielsen, eventual vice president for finance, was brought on board to manage the college's food service program.

Seventy-Fifth Anniversary Celebration

Houghton's fiftieth anniversary, in 1933, fell in the midst of the Great Depression and apparently passed with little fanfare. But the campus environment just before 1958 as the seventh-fifth anniversary approached was much different. Enrollment was large and getting larger, the financial picture (though always tenuous) was brighter, several new buildings were up or being built or designed, and the survival of the institution, though never guaranteed, seemed highly probable. As a result, plans were begun to celebrate this milestone. Kenneth Wilson, who had attended Houghton in the late '30s and subsequently achieved distinction as writer and editor of the *Christian Herald* (and would later serve on the faculty for a year), was asked to polish a historical review of the college, *Consider the Years*, written primarily by Ruth Luckey.

The celebration occurred in two installments. The first was during Founders' Day week in October 1957, and the second in April 1958, near the actual anniversary. Kenneth Wilson, speaking in the old chapel, delivered the Founders' Day Address, "The Story in the Stones," and received an honorary doctor of letters degree. Other events included a concert by the Buffalo Philharmonic Orchestra, a Purple-Gold football game, and a special church service.

The greater celebration took place on April 21–26, 1958. Dr. Paul S. Rees, radio minister and pastor of the First Covenant Church of Minneapolis, spoke in Thursday's chapel on the Wesleyan contribution to evangelism. That evening, at the special Anniversary Convocation, Dr. A. W. Tozer, pastor of the Alliance Church of Chicago, presented an address titled "Consider the Years of Many Generations." During Friday's chapel, the Rev. George Failing, editor of Sunday School materials for the Wesleyan Methodist Church and former director of public relations at Houghton, gave an anniversary lecture on Houghton's contribution to evangelism, and copies of Kenneth Wilson's commemorative book, *Consider the Years*, were presented to all chapel attendees. At the conclusion of the chapel, the college bell was rung seventy-five times in celebration of the anniversary. On Friday evening, there was a special concert by the College Choir, which performed a new work by Dr. Charles Finney, followed by performances of the faculty woodwind quartet, the faculty string quartet, and several soloists.[56] Also, throughout the school year the *Houghton Star* featured a historical column written by Professor Ray W. Hazlett, who had known personally many of the turn-of-the-century personalities.

Revivals in 1951 and 1959

Houghton experienced notable revivals in 1926 and 1942, both reported in earlier chapters. But in 1951 there occurred the greatest revival in Houghton's history. One source hinted that the missions emphasis provided by returning veterans was a catalyst; another traced the revival all the way back to the praying in the 1930s by a visiting evangelist. George Wells cites the activities of an unidentified faculty member who wrote to all on faculty and staff as summer ended, urging prayers for a great revival.[57] Summer outreach teams and returning students began to share this burden, and many in Houghton's constituency added their prayer support as the semester began. Obviously, many forces combined, and the campus was spiritually ready and receptive.

The revival began after a visiting evangelist led an undistinguished series of meetings from October 20 to 22. On the final Saturday evening, a group of students left the session to carry their joys and burdens to Gaoyadeo dormitory, triggering a prayer meeting that lasted past midnight. On Sunday night, some men from one rooming house started a prayer session that soon overflowed the available space and was moved to the village church, where the revival really flowered. The session continued until 5:30 a.m., and attendance was reported at between two hundred and five hundred. Individuals left the session to "compel" roommates and friends to attend, and soon faculty members and community people joined in.

Dean Arthur Lynip reported on what he saw:

> The leader [of the special meetings] was terribly bossy and cruel in whipping the congregation of students, saying "You don't want to be saved. You do not want to lead a godly life." . . . I disliked every minute of the meetings . . . [and] I went to bed disgusted at the meetings. . . . We were living across the street from the church . . . and along about 10:30 or 10:45 I could hear quiet voices . . . and here were kids going to the church. I got dressed and went over and here were fifty to seventy-five kids up around the altar area and in the first darkened seats. [The news] spread over the campus until about two and three in the morning. The church had a couple hundred people in it. . . .[58]

The next day, classes were modified or suspended to permit *ad hoc* chapel sessions, and evening sessions were held to allow students under conviction to testify. Phone calls were made to parents and to home churches to report what was happening on campus, and on Wednesday, a team visited the Buffalo Bible Institute in West Seneca to personally share the good news. Friday's Founders' Day service was modified to allow students to tell of their experiences following the main speaker. The awakening was contagious: ministers who heard about the revival visited the campus, and many Houghton students went forth to share their experiences with churches in nearby communities and in the cities of Buffalo and Rochester. On the evening of October 28, over two hundred students, in small teams, spoke and sang in churches of many denominations.

Two weeks after the revival began, evangelist Jim Vaus (a former gangster converted in a 1949 Billy Graham evangelistic meeting in Los Angeles) spoke in a series of chapels on the importance of feeding regularly on God's word. His emphasis on reading and memorizing Scripture helped establish a solid foundation under the new conversions and rededications. Also, he placed great emphasis on restitution, drawn from his own experiences involving tens of thousands of dollars in electronic equipment he'd "boosted."[59]

Though smaller in scope and effect, another revival took place in the 1958–1959 school year during the March special services, with Dr. O. G. Wilson, editor of the Wesleyan Methodist Church's denominational magazine, as evangelist. One night during the week there was a spontaneous all-night prayer meeting, and during and after these special services there was a great spiritual revival on campus and in the village of Houghton. In the words of Willard Smith, "Many were converted, others were restored to a vital Christian life, and others were called to definite Christian service."[60]

Academic Programs

When Houghton was granted its absolute charter in 1927, both the music department and the theology department were part of the seminary. Following the state education department's review of the college, the music department was elevated to college level (theology followed several years later) and a public-school music course was introduced. Initially, Houghton's music program was a twenty-four-hour major that had the same general education requirements as other degrees. In 1945, the bachelor of music program first appeared in the catalog, requiring 128 total hours with forty-one hours in "background courses" (formerly called "academic courses"). Performance majors were required to take thirty-two background hours.[61]

In April 1946 Houghton received associate membership in the National Association of Schools of Music, and full NASM accreditation was granted in January 1948.[62]

One measure of the acceptance of Houghton degrees for graduate school admission can be found in an outcomes table in the 1953 report to Middle States. Assembled in December 1951, the report identified by institution the number of Houghton graduates from the classes of 1946 to 1950 enrolled for graduate study (plus those from 1951 who had been accepted). The summary note says that 374 Houghton College graduates for those years attended 113 different institutions; because some attended more than one, 431 institutional placements were recorded. Leading the list: twenty-six in Asbury Theological Seminary, twenty-five in Eastern Baptist Theological Seminary, twenty-two in Columbia University, twenty-two in Syracuse University, and twenty in Geneseo State Teachers College. At the other end of the scale, fifty-seven institutions reported enrolling one Houghton graduate each, at sites as diverse as Notre Dame, Drexel, Walla Walla, McGill, and L'Alliance Francaise.[63]

The years from 1946 through 1962 saw some of the greatest changes and greatest growth in Houghton College's history. A tiny college that had barely managed to survive World War II was now coming into its own as a liberal arts institution worthy of its sought-for state, regional, and national reputation. But the next ten years would bring other difficulties that would challenge both the academic community and the entire Wesleyan Methodist Church.

Construction
and Merger

Transformation in the 1960s

Much as each of the preceding eras saw major changes in the college, so did the era of the 1960s. Out in the greater world, the hippies and flower children of the drug culture were having their influence, though their derailed morality and their pharmacological excesses mostly passed by Houghton's serene copse of academe. The same bypassing of effects was true for the mid-decade start of American involvement in the Vietnam war, a conflict escalating since the end of World War II. But Houghton felt clashes and changes of its own kind.

The first, of course, was the continued growth of the student body as the baby-boomers began to enroll and the pressures that this brought on Houghton's physical plant and faculty. Table 13 shows the growth in enrollment.

TABLE 13	Enrollment at Houghton College, 1962–1971		
Year	Men	Women	Total
1962–63	386	571	957
1963–64	411	589	1000
1964–65	458	614	1072
1965–66	482	610	1092
1966–67	501	636	1137
1967–68	498	664	1162
1968–69	506	655	1161
1969–70	513	657	1170
1970–71	505	693	1198
1971–72	494	716	1210[1]

As the numbers of students grew nationwide, a faculty hiring race developed. Like its sister institutions, Houghton needed more teachers; because of its pay structure, however, it was not able to compete for those with doctoral degrees and was forced to hire master's-degree holders. In the ten years from 1959 to 1969, Houghton's faculty grew by 75 percent, while the percentage of doctoral faculty declined by a third. Table 14 illustrates this shift.

TABLE 14	Distribution and Percentage of Earned Degrees, Houghton College Faculty[2]									
Degrees Earned	1929–1930		1939–1940		1949–1950		1959–1960		1969–1970	
	No.	Percent	No.	Percent	No.	Percent	No.	Percent	No.	Percent
Doctoral Degrees	—	—	5	17.2	12	25.5	20	45.5	23	29.9
Master's Degrees	10	38.5	14	48.2	20	42.6	17	38.6	38[*]	55.9
B. Mus. Degrees	3	11.5	2	6.9	7	14.9	0	—	0	—
A.B. & B.S. Degrees	10	38.5	6	20.7	7	14.9	7	15.9	9	11.7
Non-Degree Faculty	3	11.5	2	6.9	1	2.1	0	—	1[**]	1.3
Total teachers	26		29		47		44		77	

[*]Five of this number had completed doctoral requirements but had not received the degree. If their number is shifted to the doctoral box, the percentages become 36.4 and 49.4 respectively.

[**]This faculty member was the fine trumpeter Keith Clark, who played "Taps" for John F. Kennedy's funeral.

The issue of adequate and satisfactory housing also affected the hiring situation. Houghton's housing stock had not expanded as rapidly as did its population in the two decades following the war:

> As the summer of 1965 drew to a close, the college faced a serious housing shortage for new faculty and staff members. Some of them refused to come if housing was not available within the Houghton community. Therefore, Dr. Smith proposed the building of four one-bedroom and four two-bedroom units on college property on Centerville Road. By using prefabricated construction it was estimated that new units could be ready for occupancy in four months. . . . Work began by the end of March 1966 and by the middle of May, two buildings containing four apartments each were up and ready for internal finish work. Based on the pledge of the college to provide housing, several prospective employees accepted temporary housing within or outside the community. All the apartments were ready for occupancy by August 1966[3]

Concurrently, one non-financial situation involving conservative Wesleyan Methodist expectations also affected the hiring picture. The garment and adornment conflict flared in the early 1960s, and the distaste of going to work within what might appear to be an ever-narrowing sectarian environment (to be discussed in chapter 15) may well have added to the negative aspects, even for lifelong Wesleyans Methodists. Did collegiate morality hinge on the wearing of engagement rings or even wedding rings? Were academic standards compromised by short-sleeved dresses or stocking-free legs or jeans or beards? The emphasis on legalism by certain sectors of the college's constituency was becoming problematic for administrators and faculty. (This controversy is discussed in more detail in chapter 15.)

Construction

As the physical plant felt the crunch of increasing enrollment numbers during the post-war span of years, as addressed in the preceding chapter, a construction boom began. Just four weeks before the end of 1959 the new John and Charles Wesley Chapel was dedicated. The magnificent 1,200-seat auditorium was a welcome change from the relatively tiny, second-story space in Fancher Hall with its single set of access stairs. The new 3,153-pipe Holtkamp organ, dedicated some twenty-eight months later, brought a new dimension to musical programs in general and worship services in particular.

The men and women who kept the college plant operating rejoiced in the opening of the new maintenance center in the spring of 1960, allowing the small maintenance shops scattered around the campus (including one in the basement of the music building) to be consolidated. And a year later Shenawana dormitory was dedicated, allowing many men to live on campus instead of in shower-less homes in the village.

Willard Smith reported the flurry of physical-plant expansion activity during 1964:

> At the opening of the February semester, college girls moved into the top two floors of the new East Hall East Wing. The dedication of that wing occurred during June commencement. . . . There had [also] been a rush of construction work to ready the new Presser Hall basement recital room in the Wesley Chapel for dedication during commencement. During the summer, major development of the Stebbins Athletic Field area began. During the early and late fall, shrub and tree clearance was completed on the Stebbins Farm ski slope. Inside finish work and placement of new shelving and furniture in the new library was carried forward and completed in time for the October dedication of the new facility. During the summer the campus sidewalks were torn up and the route used for the placing of a heavy duty powerline plus communication lines for service of the new library and other buildings (present and proposed) on the campus.[4]

Concerning the planning for the library, librarian Esther Jane Carrier was not impressed with the credentials or performance of the architect, the same man who had designed the chapel. She felt he had no experience whatsoever in library design, and she took it on herself, fresh from her library-science doctoral research, to contribute all she could. "I spent hours and hours. I cut every piece of furniture out to scale, every row of stacks, every desk, every carrel, every table, cut everything out to scale and pasted it on the plans to see if it would really work or not."[5] Still, a number of features such as the isolated downstairs classroom and the small stairways (similar to the ones in the chapel) were dictated by the architect, with endorsement from senior administrators. There was little support for open stacks; because of the campus tradition (dating from the days when the library was in the Fancher-Woolsey) of keeping the stacks closed, the leadership felt there was no need for stairways capable of high traffic.

One of the big challenges once the library was ready for occupancy was moving the library collections of more than fifty-two thousand volumes plus microfilms, bound periodicals, and other items[6] from their several locations: second, third, and basement floors in Luckey Memorial Building, a small storage room in the chapel basement, and the old Pantry on the future site of the Science Building.[7] Though a story has grown about a bucket-brigade passing handfuls of books from person to person from one building to another (a yarn apparently rooted in a photograph made to illustrate the need for the move), Dr. Carrier reported a different version. The maintenance staff had built a series of small trough-like book carriers, and a back-and-forth parade of volunteers walked their troughs-full into the new space, putting each load where Dr. Carrier had already marked the shelves. The move had been scheduled for August before students returned, but the need to paint the old shelving (little new equipment could be afforded) and then wait for the paint to dry during a very muggy August delayed the work. When school began, groups of students were assigned after chapel to proceed to Luckey and start carrying books.[8]

Life in the new library was made difficult in the first semester by the fact that no telephones had been installed, and the librarians had to walk through nearby buildings during chapel time to find not-in-use phones. But this changed abruptly in the second semester, when class registration was carried out in the library's reading room area close to where the Science Building now stands, and phones showed up overnight.[9]

One circumstance brought a bit of sadness to those who appreciated the rustic beauty of the campus. During the middle '60s, Dutch elm disease killed more than a dozen of the big American elms on the campus, and these hulks had to be cut down for campus safety. With the usual adroit planning that outside agencies manage, Davey Tree did the felling work during registration week in 1967, and Willard Smith and friends had to cut up and remove the downed trunks.[10]

Several other major construction projects soon went through their fund-raising, planning, and ground-breaking stages. Business manager Willard Smith reported on his role in these activities:

After the celebration of the [1967] commencement activities, Dr. Smith focused on planning new building projects. The science building plans were in the engineering stage, which required frequent sessions with the Beardsley architectural firm. Initial plans were being developed for a multistoried dormitory in the Houghton Creek area on the west side of the campus. . . . The campus center planning was continued. . . .[11]

The big activity at the opening of the fall semester of 1968 was the beginning of construction of the new science building. During the spring and summer the [former] home of the college presidents, the Pantry, and the Barnett house on the building site had been stripped and burned as training projects for the Houghton and Fillmore fire companies. . . . The successful bidder [for the science building] was the Decker Construction Company at $2,032,000, which was $160,000 over estimate.[12]

The 1960s brought the dawn of the computer age to the college. Attending to college financial affairs, including student accounts, was costing immense numbers of hours for hand-posting account sheets, and senior administrators began looking for a better way. But the Luddite spirit which lurks beneath the surface in all liberal arts colleges quickly popped up: the early plans to bring in computer technology to enhance administrative and research work was seen as a problem that stimulated a great amount of campus debate. To help clear the air, the college trustees voted to hire a consultant to assist in developing a practical program with adequate supporting hardware.[13] Soon a contemporary computer system (an IBM 1130), using punch-card data input, was designed, purchased, and installed in Russell House near East Hall. (Later, in 1969 it was re-installed in a state of-the-art computer room in the new science building.) Work stations were located in selected offices in the administrative areas. Said the business manager, "The office installations [began] to produce results in greater office efficiency.[14] Of course, the budget-stretching new equipment also meant new staff, and a director of the computer center was promptly hired.

Curricular Changes

In its self-survey of 1965, Houghton reported an extensive listing of curriculum and program changes during the preceding decade. The list includes:

- 1957: department of biology organized; sociology major added
- 1958: elementary education curriculum organized

- 1959: political science minor added
- 1960: writing major added; music added as liberal arts major; business administration major added; German major reinstated
- 1961: philosophy major added; minors in physical education and linguistics added
- 1962: economics minor added[15]

From the students' standpoint, one of the great accomplishments of the decade was the official ending of Saturday classes in academic year 1967–1968. It was not, however, a sudden change by decree. Instead, first one faculty member moved his schedule to Monday-Wednesday-Friday, and others began to follow suit. Tuesday and Thursday soon became the home of two-hour and four-hour classes, and eventually the faculty made the five-day week official.[16]

Interestingly, the change, which had been frequently discussed in faculty meeting and in the pages of *The Star*, was sanctioned during the year that president Stephen Paine was on a well-earned and sorely-needed sabbatical, and vice president Robert Luckey was serving as acting president. And equally interesting, some alumni felt that this schedule modification had some negative effects: because of Saturday classes, students had tended to stay in Houghton on weekends, which strengthened attendance at Friday night concerts and other campus activities—and contributed to the dynamics of the weekend dating situation, one of the main dimensions of Houghton's status as a "match factory." Having Saturdays class-free meant greater weekend flight was possible for students and faculty. As a result, Houghton's status as a residential college, with weekend cultural events and worship services as an essential component of students' liberal education, was diminished. "The momentum created for change disregarded the carefully constructed network of rationales which had forged a vision for college (in the ancient sense of the word). . . . The consensus and the momentum were for change. . . ."[17]

Self-Survey of 1965

It appears that the Middle States Association of Colleges and Secondary Schools extensively revised its re-accreditation expectations in the years before the mid-1960s, and as a result Houghton's report of its self-survey of 1964 and 1965 combines both statistical data and detailed scrutiny of college situations and conditions.

At the front of this self-study volume can be found a listing of the near-term objectives of the college, presented as "General Lines of Development." This list includes such items as

- a continued emphasis on the liberal arts;
- additional endowment of one million dollars;
- salary increases of three hundred dollars per year;
- discriminating application of fifteen-hour hour standard teaching load;
- completing a campus master plan;
- completing a science center, physical education center, and campus center.[18] [Note: these building were opened in 1970, 1980, and 1972, respectively.]

The philosophical posture of Houghton College was addressed rather forcefully in the *Houghton College Self-Survey* of 1965. Quite aware of the legalistic brouhaha festering in the denomination's background, the authors said this about Houghton College:

[It adheres] in general to the Graeco-Roman and Judaeo-Christian scheme of values. [It is] inclined to rely heavily on history as a light for understanding the present and to shy away from improvisations prompted by expediency. Socialistic trends are resisted. Progressive education has not found favor. Communistic doctrines are regarded as destructive to personal freedom. Unrestricted centralization of power is generally considered an evil. The abuses of capitalism are not defended, but the freedom of the individual is urged.

"Life-adjustment," a widely accepted educational objective in America for several generations, is less a goal . . . than is Christian "life-confrontation," for it is believed that our form of government and our civilization have come to the brink of disaster because we have not taught our young people to face the issues of life in the light of Christian principles. . . . The evangelical approach to correcting the ills of our day calls for a citizen to accept his own personal accountability to God for his life and in the knowledge of that accountability to take his stand daily for that which is consonant with moral rectitude.[19]

One of the largest sections in the one-hundred-page self-survey report is devoted to a review of library holdings. This effort was undertaken at the strong urging of librarian Esther Jane Carrier and with the initially ungracious cooperation of the faculty, several of whom objected to having to spend time in the library reviewing and appraising the collections relative to their specific academic disciplines.[20] The subject-area holdings were described as "barely adequate," with the exception of the elementary education collection, which had been recently enlarged thanks to a $10,000 grant from the Kellogg Foundation. To put this sum in perspective, the library acquisitions budget for many years was $3,500 and only since 1959 had been increased by $500 to $1,000 each year.[21] The library's total of approximately fifty-two thousand volumes was adjudged to be about three-quarters of the minimum collection size expected for a college of Houghton's enrollment.

Another large section of the report dealt with the review and evaluation of academic programs. The text seemed gently (and justifiably) self-congratulatory, with very few recommendations of any great magnitude. The largest involved some suggestions for new majors, new courses, and new faculty.

Faculty workloads and salaries drew more pointed observations. Though there was some concern over the standard fifteen-credit teaching load, the prime suggestions for amelioration included allowing a research project to replace one three–credit course, or arranging schedules so the number of preparations could be reduced from five to four or three. The irony in this approach is that faculty lesson plans tend to persist from year to year, while the tasks of professional reading in the discipline, platform hours, papers to be graded, and student conferences are the real essence of workload.

The February 1965 report of the Middle States visiting team singled out faculty workload and salary conditions as needing special attention. Said the team, "it is [our] unanimous and strong recommendation . . . that the primary area in which Houghton College must strengthen its program and personnel is the area of faculty teaching loads, salaries, and development."[22] Money had not been a faculty-generated concern, and the team noted that it heard no complaints from faculty on this issue. But the team was concerned about the effect of the arduous workload on professional development and maintaining disciplinary currency, and it felt that Houghton would not be able to compete for new faculty under its limited pay scale. At the same time, the team recognized that increased funding to achieve the salary and workload changes would be another critical issue, but it was persuaded that Houghton's donors would rise to the opportunities. Also, the team was concerned about the disproportionate funding for freshman honors scholarships, feeling that too few awards were need-based and the overall effect of Houghton's largesse was to consume funds needed in other areas, such as faculty salaries.

In the self-survey, the average faculty salaries for each of the three faculty ranks were reported for the latest three years (see table 15). These figures do not include the extra increment of two hundred dollars for marriage and one hundred dollars for each for dependent child.[23] Fringe benefits in 1965 included a five percent match by the college for TIAA retirement funding, a 50 percent tuition discount for dependents, sabbatical and graduate study aid options, and shared-premium life insurance. Health insurance was funded by the individual. (Later, an *ad hoc* committee recommended and the college approved a health insurance program provided by Aetna and funded by the college.[24])

TABLE 15	Basic Salaries by Faculty Ranks, 1962–1965[25] (Figures in parenthesis indicate number of full-time faculty)		
Faculty Rank	**1962–63**	**1963–64**	**1964–65**
Instructor	$4,330 (11)	$4,583 (6)	$4,777 (7)
Associate Professor	$5,000 (20)	$5,333 (24)	$5,500 (23)
Professor	$6,100 (17)	$6,400 (23)	$6,620 (24)

Several months after the Middle States evaluation team's visit, the college was asked to provide within two years further information on certain items, especially faculty load and salaries. Dr. Paine reported that about half the full-time faculty at that point had twelve-hour teaching loads, with the balance at fourteen or fifteen hours. No information was offered on how many of these lighter loads were in addition to research projects or other responsibilities. The division chairs typically taught nine hours in addition to their divisional duty.[26]

As was true in the case of Saturday classes, faculty loads slowly were reduced over the next few years. One source indicated that it began with faculty who were in "special situations," who needed more time to develop a new course or serve in some special campus capacity. The advent of Winterim in 1971, a short in-between term in January, may have led to a 12-3-12 rhythm, which later became a 12-12 load.[27] Concurrent with this was the continually growing expectation of enhanced academic demands within the offered courses, requiring on-going faculty personal upgrading.

The faculty rank of assistant professor was reinstated after 1965, and salaries were boosted for each faculty rank, as reported in table 16.

TABLE 16	Faculty Salary Increases and Ranges Following the 1965 Self-Survey[28]			
Faculty Rank	**Salary Increase 1965–66**	**Salary Increase 1966–67**	**Salary Increase 1967–68**	**Basic Salary 1967–1968**
Instructor	$300	$200	$500	$5,400–5,900
Assistant Professor	$300	$300	$500	$6,000–7,700
Associate Professor	$700	$400	$600	$6,800–7,600
Professor	$900	$400	$700	$7,700–8,500

Finances at Houghton College had always been tight, terribly so in the early years. But even in the relatively flush post-war days money was still scarce, especially considering the need to erect new buildings for the burgeoning enrollment and to fairly remunerate the continuing faculty members and attract new ones. Also, during the 1960s, inflation was ravaging the college budget, even as changes were needed.

In 1971, the Local Board of Trustees approved a new pay scale aimed at reducing some of the relative disparity of Houghton salaries compared to those of similar institutions.

TABLE 17	Houghton College Faculty Salary Scale for 1971–1972[29]	
Faculty Rank	**Amount**	**Change**
Professor	$10,100–11,100	+$600
Associate Professor	$,9000–10,000	+$600
Assistant Professor	$7,900–8,900	+$500
Instructor	$7,000–7,800	+$400
Base salary additions: $400 for doctor's degree, all ranks $200 for master's degree, assistant professors and instructors only $800 for division chairs $200 for department chairs $200 for head of household $50 for each dependent child		

As had always been the case at Houghton College, the salary scale was quite compressed, with less than 60 percent separating the base salary of a new instructor from a senior professor. Even under the new scale, Houghton faculty were paid only approximately two-thirds to three-quarters the average salaries of public secondary-school teachers (and several staff members were receiving the federal minimum wage). Eighty-nine years after its founding, Houghton continued to be a place of sacrificial and near-egalitarian service.

The Middle States visiting team in 1965 also was convinced that "too many routine decisions are carried to both the Local Board of Trustees and the Local Advisory Board."[30] The recommendation was to pass the simple tasks to an appropriate administrator to conserve valuable board time.

College and Community Projects

Houghton College has always been a major and integral component of the Houghton community, and items affecting one almost always affect the other. Utilities have always played a central role, especially water—both fresh and waste.

The enlarged college enrollment overtaxed the outdated and too-small college septic system. And in the village, as at the college, residences were dependent on septic tanks. Modernization became an imperative; during the 1964–1965 school year . . . both the federal and the state government agencies were insisting that Houghton College in particular and the community in general must do something to solve the septic tank effluent water runoff. Because of the absence of a sewer system, the runoff was contaminating Houghton Creek and the Genesee River. Not only could no more building permits be allowed but a government order had been issued to cease the discharge of untreated water into the streams.

> The college filed application for government aid to build the [sewer] system conditioned on the establishment of a sewer district. The government grant was approved and the sewer district was organized and approved by a vote of residents in the area.[31]

Because of the new buildings on campus, the college's insurance coverage had to be revised. But the underwriters were concerned about the inability of the current water reservoir to handle demands from a major fire, and they required a new nine-hundred-thousand-gallon water reservoir to be built if the favorable insurance rate was to be maintained. This expense was more than the college could bear, and the conviction developed that the fiscal burden of the water system needed to be shifted to a community water district, where a local bond issue could encompass the financing. Willard Smith reported that the engineering firm assigned to work on the proposed sewer system came through with plans and an estimate of $800,000. Subsequently, the Caneadea town board authorized Dr. Smith to proceed with the legal work and authorized filing applications for state and federal assistance to help finance the project.[32]

During the last week of January 1968, the good news came from the New York Public Service Commission that approval had been given to form a Houghton Water District. As a result, "the college and community would experience more than the usual amount of construction during the year; a $200,000 water tank project, a nearly $2,000,000 sewer project, and a more than $2,000,000 science building construction."[33]

Another 1968 event relating to dorm fire protection was the acquisition by the Houghton fire company of a snorkel truck, required because of the relatively high-rise (for this rural area) buildings filled with people. The college made a significant contribution to the snorkel's purchase, hence the "Home of Houghton College" sign on the snorkel's boom.[34]

About a year later, administrative efforts were focused on resolving the telephone communications problem on campus. For several months, the business manager worked with the college architect and the local and area telephone companies to develop a comprehensive telephone system for the college including intra-campus and outside telephone service. The planning committee decided to merge the college intra-campus system with the outside telephone system, a project that called for a telephone substation on campus with initially three hundred telephone lines serving the campus.[35]

Financial Stresses

As a result of the recommendations of the Middle States evaluation team following the self-survey of 1965, college salaries were raised significantly. This had a serious effect on the budgets, as did the decision by the trustees in the 1966–1967 school year to permit an intercollegiate athletics program to begin in the fall of 1967. The business manager reported that he had a difficult job reworking the college budget to handle the salary boosts and add start-up funds for the intercollegiate athletics.[36]

More budgetary challenges arrived in subsequent years. In 1968, a heavy part of planning for the 1969–1970 school year was dealing with the stresses of inflation combined with the added operating expenses of an expanding physical plant. Unfortunately, in the eyes of the business manager, budget building in the '60s was also made more difficult than usual because a disproportionate amount of time of the Administrative Committee was spent on debating prudential rules (dress and jewelry). In addition, he faced budgetary turmoil when "certain departmental and divisional interests mustered enough votes to make significant line changes which were utterly unrealistic."[37]

The effect of unrealistic budget demands showed up in November 1969, when Houghton College experienced a financial crisis because of a shortage of general-fund cash.

> The problem developed because of the unwillingness of the college administration and the trustees to fund the many projects which related to new buildings on campus: extension of water, sewer, electric, and communication lines, walks, parking, grading, seeding, and landscaping of the new building sites. In November, a $50,000 bill arrived for the electric switching gear and new electric lines to serve the new buildings. When this was added to the many thousands of dollars already spent on unfunded off-site work, the operating cash was used up and borrowing was the alternative. However, banks at that time were reluctant to make such a loan to the college.[38]

Some good news regarding construction funding arrived during the week of July 13, 1969. The first item was a telegram that announced the granting of New York State Dormitory Authority financing for the new Campus Center at $1,125,000. Later that same week, the college received $501,000 in shares of Anchor Concrete Company stock. One half of that gift was for a scholarship fund and the other half was to apply to the new Campus Center project.[39]

One move that was contemplated by the state legislature had budget-bursting potential, but the danger was narrowly averted. As Willard Smith reported,

> The New York State colleges and universities had been called together [in February 1969] on an emergency basis because there was a drive in Albany to get legislation which would require all institutions receiving any form of state or federal scholarship aid to

use only union employees. . . . The all-day meeting was held at Columbia University. It was very informative and pointed out that the cost to the institution of unionization would be a fiscal tragedy. Subsequent to this meeting an organized appeal was addressed to the legislators, who defeated the legislation.[40]

In 1952, Houghton had helped organize ESFILAC, the Empire State Foundation of Independent Liberal Arts Colleges, a cooperative fund-raising effort. Houghton's portion of ESFILAC income was never great, though the annual sum eventually reached thirty thousand dollars, to be used for capital projects. However, the pressure to strengthen faculty salaries led to dividing the income between capital projects and faculty pay by 1972.[41]

Merger with the Pilgrim Holiness Church

While the Wesleyan Methodist Church evolved in an almost linear descent from the Methodist Episcopal Church, the Pilgrim Holiness Church grew out of a braiding together of numerous affiliated-church strands of the holiness movement. This movement began after the Civil War, when a spiritual awakening blossomed among the established churches in America (especially those of the Methodist family).[42] Born in revivals and spread the same way, it was labeled "the holiness movement" because of to the emphasis placed on the doctrines of Christian perfection and the second-blessing experience of holiness.[43] Both Charles G. Finney and Dwight L. Moody were associated with the holiness movement.

While its roots were in the "Methodist family," the holiness movement was truly interdenominational, drawing Christians from many different backgrounds. As one writer stated, "They said that whether a man was Arminian, or Calvinist, whether he was an immersionist or an effusionist, whether he was an Episcopalian or a Congregationalist, if he was a Christian his right and privilege was to seek to be made perfect in love and to receive this grace by faith now."[44]

The first evidence of the genesis of the denomination was the inauguration of the International Holiness League and Prayer Union in September 1897. The name was subsequently changed to the Apostolic Holiness Church, and later to the International Holiness Church. The church's prime objective was world evangelization, and its primary vehicle for doing so was gospel preaching, not social work. Reflecting its interdenominational character, its first missionaries included men and women who belonged to the Methodist, Friends, Wesleyan Methodist, Free Methodist, Presbyterian, and independent holiness churches, and the Salvation Army."[45]

Equally strict in directed conduct to the Wesleyan Methodists, members of the Holiness union were expected to pledge to "walk in the ways of 'righteousness and true holiness all the days of our life,'" and to abstain "from the sale and use of intoxicating liquors and tobacco in all forms; to avoid places of worldly amusements, such as dances, shows, theaters, horse-races, baseball games, and places where gambling is indulged in."[46]

In the years between 1897 and 1922, Apostolic Holiness Church missionaries continued to be drawn from a variety of churches, linked together by their vision of mission and their dedication to holiness concepts. Individual churches that united in the Pilgrim Holiness Church had been organized before or near the turn of the century, and most grew out of camp meetings or revivals. Initially, small aggregations of holiness churches began to band together in larger groupings, changing names as they went, and in 1922 the Pilgrim Holiness Church was created by the merger of the Pilgrim Church of California and the International Holiness Church. Over the next years, several other small church-groups elected to unite with the Pilgrim Holiness Church, even as late as the 1960s.

The idea of merger with Wesleyan Methodists occurred briefly in the early twentieth century but nothing came of it. Later, during World War II, as resources became ever tighter and a spirit of cooperation seemed to pervade America, the two denominations established a joint Commission on Church Union, which met at Indianapolis on October 11, 1944. According to Pilgrim Holiness records, "The matter of union was not pushed, and the idea of merger was to lie dormant for some time."[47]

The beginning of a serious joint effort toward merger occurred on March 6, 1944, when a joint meeting of merger commissions from the Pilgrim Holiness and Wesleyan Methodist churches took place. The sessions' summary reported "a congenial air was in evidence. . . . The meeting . . . concluded with the agreement that there seems to be good climate for merger. . . ." Subsequently, a joint merger commission produced a document titled "Basis for Merger," which was released to both denominations on April 23, 1966.[48]

Following a pro-merger vote by the Wesleyan Methodists, the Pilgrim Holiness Church voted on June 16, 1966 to approve the merger and convene a merging conference.[49]

On June 26, 1968, the Pilgrim Holiness and Wesleyan Methodist churches merged into The Wesleyan Church. Pilgrim Holiness membership in 1968 was 56,763 worldwide, and Wesleyan Methodist membership was 48,344 full members plus 10,696 associate members and 6,519 junior members (representing a drop after the defection of the Allegheny and Tennessee conferences).[50]

Houghton's Buffalo Campus

In 1968, an opportunity came to Houghton College to add a small campus in the southeast Buffalo suburb of West Seneca. The property was that of Buffalo Bible Institute, which had been organized in 1938 at a Main Street location by Dr. Herbert M. Lyon, who subsequently moved the institute to Delaware Avenue. On July 1, 1957, BBI had merged with Buffalo Bible Conference and moved to BBC's thirty-four-acre site, a former amusement park adjoining Cazenovia Creek just off Union Road.[51] BBI subsequently reorganized as a school of higher learning and on February 27, 1959, was provisionally chartered by New York to offer three years of college-level work.[52]

By 1968, BBI was in dire financial straits. With an annual budget approaching $150,000, it faced a growing shortfall, and by the summer of 1968 was searching for $15,000 to cover current bills. (In addition, there was a property mortgage balance of about $45,000.[53]) According to a letter by then-president Dr. James Bedford, it was costing BBI $3,000 per year to educate its students, versus $2,000 per year for Houghton.[54] The major factor was the lack of students; only sixty-five were enrolled in September 1969.

By 1968, Houghton College had reached its twelve-hundred-student planned maximum, and space was once more becoming tight. The option of having another campus in the edge of Buffalo was appealing, for it would offer additional student space while allowing easy access to Buffalo facilities for programs such as social services, business, and teaching. That year, leaders at Houghton and BBI discussed the possibility of creating an institute for Christian social service.[55]

The merger was achieved on September 1, 1969, with the former BBI board assuming responsibility for the campus's debts while Houghton College picked up payroll, maintenance, and other costs. Houghton's charter was officially amended on July 30, 1970.[56] E. Harold Shigley, who held an EdD from Indiana University, was hired as academic dean of the new unit.[57] His wife, however, had continued to work at Marion College and the family home was there, so the new dean resigned after one year, and he was replaced by Houghton alumnus Clifford Garrison '57, holder of a PhD from SUNY at Buffalo.[58]

The Houghton trustees and administration had grand ideas for this new site, and an architectural firm, Beardsley and Beardsley, was hired to draw up a master plan for a facility that would hold five hundred to one thousand students.[59] The Founders' Club Banquet program for November 5, 1970, states the following:

> The Buffalo Campus . . . provides an ideal setting for a campus to accommodate one thousand students . . . The Master Plan calls for maximum density of construction to preserve the park-like setting of the campus. Proposed buildings are interconnected by glass curtain corridors. Designed for phased construction, the campus plan calls for buildings that will ultimately cluster around a striking chapel. . . . Architectural interest will be heightened by a tiered effect—single and two-stories academic buildings towards the front of the property, high-rise men's and women's residences to the rear.[60]

However, enrollment at the new facility remained below the fancied target by a factor of ten, and Houghton was experiencing its own financial constraints. Development at the Buffalo campus was very slow. In fact, the new campus proved to be a continuing strain on the Houghton budget.

Other Changes

During the last decade of the Paine era, faculty began to be more assertive and to deal more with issues of collegiate education rather than questions of student affairs. With Paine's concurrence and under his leadership, the prior practice of taking general faculty meeting time to discuss all business shifted to allowing committees to handle many of the routine matters. While student activities continued to be of concern (one faculty member reported that far more faculty-meeting hours were spent discussing skirt length than true academic matters), the faculty also began to decide issues of course attendance, extension education, credit for training received in the armed forces, electives and minors, SATs, general education, and other issues relating to the college's academic program. By 1972 the college was educationally very similar to other liberal arts institutions, especially those that maintained a Christian distinctive.[61]

In 1972, Houghton's six academic divisions offered these majors:[62]

- Division of English: English, Humanities, Writing
- Division of Foreign Languages: Classics, French, Greek, German, Latin, Spanish
- Division of Science and Mathematics: Biology, Chemistry, Mathematics, General Science, Physics
- Division of Social Studies: Business Administration, History, Sociology, Social Science (Elementary Education)
- Division of Psychology and Education: Elementary Education, Physical Education, Psychology
- Division of Religion and Philosophy: Bible, Christian Education, Philosophy, Ministerial Religion
- Division of Fine Arts: Church Music, Music Education, Theory, Applied Music (Brass, Strings, Woodwinds, Piano, Organ, Voice)

Also, minors were available in speech, economics, political science, and art.

Choosing a New President

A discussion of the selection of Stephen Paine's replacement and the effects of that choice must await the sequel to this volume, probably in another fifty years. Nevertheless, because the selection itself took place in 1971, a summary of the details can be offered here.

Stephen Paine, speaking in a closed session of the Local Board of Trustees on June 2, 1971, reported that he felt what he considered to be the "nudging along of the Lord" and asked that someone else be found to take over the reins of the presidency.[63] At the root of his request lay his recent back troubles and the early stages of Parkinson's disease (which had been diagnosed just the day previous).[64] Board chairman Daniel Heinz asked that it be a matter of prayer overnight and declared it to be the first item of business in a another closed session in the morning. In that session, Dr. Paine's request to retire in 1972 was honored, and Dr. Robert Luckey was asked to serve as interim executive vice president of the college, relieving Stephen Paine of some of the job stresses.[65]

Subsequently, a presidential candidate research committee was named, to include the president of the Student Senate, the president of the Alumni

Association, the chair of the Division of Religion and Philosophy, the academic dean, the general secretary of Wesleyan educational institutions, and five members of the Local Board of Trustees.[66]

In another closed session during a subsequent board meeting on October 14, 1971, research committee chair Daniel Heinz reported that criteria of evaluation had been adopted for reviewing all thirty-nine individuals named for presidential consideration. Four names were advanced for consideration by the board: Robert Luckey, Bert Hall, Melvin Dieter, and Wilber Dayton.[67] The next day, after a "screening of opinion" from the division chairs, the board held a straw vote to establish preference, followed by an official vote to elect the new president.[68] Thus, within twenty-four hours of the naming of candidates, a new man was chosen. Dr. Dayton was contacted in person by Daniel Heinz at Marion College and informed of his appointment, even though he had not submitted an application for the post.[69] He attended his first session with the Local Board of Trustees on December 17, 1971.[70]

The retirements of both Stephen W. Paine and Willard G. Smith in 1972 were actions that served to bring this era of Houghton's history to a close. Dr. Paine subsequently turned most of his attention to his Bible translation work, leading to the publication of the NIV New Testament in 1973 and the full NIV Bible in 1978. Dr. Smith, who had built a new, smaller house near the campus and originally planned to move into it as he pursued his many local interests, was enticed to spend six years in Marion, Indiana, as general treasurer for The Wesleyan Church. Houghton awarded Willard Smith an honorary doctor of laws degree in 1972, and Stephen Paine received a doctor of humane letters degree in 1976.

In a letter to his former associate Arthur Lynip, written during his first month of retirement, Stephen Paine said, "I can testify personally that the Lord gives wonderful peace and a degree of relief to be out of the fray."[71]

TWELVE

Making Decisions

Governance and Administration

I f one were to ask a typical member of the Houghton academic community who above the president makes the final decisions, the probable response would be, "The trustees." And, in essence, that answer is correct, but there is more to the situation. However, before a full answer is offered, it would be well to explore the history of Wesleyan Methodist governance, starting even before Houghton Seminary was incorporated in 1883.

Governance from the Wesleyan Methodist Viewpoint

In their early years, Wesleyan Methodists had such an aversion to a formal church hierarchy and were so congregational in their local church polity that they called their affiliated churches a "Connection" and did not allow a denominational governing structure beyond the few days of the quadrennial General Conference. There was no central administration except for that provided by the publishing agent, the denominational editor, and men handling a few other designated tasks. Although the limited governance of the several annual conferences persisted from session to session, the president of the quadrennial General Conference held his post as conference moderator only for the few days' duration of that conference, and a new president had to be elected each four years.

The first continuing denominational service board was created and appointed in 1844 to oversee the new Wesleyan Methodist publishing house, then in New York City. Called the Book Committee, its eleven members were drawn primarily from nearby churches.[1] In 1848, the Book Committee membership was revised to consist of six pastors (to include the connectional agent and the editor) and six laymen from the New York City area, appointed by the New York Conference.[2]

A slight governance change took place in 1852, when the duties of publishing agent and editor were combined into one office, and eleven men were to be nominated by a special committee to serve on the Book Committee, with the slate then elected by the General Conference. The publishing house, called the Book Concern, was moved to Syracuse the next year.[3] In 1856, the committee was again changed to include twelve members, with the connectional agent and editor added (apparently the posts had been re-separated; they would be recombined from time to time through 1874).

During the Ninth General Conference in 1875, prompted by a bequest left to "the officers of the General Conference as agents," those assembled approved a resolution stipulating that the president and secretary of the General Conference would continue to hold office until their successors were elected in four years.[4] Their duties between General Conferences were rather limited, consisting primarily of signing papers and channelling most legal and financial matters to the Book Committee. This change formed the first step toward creating permanent administrative machinery that would be more adequate for the evangelical work that the denomination was seeking to do.

Subsequent to the Tenth General Conference in 1879, the Wesleyan Educational Society was incorporated in New York as a receiving agency for donations and bequests made for educational purposes.[5] The charter listed the tasks of the society as "the securement, management and disbursement of funds and property in such a manner for the Wesleyan Methodist Connection of America as shall confer a Christian education without regard to sex or nationality."[6] While all interested Wesleyan Methodists could be members of the educational society, fifteen trustees were elected annually to lead and manage the organization. Initially, only Wesleyan Methodists from in and around Syracuse attended the meetings, but in 1891 steps were taken to provide for denomination-wide participation.[7]

With the creation of a new denominational position, that of general missionary superintendent, the membership of the Book Committee was expanded to fifteen.[8]

Following 1891's Thirteenth General Conference, the denomination was incorporated under New York law as the "Wesleyan Methodist Connection (or Church) of America."[9] The Wesleyan Methodist Educational Society was put under the direct supervision of the fifteen-member Book Committee (acting as a general board).

In 1895, the Fourteenth General Conference of 1895 designated the Book Committee as the Educational Society and decreed that all educational work of the denomination must be under the control of this society. This same General Conference also provided for the election of a local board of managers for each institution, operating under the final approval of the Book Committee.[10]

In June 1896, some thirteen years after its incorporation, Houghton Seminary was officially passed from being the property of its own Lockport Conference board of trustees, as incorporated by the state, to supervision by the Wesleyan Methodist Educational Society ("a body identical in membership with the Book Committee").[11] While the connectional agent continued to be the denominational treasurer, the seminary president was granted authority to handle local financial matters, bearing the title "sub-treasurer."

At the General Conference in 1907, the Educational Society was strengthened for a few years by the creation of the position of educational secretary.[12] Silas Bond, then president of Houghton, was chosen for this post, and his departure in 1908 opened the way for calling James S. Luckey as Houghton's new president.

In June 1923, at the Twenty-First General Conference, it was decided that the practice of trying to provide financial support for the then-four Wesleyan Methodist colleges though a general budget for education was not feasible. The solution was to apportion the territory of the denomination by assigning certain annual conferences to the four schools. Houghton's district included these seven annual conferences: Allegheny, Canada, Rochester, Champlain, Lockport, and Michigan.[13] (When the Middle Atlantic Conference was organized, it was added to Houghton's district.[14]) This General Conference also approved the organization of a local board of managers for each college, to be nominated by the conferences in each college's district and elected by the Book Committee. While the president of the college was to be an ex-officio member, membership by any faculty member was prohibited.[15] The duties of the four local boards of managers were to include planning for financing the colleges, hiring administrative officers and faculty, determining salaries, and the working out of general policies.[16] (Of course, any items initiated by the local board had to be ratified by the Book Committee before being implemented.) Concurrently, each college was permitted to appoint its own treasurer and keep books locally. Previously, each president acted as a sub-treasurer for the denominational treasurer, and the official books were all kept at headquarters in Syracuse. This system had proved to be increasingly cumbersome, and the change was welcomed.

Ever since its organization in the 1840s, the Book Committee had seen its duties constantly broadened to include far more aspects that merely Wesleyan Methodist publications. Eventually, in 1947, the Book Committee was renamed as the Board of Administration, and under this label it would continue to serve as the general board for all the colleges.[17]

At the Twenty-Ninth General Conference in 1955 (and as a result of pointed urging by the Middle States Association of Colleges and Schools), the Local Board of Managers at each college was renamed as the Local Board of Trustees, and the board's duties were revised. Now each local board was required to keep its college's expenses within the estimated annual income as determined by the general board, and it was authorized to employ teachers and staff, set salaries, invest funds, initiate capital projects, bind the college through contracts and instruments of indebtedness, supervise academic policies and standards, and determine all business policies.[18]

In 1959, the General Conference approved a major administrative change for the Wesleyan Methodist Church. Leadership of the denomination's many activities was proving to be far more work than one man could handle. Now three general superintendents were to be elected, and later each one was assigned to chair a "commission" relating to the three major areas of service: Christian education, evangelism, and missions.[19] This arrangement persisted until the merger with the Pilgrim Holiness Church in 1968, when a fourth general superintendent was added. (Incidentally, the post-merger administrative unification efforts led to a number of other changes, most of which must be addressed in the sequel to this volume.)

One of the problems inherent in the denominational arrangements for college administration was cited in the 1965 *Self-Survey*. The authority of the board, under New York law, was a key issue, and conforming with that law while sustaining denominational control presented an administrative challenge. The proposed modification, which came to pass in 1969, included language that would assure that Houghton College could never secede from the church.

The Board of Administration of the Wesleyan Methodist Church is the legal board of trustees for Houghton, as it is all other institutions related to the denomination. This board primarily holds title to the property, executing any legal documents requiring official board action, and receives major reports of the operation of the institution. . . .

The actual governing body [of Houghton College] is the Local Board of Trustees, consisting of fifteen members, two each from the seven annual conferences to which Houghton is related, and the president of the institution. The members of this board . . . all seem to be substantial business and professional men, half of them Wesleyan Methodist clergymen, who have a pride in and a devotion to Houghton.

Consideration is being given to the possibility of transferring the title of the property to the Local Board of Trustees, thereby making it the actual legal board. If this is done, the election of members to the Board of Trustees would be transferred from the seven annual conferences to the Board of Administration of the church in order to guard against the eventual danger of some future board of trustees taking action that possibly would separate the college from the church.[20]

General superintendent emeritus Lee Haines provided some background on this issue of strong denominational control:

The contrasting effort to bind the colleges closely under denominational authority was a result of the "Union Movement"[21] following the Civil War. One costly outcome of that was our loss of Adrian College in Michigan—now a nominally United Methodist institution. Two things were stamped in the Wesleyan Methodist psyche in that experience: a fear of mergers, and a determination to bind future schools so that there would never be another one taken from us.[22]

Dr. Melvin E. Dieter, then General Secretary of Wesleyan Institutions, explained Houghton's unique board structure during a 1973 visit to the campus. The minutes of the Local Board of Trustees state the following:

[Dieter] explained the difference in the operational structure of the Houghton board from that followed in other Wesleyan colleges because of the N.Y. State requirements. The Board of Trustees at Houghton College is composed of thirteen members of the General Board of Administration of The Wesleyan Church. This Local Board of Trustees is appointed by the General Board of Administration with representatives of the GBA, the districts served by Houghton, and nominations from the LBT. There are five members serving on both the Board of Trustees and the Local Board of Trustees.[23]

The issue of Wesleyan Methodist control and loss of both Adrian College and Wheaton College deserves discussion here.

One of the sore points in Wesleyan Methodist history that has shaped denominational attitudes for almost 150 years was the loss of Adrian College. Adrian College was established at Adrian, Michigan, in March 1859 by the Michigan Conference of the Wesleyan Methodist Connection.[24] Local citizens had offered a tract of land and pledged thirty thousand dollars to erect suitable buildings.[25] When the offer was accepted, Rev. Asa Mahan was selected as the founding president. Five years later, Adrian was the site of the Sixth General Conference, the conference at which a strong anti-secret society resolution was passed (though it cited only the Masons and Odd Fellows as anathema.[26] It wasn't until 1879 that membership in all secret societies was proscribed.) It was at this conference that the idea of exploring union with the Methodist Protestant Church (an earlier secession group from the Methodist Episcopal Church) and two other small bodies was suggested, though without conference approval, and this unofficial union movement became a factor in the loss of Adrian.

Adrian's incorporation document from the State of Michigan stipulated that total funding of the college was to reach one hundred thousand dollars within five years, or, failing that, "the majority of the board of trustees shall be selected from any religious body" that would agree to raise the funding to that level or more. While the Wesleyan conference asserted that it had satisfied the financial requirement, the trustees decreed otherwise and soon the college was passed to the Methodist Protestant Church, with all financial input from Wesleyan Methodist sources lost.[27] Wesleyan Methodist attempts to secure a financial settlement were ignored, and the loss of both the college and the funds sorely rankled the denomination.

Financial duress also cost the Wesleyan Methodists ownership of the institution that became Wheaton College. Founded in the 1840s at Wheaton, Illinois, and chartered in 1848 as the Illinois Institute, this school came under the control of the Illinois Wesleyans around 1852. The effects of the national financial crisis in 1857 led Wesleyans Methodists to seek assistance from other groups, and soon the Congregationalists joined in the work. Then, in 1860, the institute's original charter was replaced by a new one for Wheaton College, at which point control of the school passed to the Congregational Church, which held the majority of seats on Wheaton's board of trustees.[28] Interestingly, the transition included a covenant to hold and teach the reform principles as advocated by the Wesleyans. Jonathan Blanchard, the first president of Wheaton (and the great-grandfather of Houghton's Stephen Paine[29]), was also pastor of the Wheaton Wesleyan Methodist Church. The Wesleyan Methodists later established a denominationally-funded school of theology at Wheaton, but this too did not survive.

Governance from Houghton's Standpoint

The First General Conference in 1844 strongly encouraged education for Wesleyan Methodist youth and placed the responsibility for establishing schools in the hands of the various annual conferences. From such an arrangement came Houghton Seminary, in 1883.

While a number of other schools had been proposed (and a few established) under other annual conferences, the conferences seemed to have had little control over these schools, and none survived. (A brief recap of these schools may be found in appendix D.) The early failures contributed to the awakening of Wesleyan Methodist leaders to their need for some form of effective central church government, but this was slow to be developed. As mentioned above, at the General Conference in 1875 a denominational president and secretary were elected to hold office throughout the next four years, providing some degree of leadership between General Conferences beyond that provided by the publishing agent and editor.[30]

A reading of Houghton Seminary's petition for incorporation (see appendix C) establishes that twelve men from the Lockport Conference were listed as trustees, and at the beginning they held the corporate authority granted by the state. But the impetus to organize the seminary had come from the Wesleyan Methodist denomination, through connectional agent Rev. D. S. Kinney and the Book Committee, which acted as a higher-level board of trustees. When, in 1895, the denomination decreed that all Wesleyan Methodist schools were to be placed under the ownership of the denomination and the administration of the Education Society, another layer of supervision was added to the structure (until the Lockport Conference board was dissolved). But the membership in the denomination was not large, and the men at the different levels tended to know each other, which kept decision-making reasonably uncomplicated and held any contemplated actions within the bounds of denominational expectations.

In practice, the school was run by the principal, who initially was a Wesleyan Methodist pastor with an appointment to serve at the seminary. Since the seminary was chartered by the Lockport Conference, the designation of someone to head the school came from conference resources or at the request of the conference (see chapter 4). When the fourth principal, the Rev. J. R. Hodges, departed suddenly (he claimed he was pressured into taking the post and swiftly resigned to return to his ministry), it led to a promotion for young James S. Luckey, at that time teaching in the seminary. J. S. Luckey was the first non-pastor to hold the principal's post, which was soon changed in name to "president." His tenure of thirty months was followed by that of the Rev. Silas Bond, who served for twelve years until being promoted to the post of educational secretary of the Wesleyan Methodist Connection. Bond later became founding president of Miltonvale Wesleyan College in 1909. (A listing of Houghton's leaders appears in appendix I.)

Early catalogues of Houghton Seminary list no administrative aides to the president, and President Luckey's duties included being "chief executive, treasurer, teacher, purchasing agent, overseer of repair and construction, publicity agent, and advisor to the students."[31] Willard Smith reported that President Luckey taught a two-thirds load of classes and that his office staff consisted of two student helpers who worked for tuition and board. In essence, this exhausting depth of responsibilities continued until Luckey's death in 1937.

(One evidence of the demand placed on college leadership is mentioned in the history of the music building. When the music department began to grow rapidly after the public school music course was approved, the local board of managers recommended in 1932 that a music building be constructed, *provided that the music faculty could raise at least one-third of the construction costs.*[32] The thought of levying any current department's faculty for such a fund-raising effort is mind-boggling.)

In 1923, the position of dean of the college was established, though for the next fifteen years the holder of that office taught a customary full load of fifteen academic hours. It was not until the rapid expansion following World War II that the dean's teaching commitment was cut to two courses per semester.[33]

Willard Smith reported that the first business manager was added to the staff in 1940, though problems with the individual triggered his departure, and college economics led to leaving the post vacant from late 1943 to early 1945. The next man to serve as business manager was also given the responsibility of public relations. In mid-1948, however, this latter duty was passed to others because the task of serving as college treasurer, finally consigned from the denominational treasurer's office down to the college, was delegated from the president to the business manager.[34]

The growth of the college meant more hands were needed to accomplish the many jobs ancillary to teaching. Where in 1923 the full-time non-faculty staff included just a janitor and the dining hall matron, by 1950 there were forty-two nonfaculty workers, including four administrative assistants, fifteen secretaries, two dining-hall supervisors, twelve men in campus maintenance and operations, and nine others assigned to a variety of tasks.[35]

Another governance modification was the formation of the Local Advisory Board, under the provisions of the 1948 Houghton College constitution. This group was separate from and subordinate to the local board of managers. The LAB, as it was known, was "charged with establishing policies relating to the internal business management and care of the physical plant,"[36] and was tasked to make recommendations concerning the employment of faculty and staff. This group was comprised of the college's president, vice president, academic dean, and business manager, plus the five or six division chairs and three members elected by the faculty. The group was relatively toothless in terms of being able to spend money: any obligation or encumbrance in excess of a meager five hundred dollars had to be ratified by the trustees.[37] Houghton was the only Wesleyan College to have such a board, a situation that was of great concern to the Middle States team in 1975.

In his 1951 doctoral dissertation, Professor J. Whitney Shea provided a then-current picture of the college's administrative structures:

Wesleyan Methodism broke with the mother (Methodist Episcopal) church in 1843 over the question of slavery and the "autocratic" form of [church] government. A congregational pattern of church governance [essentially as established in 1843] prevails today in Wesleyan churches. Local churches are autonomous bodies held together by the annual conference. These annual conferences . . . send delegates every four years to the general conference session. This session elects the general conference president and the board of managers for the quadrennium. The executive committee, chosen by the board of managers of the Wesleyan Methodist Church, . . . is also the board of trustees for each of the church colleges. It acts largely as a coordinator and instigator of broad general policies.

Policy making for Houghton College originates on two levels: the Local Advisory Board and the college faculty, depending on the nature of the case. The Local Advisory Board has to do with the fiscal policy and all problems to be referred to the next higher echelon, the Board of Local Managers. The faculty is concerned with any of the academic and disciplinary problems. As a matter of custom recommendations from the disciplinary deans are approved without discussion in faculty meetings except in a few cases.

Proposed changes in educational policy are first submitted to the Educational Policies Committee composed of the six college division chairmen (English, Foreign Languages and Literature, Social Sciences, Sciences and Mathematics, Theology and Christian Education, Music and Art), the registrar, and the dean of the college. Recommendations by this committee must be approved by majority vote of the faculty.

The Local Advisory Board is also composed of the division chairmen and the dean of the college. In addition three members-at-large from the faculty are elected annually by the faculty. The business manager, the public relations officer and the college president complete the board membership. An Administrative Committee (college president, business manager, public relations officer, dean of the college) meets informally as occasions arise, and decisions made are approved by the Local Advisory Board at its next regular meeting, every two weeks.

Annual recommendations regarding faculty and staff changes and any policy changes or requests for fiscal arrangements must be approved first by the Board of Local Managers before presentation to the Church Board of Trustees. This group meets annually in January on the college campus. It is composed of a minister, elected by the Wesleyan Methodist Church Annual Conference, from each Conference in the Houghton district (Alleghany, Canada, Champlain, Lockport, Michigan, Middle Atlantic States, and Rochester conferences). It has the power to suggest or alter recommendations submitted by the college Local Advisory Board.[38]

Alan Graffam reported that during the Paine era faculty began to shift their administrative attention from questions of student affairs to issues of collegiate education. Instead of spending time in general faculty meetings discussing all sorts of business, under Stephen Paine's leadership a system of committees handled much of the faculty business. While student activities remained matters of concern, faculty members also began to decide issues of course attendance, extension education, credit for armed forces training, electives and minors, SATs, general education, and other issues which related to the college's academic program. By 1960 the college's structure and governance was educationally very similar to other liberal arts institutions.[39]

One can readily agree that Houghton's governance structure was both awkward and somewhat confusing. To recap: at the top was the General Board of Administration, formerly called the Book Committee. Below it was a separate board of trustees for each of the Wesleyan colleges (of which the college president was a member), called the Local Board of Trustees. Then, below this but also including Houghton's president, was the Local Advisory Board. On the same level but at the other side of the college's organizational chart was the Administrative Committee, which included only the senior local administrators. The faculty, with its shifting number of committees, was the next level down.

Not only was the Local Advisory Board unique to Houghton, so was the establishment of a subset of the General Board to serve as a special headquarters-level board for Houghton. This unusual adaptation came about because the counsel for the University of the State of New York ruled that the General Board as constituted was too large (according to New York law) and not local enough to be a proper New York board of trustees. However, instead of working to transfer property-owning and president-appointing powers down to the Local Board of Trustees, Stephen Paine was led to ask that a portion of the General Board be named to deal with Houghton at the denominational level, establishing a board within a board. This unique structure appeared in the Wesleyan Discipline in 1972.[40]

While the issue does not seem to be openly discussed in any of the materials available, there is a general feeling that a paternalistic governance style was sustained from the founding of the seminary through the retirement of Stephen Paine. True, post-World War II faculty sought and pushed for a higher level of participation in conducting the educational business of the college, but the spirit of benevolent authoritarianism seems to have prevailed. Many of those who served under Dr. Paine reported that he worked hard to achieve consensus, sometimes bending to the will of the faculty but more often swinging the group to a position of his determining. Through it all, his innate humility was the major attitude, and this aspect made it easier for most contenders to support his eventual decision.

When Willard Smith was hired in 1938 to teach social science courses and direct the college's public information activities, he looked forward with enthusiasm to taking part in faculty meetings and advisory board sessions. But his anticipation soon turned to exasperation: he was "troubled by the many trivial items which came before these groups . . . a large portion of the agenda items should have been handled by the responsible administrators guided by carefully crafted policy statements."[41]

Smith's disquiet with the awkwardness and inefficiency of administrative practices grew as World War II developed, and he and his close associate, J. Whitney Shea, combined their interests and their recently-logged graduate training to analyze and resolve the situation. Together they developed a list of all the functions performed by each of the administrators, campus committee chairs, and staff members. From this they developed a list of duplicated functions and another of tasks not being done. The departure of Professor Shea for military service halted this effort, and the reluctance of Stephen Paine, as a young president, to suggest major changes to the campus leadership put the needed structural revisions on hold until after the war ended.[42] Smith also initiated a quest to develop a long-range planning system for the college, feeling that operational efficiency was being compromised by the constant need to put out fires rather than prevent them from ever starting. He described the Local Advisory Board's response to this suggestion as "courteous but cool."[43]

Willard Smith also candidly expressed his dissatisfaction with the local managerial-board structure he was forced to endure during his early days as post-World War II business manager.

> [The biggest challenge was dealing with] preacher-thinking of the board, which was a real problem because they were mostly preachers and didn't understand business. All you had to do was to be a good brother and someone recommended you and you were business manager. . . . They tried several times to find qualified business people but when they offered them the [meager] pay . . . you just couldn't hire people. . . . The mechanics meant preachers got elected . . . because each district proposed their people.[44]
>
> I found I had an audience that didn't know what I was talking about when I talked about hard-nosed business matters. I was stuck two ways: the typical academician who didn't know what I was

talking about and the board members who didn't know what I was talking about, so I had nobody to talk to. Even Stephen Paine . . . didn't understand the hard-nosed issues of the cost of deferred maintenance, the logistics of having a particular work activity to do in getting from here to there, planning ahead, design, getting the materials, executing the job, completing it. . . . [The preachers] always felt there was some cheap way to toggle the thing up and get by.[45]

In June 1947, at the Twenty-Seventh General Conference, a denominational reorganization established a full-time office of denominational president and, with the addition of some key denominational officials, a twenty-one–member board of administration. By doing so, the Wesleyan Methodists formally moved from being an affiliation of like-minded local societies to a united, year-round organization with interdependent local churches. Said McLeister and Nicholson, "The Connection . . . became a Church whose . . . programs were to be given general supervision." As part of the changes, the old Book Committee became the Board of Administration.[46]

In response to a Middle States questionnaire, a January 1953 Houghton document (a forerunner of a contemporary self-study report), states the following:

> In the fall of 1947 a special committee was set up by the Local Advisory Board of the College for the purpose of studying the administrative setup of the college. The end result was the adoption of the present arrangement as formulated in the constitution and bylaws of the faculty on January 7, 1948 . . .
>
> Prior to this time the Local Advisory Board had by custom come to include all male members of the faculty, with the president and business manager. Because of the size and unwieldiness this group a sort of inner circle or "cabinet" had come into use consisting of division chairmen and some of the older men professors. The adoption of the constitution called for a discontinuance of the larger group and established the "cabinet" as the functioning local advisory board. The president, dean of the college, and business manager were designated to serve as an administrative or steering committee for the local advisory board.[47]

A 1951 amendment to the 1948 constitution added the director of public relations to the administrative committee.[48] Subsequently, a revision in

1956 changed article V to establish the Local Board of Trustees in place of the Board of Managers:

> There shall be a Local Board of Trustees for Houghton College, composed of no less than five and no more than fifteen members from the seven conferences of the Houghton area as provided by the Book of Discipline . . .
>
> The management functions of the Local Board of Trustees in the interest and subject to the authority of the Wesleyan Methodist Church shall include the following:
> a. The employment of teachers and staff members; fixing of salaries and duties.
> b. The investment of funds.
> c. The initiation of capital projects.
> d. The binding of the college by contracts and instruments of indebtedness.
> e. Supervision of overall academic policies and standards of conduct.
> f. Determination of business policies.[49]

In 1962 the constitution was subject to many tweakings to adjust for changes in nomenclature, duties, and titles. The most significant seem to have been the renaming of the director of public relations as the vice president in development and the re-identification of the Board of Administration of the Wesleyan Methodist Church as the General Board of Trustees of Houghton College.[50] Also, the dean of men became the dean of students, though the dean of women retained her title and apparently became a subordinate of the dean of men.[51]

In an interview conducted in 1985, Dean Robert Danner asked Robert Luckey, "In the era from 1935 to 1955, to whom did the dean of men and the dean of women report?" Luckey responded,

> There probably were two places where they had accountability. One of course was directly to the president. The second was to . . . a disciplinary committee or some sort of faculty committee. There was very little administration as such, other than direct lines to the president. So I'm sure the dean of men and the dean of women reported directly to the president, and probably major discipline matters were made in conjunction with the president or at least the

president's full knowledge. . . . In matters of policy, let's say in matters of prudentials, I would suppose there was quite a bit of faculty input. I would say a major change of rules, for instance, would require faculty action, and probably faculty action was more important even than trustee action, unless it actually impinged on the church or something of that kind.[52]

At the Thirtieth General Conference in June 1959, the matter of local boards of trustees was addressed by a specially-appointed committee. This group recommended that an alternative plan be offered to each Wesleyan Methodist college desiring to use it: that a separate board, operating under the denomination's Board of Administration and elected by it, be approved upon petition and presentation of a charter for such board.[53] The new board would have wider membership and a better balance between clergy and laymen. Under this plan, the terms of the board members would expire on a rotating basis, and the board would be granted more authority to supervise, manage, and conduct the business of each college. One prime factor in offering this option was pressure from the state and regional accrediting authorities.

At this General Conference, the church's administration was revised to include three general superintendents, and a written church constitution was adopted.

As discussed in chapter 11, the self-study of 1965 and the subsequent report of the Middle States visiting team forced the college to look long and hard at its administrative policies and practices.

Student Participation in Governance

In an essay in the 1972 *Boulder*, John Jordan sought an expanded voice for students in campus governance and expressed his concern about the wholly dominant role being played by the board of trustees. He said:

The proposal on "controversial" campus speakers was the Senate's first attempt to deal with the College in its liberal arts perspective. The issue was debated throughout the entire local governmental structure, winning the support of the Faculty and the Student Senate. But the defeat of the proposal by the Trustees taught the Senate a reality of Houghton politics—the Board is the Boss. . . .

The control held by the Trustees raises one problem in particular: that of communication. The Trustees are on campus for one or two weeks per year. During this time, they are involved in meetings and planned programs. This leaves very little time for conversation and interaction with the faculty, staff, or students. Thus, most of the information by which decisions are made is given to the Trustees by the College President. I seriously doubt the ability of any one person to correctly reflect all campus attitudes, emotions, and approaches to the dozens of issues the Trustees have chosen to decide.[54]

It was not until after the presidency of Stephen Paine's successor, Wilber Dayton, that the new college constitution included students on all college councils and major committees. Daniel Chamberlain included students in the governance discussions conducted prior to the college's reply to Middle States in 1977.[55]

Houghton Seminary

When the college received its provisional charter in 1923, the seminary began to be operated as a separate unit but under a common president. This was seen as a compromise at best, and at the pointed urging of the Middle States Association, the regional accrediting agency, the seminary/preparatory school was put on separate footing as a self-sustaining entity called Houghton Academy. Oversight responsibility was assigned to a seventeen-person board of directors that answered to the Houghton College Local Board of Trustees. The Rev. J. Walden Tysinger was named president of the academy, a post he held for seven years, and a new campus for the academy was planned southwest of the college campus, on the site of what once had been Vetville.[56]

In May 1957, Houghton Academy broke ground for its new school building.[57] The academy's eventual move into the new facility, in 1959, meant classroom and office space in Fancher Hall was released for college use.

Houghton's Academic Organization

In 1934, the faculty and curriculum of Houghton College were regrouped into six academic divisions from the original single-unit structure, probably with the pointed encouragement of Middle States. Concurrently, there was an expectation that each division would be headed by a person holding a doctorate in an appropriate subject area. Those on board at the time were Dr. Pierce Woolsey (Division of Foreign Languages and Literature), Dr. Samuel Small (English Language and Literature), Dr. Raymond Douglas (Sciences and Mathematics), and BD-holder Frank Wright (Philosophy and Religious Education). Dr. Stephen Paine was soon to be named academic dean. Only Music (Ella Hillpot) and Social Science (Bessie Fancher) lacked doctoral heads, though both incumbents were legendary for their professional competence and educational effectiveness.[58]

Long-time faculty member Edward Willett expressed his convictions about the value of having the college organized into six academic divisions rather than the subsequent realignment into a far greater number of academic departments, a change made in 1992, long after Stephen Paine's retirement:

> This college succeeded in doing what it did after 1925 as a four-year college because it was structured into divisions. The division structure allowed professors to cross over disciplinary lines. They could be trained in more than one area. That was true of Whitney Shea. He was a sociologist . . . but he was also an economist [and he taught in both areas].[59]

From an external perspective, administration of Houghton Seminary and then College progressed from the Lockport Conference board of trustees through supervision by the Book Committee and the Wesleyan Methodist Educational Society, to a multi-layered arrangement involving the Book Committee and eventually a subset of the denominational Board of Administration, a Local Board of Managers, and Houghton's Local Advisory Board, aided by the Administrative Committee.

Internally, Houghton was first operated solely by the principal or the president. Later, a number of faculty committees were developed to handle all sorts of campus matters. Task division began with the identification of an academic dean and then deans of men and of women. It was not until after World War II that various academic services functions were stipulated, and the 1948 college constitution formalized a structure that resembles the one existing at the end of the twentieth century, though there have been many modifications and adjustment.

College Days

Students and Student Life

S tudents are the college's lifeblood. But students do not live in a void, and surrounding them (to mix a metaphor) is a rich tapestry of academic work, social life, community and on-campus housing, athletic activities of one sort or another, religious endeavors, academic-year events, and even pranks and shenanigans. Nevertheless, the students themselves deserve consideration, and we will encounter them in a variety of ways.

As you will recall from chapter 4, the charge that Rev. D. S. Kinney gave to Willard Houghton was that the denomination wanted to "plant a first-class seminary in these parts to accommodate the children of our people,"[1] leaving us with the conviction that the first audience (and the audience for which Wesleyan Methodist money would be available) was church-family children. But Willard apparently had a broader vision: he wanted to offer a suitable education to all who would enroll and abide by the seminary's rules. Narrow sectarianism was not his goal. In fact, his vision included helping to change human behavior and to move mankind toward perfectionism. As he traveled the area seeking funds for the yet-to-be-opened Houghton Wesleyan Methodist Seminary, he said this school should be "high in standards, low in expense, fundamental in belief."

Geographic Sources

In chapter 4, the geographical sources of Houghton students around 1900 were presented by Willard Smith (see table 7). For more recent years, a review of selected Houghton College catalogs produced the data shown in table 18. From the beginning, New York State provided about three-quarters of the students, with most others coming from the states in Houghton's assigned district. There were, however, representatives from other states and later some foreign countries.

In the early years, it appears that the greatest appeal was to students who lived within a few hundred miles of the campus, which meant New York, Pennsylvania, and southern Ontario. The college's accreditation likely widened the audience, but the effect of World War II on travel and student availability kept attendance in the pre-war mold.

TABLE 18	Geographical Sources of Houghton College Students in 1925, 1935, and 1945[2]					
State or Country	1925		1935		1945	
	Number	Percent	Number	Percent	Number	Percent
New York	78	74.2	250	87.1	216	73.0
Pennsylvania	19	18.1	19	6.6	38	12.8
Canada	0	0	2	0.7	0	0
California	1	0.9	0	0	0	0
Connecticut	0	0	0	0	1	0.3
Delaware	0	0	0	0	2	0.7
Iowa	0	0	1	0.3	0	0
Maine	0	0	0	0	1	0.3
Massachusetts	0	0	0	0	4	1.4
Michigan	2	1.9	8	2.8	9	3.0
Missouri	0	0	0	0	1	0.3
Nebraska	0	0	0	0	1	0.3
New Jersey	1	0.9	4	1.4	10	3.0
North Carolina	0	0	1	0.3	0	0
Ohio	1	0.9	1	1.3	8	2.7
Oregon	1	0.9	0	0	0	0

State or Country	1925		1935		1945	
	Number	Percent	Number	Percent	Number	Percent
South Dakota	0	0	0	0	1	0.3
Vermont	1	0.9	0	0	2	0.7
West Virginia	0	0	1	0.3	0	0
Total	105		287		296	

Points of origin for students changed significantly after the war, as Houghton attracted more students from other states in its district, such as New Jersey, Michigan and Massachusetts, and as students from farther afield began to arrive. Addresses such as Hawaii, Japan, the Philippines, Nigeria, and Vietnam appear in the catalog. Houghton College was no longer just a tiny local institution but was achieving much wider recognition.

TABLE 19	Geographical Sources of Houghton College Students in 1955 and 1965[3]			
State or Country	1955		1965	
	Number	Percent	Number	Percent
New York	303	49.9	610	57.2
Pennsylvania	123	20.3	170	15.9
Canada	13	2.1	9	0.8
California	1	0.2	0	0
Connecticut	7	1.2	9	0.8
Delaware	0	0	10	0.9
Florida	2	0.3	4	0.4
Georgia	0	0	3	0.3
Hawaii	1	0.2	0	0
Illinois	5	0.8	3	0.3
Indiana	2	0.3	6	0.6
Kansas	0	0	1	0.1
Maine	5	0.8	9	0.8
Maryland	8	1.3	7	0.7
Massachusetts	14	2.3	20	1.9
Michigan	19	3.1	36	3.4

State or Country	1955		1965	
	Number	Percent	Number	Percent
Minnesota	1	0.2	1	0.1
Montana	1	0.2	0	0
Nebraska	1	0.2	1	0.1
New Hampshire	0	0	2	0.2
New Jersey	51	8.4	96	9.0
North Carolina	5	0.8	3	0.3
North Dakota	0	0	1	0.1
Ohio	20	3.3	30	2.8
Oregon	0	0	1	0.1
Rhode Island	0	0	2	0.2
South Carolina	2	0.3	1	0.1
South Dakota	1	0.2	2	0.2
Tennessee	2	0.3	1	0.1
Texas	0	0	1	0.1
Vermont	6	1.0	6	0.6
Virginia	2	0.3	6	0.6
Washington	0	0	1	0.1
Washington, D.C.	1	0.2	3	0.3
West Virginia	1	0.2	1	0.1
Wisconsin	1	0.2	0	0
Wyoming	0	0	1	0.1
Other Countries	9	1.5	10	0.9
Total	607		1067	

Denominational Affiliations

Willard Smith also tabulated the reported denominational affiliations of students for the years for which such data were available, drawing his numbers from records kept by the registrar. Table 20 presents data from selected years, to show trends.

Denomination	1929		1936		1939		1944		1949	
TABLE 20 — Denominational Distribution of Houghton College Students, 1929–1949[4]	No.	Percent	No.	Percent	No.	Percent	No.	Percent	No.	Percent
Baptist	41	17.5	66	16.6	78	16.6	58	17.4	206	26.2
Catholic	5	2.1	8	2.0	8	1.7	1	0.3	0	0
Congregational	3	1.3	9	2.3	8	1.7	7	2.1	12	1.5
Episcopal	6	2.6	8	2.0	4	0.9	4	1.2	6	0.8
Evangel./Un. Brethren	2	0.9	0	0	20	4.3	18	5.4	30	3.8
Free Methodist	6	2.6	14	3.6	14	3.0	5	1.5	11	1.4
Methodist	51	21.8	98	24.9	104	28.2	56	16.8	87	11.1
Presbyterian	10	4.3	28	7.1	38	8.1	13	3.9	64	8.1
Wesleyan Methodist	65	27.2	78	19.8	68	14.5	75	22.5	156	18.5
Other Denominations	11	4.7	NA	—	131	27.9	57	17.1	131	16.6
No Church	33	14.1	NA	—	90	19.2	39	11.7	25	3.2
Total Registration	234		394		469		333		787	

Some twenty years later, Lois Ferm analyzed the denominational affiliations of the families of freshmen and seniors at the five Wesleyan liberal arts colleges in 1969. She found the overall ratios somewhat different from the percentages at Houghton, especially regarding Wesleyan and Baptists. It appears from her data that the other four colleges drew more heavily from Wesleyan sources, supporting the idea that Houghton was not perceived as conservative enough for many orthodox Wesleyan Methodist families.

Stephen Paine's biographer, Miriam Lemcio, offered another thought:

> It is a fact of life that most colleges become more liberal than the denominations which founded them. This is especially true when these institutions of higher learning attract students from other Christian traditions. It is always harder to maintain standards among heterogeneous groups whose knowledge of and loyalty to the parent body is minimal.[5]

TABLE 21	Family's Religious Affiliation for Five Wesleyan Colleges[6]	
Denomination	Freshmen	Seniors
Wesleyan*	41.6	37.8
Baptist	18.2	20.5
United Methodist	8.5	8.0
Reformed (Lutheran, Presbyterian, etc.)	5.6	5.4
Christian and Missionary Alliance	3.9	3.9
Pentecostal	1.4	1.5
Other Protestant	6.1	9.8
Greek or Roman Catholic	1.2	0.6
No Church Affiliation	4.0	5.6
No Response	9.5	6.8
Number Surveyed	719	336

*The survey instrument combined Pilgrim Holiness, Wesleyan, and Free Methodist.

TABLE 22	Houghton Student Denominational Affiliation, 1979–1980[7]	
Denominational	Number	Percent
Baptist	276	25.1
Wesleyan	176	16.0
Non-Denominational	118	10.7
United Methodist	102	9.3
Christian and Missionary Alliance	85	7.7
Presbyterian	60	5.5
Roman Catholic	26	2.4
Free Methodist	20	1.8
Assembly of God	19	1.7
Lutheran	12	1.1
Congregational	11	1.0
Other Denominations	160	14.6
No Denomination Given	34	3.1
Total	1099	

Though a search was made of the library, the archives, and many offices, student denominational data for Houghton for the years 1950 through 1972 appear to have disappeared. The only bright spot involved the fact that a report covering the years 1979–1980 through 1983–1984 was discovered. Information from 1979–1980 appears in table 22.

Houghton and Wesleyanism

Alumnus Arthur Lynip, who arrived at Houghton as a student in 1934 and served as academic dean from 1950 to 1966, felt that one of the questions he and his peers faced was "How Wesleyan is Houghton?" Here is his answer:

> You had questions about denominational control. Was it a Wesleyan college? I felt as a student and then later on, it was remarkably relaxed in terms of insisting on one doctrinal emphasis. Even the chapel speakers, though there were some that were strongly and colorfully Wesleyan, there were others, and so my impression was that the college was marginally Wesleyan. When I was dean I thought it was very important to get to the Wesleyan students and say this is your school, and you should not be strangers here at any point. We tried to have a Wesleyan orientation program where they were encouraged to believe that they should be at home. I think that that was a major problem with Houghton—a Wesleyan school but to a large extent, the students were non-Wesleyan, maybe two-thirds of them were non-Wesleyan.[8]

Dr. Harold Kingdon provided some additional impressions of Houghton in the 1960s.

> There was considerable emphasis on externals (proscription of jewelry and make-up; women not allowed to wear slacks to class, etc.). Claude Ries emerged from the ultra-conservative Allegheny Conference of the Wesleyan Methodist Church and endeavored to walk a tightrope, which on the one hand attempted not to offend the conservative constituency, yet realized that Wesleyan Christianity was much more than prudentials.
>
> While enjoying high esteem throughout most of the denomination, Houghton College was viewed very skeptically by the Allegheny Conference because we were too "liberal." One classmate of mine from that conference attempted to return as a pastor,

but was not welcome. Claude Ries was caught in the middle. He had a passion for genuine biblical spirituality and for quality preparation for preaching, all blended in with high academic standards. Stephen Paine also did his utmost to walk that tightrope.

I interpret many of the frustrations, conflicts, and "experience based" struggles of the C. A. Ries era as devolving from attempts to placate this very vocal and numerically strong segment of the Wesleyan Methodist Church. It did, after all, provide students as well as financial support. The tightrope snapped in two, of course, when the Wesleyan Methodist Church merged with the Pilgrim Holiness Church, and the ultra-conservative segments of both denominations voted with their feet and became independent groups.[9]

Student Life in Seminary Days

That Houghton Seminary offered its education in a controlled environment was made clear by this announcement in the seminary's catalog for 1888–1887:

Moral surroundings: parents and others are usually anxious to know about the moral surroundings of a school before sending children. We are very confident that for good moral influence Houghton cannot be excelled. There are no saloons, gambling places or theaters to corrupt the young people. We are fully aware of the evils of a corrupted youth, and we shall labor assiduously to send forth from this institution young men and young ladies in whose minds are instilled the principles of sobriety and morality.[10]

Religious exercises: Religious exercises are held twice a day in the Seminary chapel. Students are required to be present. In addition to these exercises a students' prayer meeting is held every Tuesday evening in the chapel, and students are earnestly exhorted to attend. It is believed that these meetings will prove a source of great spiritual strength to many.[11]

Students who enrolled in the seminary were expected to observe a very specific list of rules and an even more specific set of prohibitions. Concerned parents could be assured that, from the school's viewpoint, Willard Houghton's "strict and reformatory standards" would appropriately regulate conduct. According to the *Houghton Seminary Circular* of 1886–1887:

The rules of the school will be enforced with firmness, yet such methods will be adopted as will secure a voluntary self-government. It is expected that students, while in attendance, will deport themselves as ladies and gentlemen. The following are the rules adopted:

1st. Registry of names at the office on entering the school.
2nd. Adjustment of bills—one-half in advance, and the remainder at the middle of the term.
3rd. Strict observance of study hours.
4th. Attendance at church on the Sabbath.
5th. Punctual attendance upon all regular exercises.
6th. Attendance at chapel exercises.
7th. Observance of temporary prudential rules.
8th. Habits of good order and propriety at all times.
9th. Occupants of rooms shall be responsible for disorder in them, or injury to them.
10th. All excuses from duty are to be obtained *beforehand*, in all possible cases, and in no case must they be deferred later than the following Tuesday.

Prohibitions
1st. Unpermitted association of ladies and gentlemen.
2nd. Visiting, or receiving company on the Sabbath.
3rd. Smoking or chewing tobacco on the premises, or the use of all intoxicants, profane or obscene language.
4th. Attendance upon dancing, play parties, skating rinks, theatres, horse races, etc.
5th. All games of chance prohibited.
6th. Leaving school or town without permission.
7th. Dropping any study without permission.
8th. The use of gunpowder and explosives, and the carrying of fire arms.
9th. Visiting billiard saloons, drinking saloons, and kindred places.
10th. The organizing of secret societies among the students.[12]

In keeping with Willard Houghton's objective of affordable education, the *Circular* said:

Tuition is put down very low to meet the pressure of hard times, and almost any one can, at these low prices, obtain an education. Preparatory year, (which embraces all the common English branches,) per term of thirteen weeks, $4.00.

All higher branches per term, $6.00.

Students are required to pay at least a half-term's tuition in advance.

Good board can be obtained in private families for $2.50 per week, rooms furnished. Students who wish to board themselves can find good rooms.[13]

To be a Houghton student in the 1880s was a rather restricting experience, especially as seen through modern eyes. Here's one alumna's retelling of her mother's student-days story:

What was life like for young people in this town where every thought and almost every breath seemed some way bound to religion? There were no athletics. Games of contest between schools not permitted. There was no gymnasium, no physical education classes. In winter there was some skating or sliding down hill or sleigh rides, not usually indulged in much by girls. Mother could neither skate nor swim. Swimming was not considered entirely ladylike. Of "worldly entertainments" there were none. But young people generally managed to have some fun some way.

This was the age of the Gibson girl look, when women wore large hats with flowers on them, sleeves with voluminous puffs at the shoulders, full skirts with a bustle at the back. There were none of these things for Mother. In a picture I have of her at 13 years of age she is wearing a very plain dark dress, long sleeves with no fullness, fitted bodice, high at the neck, buttons down the front, skirt not skimp but not fashionably full by any means and, of course, no bustle. Her hair was drawn straight back from her face and undoubtedly worn in a simple bun behind. She looked very sober for a thirteen-year-old.[14]

Students enrolling in the seminary in the 1880s often faced more formidable economic and residential challenges than did their successors in Houghton's early college years. Alumna Roberta Grange tells of the travails faced by her mother, Pearl Ingersoll:

When my mother was fourteen years old (1888) she came to Houghton to attend the small denominational school founded by Willard Houghton. The school was in one brick building on a hill overlooking the Genesee Valley and the little village of Houghton. It was called a seminary. Willard Houghton, in his work among the children of the church, had been impressed with the need for a church school where the poor boys and girls of the church and of the surrounding community could get an education.

Mother was to work for her room and board with a family in the town. Her older sister, Rachel, had lived with this same family previously. They expected mother to be like her sister, a strong, well-developed girl for her age. Mother was little and "skinny" for her age. They took one look at her and said she would not do. They couldn't keep her. Mother was heartbroken. She wanted desperately to go to school.

She went up to the school to classes and to tell them she could not stay. She cried so heart-brokenly that President Dodd talked to her. He told her to attend classes that day and after school he would go with her to see if a place could be found for her to stay. He took her to a farm home just south of the school and the people there agreed to take her in to work for her room and board. . . . The mother of the house had a somewhat acid tongue. She was quick to criticize and sparse with praise. Mother arose around four in the morning and worked hard to please for she wanted desperately to go to school.

The school year was divided into eight-week sessions at that time. A student enrolled for one session at a time. As a session neared an end, Monny [the housemother] would try to talk Mother into not going to school the next session, just keep working for her. She would pay her a dollar and a quarter a week when she didn't go to school. She would tell Mother she couldn't spare her to go to school and if she would just stay out this session she would let her go to school next session. . . . So it continued on and off until Mother was seventeen.[15]

To work for room and board, and even for tuition, was very common in those days before state and federal grant and loan programs. In fact, it was common in the early years for a family to mortgage its farm or home, or later on, to sell its only auto, to help finance a seminary or college education, believing that to exercise this then-rare privilege was worth such a sacrifice.

An early catalog offers this note:

Opportunities for self-help: Many students are attending Houghton Seminary who pay all or a large part of their expenses with the work they are able to do in term time and during vacations. At the dormitory, nearly every young woman, who desires to do so, is allowed to earn a part of her board. Several of the farmers in the vicinity of Houghton take a young man to work for his board. Then in many other ways, students are able to get work a part of the time, especially on Saturdays. As a rule the opportunities for earning all of one's board are not open to new students, as such places are secured as soon as known by the students already on the ground; but any student with good health and a willing hand stands a good chance of earning a large part of his expenses after the first semester. A student who has money enough to pay his expenses for one semester need not hesitate to make the start.[16]

With the opening of Besse Hall (later named Gaoyadeo) as a women's dormitory in 1906, food service and rooms for women were available on campus. The catalog for 1905–1906 summarized the opportunities and expectations involved in this new facility:

Room and Board: . . . The Ladies' Hall is provided with ample and modern accommodations for all the young ladies. It is heated by steam and lighted by gas and is conveniently located near the college building. All young ladies are expected to board in the hall except those who work for their board, board themselves, or have homes in town. Special permission must be given to any who have good reasons for boarding elsewhere. Young ladies are expected to attend to their own washing and ironing in the well equipped laundry in the building either by doing it themselves or hiring it done, and to care for their own rooms. Each shall provide herself with towels, soap, bed linen, one pair of blankets, comfortable, counterpane, apron and sleeves, dust cap, and napkin and ring, all of good quality and perfectly clean, subject to the inspection of the Matron. All other necessary articles are furnished by the institution. The price of board, furnished room, heat and light shall not be more than $2.50 per week, and as much less as possible. Those coming to the dining room for table board only shall not be charged more than $2.25 per week, single meals fifteen cents. Board is always to be paid in advance, except by special arrangement. All students are expected to be at their meals on time and to remain to devotional exercises. . . . Marring or defacing the rooms or building by driving nails into the walls or marking with pencils is positively forbidden.[17]

A young man who came to the village in 1907 to begin his studies in the Houghton Seminary described what he saw on the day after his arrival by train:

I arrived at Houghton on Friday evening of the week before school began . . . . I had a chance to look around the village which was destined to be my home for the next seven years. . . . Uncle Clark [Bedford]'s house was built on the edge of the school campus which encompassed most of the plateau [above the Genesee River valley]. Across the street was one brick house owned by J. N. Bedford, Uncle Clark's uncle. . . . On the campus were three buildings. The first was the main school building: a large rectangular structure of red brick with a slate roof and trimmed in white, facing east overlooking the Genesee River Valley. The front entrance was dominated by high stairs leading to a large portico, enclosed on either side by white banisters, and from which rose several large round white columns to support the roof and cupola which held the school bell. Just beyond the main building was another, also made of red bricks, which I learned was the girls' dormitory and about a hundred yards behind the school building was the President's house, also made of red bricks. . . . The road followed the brow of the plateau, then down a steep incline in front of the dormitory, crossing a bridge at the bottom over Houghton Creek and curved around to meet the main road which was dirt and followed the river through the village, running south to Caneadea and north to Fillmore. Houghton Creek, a small boisterous stream, came running down from the hills in back of Houghton, through the village, and emptied into the Genesee River.[18]

This same student also describes residence life for men:

Most of the girls in the school lived in the dormitory, but the boys had to find rooms with private families in the village. Many of these boys got their meals at the girls' dormitory. Some of them were lucky enough to get jobs waiting on tables for their board. Almost every house in the village rented one or more rooms, and Aunt Nell [Bedford] was no exception. Besides me, there were four or five other boys who roomed there . . . Theo and Gail Thompson . . . Glenn Carpenter and Charlie Pierce. . . . The school enforced [regular study hours] from 7:00 to 9:00 pm every evening except Sunday. . . . near the end, before going to our rooms to sleep, we would hold a "bull session." We talked about the school, the teachers and whatever was current. Of course, there was no radio and only a day old newspaper in the school library, so the news of the world was far away.[19]

Literary Societies

As was common in higher education in the years from the Civil War to 1900, students took it upon themselves to organize activities that would augment their classroom learning. Since the operant word in nineteenth-century pedagogy was "recitation," learning involved much done by rote, and students craved a more active involvement in the education process. At Houghton, two literary societies, the Neosophic and Philomathean, were organized before 1900 to give students training in literature, parliamentary practice, and public speaking. According to the catalog for 1907, "The literary exercises consist of debates, orations, essays, and readings. All students who expect to graduate are required to become members of one of these societies. A meeting of each is held every Friday evening. Both ladies and gentlemen are admitted to membership."[20]

Another aspect of student life, one that is little documented and has begun to slip from memory, is the official training provided in etiquette. According to a former dean of women, part of her job was to conduct regular training sessions for the women in her dorm. These occurred several times a semester and addressed many issues related to lady-like conduct. In addition, the dean of women was to present an etiquette chapel once a year. During one of these sessions in the late 1940s, Dean Elizabeth Beck gave a quiz to students and faculty alike. She reported that at least one student class scored better on the quiz than did the faculty.[21]

Ever since Harvard's organization in 1636, students have felt called to test the confines imposed by college administration. The tradition continued at Houghton, where it appears that students were wont to push the limits of expectations for the campus publication, *The Houghton Star*. The Advisory

Board minutes report for February 8, 1922, that it was "voted that Professor Whitaker and Professor Wright read all the proof of the Houghton Star."[22] This issue again became lively in the 1960s, when an assertive editor and a sympathetic faculty advisor had several conversations with President Paine about print propriety.

Miriam Paine Lemcio provided an insightful note on the ongoing contest between students and administration:

> Working with college students exacts great patience. For while they possess many mature attributes, they are still in transition from adolescence to adulthood. Although their time at the college will last but four years, they are often intent on molding its long-term policies according to their immediate perceptions of what ought to be standard. Particular matters can quickly burgeon into universals, and the boundaries between reason and emotion are not finely drawn. As a result of this changing clientele, teachers and administrators must be willing to explain to each new generation how things are.[23]

Incidents involving student discipline surfaced from time to time in various alumni, faculty, and administration interviews, though many of the details are wrapped in the cloak of confidentiality. The incident of the air rifle was presented with more particulars.

> During the spring of 1945, the breaking of street lights in the campus area became a major problem. The local electrical provider, Rochester Gas and Electric, told the college that anyone doing this would be arrested and fined, and also stated that it was up to the college to find and apprehend the culprit.
>
> Lacking a college watchman, the business manager became the overnight sentry, and at 2:00 a.m. the next night he caught a sophomore music student with a BB gun popping out the lights. (The boy's father, a pastor, subsequently engaged in a series of abusive phone calls attacking the college administration and defending his son.) The boy was hauled before the local justice, who allowed him to continue his education as a violinist but sentenced him to spend nine hours a week, for ten weeks, in a community work project, using a five-pound sledge to break up creek stones for village road patching. The boy later thanked the business manager and the college for the positive way in which his offensive conduct was censured.[24]

Returning Veterans and the Smoking Issue

Ever since abstinence from the use of tobacco became an element in the Wesleyan Methodist Discipline following the Civil War, the issue of illicit smoking has popped up from time to time at Houghton. One incident involved a returning vet who had visited Houghton College upon the urging of friends and talked with several people, including the dean of men. Though the vet, a survivor of the horror of the Normandy invasion, did not smoke while he was on the campus, he apparently expressed some position regarding smoking that aroused the dean's hackles.

Shortly after returning home, he received the following letter from Houghton's dean of men:[25]

> Dear Mr. Paul Cherndon [*not his real name*]:
> While I have accepted your room reserve and am putting you on our reserve list, I am impelled to make further inquiry as to your use of tobacco in any form. Houghton College students are not permitted to use tobacco, and we would not care to have anyone among us who would publicly sanction its use. I wish you would face this squarely and give me a frank expression of your feelings on this matter. If you feel that you cannot meet our requirements in this matter and will return enclosed receipt your money will be refunded.
> Sincerely yours,
> *(Signed)* F. H. Wright

The vet subsequently replied that he would have no trouble giving up smoking, and as he rolled through Fillmore on his way to matriculate, he heaved his "last" cigarette out the window. He later commented that there was quite a battle between those who admitted they smoked but could quit (but couldn't) and those who didn't admit they had the habit but did and kept on with the habit. He says he did quit for two days—"but a number of vets and non-vets living in Hazlett House smoked.

"Dean Wright mentioned from time to time in chapel that 'not all that smoke coming out of the blue chimney in your place is woodsmoke.' So we met under the beautiful evergreens on the sidehill opposite Luckey Building and took care of that problem."

"Paul" was converted during one of Houghton's revivals and finally gave up the habit. He later returned to the college to serve as a faculty member for multiple decades.

Special Degrees in 1955

In the years before World War II, just to have attended college was a significant achievement, and many of those who started at Houghton departed after a year or two. World War II, however, wrenched many from their academic track and sent them off to war. Some came later back to finish degrees; some with enough credits moved directly to advanced professional schools sans a bachelor's degree.

Of this latter group, four former Houghton students received baccalaureate degrees under a new "in absentia privilege" inaugurated in November 1955. This privilege, to award degrees to those who amassed at least ninety credits before seeing their education interrupted by World War II, was extended to those who had completed at least two years of professional education in the fields of medicine, veterinary medicine dentistry, law, engineering, and nursing. The recipients included Melvin E. James, Harold C. Livingston, Malcolm D. Phillips, and Edwin T. Presley.[26]

The Flu Epidemic of 1957

Rarely have student health issues been of such magnitude as to claim the attention of the campus for more than a day or so. One of greater significance hit in the fall of 1957, when an epidemic of Asian flu struck the student body. Over a ten-day period, nearly 350 students were stricken. Willard Smith described the situation:

> Everybody in the community with any nursing experience (and some without experience) were called in to care for the sick. Army hospital beds were set up in the lounges of Gaoyadeo and East Hall. Students were evacuated from the main floors of Gaoyadeo and East Hall and the areas were turned into wards for the ill. Medicine and related supplies had to be secured on an emergency basis. Special crews were organized to feed the sick and perform the support services. At the peak of the epidemic during the middle of October there were nearly two hundred students ill at one time. . . Typical confinement with a serious temperature was three to five days.[27]

Eventually the epidemic subsided, but classes were disrupted for a time and a general aura of fatigue seemed to pervade the campus for a few weeks.

Religious Endeavors

The fact that Houghton College is a denominationally-affiliated and supported college does not mean that the religious life of the campus proceeds on an even keel. Fortunately, any theological low points have been minor—and more fortunately, the several revivals have been of exceptional benefit both to the individuals and to the institution. The first major revival occurred in 1926 and was discussed in chapter 7. Another happened in 1942 (see chapter 9). Houghton's great revival took place in 1951 (see chapter 10), followed by a fourth revival in 1959.[28]

A better indicator of the enduring effects of religious life at Houghton may been seen in the report of the missionary labors of Houghton alumni, as reported in the next chapter.

Athletic Activities

Sports activities were not a significant part of student life in Houghton's early days, primarily because Wesleyan Methodists typically held athletic competitions in low regard.[29] Some of the more conservative members of Houghton's early faculty judged athletics of any form to be frivolous behavior. One student, who arrived in 1907 to attend the seminary and went on to graduate from Oberlin, reported an illuminating incident. It seems that two students were playing toss-and-catch with a football on a sunny weekday afternoon, and a passing faculty member advised them to "bury the football and be rid of that evil thing."[30]

Some faithful Wesleyans, however, espoused inconsistent positions: Dorm matron Bertha Grange, who sometimes spoke glowingly about the exploits of her football-star nephew Red Grange, the famous "Galloping Ghost" from the University of Illinois, often declared to Houghton students how evil interscholastic sports were.[31]

Another (and logically limiting) factor was the almost complete lack of facilities. Though in 1908 a classroom was set aside as an exercise area, no formal gymnasium facility existed until 1917. Boys from the early part of that era would carry equipment to the old seminary building where they would play winter basketball. However, Willard Smith reports that by 1909 there were athletics associations offering intramural competition in baseball, basketball, tennis, physical culture drills, military drills, and skating and swimming in season.[32]

For many years sports were available only on an intramural level, though some of the male students managed *sub rosa* participation in town-team baseball. There was a denominational perception that other church-related institutions had allowed sports programs to the detriment of their religious development, and the leadership at Houghton did not contemplate permitting their school to follow a similar pattern. The issue of participation in intercollegiate athletic competition was raised from time to time, especially following the influx of World War II veterans, but it was not until 1967 that Houghton teams were allowed to participate in such competition.

According to a post-war academic dean, "Students were somewhat unhappy because they didn't have intercollegiate athletics. Dr. Paine held out against that partly for the sake of the Allegheny Conference, partly because he felt there were a great many more students involved in athletics with the intramural program."[33] According to historian Alan Graffam:

The intramural program was sufficiently complete . . . that the administration felt that intercollegiate sports were not necessary. Each class fielded teams in various sports, and the best players from these teams were chosen for the Purple and Gold teams which then provided additional competition for better athletes. The quality of the intramural activity for both men and women became nationally recognized. *The Star* reported the continuing competition between the Purple and Gold squads in the same manner as it might have for intercollegiate sports.

This [Purple and Gold] intramural organization was first developed in 1918 and continued until 1968 when intercollegiate sports were introduced. A complete [though less formally structured] intramural program continues.[34]

Propriety extended into the sorts of activities that were to be permitted in athletic-oriented coursework. In a decision rendered in February 1961, the Houghton College Local Board of Trustees recommended "that the course in elementary games offered by Houghton College include rhythmics but only through musical games and not include any folk or solo dancing."[35]

Appropriate dress for athletic endeavors as well as class attendance was an ongoing issue of concern, and on June 13, 1921, the Local Advisory Board "voted to recommend that a clause or paragraph be inserted in the Seminary Catalogue explaining our position on dress."[36] The resulting paragraph expressed a decidedly conservative posture:

The policy of the school is to encourage simplicity and modesty in dress. The Board of Education and the Faculty view with alarm the modern trend of fashion that exposes the body to the gaze of the public, and they most thoroughly approve the stand that some schools and some pulpits are taking against this evil. Hereafter students will not be permitted to attend either class exercises or the evening gatherings in dresses made with extremely short skirts, or with extremely low necks, or made of transparent material unless the body is properly covered with undergarments. The principle of this shall apply to all gymnastic suits, both of men and women, and such suits must be approved by the President and the Physical Directors.[37]

Graffam reports that the first serious discussion of athletics is cited in the faculty minutes of 1909, and a faculty committee was named to oversee the matter. The seminary leaders seemed to support the idea of athletics, though this support was not translated into an organized program for several years. In 1909 a baseball diamond was built, and in 1917 a gym and pool were dedicated. The question of intercollegiate games was considered in 1911 and again in 1917, but no specific action was taken. In 1933 the idea was proposed to allow a non-precedent setting baseball game against Chesbrough Academy (now Roberts Wesleyan College). A faculty committee presented this idea through the campus board to the Wesleyan Book Committee at Syracuse, and received this answer: "[Received] a petition from Houghton College asking that they be permitted to engage in athletics to the extent of entering into games with Cheseborough [*sic*] Junior College. The Book Committee by unanimous vote expressed themselves as being opposed to intercollegiate games on the part of any of our schools."[38]

The baseball game did take place, as reported by one alumnus from the '30s, now a retired school principal. Recalling the days when even the appearance of participating in intercollegiate athletic competition was proscribed, he describes how student inventiveness got around the problem. But doing so led to a unique honor for this man:

I can remember the year that they had a baseball game with Roberts [then Chesbrough Seminary]. There weren't any intercollegiate sports at Houghton, so we had to have one person from Roberts play on Houghton and one from Houghton play on Roberts so it wasn't an intercollegiate game. I was a sophomore that year (around 1934). Chet Driver was a senior. He decided he was going to be captain of the Houghton team. Bill Farnsworth was a terrific pitcher, from Fillmore. Chet wanted to play on the Houghton team, so he put me on the Roberts team. It kind of irked Bill, and his cousin Dick was catcher, and they wanted me to play on the Houghton team. This irks them yet, because I got two hits off Bill that day and won for Roberts. They were sore . . . I was the only Houghton player ever to win a game for Roberts.[39]

Stephen Paine's arrival in 1933 brought new life to the Houghton Forensic Union, and intramural debating flourished on campus. One topic truly reflected contemporary student concerns: "Resolved, that Houghton College should sponsor a system of intercollegiate athletics."[40] It was reported that the debate drew enthusiastic interest, but it would be more than three decades before the first intercollegiate athletic competition was held.

Graffam's analysis of the athletics situation continues:

There were other problems associated with athletics. The strict control of male-female relationships and the Wesleyan concern about propriety in clothing raised questions of modesty in attire. In 1910, for example, the faculty refused to allow the female students to play basketball with male students in attendance. In addition, there was limited support from the denominational constituency. In 1916 a Wesleyan church in Lockport protested a field day as detrimental to the development of Christian character. This raised discussion among the faculty as to appropriate dress and events if the field day was to be held. Luckey dispatched two professors to Lockport to meet with the church and discuss the issue with them.[41]

Still, sports were always an extra-curricular part of student life, and innovative methods to find opportunities and venues were called for.

Houghton had no gymnasium [in 1907], but a year before I entered, a group of students who were interested in playing basketball had gone to the old Seminary building which still stood on a hill about a mile from the campus and had cleaned out the auditorium, which was on the second floor, and put up baskets at both ends. There was no heat and in the very cold weather it was hard to hang onto the ball, but it was a place to play. We had a small portable kerosene stove which we put in the old office, a small room which gave us a place to dress.[42]

Because of the growth of the student body in the post-war years, the old gym became badly crowded and outdated, especially the plumbing. Houghton's intercollegiate basketball games were played off-site, including using the new gym at the Houghton Academy after 1965. It was not until 1978 that ground was broken on the campus for a truly satisfactory athletic center, which opened in 1980.

Student Life in the 1950s

Alumnus Stanley Sandler '60 offered a reminiscence of campus life in the '50s during a Houghton history chapel talk in 1999:

TV's raw slice of life offered "I Love Lucy" or "Leave it to Beaver" or "Father Knows Best." . . . Packards and Kaisers and Hudsons were innocent of seat belts, warning bells, or interlock systems. . . . A pay phone was a real enclosed booth to give you some privacy, the cord wasn't armor-plated, and a local call was a nickel. . . . You'd better finish your college education or the draft would get you, and you might spend the next two years in Korea, shaving with cold water out of a helmet liner at 4:00 a.m.[43]

[We had] four-to-a-table sit-down waiter service for each meal. . . . The food was very good, from the college farm, typical 1950s meat-and-potatoes, say pork chops (one chop per person), mashed potatoes and string beans, with cake and coffee following. You don't like pork chops? Too bad; you'll have an opportunity to pray for better food next time. At the end of dinner, the waiters would pass out hymn books, and we would have devotions.[44]

I found it no big deal to embark on post-secondary education. And without any sort of [federal] government help. No one then left college in debt. (In fact, I remember much later the first student I knew who would be leaving the college with education debts hanging over his head.) A student didn't need government aid; enough could be made in various summer jobs for the coming year. . . . At the time, it cost something like one thousand dollars per year for tuition, room and board. . . . And there were those at the time who worried that Houghton was pricing itself out of the market.[45]

Houghton then had some superb teachers, who taught for salaries as low as those serving in holy orders. The ones I remember most are Dr. Charles Finney, a rare Fellow of the American Guild of Organists and stout battler against cheap gospel ditties; Ray Hazlett, English professor with no PhD, who violated most of the pedagogical rules laid down at East Walla Walla Teachers College, slouching in his chair behind a desk. . . . Then there was Doc Jo, in her zeal for Christian missions and English, combining both in scholarly vigor; the saintly vice president and chairman of the Theology Department, Claude Ries; and Dr. Bob Luckey, who could make even mathematics exciting.

Social life was very important then, because there was practically no place to go beyond the campus . . . Houghton's women's "uniform" of the day was basically skirts and blouses; no jeans, and no sleeveless outfits. Men had no dress code, but tended to favor chino pants and oxford-cloth, button-down shirts. . . . Houghton . . . did permit, almost by default, a modest amount of actual physical contact between the sexes, and one could find couples blissfully walking hand-in-hand (which meant they were "going steady") and even kissing (called "scrunching") in dark places.[46]

The prohibition of matrimony became an issue following World War II. During his interview, Dr. Bert Hall commented that one of the toughest tasks he had to do (probably in 1955) was to notify a student, less than six weeks before his expected graduation, that he was being dismissed from Houghton because he had violated the "no marriage while an undergraduate" rule by getting married over Easter break. Asked by the interviewer if this was a Wesleyan Methodist expectation left over from the early years, Dr. Hall replied, "No, it was a local Houghton rule."[47]

The rationale for this rule remained a mystery until Elwood Zimmerman, who attended Houghton from 1960–1962, provided some background for the college's matrimonial ban for students. Elwood had roomed in the Paine home for two years, and he developed a closeness with the president and his family. His comments:

You didn't really argue anything with Doc Paine—at least, not successfully. He always knew where he stood already on most any issue. Changing his mind wasn't really possible, but as a brash young man I didn't understand that. Near the end of my second year I spent about an hour trying to convince him that the rule against underclassmen getting married was outdated and should be waived in my case. . . . Dr. Paine very patiently explained how the rule was laid down right after the war when so many married veterans arrived that there was no housing for any more married students. Something had to be done, so the infamous rule—repealed soon after my time—was laid down.[48]

Characteristics of Students at Wesleyan Colleges

In her 1972 dissertation for a PhD at the University of Minnesota, Lois Roughan Ferm '39 analyzed the characteristics of students at Wesleyan colleges. Since this study was completed during Houghton's final year with Stephen Paine at the helm, her findings serve as one form of report card for the college. (Note: while her data were drawn from surveys of students at Bartlesville, Central, and Miltonvale Wesleyan colleges, and from Marion and Houghton colleges, Houghton students provided nearly half the responses. A more extensive discussion of her work and findings appears in appendix N.)

Here are the conclusions she reported from her study:

1. The students who select Wesleyan colleges generally come with rather limited types of social and educational experiences.
2. The largest percentages of students attending Wesleyan colleges come from spiritually-oriented homes and churches.
3. Wesleyan colleges attract students who have achieved well academically in their high school work with a good many also giving evidence of participation and leadership in non-class activities.
4. Senior students strongly motivated by parents come to college with two dominant aims, namely to gain liberal learning and preparation for a vocation.
5. Senior students in these colleges do not differ from freshmen in their goals and outlooks.
6. Most students are satisfied with their choice of a small coeducational and religiously-oriented college, and say that they would make the same choice again.
7. Wesleyan colleges rank lower than other denominational and private (independent) colleges in students' perceptions of the learning environment provided for intellectual growth and development.

8. These colleges rank between the denominational and the private colleges in the climate furnished for out-of-class activities.[49]

Overall, one may surmise that Houghton students were in very many ways like students at other colleges and universities, with perhaps a bit more tendency to rank toward the middle of the pack; those who were painfully bright or academically limited tended to seek their education elsewhere. The biggest difference, of course, was the theological dimension. Houghton students almost exclusively came from Christian homes and were steeped in the Christian ethos. Except in a few cases, they accepted and fit comfortably under the expectations for student behavior. But they also remained healthy young adults, pushing (however gently or aggressively) against the constraints and exercising their right to make mistakes and then grow in the safety of the college milieu.

Without question, Houghton students through their lives and achievements have affirmed the essential reason for Houghton's existence: to provide a Christ-centered liberal education.

FOURTEEN

Going Forth to Serve

Alumni and What They
Have Done

Houghton exists as an institution dedicated to providing for its students a strongly academic, avowedly Christian education in the liberal arts and sciences. The few years a student spends at Houghton, however, comprise but a small fraction of each individual's life, so the application of that education to subsequent careers and callings is far more germane to Houghton's ideal of producing Christian scholar-servants.

At the outset, be advised that it is impossible for any writer to deliver a document that lives up to full implications implied in the title of this chapter. Many factors underlie this situation: the college has not pursued the impossible task of maintaining an exhaustive list of alumni and what they have done; alumni change their careers or conduct multiple parallel careers; some almost-alumni who became great achievers ended their Houghton days prior to graduation because of war, finances, or other factors; and no single book would be large enough to hold all the major details, even if they were available. But it is accepted common knowledge that Houghton alumni have gone forth in many forms and areas of missionary[1] and Christian service outreach, in variegated civilian careers, and in the military, including serving in all wars of the twentieth century.

Some selected assortments of information, however, are available to be shared. First, as part of this study, a directory of baccalaureate graduates, 1925–1972, was compiled from several sources. Subsequently, a tabulation was made of the numbers in each class year (see table 23).

Houghton alumni live—and are buried—on all the habitable continents, and, to use a scriptural term, their names (and accomplishments) are legion. Houghton men and women have made a difference, though the full greatness of their effect shall be known by none this side of glory.

In an attempt to provide some measure of indication of alumni accomplishments, selected individuals were asked to consider the roster of graduates for their class and draw from memory and from other records details about the lives of their fellow graduates. Also, a number of alumni interviewed for this book were asked to sum Houghton in one sentence. Their responses are reported in appendix K.

TABLE 23	Number of Baccalaureate Degree Recipients by Class Year, 1925–1972[2]				
Year	Number	Year	Number	Year	Number
1925[a]	20	1941	78	1957	120
1926	15	1942	82	1958	134
1927[b]	26	1943	77	1959	106
1928	31	1944	61	1960	128
1929	33	1945	42	1961	142
1930	29	1946	54	1962	140
1931	28	1947	93	1963	168
1932	61	1948	94	1964	207
1933	60	1949	160	1965	239
1934	48	1950	177	1966	194
1935[c]	49	1951	148	1967	216
1936	61	1952	152	1968	234
1937	45	1953	114	1969	290
1938	81	1954	123	1970	228
1939	83	1955	120	1971	230
1940	75	1956	115	1972	230
				Total	5441

[a] Provisional New York charter granted on April 7, 1923
[b] Absolute New York charter granted on June 30, 1927
[c] Accreditation granted by Middle States Association on November 29, 1935

One other barometer, though it involves a limited number, is to consider those who were awarded honorary degrees by the college in the years from 1936 through 1972. Fourteen of the 142 are Houghton grads, and at least two more—George Beverly Shea and Alton Liddick—studied at Houghton before being called elsewhere. A more detailed listing may be found in appendix H.

And then there were those who came from other colleges to devote a large part of their lives to Houghton, becoming in a very positive sense Houghton alumni. Two of the greatest academic immigrants were Oberlin alumnus James S. Luckey (who graduated from Houghton Seminary) and Wheaton grad Stephen W. Paine. But a check of the faculty directory for 1884–1972 shows about 30 percent of all faculty listed (467) came from Houghton, and among the seventy-one with twenty or more years of service, 48 percent were Houghton graduates.

In the 1953 collection of data for the re-accreditation study by Middle States, 639 alumni from 1946 to 1951 reported on their occupations as of December 1951. The categories listed in table 24 are those found in the report.

TABLE 24	Occupations of Houghton Graduates, Classes of 1946–1951[3]	
Field	**Number**	**Percent**
Full-Time Graduate Study for Professions	122	19.1
Proprietors, Managers, Executives	3	0.5
Professionals and Semi-Professionals		
Ministry	86	13.5
Missionary Work	32	5.0
Choir Directing	1	0.2
Teaching: Christian Institutions	25	3.9
Religious Education	6	9.4
Teaching: Public Schools	134	21.0
Medicine	1	0.2
Dentistry	1	0.2
Nursing	5	0.8
Law	3	0.5
Librarianship	13	2.0
Engineering	6	0.9

Field	Number	Percent
Chemistry	7	1.1
Physics	2	0.3
Research Technology	4	0.6
Radioisotope Research	1	0.2
Social and Personnel Work	8	1.3
Civil Service	1	0.2
Editorial Work	1	0.2
Clerical, Sales, Kindred Work	55	8.6
Craftsman, Foreman, Kindred Work	6	0.9
Farming; Skilled and Unskilled Labor	14	2.2
Military Service	20	3.1
Full-Time Housewives	69	10.8
Unemployed	9	1.4
Total	639	

Some Representative Classes

To provide examples of the variety of fields entered by Houghton alumni and rough percentages in each field, three Houghton graduating classes were examined.

1943

The class of 1943 was reported by Dr. Katherine Lindley '43 with the assistance of several of her local friends. In that class, teaching was identified as the career of nearly a third, with ministry and missionary work totalling about half that number. An attempt was made to follow the occupational categories from the 1946–1951 survey, and some alumni with two-aspect careers were arbitrarily assigned to what seemed to be the most appropriate category. Also, Dr. Lindley remarked on the relatively high number of her classmates who returned sooner or later to serve at Houghton College, listing eleven names.

TABLE 25	Occupations of Members of the Class of 1943[4]	
Field	**Number**	**Percent**
Proprietors, Managers, Executives	1	1.0
Professionals and Semi-Professionals		
Ministry	7	7.4
Missionary Work	7	7.4
Primary/Secondary Teaching	21	22.3
College Teaching	7	7.4
Medicine	9	9.6
Nursing	2	2.1
Law	1	1.9
Librarianship	3	3.2
Engineering	1	1.0
Research/Laboratory	5	5.3
Clerical, Sales, Kindred Work	2	2.1
Craftsman, Foreman, Kindred Work	1	1.0
Farming, Skilled and Unskilled Labor	2	2.1
Homemakers	5	5.3
Unknown	20	21.3
Total	94	

1960

Members of the class of 1960 (not all of whom graduated from Houghton) were recalled by Dean '60 and Carmen VanderVeen '60 Liddick, using records that Dean had assembled in his years as an administrator at Houghton and assisted by some friends. Again, an attempt was made to follow the occupational categories from the 1946–1951 survey.

Several members of the class of 1960 achieved a measure of national prominence. Anthony Yu from the University of Chicago (who served as senior class president and won Houghton's first Danforth Fellowship) and David Sabean of UCLA, both history majors, were inducted in 2000 into

TABLE 26	Occupations of Members of the Class of 1960[5]	
Field	**Number**	**Percent**
Proprietors, Managers, Executives	8	5.4
Professionals and Semi-Professionals		
Ministry	12	8.1
Missionary Work	9	6.1
Primary/Secondary Teaching	45	30.4
College Teaching	15	10.1
College Administration	5	3.4
Medicine	3	2.0
Dentistry	1	0.7
Nursing	4	2.7
Librarianship	1	0.7
Music	3	2.0
Aviation	2	1.4
Engineering	2	1.4
Physics	1	0.7
Research/Laboratory	1	0.7
Social and Personnel Work	1	0.7
Civil Service	4	2.7
Authors/Editors	2	1.4
Clerical, Sales, Kindred Work	2	4
Craftsman, Foreman, Kindred Work	1	0.7
Military Service	1	0.7
Homemakers	4	2.7
Unknown	12	8.1
Total	148	

the American Academy of Arts and Sciences as "exceptional achievers" for their work. Neurologist Eugene D. George served as an advisor to the U. S. Surgeon General. Robert MacKenzie, of Houghton trumpet trio fame, was honored for his leadership in the music business. Carolyn Paine Miller, a one-time prisoner of the Viet Cong, was the first woman member of the Wycliffe board and first woman president of the Summer Institute of Linguistics. Joy Bodunrin Udo, a Nigerian, was the first Protestant principal of a Catholic teachers' training college and the first woman in Nigeria to supervise a fifty-eight-school district; she retired as chief inspector of post primary education for the education board of her state. Ronald Enroth, professor of sociology at Westmont College, Santa Barbara, California, is an internationally known authority and author on cults and spiritual counterfeits. Robert Norberg, an Emmy nominee, is senior recording engineer at Capitol in Hollywood specializing in restoration of vintage recordings. Stanley Sandler became a respected historian with more than ten books published. Three members of the class were named Houghton College Alumnus of the Year, and three others were named Distinguished Alumni.

1972

The class of 1972 was deemed too large for a single person to recollect and report the occupational fields entered, so a survey was sent to all class members for whom we had addresses. Approximately 175 letters went out, and thirty-six responses were received. Surprisingly, the typical '72er knew of only three or four classmates, and the occupations of less than half the class were reported. Fortunately, a conversation with one classmate working at Houghton led to some outdated (but usable) alumni files, where additional data were secured. From those two resources we compiled the results presented in Table 27.

Alumni among the Centennial 100

In 1983, as part of Houghton's centennial celebration, the college selected and honored one hundred individuals who had exemplified Houghton's ideals by demonstrating "effective ministry or service, uniqueness, longevity or extent of service." These were persons who distinguished themselves professionally or who had rendered distinguished service to the college. Of that one hundred, sixteen were faculty and staff non-alumni. The other eighty-four, all alumni from the seminary or the college before 1972, are listed in appendix N.[6]

TABLE 27	Occupations of Houghton Graduates, Class of 1972[7]	
Field	**Number**	**Percent**
Proprietors, Managers, Executives	35	15.4
Professionals and Semi-Professionals		
Ministry	23	10.1
Missionary Work	4	1.8
Primary/Secondary Teaching	57	25.1
College Teaching	8	3.5
College Administration	8	3.5
Medicine	4	1.8
Dentistry	1	0.4
Nursing	2	0.9
Law	5	2.2
Engineering	1	0.4
Research Laboratory	4	1.8
Social and Personnel Work	12	5.3
Authors/Editors	2	0.9
Clerical, Sales, Kindred Work	7	3.1
Craftsman, Foreman, Kindred Work	3	1.3
Military Service	1	0.4
Homemakers	7	3.1
Unknown	43	18.9
Total	227	

Alumni and Missions

Another dimension of alumni service involves the number who have gone into missionary service. The histories of Houghton College and of missions have been intertwined since the founding of the seminary, and hundreds of individuals have applied their Houghton education to Christian work both in the United States and abroad. Dr. Paul Shea '69 compiled a history of missionary (and Houghton alumni) work in the small West African country of Sierra Leone, and his essay is presented as one example of the special service and influence of Houghton alumni. While the time period he covers extends somewhat beyond the terminal date of this study, Shea's essay is included here in its entirety.

At the Eleventh General Conference of the Wesleyan Methodist Connection in Syracuse, N.Y., in 1883, Rev. Willard J. Houghton reported on the progress of the newly-founded Houghton Seminary. The conference received an offering of seven hundred dollars in cash and pledges for the new Houghton Seminary building. At this same gathering a motion was passed authorizing the collection of funds to be held in trust until such time as a work might be started in foreign lands. Houghton and Wesleyan foreign missions already had common bonds.

At the next General Conference four years later, a native Sierra Leonean, J. Augustus Cole, convinced the Wesleyans to make Freetown in West Africa their first mission endeavor. The conference appointed a missionary agent, Rev. A. W. Hall, and authorized him to raise funds with Cole and then make the first exploratory trip to Africa. In 1889 Hall sailed on his famous excursion, chronicled in a little book published in Houghton that same year: *Three Hundred Miles in a Hammock or Six Weeks in Africa*. As a result the Wesleyans affiliated with St. John's Church in Freetown, Cole's English speaking church, comprised of descendants of repatriated freed slaves. (The story of those days in Sierra Leone's history from 1789 to the late 1800s was well told in Houghton's Chamberlain Mission Lectures in February 2002 by scholar Andrew Walls.[8])

Rev. Hall realized that the coastal city of Freetown was well christianized, but his inland adventures revealed great needs and gave promise of open doors to the un-evangelized indigenous interior tribes. He wrote of the potential harvest of souls:

Although their objects of worship and superstition were in endless profusion and their idols prominent in every village, still they confessed no hope of eternal life, and were anxious to be taught of God. Such clamoring for the Word of Life and respectful and earnest attention to the truths expounded, made me keenly feel that dereliction of duty on the part of the church of Christ was not chargeable with the guilt of disobedience alone, but with deep inhumanity in withholding Christ as the hope and help of the lost. When will the church stop its harvest of wealth and turn to the harvest of souls?[9]

Within six months of Hall's return the first party of Wesleyan missionaries, Rev. and Mrs. Henry W. Johnson, their son Irwin, and Miss Alice Harris, M.D., sailed for Sierra Leone. By this time also, a Houghton area native, Mary Lane (who as a four-year-old first met Willard Houghton in the 1870s), enrolled at the Houghton Seminary. She graduated in 1893 and while teaching in the school sensed God's call to missions in Africa. By the summer of 1900 she was on her way to Sierra Leone, where she married missionary widower George Clarke and became the first of a flood of Houghton graduates who answered the call to serve in the Wesleyan church's first overseas mission field.[10]

Tracing the Houghton impact on world missions would be a mighty task, but a short review of the perhaps unique and certainly amazing contribution of Houghton alumni on one country, Sierra Leone, seems doable. Before that abbreviated story we must hasten to say that there are many other chapters in the saga of Houghton and global mission. Perhaps the most well publicized is the major role Houghton grads have played in leadership and labor of Bible translation with Wycliffe Bible Translators. It appears true that no other single school of this sort has contributed more personnel to Wycliffe than Houghton College. The current president of SIL (an affiliated association of linguists), Carolyn Miller '60, and past president Frank Robbins '49 are Houghton alumni. There are well over one hundred Houghton graduates currently serving with WBT.

Other alumni have served or are now serving in leadership roles in numerous mission organizations. To name a few and leave out many is too risky. Houghton people have led in evangelism, literature, media, theological education, medical work, community development, and modern technology on every continent. Someone might ask how many Houghton alumni have served as missionaries? The honor roll that once hung in a prominent place in the old Woolsey-Fancher complex (and now resides in the archives) lists up to 240 missionaries from 1900–1950. An attempt almost ten years ago to round up names for the second half of the twentieth century found nearly four hundred alums in active service.[11] With the rise of short-term missions, some for several years of service, this number likely is much too small.

Back to our story of Houghton and Sierra Leone. Over one-third of the ninety-four Houghtonians who went to Africa in Mary Lane Clarke's footsteps up to 1950 ended up in Sierra Leone. Twelve with Sierra Leone connections have been recognized by this college with honorary doctorates—Frank Birch and his twin children Marion and Marilyn are three of that number.[12] Queen Elizabeth II personally designated two Houghtonians as Members of the British Empire—Ione Driscal '27 for educational service and Marilyn Birch '44 for medical work. A close estimate lists sixty Houghtonians serving in Sierra Leone in the twentieth century.

The beginnings were anything but glamorous in that country, another of those places designated "the white man's grave." A least a dozen Wesleyan missionaries are buried in Sierra Leone, and many more died on American soil of Africa-spawned illnesses. The most shocking death perhaps was that of 1895 theology department graduate Willard C. Boardman. He entered Houghton Seminary in 1884, the year after it was started, and a year before graduation he wrote in his diary that he would not be surprised if he were in Africa some day. He arrived in Sierra Leone with his wife in February 1902. A month later, two missionary men with deadly fevers were fighting for their lives: George Clarke survived, but Boardman's last words were, "Jesus, blessed Jesus!." He died March 27, 1902. Houghton friend James S. Luckey, who enrolled in the school the same year as Boardman, wrote, "Like David and Jonathan we lived and worked together, sharing the same table, sharing each other's joys and sorrows, and when he was called to meet the Blessed Jesus, it seemed that a part of my life had gone out."

Boardman was not alone. John and Lizzie Ayers graduated in 1901 and 1902. They departed for Sierra Leone in June 1905, four months after their wedding. Her immediate sickness required a sudden return home. He remained but died six months later, and another gravestone was added to Sierra Leone's Kunsho graveyard. Educator Marie Stephens died two months into her second term in 1906. Other Houghtonians moving to heavenly reward from Sierra Leone were J. Hal Smith, Miriam Churchill Sprague, and Miriam Day, who was in Sierra Leone one year before becoming the last of those pioneers to die on the field.

One marvels at the strength of God's call and the resolve of obedient response. Someone declared that missionaries packed their belongings in wooden crates purposely cut to size in anticipation of the need for a coffin. Their sacrifice remains an inspiring legacy.

Houghton missionaries to Sierra Leone also taught us about strategy. The Wesleyans in Sierra Leone forged a balanced method in missions.

Africans were trained as evangelists and over the years carried out much of the work of evangelism.[13]

In 1891 God directed them to begin the work in the northern village of Kunsho at the crossroads of three great northern tribes—the Temne, Limba, and Loko. Other outposts were opened as numbers of volunteers increased: Masumbo, home of a girls' school in 1895; Kamabai in 1908—site of the relocated girls' school and eventual Bible school and full-fledged co-ed secondary school; Binkolo, in 1920, where the first established church was chartered and a boys' school was located; Kamakwie in 1919 where the medical work would take root and the famous Kamakwie Wesleyan hospital was founded. It became the place of service for seven Houghton doctors: S. I. McMillen (staff), Marilyn Birch '44, Robert Benniger '48, Gus Prinsell '48, Wilbur Zike '53, Charles Paine '54, and James Tysinger '65. Numerous nurses also ministered in Christ's name at Kamakwie and in clinics, including Esther Smeenge '47, Ruth Pierson '65, Eila Shea '66, and Evvy Hay Campbell (honorary). Houghton superintendent of buildings Robert Fiegl helped construct facilities in Kamakwie.

Gbendembu opened in 1920 and became the heart of Wesleyan work with schools, printing press, radio ministry, and Bible school training. Serving there from Houghton were Price '31 and Helen '25 Stark, Alton '35 and Aileen Shea (staff), Warren and Ella Woolsey (both '43), Marion Birch '44, Margaret Paine Swanson '53, Francis '64 and Leni '65 Strong, Pat '68 and Joe '72 Estes, and Steve and Audrey Pocock (both '79).

Other Houghton alumni contributed in general evangelism or theological education over the years including: George '42 and Mildred '40 Huff, Harold '52 and Marbelle '53 Chapman, Paul '53 and Donamae '55 Dekker, Don Kinde '58, and Paul and Deborah Shea (both '69). And while these listings do not include all, they indicate the astonishing numbers from a school the size of Houghton on a single country and single mission.

A more detailed report on six who contributed to the Houghton missionary legacy in Sierra Leone will provide an overview of the work in that country—two "Pioneers" (1900–1940s), and four "Partners" (1940s– 1990s).

Mary Lane Clarke, 1893

Houghton Seminary alumna Mary Lane Clarke played a major role in establishing Wesleyan missions and in forming the Houghton missionary service tradition. She served from 1901–1915 and then returned for two terms in her seventies! She was a noted teacher in both general education and theological training. She translated many hymns and the Gospels in the

Limba New Testament project. Her notes are preserved in the Wesleyana Collection of the Willard J. Houghton Library. Perhaps she is best known as co-founder, with husband George Clarke, of the Young Missionary Workers Band, a denomination-wide movement of children interested in missions. They based the work on Zechariah 4:6: "Not by might, nor by power, but by my Spirit, saith the Lord of Hosts." And that Spirit did marvelous things, including funding the first two single missionary teachers to Sierra Leone, and funding the construction of portions of Kamakwie hospital. Over the years over five million dollars was raised by children for Wesleyan missions out of the "penny-a-meal" concept instigated by the Clarkes. Who knows the numbers of missionaries mobilized out of YMWB ranks? Mary Lane Clarke spent her golden years living in Houghton as one of our "patron saints." She died at age ninety-seven and is buried in Houghton cemetery.

Ione Driscal '27

In addition to her Houghton degree, Ione earned master's degrees in elementary education and religious studies. She served as a teacher and principal in Africa from 1933–1963. In Houghton she was a campus "all-'rounder" participating in the *Star*, *Boulder*, and sports. In later furlough years she served as dean of women at both Houghton and Taylor University. Her contributions in Sierra Leone focused on schools, building the fine reputation of Wesleyan schools. It is known that close to 90 percent of Africa's leaders at independence were educated in mission schools. Sierra Leone was no exception. In 1957 the British Queen pronounced Ione a Member of the British Empire. She was a discipler of many leaders, including the first national superintendent of the Sierra Leone Wesleyan Church, Rev. Y. Martin Kroma. She had paid the young Kroma's school fees in 1948–1949, and he never forgot his "mother Ione." Kroma, after years of service to the nation and church, was one of the casualties of the recent ten-year horrors of civil war.

Many more pioneers are worthy of mention, including those who gave their lives as mentioned earlier. We could also name Alice and S. I. McMillen. Beginning in 1929 they were leaders in theological education and medicine in Sierra Leone. Alice was an ordained minister who directed the Mt. Loma Bible School at Kamabai. Physician husband S. I. helped move Kamakwie from bush clinic to the major health facility in the remote north of the country. Later, the McMillens had major effects on the Houghton campus as dean of women, Bible teacher and college physician, and both as authors.

Marilyn Birch '44

In the years from 1940 to 1990, the national church certainly took leadership in evangelism, discipleship, and training, but outstanding missionaries helped shape the nature and mission of the church. Marilyn Birch and her twin brother Marion were practically natives of Sierra Leone, having been raised there from infancy by their missionary parents, Frank and Zola Birch, who arrived in early 1919. Both were fluent in the language and at home with the culture of Sierra Leone. Marilyn went from Houghton to medical school at the University of Michigan and then served at Kamakwie Hospital from 1950–1975. She was a gifted eye surgeon and served as hospital administrator for many years as well, designing the new facilities built in 1959–1961. Nothing short of her journals of her exceptional experiences (hopefully to be one day published) can describe the impact of her life and work. Queen Elizabeth II inducted her as a Member of the British Empire during a state visit to Sierra Leone in 1961. A sister-mission medical colleague, Dr. Hugh Maclure, described with amazement and appreciation the facilities and equipment at this jungle hospital in Kamakwie:

> This mountain of paraphernalia reflects the influence of Dr. Marilyn Birch, Marion's twin sister. I suspect that on leave this extremely capable and competent lady must deliberately play the unaccustomed part of needy missionary so that her gallant medical friends all rally around and dutifully donate mountains of equipment for Kamakwie hospital. The reputation of this center in Kamakwie is a tribute to her many years of leadership.[14]

In one of Marilyn's countless stories she narrates the miraculous healing of a little boy, Joseph Konteh, whom she ran into in the village of Laia, over the hills behind Kamakwie.[15] He was struggling for life but could be cured with common medicine, which Marilyn administered under her tender care during a night of uncertainty. Joseph survived, went on to be educated in Wesleyan primary and secondary schools, and felt the call to pastoral ministry. His uneducated mother allowed him to be "given to God," for after all, through Marilyn's hands, God gave him back to her. Today, Joseph Y. Konteh is the head of the Wesleyan Church in Sierra Leone, which includes more than twenty-five thousand believers, many won to Christ through the medical outreach and this amazing missionary, Dr. Marilyn Birch.

One does dislike focusing on one particular medical hero . . . there have been so many. Gus '48 and Louise '50 Prinsell come to mind. Gus and

Louise served at Kamakwie from 1957–1964 until illness brought them home to Houghton, where he served as college physician, and both remain as praying pillars in this community. Following Mary Lane Clarke's lead, Dr. Gus triggered a homeland ministry that has sustained medical missions long after his hands-on work ended. He founded the Wesleyan Medical Fellowship, a network for prayer, mobilization, and support with over 500 members, which has contributed thousands of dollars for hospitals in Zambia, India, Haiti, and Sierra Leone, among other projects.

Marion Birch '44

The second Birch twin went on for a graduate degree from Wheaton College and served in Sierra Leone from 1950–1978. Marion was the gifted linguist, translator, and evangelist. He was so keen on the Temne language that his wife, Marge, reported occasionally overhearing a comment from one national to another when they did not realize that they were understood. They would say, "He was born here. . . . He talks our language. He speaks like his mother was a Temne. He can even 'pull' parables from our elders that we have forgotten. He loves us. . . . He is one of us." They affectionately called Rev. Birch "Pa Kamara" or "Pa Batch." Paul Shea inherited Rev. Birch's last vehicle, an old green Mazda pickup truck with license "NB 960." As he drove up and down the dusty roads, school children recognized the color or the plate and ran after the vehicle shouting "Pa Batch, Pa Batch."

Rev. Birch was much more than a friendly folk hero to young and old. He was a keen mission strategist with deep knowledge of African traditional religion and Islam, and he held clear ideas of how to evangelize people steeped in either or the more common folk combination of both. His method was to spend days at a time in a single village or region, often with Bible-school student evangelists (for many years he trained pastors in Gbendembu) along to observe and assist during dry-season evangelistic treks. Preaching followed a careful story-telling pattern from the book of Genesis—creation, the Fall, the promise, through the prophets, and finally to the Gospels and the story of Jesus. This method has received across-the-board endorsement in mission circles today.[16]

Pa Birch took this approach a step further with film evangelism way ahead of its time. Early on he began lugging heavy equipment from village to village, and city to city, holding week long campaigns. He followed the same narrative approach finding films of creation, the power encounter of Elijah and Baal, and old precursors to the "Jesus Film" on the life of Christ. He also spearheaded production of homegrown true-story dramatizations including the film, "Amadu," telling the story of Muslim Amadu H. Kanu becoming a Christian and eventually a Wesleyan evangelist and pastor. These methods won whole villages to Christ and led to church planting. In his last on-field years Rev. Birch blended these methods with the very fruitful Metro-Move strategy and helped launch the first Wesleyan indigenous churches in the capital city, Freetown, in 1977–1978. Today there are more than ten churches in the metropolitan area as a result.

The accomplishments of this model missionary are too numerous to report, but mention must be made of his large spirit. He was influential in the formation and strength of both the broader ecumenical United Christian Council of churches and the spirited Evangelical Fellowship of Sierra Leone. He promoted and administered the nationwide New Life for All campaign in the 1960s and introduced the appointed national director, Wesleyan pastor and Houghton graduate from Sierra Leone, Rev. Sedu Mans '64.

Marion and wife Marjorie were experts in the local flora and fauna, and no description of their lives would be complete without mention of his love for the extraordinary outdoors. In his own words, he reports his knack for combining mission and adventure:

> Much of the day we would fish for Nile perch and tiger pike, scrappy game fish. Wife Marjorie holds the record in our family landing a forty-four-pounder. A fillet of perch hot from the campfire on a moonlit sandbar is really a tropical treat! While fishing we would occasionally see a huge croc take to the water, or give a wide berth to a snorting hippo. We would notice a slim green mamba hang by its tail from an overhanging branch to sip from the river's surface, or observe an otter take a quick duck and soon surface with a fish flopping between its teeth. In the evening however, we often went to the nearest village to fish for men. Our bait was the Gospel visualized in color on a screen.[17]

Fishing for men paid off. Retired assistant national superintendent Rev. Mallay Kargo remembers being one of those student traveling evangelists. "Even when he went fishing he would gather people in the evening. He was the first white man to preach God's word in my village. He was patient. He would go over the Word until we understood it. He invested his time in us."

Maclure summarizes the weight of the Birches' lives: "Veteran missionaries like the Birches are a rare and endangered species, surviving here and there in spite of the schooling, health and other problems which sit the rest of us down earlier."[18]

When one Paramount Chief, Kande Saio, heard of Marion's death in 1993, he said, "He was no hypocrite. We enjoy the fruit of his labors today. The body of Pa Birch should be brought back to Sierra Leone where he belongs."

Warren '43 and Ella '43 Woolsey

It's best to hear Warren and Ella tell their own story of him growing up as a professor's cynical child at Houghton, of them being classmates at Houghton during the war years, his "decision" to seriously follow the Lord in his junior year, his military duty in Europe, and their subsequent marriage and preparation for missionary service. There are many fascinating and deep twists and turns. It was Rev. Marion Birch who recruited them to teach in the Bible School in Gbendembu, Sierra Leone.

With graduate studies at New York's Biblical Seminary in hand plus financial support from Houghton Church and the college Foreign Missions Fellowship, they were on their way to Sierra Leone in 1950 and served until 1966, three terms up-country in theological education and field administration, and a fourth term near Freetown, founding the interdenominational Sierra Leone Bible College. The latter assignment was brought about by evangelical cooperation and futuristic thinking. The leaders of the future church needed broader and higher education as the nation sprang into independence in 1960. God provided a former British WWII military base and Prof. Woolsey's skillful teaching and administration, admired by a broad spectrum of the Body of Christ in the nation. Since its beginning in 1963 Sierra Leone Bible has produced many strong leaders in the churches across Sierra Leone—leaders who stood firm in the midst of the worst horrors imaginable in the 1990s.

Through much prayer, led by dear national pastor Rev. Bai Bangura, Warren survived in Gbendembu a near fatal attack of typhoid fever in 1957. That resulted in a home-side stint teaching Bible and theology at Houghton College in 1958. With a capable replacement for SLBC in Rev. Don Kinde (Houghton '58), family concerns including his widowed mother to care for, and a sense of God's release from Sierra Leone, Woolsey joined Houghton's religion department full-time in 1966 and served until 1992. His effect here on preparing and motivating future missionaries is the rest of the story. This was a man who would modestly estimate his role in missions, but who was pivotal in preparing the Sierra Leone church for the challenges at the end of the twentieth century.[19] In a 1994 survey of missionaries, Warren and Claude Ries were named by one in seven as being most influential in the missionaries' choice of a career. The other nominations were spread over seventy names.[20]

What was the role of missionaries in Africa? Warren Woolsey described it this way:

> In this task the special role of "foreigners" can be described in several ways. They may serve as a "catalyst," i.e. "a substance which initiates a chemical reaction and enables it to proceed under milder conditions than otherwise possible." (Webster's New Intercollegiate). This is best done, not by making pronouncements, but by raising questions. They may serve as a "source of alternatives," suggesting solutions which the church has tried in other times and places. In this process the contribution of those who have had a different and perhaps wider experience may be especially helpful.[21]

The success of Houghton's missionary ambassadors to Sierra Leone in these roles can best be judged by the perseverance of the church in the midst of a horrible ten-year holocaust in the 1990s. God built His church, and the gates of hell could not prevail. One must agree with Yale scholar Lamin Sanneh that "the missionary contribution of outsiders to the modern reawakening of African has few parallels and should stand as a monument to the scaling down of cross-cultural barriers."[22]

Today, Houghton trustee Joanne Lyon and the World Hope organization are gently moving alongside as today's partner to help our brothers and sisters rebuild from the embers of war. Some have returned to this field to offer short-term assistance, including doctors Gus Prinsell and Charles Paine, nurse Ruth Myering Pierson, and Don and Joan Kinde.

Houghton alumni and the people of Sierra Leone have had a close, remarkable, and lasting relationship. May God be thanked for this story of a great cloud of witnesses. (A listing of Shea's reference sources appears in the bibliography section.)

Growth and Tension

Issues of Contention

W esleyans, under all their organizational names since the 1840s, have
not been strangers to contentious issues. Only a few of these issues,
however, managed to affect the seminary and the college to any degree.

In chapter 2, the denomination-shaping concerns of anti-slavery, disgust
with the misuse of power by the Methodist Episcopal bishops, and Wesleyan
concepts of free will and church polity were discussed. Each of these
considerations helped inform the development of the Wesleyan Methodist
church, though by the time of the founding of Houghton Wesleyan
Methodist Seminary in 1883 they were essentially background aspects. Even
the issue of slavery, which essentially vanished in 1865, was not replaced by
an active interest in integration, probably because of the exceptionally small
proportion of blacks in Houghton's recruitment area. Equal rights for both
sexes and all races was merely a fact of life at Houghton.

Among the public-morality tenets of the early Wesleyan Methodist
Discipline were two that would bear in modest degree upon Houghton: the
positions taken against secret societies[1] and against the use of alcoholic
beverages. The former is essentially a moot point for current Houghton
students and faculty, since tongue-in-cheek campus attempts at Greek-letter

societies have involved neither secrecy nor success.[2] The latter, the prohibition of beverage alcohol, continues both in the *Discipline* and in the campus statement of community responsibilities, though a few contemporary Houghton students (like some of their predecessors) test the rules from time to time, and their clandestine efforts challenge the authority and enforcement ingenuity of the student life staff.

A third issue involved the use of tobacco. It may be surprising to learn that the Wesleyan plank against tobacco (as a "filthy and poisonous narcotic") was not firmly written into the *Discipline* until after the Civil War.[3] Tobacco continues to be a proscribed substance, less so in its "filthy weed" persona than because of the major health risks its use entails. Doctrinally, Wesleyans actively subscribe to the ideal of a highly moral life.

There were issues, however, that did have an effect on the life of Houghton College. Among these are the role of women, hill-village relations, Calvinism versus Arminianism, responses to church union attempts, emotional conversion experience vs. personal relationship, liberal arts college vs. Bible school, and the issue with the most disruptive impact, the adornment and garment controversy.

Role of Women

One contentious issue that has affected the college throughout it existence is the role of women in the church, in academe, and in life. The Arminian concepts of free will and self-determination, extending forward from the ministries of the Wesleys, tended to elevate the potential and status of women to be closer to those of men, in contrast to their second-rank position in the more traditional, Calvinistic churches. Yet Wesleyan men were ambivalent about how far these opportunities should go. At their 1867 General Conference, Wesleyan Methodists endorsed the idea of granting to women the right to vote, but women were not commonly advanced to denominational leadership positions for nearly another century.

Curtis Johnson, writing in *Islands of Holiness*, observed that in the early eighteenth century, "Women were more prone to evangelicalism than men . . . [and] women were central to evangelical religion . . . Even though females were given few leadership opportunities in the official church hierarchy, they were the heart and soul of local congregational life."[4] Women responded to evangelistic revivals in greater numbers than did men, and women took a primary role in training their children, especially their daughters, toward salvation and church membership.

Traditionally, men and women were consigned to rather carefully defined arenas of service. From the time of America's colonization until the domestic turmoil of the Civil War, American and European culture was divided into two distinct and almost wholly separate spheres: the public sphere, which was the domain of males, and the domestic sphere, more than figuratively the home of females. One source even offers this pronouncement by Martin Luther (1483–1546): "The world has need of educated men and women to the end that men may govern the country properly and women may bring up their children, care for the domestic, and direct the affairs of the household."[5]

Historian Jill Conway delineated the early nineteenth century "division of labor between the sexes":

> Males were thought of as having political and economic responsibilities; they were to be citizens and provide the economic support for the family. Women . . . were to have responsibility for the administration of the domestic establishment . . . to play the primary role in educating the young . . . to serve as moral guardians of the young.[6]

This division of expectations had not changed markedly when the Wesleyan Methodist Connection was formed, and it persisted in many ways through the next four decades before the chartering of the Houghton Wesleyan Methodist Seminary. Thomas Woody, in his landmark text, *A History of Women's Education in the United States*, cites the work of Charles Butler:

> [Butler] found the duties of women, in 1851, to be "First, in contributing daily and hourly to the comfort of husbands, of parents, or brothers and sisters, and of other relations, connexions, and friends, in the vicissitudes of sickness and health, of joy and affliction. Secondly; In forming and improving the general manners, disposition, and conduct of the other sex, by society and example. Thirdly; In modelling the human mind, during the early stages of its growth, and fixing, while it is yet ductile, its growing principles of action. Children of either sex are, in general, under maternal tuition during their childhood, and girls until they become women."[7]

As schooling opportunities for both boys and girls expanded rapidly in the nineteenth century, so did the opportunities for women to train and serve as teachers. Because teaching was one of only three main non-domestic occupations for women (the other two were work in the cloth mills of New England and nursing), eminently competent women were available for teaching positions in the new seminary.

Many Wesleyan Methodists agitated in favor of ordaining women, and at the Tenth General Conference in October 1879, the question of licensing and ordaining women was officially brought forward. It was decided that it was proper to license them to exhort and preach, but not to ordain them.[8] Then, at the Thirteenth General Conference in 1891, the question of the ordination of women as elders in the church again came up. Without much debate the rule forbidding their ordination was repealed, but supporters could not enact a church law favorable to such ordination. The whole subject was left as if there had been no legislation on the subject, and any annual conferences that wished to ordain women did so on the ground that what was not forbidden might be done.[9]

A former general superintendent and historian of The Wesleyan Church commented:

> There was a bit of controversy within the Wesleyan Methodist Church as to whether women could be ordained. At one point they adopted a rule that went into the *Discipline* saying that they could be licensed but they could not be ordained. Then that was stricken out, and it was left up to each annual conference. My wife, in her research, has on file records of 1200 ordained Wesleyan women ministers.
>
> And the heyday of Wesleyan women in the ministry would have been probably in the '20s, the '30s, and the '40s. From that point on it dropped off very sharply. There was a tremendous decline in the number of women in the ministry.
>
> One of the reasons, I think, was the fact that we became members of the National Association of Evangelicals, many of whom were either fundamentalists who completely ruled out women, or even old-line Calvinistic churches that did not consider that to be biblically appropriate. We came under their influence and the influence of the literature that flooded the market from fundamentalist groups against women in leadership. It had a profound effect.[10]

Nowhere in the early records of Houghton Seminary is there any evidence of the proposed school being anything other than an equal-sex-opportunity educational institution, which was in agreement with the 1844 Wesleyan

Seminary Founder, Willard J. Houghton
(Portrait by Aileen Ortlip Shea; Photo by C. Nolan Huizenga)

President James S. Luckey
(Shea/Huizenga)

President Stephen W. Paine
(H. Willard Ortlip/Huizenga)

President Daniel R. Chamberlain
(Shea/Huizenga)

President Wilber T. Dayton
(Shea/Huizenga)

1973 Aerial View of Campus
(Houghton College photo)

The Class of 1925, Houghton College's First Graduates

(Houghton College photos)

Mark R. Bedford
President

Earl H. Tierney
Vice-President

Rachel Davison
Secretary

Edward Williams
Treasurer

Esther Haynes

Alice Jean Hampe

Keith G. Farner

Laura Steese

Allen Baker

Mamie Churchill

The Class of 1925, Houghton College's First Graduates

(Houghton College photos)

Helen Davison

Arthur Bernhoft

Laura Baker

Herbert Lennox

Clarice Spencer

Josephine Rickard

Fred Bedford

Mary Williams

Kenneth Gibbin

Pearl Russell

Original Seminary Building
(Houghton College photo)

**Commencement Procession
of 1925 Graduates and Faculty**

Methodist educational report. Men and women faculty were employed in roughly equal numbers. However, leadership positions were reserved for men, in part because the first principals of the seminary were pastors, and pastors (even in the "liberated" Wesleyan Methodist Church) were men, and in part because, while women had the trained skills and socio-biological attributes to be teachers, the firm hand of a man was supposedly needed at the top. This situation essentially continued into and through the college's World War II years, though there was one notable exception at the seminary's helm: the stalwart Philinda Sprague Bowen.

Philinda Sprague was born in 1867 and studied at Geneseo Normal School in the late 1880s. She accepted a teaching position at Houghton Seminary in 1889. In 1892 she married James Bowen, who later was called to the ministry and then to denominational headquarters in Syracuse. After James's death in 1908, apparently from a form of meningitis, Philinda returned to Houghton and resumed her work as a teacher in the seminary to support herself and her two sons. She is reported as being an exceptionally strong and determined teacher, who took a special interest in orphan boys and pushed them to do their best. In her fifteenth year at the seminary, the year that Houghton College was granted a provisional charter and the separation of the two institutions began, Mrs. Bowen assumed the post of principal and continued in that capacity for twenty years. In 1942, she became the first woman to receive an honorary degree from Houghton College. She retired in 1943 and died in 1944.[11]

At the denominational level, the first woman to appear as part of the Book Committee was the Rev. Clara McLeister, who was granted honorary membership in 1923 as president of the Missionary Society. Her service continued to 1943. Ruby Reisdorph held ex-officio Book Committee membership as general president of the Woman's Missionary Society, a post she served in from 1943 to 1959.[12] But no women other than Missionary Society presidents appeared in denominational leadership positions.

At Houghton, a manual count of all 463 faculty names listed in the "Faculty Directory, 1884–1972" (see appendix I) determined that, over those eighty-six years, 56 percent of the faculty was male and 44 percent female. Among those who served the college for twenty years or more, the ratio was 68 percent male and 32 percent female, probably indicating to some extent the then current expectations of breadwinner and homeowner responsibilities for men and the childbearing and domestic commitments for women. It also may have indicated that, as Houghton sought individuals with higher degrees, a greater percentage of that resource was male.

Also, a number of faculty wives were employed in administrative and campus-service roles and therefore were not listed as faculty, even though their service (though always lesser paid) was perhaps equally essential to the existence of the institution.

One of Houghton's early female faculty, Frieda Gillette, achieved a notable milestone for women. Dr. Gillette, who served on the history faculty from 1923 to 1969, was named in 1944 as chair of the Division of History and Social Science. But this posting was only as "acting chair" for the first six years, until she reportedly told President Paine that she did not wish to remain in a halfway capacity. She also became one of three women to serve on the Local Advisory Board (a level below the Local Board of Trustees), along with Dr. Josephine Rickard and Prof. Alice McMillen. Houghton did not have a female trustee until after the retirement of Dr. Stephen Paine, when Mrs. Elizabeth Beck Gilbert Feller, who had served Houghton as dean of women from 1944 to 1951 (and whose master's dissertation involved designing East Hall) was elected to the Houghton board in 1974.[13]

While documentation is sparse, anecdotal evidence indicates that married female faculty members were purposely paid less than their male counterparts, on the rationale that the husband had to provide the home, and the wife was merely working because she wanted to. Of course, the reality of Houghton's pragmatic parsimony regarding faculty and staff salaries may have been a factor in the decision, but the underlying issue was women's wages.

On the issue of woman as pastors, McLeister and Nicholson report that from the very beginning some Wesleyan Methodist churches ordained female ministers. However, not all churches in the Wesleyan Connection supported the idea, and when draft resolutions either to bar or to approve the ordaining women were presented at General Conference, a compromise was reached: licensing or ordaining of female ministers was left to the annual conferences or local districts, while denominational ordination of women as elders was not contemplated.[14] The number of women licensed reportedly was not large, though (as mentioned earlier) 1200 Wesleyan Methodist women preachers were identified by one researcher. Some, of course, were pastoral spouses whose preaching credentials served to expand their family's ministry. But, a number of these female ministers were independently active in church planting and in evangelical crusades.[15]

Hill-Village Relationships

Relations between the Houghton academic community and the surrounding (and supporting) communities have ranged over the years from mutual misunderstanding and suspicion, to near animosity, through reciprocal live-and-let-live, to an environment of general acceptance and affability. One early alumnus, at age 103 the oldest person interviewed for this project, offered this observation:

> The communities around were sort of resentful to the college. The reason was pretty much this: The Wesleyan church had preachers who spent a lot of time preaching against women's wearing jewelry, furs and hats; long sleeves and long dresses were worn. . . . They'd get up in the aisles and screech and yell, and that gave a black eye as far as the community was concerned. They thought the college was just like what they saw in church."[16]

Houghton, especially in the early days, perceived itself as an island of holiness in a sea of sin, and it proclaimed its self-isolation in an attempt to attract students. Seekers of a purer way of life were drawn to move to the community, but their isolationism and aloofness (at least in the eyes of the next ring of population) was not a positive force.

Houghton apparently worked at maintaining a distance between the school and the community. A 1912 request to use the ball field on Independence Day drew this statement from the Educational Society:

> In regard to the request from the citizens of Houghton for the privilege of playing ball on the athletic field July 4th, we recommend that the request be granted with the distinct understanding that the said permission extends only to July 4, 1912, and that each person must comply with the rules of the Athletic Association or withdraw from the game. Furthermore, the permission is to the players through the persons signing this request, who are responsible to see that these specifications are carried out.[17]

One lifetime resident of the area, a man with at best tangential contact with Houghton, recalls riding in the 1920s through Houghton with the family lawyer and being told, "We're going right through the streets of glory now."[18] This insular attitude was also reflected in a description of Houghton shared by a class of 1934 alumnus. After designating Houghton as "a little isle of decency," he said: "Piety hill, I suppose, was the general impression about Houghton, straight-laced, but nonetheless respected." He went on to add an anecdote: "Around 1931, as I was walking north from Robert Molyneaux's place on the south side to our home on the north side [on Old Centerville Road], some young people driving south stopped and offered me a ride. 'Well,' I answered, 'I am not going your way.' Laughing, they shouted, '*Nobody* in Houghton is going our way!'"[19]

A former college treasurer, who moved to Houghton in 1908 and spent most of his working life here in the Genesee Valley, recalls "I grew up when Houghton kids weren't supposed to go to Fillmore, and people weren't supposed to fellowship with anybody down there lest they be guilty of being contaminated." He felt it was all a part of coming out from the world and being separate. And the climate changed very slowly:

> When I started [working] at Houghton, there was an aloofness between the college and the surrounding business community. They referred to Houghton as the "new Jerusalem" and used other disparaging remarks. In the 1940s I became a member of [several community agencies] and made a consistent effort to befriend the business and professional leaders. This involvement was not easy in that it required time and effort, which were in short supply in view of Houghton's demands. But we witnessed a beautiful change in attitude toward Houghton. Other Houghton people got the vision and aided in this effort.[20]

Another veteran staff member reports that the behavior of some Houghton persons did not enhance community attitudes:

> [Speaking of a lady from Fillmore who used to do her hair] She would say that Houghton people are the most difficult to work with. They come in, and they are very fussy. . . . Then Houghton students go down there and they steal. . . . Some Houghton people are very hot-headed. . . . That's too bad, you know, because as a Christian community we should be different.[21]

Willard G. Smith and J. Whitney Shea led the move into fellowshiping with the community by joining the Fillmore Rotary early in World War II. But both were condemned by members of Houghton's Wesleyan congregation for compromising their Christian stance. Smith describes their status as being "carbuncles under the saddles of the traditionalists."[22]

As a result of this negative backlash, when Houghton professor Whitney Shea returned from the broadening experience of World War II military service and completed his doctoral dissertation, *Houghton College and the Community*, at Columbia University in 1952, he reportedly did not want a copy of it in the Houghton library lest someone in the college or the community read it and be affronted by the statements he made or the conclusions he reached. The document, a duplicate of which now may be found in the college library, explored the steps needed for Houghton College and the nearby community of Fillmore to work together through effective adult education for general betterment, and it was a seriously-intended vehicle for progress. In the preface to his study, Whitney Shea thanked "Houghton College and Fillmore Community who, in general, are the unsuspecting subjects of this report."[23] A contemporary reading fifty years later finds little cause for concern over any potential negative reaction, though several statements might have borne a sharp edge in 1952:

> The college dominates the village. Faculty and staff men and women play dual roles as members of the Houghton College team and as townspeople. Those strictly unconnected with the college find themselves in the minority and often are at a loss as to what the college is trying to do to them. "We" and "you" feelings of identification develop unbeknown to "busy" faculty and staff members who find little time for community socializing; so the townspeople on the outside looking in guess as to the goings-on.[24]
>
> Down through the years as a minority group, the tendency has been for the Wesleyan Methodist Church and its colleges to withdraw from the world, to become self-centered, other-worldly minded, to emphasize values in individual experiential salvation to the exclusion of the social gospel. . . .[25]
>
> Any attitude of passivity in community affairs on the part of Houghton College grows out of this personal and institutional in-group consciousness, a feeling of exclusiveness and set-apartness, magnified through time by the overemphasis on liberal arts "works," by some college intellectual "purists," and some accrediting institutions. Specialists in religion, like specialists in education, ofttimes lose the participant-observer point of view, the overall holistic approach, and [they] polarize pet interpretations.[26]

At the mid-twentieth century point, relations were not what they could and should have been. But aggressive actions over the next two decades on the part of concerned individuals, including President Paine, significantly improved the situation.

Calvinism versus Arminianism[27]

John and Charles Wesley led in developing the pietistic sub-strain of Anglicanism, which did not set well with the Church of England's ecclesiastical authority, and this contentious difference was a factor in the founding of Methodism. Later, in the era of post-Revolution expansion in America, the Wesleyan commitment to Arminianism within the Methodist Episcopal church cast it into theological opposition to the established, tax-funded churches of New England—Congregational and Presbyterian—and to the Calvinistic Baptists. However, as the floodtide of pioneer movement into the lands of the west began in the early 1800s, the emigrants' quest for freedom, self-government, and personal choice opened the way for much wider acceptance of Arminian theology. According to Curtis Johnson:

> By the early nineteenth century Calvinist ideology was incongruent with the experience of most Americans. The doctrine of election, held dear by Presbyterians, Congregationalists, and Baptists, did not fit the image most citizens had of themselves. . . . By the late 1820s universal white suffrage was a reality. Men could choose their leaders and, through representative government, establish public policy. Why, then, could they have no control over their own salvation? . . . [Through the movement toward Arminianism] thought and experience were once again brought together, and religion was revitalized.[28]

This set the stage both for the growth of Methodism via the Methodist Episcopal church and for the eventual Wesleyan challenge to the episcopal power structure of that church.

Oddly enough, though Arminianism versus Calvinism was a significant issue in the early and mid nineteenth century and then seemed to subside, the conflict appeared again at Houghton in the 1930s[29] and 1940s. One factor is that, while Houghton always was a college with Wesleyan Methodist control and support, Baptist students outnumbered Wesleyan students by a ratio of three or four to one. For whatever reason (perhaps as a result of the campus revivals of the 1940s or perhaps the outspokenness of the returning veterans), the Calvinism versus Arminianism debate suddenly flowered. Collaterally, the issue of eternal security also was injected into the dialogue. The fervor of the discussions reached a point where, to cool the passions, president Stephen Paine reportedly gave a chapel message on the situation, then wrote a strong editorial in *The Star* saying "we would agree to disagree" and exhorting students not to have any more heated public discussions.[30]

Church Union Attempts

Throughout the history of The Wesleyan Church, there have been several attempts at uniting with one or more of the smaller denominations of like faith, ostensibly to increase numbers and thereby multiply effectiveness. Those unions considered after the seminary was organized in 1883 never seemed to be a big issue on campus, though they inspired fiery rhetoric within the denomination.

The earliest attempt at union with another church began almost twenty years before the Houghton Wesleyan Methodist Seminary was chartered. At the General Conference in 1864, a small group (unauthorized by the Connection) joined in calling for a convention of non-Episcopal Methodists, to be held in 1865. The main focus was on a potential union with the northern, anti-slavery branch of the Methodist Protestant Church. Those assembled agreed to meet again in 1866, at which time specific proposals could be drawn up to present to the various conferences. But in the two years between the 1864 Wesleyan Methodist General Conference and this assembly, widespread antipathy to the proposed union developed among Wesleyan Methodists, who feared disruption of denominational unity. At a special conference in 1866, called to explore the union issue, Methodist Protestants outnumbered Wesleyan Methodists by about four to one,[31] and the resulting proposed program of union disregarded Wesleyan sensibilities against liquor consumption and secret societies and did not support other reform issues. When the Wesleyan Methodist annual conferences rejected the proposals, feeling ran high among the defeated pro-union group, and a number of preachers (including pioneer Wesleyan Methodist pastors such as Luther Lee, Lucius Matlack, John McEldowney, and Cyrus Pringle) and several congregations subsequently reunited with the Methodist Episcopal Church.[32] The report of the 1867 General Conference sums the official view:

Repeated propositions for organic union with other bodies upon the basis of accommodation and compromise, produced internal frictions and feuds, alienated affections, induced despondency, savored of restless instability if not weakness, rendered us less cohesive and more subject to disintegration. . . .[33]

Thus were sown the seeds of conservative Wesleyan distrust for any future attempts at union.

In the decade that followed the failure of union, the steady hand of connectional agent and editor Rev. Adam Crooks helped to sustain the individuals and the churches that remained in the Wesleyan Methodist fold and shaped their focus on holiness.

Without question, two of the Wesleyan Methodists' attempts to unite with other denominations had some effect on the college. The first was the extended but unsuccessful quest for union with the Free Methodist Church, and contemplation of such a union first occurred in 1903. The second was the eventually successful merger with the Pilgrim Holiness Church, first proposed in 1923.

The idea of uniting with the Free Methodists was again suggested by a visiting denominational representative who spoke at the Twenty-Sixth General Conference in 1943. He read a letter from his denomination urging closer collaboration between the two bodies and suggesting an eventual merger.[34] Wesleyan Methodists responded by appointing a commission to look into the matter and report in 1947. The commission was also instructed to explore union with the Pilgrim Holiness Church.[35]

At the Twenty-Seventh General Conference in 1947, the investigating committee was instructed to develop and present in 1951 a proposal for a plan of union, though without any official endorsement of such action. At the 1951 General Conference, the committee was instructed to "study a potential merger" with the Free Methodist Church and to develop a proposed discipline to be reviewed by the Board of Administration prior to consideration by the General Conference in 1955.[36] Stephen Paine was one of those advocating the proposed merger, and he was greatly disappointed when that effort eventually came to naught.

The extremely conservative posture of the Allegheny Conference was displayed as the Wesleyan Methodists considered uniting with this sister denomination. Women's Missionary Society president Ivah Van Wormer railed against the venture:

Finally, we tremble with fear at the thought of the result if the proposed *merger* goes through. Yes, we all realize that our leaders (God knows we have nothing against them but they are human, liable to err, and can be mistaken and led away as well as anyone) are strongly in favor, urgently advocating and doing all in their power to persuade us to accept merger with the Pilgrim Holiness Church. . . . If General Conference puts it through all of our independence and individuality will be gone. Their motive, expressed or unexpressed, is to gain a central power and control so that they can mold us into the same pattern throughout the denomination. As we now stand the conference unit still has its own independence to worship as the conscience of the conference body dictates.[37]

It seems ironic from this distance to note that the "independence and individuality" she so strongly defended was actually a carefully structured dependence and conformity to the rigid church rules within her conference, and evidenced a fear of having parallel but perhaps different constraints imposed by the hierarchy of the potential union.

The Twenty-Ninth General Conference saw the matter come to a head. While there were several points of contention (including scriptural inerrancy), one big issue apparently involved the use of the term "bishop."

The general superintendents of the Free Methodist Church were called "bishops." They did not have life tenure, being elected at each quadrennial general conference [as were the Wesleyan Methodist general superintendents]. Nevertheless, many Wesleyan Methodists feared that the term "bishop" indicated that the merger would commit the church to an episcopal form of government and vigorously opposed the merger. The vote on the merger showed sixty-two for it and ninety-six against it.[38]

Although the issue of union now appeared mortally stricken, the General Conference authorized the board to name a committee to address fraternal relations and cooperation with Free Methodists. The conference subsequently authorized the Board of Administration to study a possible merger with the Pilgrim Holiness group and even to continue the study of uniting with the Free Methodists.

In his diary, Dr. Paine wrote:

Well, after twelve years of work, the Joint Commission is ended. . . .
Two issues decided it [the vote against union]. The brethren [from certain conferences] laying the greatest claim to spirituality, do not like
the Free Methodists. Second, some of the departmental men don't rel-
ish the insecurity this could mean to their departments and jobs.[39]

While progress toward the Pilgrim Holiness union was slow, in 1966
the tiny group of Reformed Baptist Churches from Canada and eastern
Maine was readily assimilated In fact, the 1968 union with the Pilgrim
Holiness Church did not take place until after the old Allegheny Conference
withdrew from the Wesleyan Methodist Church in 1966.

Salvation: Emotional Experience versus Personal Relationship

One of the tenets of Wesleyan Arminianism was the concept of personal
and dramatic submission to the call of the gospel, and the evidence of such
an event in a person's life was the depth of emotion felt at the time of conversion. This was even more true when the "second blessing" of entire
sanctification was received, with its resulting freedom from sin. The
emphasis in the life of the believer was to be on keeping the rules and
observing all the points of the law as declared by the most legalistic
Wesleyan Methodists—and exhorting that your neighbors do the same.

One young man who spent the years 1907 to 1913 at Houghton offered
his take on the religious climate:

No one could live in Houghton all the years I did and not be influenced one way or another by the religion they taught. I had been
raised in the religious atmosphere of a Wesleyan Methodist minister's family; we had a family worship service right after breakfast
every morning, attended all church services and at age twelve I had
become a member of the church never thinking much about it, just
assuming I was a Christian. But to my surprise, I learned that in the
eyes of the strict church people of Houghton, I was not considered
one unless I could testify that I had gone through an experience of
confessing my sins and receiving the assurance that I had been for-
given. Then to publicly announcing that Jesus was my personal savior.

This was called conversion or justification. Then to live the Christian life, one had to refrain from all forms of sin, such as lying, stealing, cheating, smoking, drinking, and premarital sex. The keeping of the Ten Commandments was not enough, for each Sunday the preacher would dwell on the sin of pride, admonishing women and girls against wearing any jewelry or decorating their hats with flowers or feathers. Some even preached against the boys wearing ties.

Then the church advocated a second step called sanctification. This was another personal experience when a person entered the state of holiness. This state of grace kept a person perfect so they never sinned. There were a number of people in the church and some students who claimed they were sanctified. We boys couldn't see any difference in their lives, but they were loud in their belief. They were the ones who shouted "Amens" during the sermon and a few would run up and down the aisles shouting "Halleluiah!" Coming from a home where religion was considered a personal, calm approach to life, such actions proved very puzzling to me.[40]

Concurrently, most Wesleyan Methodists were suspicious of religion based on "book learning," which emphasized a thorough understanding of Scripture and a rational response to its claims, and involved establishing an enduring personal relationship with the God of the Bible. But at Houghton College (among other locations) a change was coming slowly. One life-long Wesleyan offered these thoughts:

In the 1930s the old guard . . . theological teachers and most of the preachers of the Wesleyan church were teaching not Bible, but experience. So you were urged to seek an experience in a certain way at a certain time and the emphasis was on rules and prudentials. There began to be a definite shift to an emphasis on salvation and Christianity as a personal relationship with God. It involves, therefore, a relationship with our fellow men and our fellow Christian, and the goal of life is to keep our relationship with God open and working that God may use us as a vehicle to be of service in any way that he can. We are not to be models of rule-keeping and law-observance; we are to be models of compassion and love and obedience. When you shift in that direction it creates an entirely different climate, and you have teachers who have emulated that, you have some wonderful preachers in the church who have emulated that, and you have a lot of adult students who have caught the vision and have helped to pass it down to the younger students.[41]

One of the great leaders in this movement at Houghton was Dr. Claude A. Ries, an exceptional Bible scholar who at one point was suggested as a presidential successor to J. S. Luckey. One contemporary observer stated:

> With few exceptions, the theological department—before Claude hit it—was experience oriented and very shallow Bible study. But Claude brought to it in-depth exegetical Bible study and dared to depart from the Arminian shibboleths which had become more important than Bible scripture. As he began to teach serious interpretation of the scripture in scriptural language, moving to the center from the extreme, experience-oriented, prudential focus preaching of the Wesleyan church and similar evangelists in the early 1900s and 1920s, he was roundly criticized for not using the shibboleths. In other words, if you didn't say "sanctification was killing of the carnal nature," you were accused of heresy. He stuck to his guns and focused on what I call an authentic John Wesley-Arminian view minus the prudential clutter that had collected and experience-seeking, seeking God in a personal relationship, making personal commitment rather than seeking an experience with certain manifestations which, unfortunately, became the focus of a number of evangelists in the 1920s. He rendered a great service to Houghton by focusing on what I consider has become our focus on Biblical Arminianism, with a tolerance for the biblical truths that are in Calvinism with the errors that are in Calvinism and to the point of even tolerating some people that are not of the extreme Wesleyan Arminian position as speakers because they were biblical.[42]

Claude Ries himself had come from the Allegheny Conference, and he was quite aware of the great importance of that conference as a source of students and financial support for the college. Because the Allegheny group also put tremendous emphasis on "externals": proscription of jewelry and makeup and of women wearing slacks to class; no jeans for men; only long-sleeved dresses for women, Dr. Ries (like Stephen Paine) was forced to walk a theological tightrope. Yet even as Dr. Ries tried not to offend this conservative constituency, he realized (and taught) that Wesleyan Methodist Christianity involved much more than strictly observing the "prudentials."[43]

While this effort to refocus on Biblical doctrines rather than traditional tenets did not sit particularly well with the more reactionary forces in the denomination, those leaders who understood the need to be aligned theologically with the teachings of scripture did not allow the emotionalists to prevail.

Liberal Arts College or Bible School

In the opinion of A. T. Jennings, writing in 1902,

> There are two extreme positions possible regarding education: first, that mental culture alone is sufficient to bring this world back to the light and blessedness of truth and righteousness; second, that the best work ever wrought in the redemption of this world from the darkness and horror of sin has been accomplished without mental culture. The whole question of education is like all other questions: neither extreme carries the full wisdom which should be applied to the problems involved; it is the medium ground which contains the truth.[44]

As mentioned in chapter 2, Wesleyan Methodists in general were quite content to be served by preachers who had the proper spiritual credentials. Unlike their Methodist Episcopal "parents" and their brothers in the Congregational and Presbyterian churches, many members of the Wesleyan Methodist church tended not to believe a college degree was essential for their ministers. According to Whitney Cross, the majority of early evangelicals accepted the guidance and leadership of traveling evangelists primarily because they were men of their own economic class and educational attainments. Of these it was said, "Theological training, in fact might be more a liability than an asset of such persons, for revivalism tended quite definitely to substitute emotion for reason and enthusiasm for knowledge."[45] At its first General Conference, however, the Wesleyan Methodist Connection came down firmly on the side of education, including in its educational report the statement that "the supposition that the Scriptures do not require Christians, and especially Christian ministers, to study and become truly learned, when circumstances will permit, is a great and dangerous error."[46]

Yes, Wesleyan Methodist leaders officially tended to favor education, but what kind? Should the seminary (and eventually the college) be a Bible school or a Christian institution of liberal arts? Denominational leaders (including Willard Houghton[47]) favored the former, and such might have been the school's bent had it not been for the leadership of J. S. Luckey. His experiences at Houghton, at Albany Normal, at Oberlin, and at Harvard taught him that a full education, developed in a strongly Christian light, would best serve students as they prepared for a life of service. Perhaps Luckey was aware that someone half a century earlier had helped to frame the argument. In 1848, a speaker at a Methodist Episcopal General Conference insisted that the denomination's schools "must comprehend the whole circle of learning and be open to all." Central to his point was the thesis that evangelical denominations which organized colleges solely for their own membership and offered in these schools an education that majored on their own peculiar views would quickly find themselves branded as "a bigoted sect instead of an enlightened and liberal church."[48]

But Wesleyan Methodists were not wholly comfortable with the concepts of a liberal-arts, truth-seeking education. At the 1923 General Conference, the Committee on Education recommended, and the delegates approved, this statement:

> We are aware that most great moves away from the simplicity of the gospel and away from the fundamentals of the faith in the various churches have had their beginnings in the school system, and we believe that it must be insisted upon that all our schools should function to produce trained Christian workers for her ranks. General education should be a secondary matter not the primary object of the church. No school under church patronage and support shall be allowed to call in question, much less deny, the position of the church on any point of doctrine or church polity. The province of the church is to declare doctrine and of the school to teach what the Church declares.[49]

In other words, we denominational leaders demand loyalty over learning; we will tell you what to think and what to teach. To have this dictum delivered in the same year that the provisional state charter was granted must have been somewhat frustrating to J. S. Luckey.

That same year, in fact, two major Wesleyan Methodist figures engaged in what was reported to be a lively debate as they rode from Syracuse to Albany. One was the Rev. John S. Willett, the first graduate from Houghton Seminary's collegiate department (1901) and denominational publishing agent from 1913 to 1935, and the other was James S. Luckey, the second graduate from the seminary (1889). According to seminary principal Philinda Bowen, who was riding in the seat behind them (and as reported by Willett's son Edward), ." . . all the way to Albany [John Willett] argued that we didn't need a four-year college, we needed a four-year Bible school. By the time they got to Albany he'd lost the argument and that's the reason we have a four-year liberal arts college."[50] Edward. Willett went on to suggest that his father had been playing the devil's advocate, and he observed that John Willett supported the liberal-arts position for the rest of his life.

Willard Smith stated:

My father [Henry R. Smith Jr.] was right on wavelength with J. S. Luckey in the feeling that an education that was academically excellent was the only type that was justifiable in a Christian school. Christianity and excellence are compatible. . . . My father, on his own expense, went in 1913 to a meeting at Princeton University, and he was thoroughly criticized by the church for having associated with a top academic institution. [However,] I have a letter from A. T. Jennings [the denominational editor] in which he comments "That it shows a lack of confidence in the spiritual stature and integrity of our men to suggest that they dare not fellowship with the academic leaders of the world."[51]

Smith went on to observe that Wesleyan Methodists "were just sure that the purest people were the people who hadn't been in college or university. To be a pure, excellent, Wesleyan, Arminian believer you couldn't be that and have gone to college, much less university, and certainly not if you got a doctoral degree."[52]

Ira F. McLiester was chair of the Houghton trustees from 1935 to 1943, and because of his roots in the Allegheny Conference, there might have been some suspicion that he would come down on the Bible-school side of the issue. Not so, according to one source: "He [Rev. McLeister] was a very cooperative man who had a great deal of confidence in J. S. Luckey, and whatever J. S. Luckey was for McLeister was for, but he was always being hammered by the other side of the issue."[53]

Houghton alumnus and thirty-five-year administrator Willard Smith shared these thoughts:

As I approached my college years I became aware of a tension between the leadership of James S. Luckey and the leadership of the Wesleyan Methodist Church concerning the character and quality of Houghton's education. Academically, President Luckey cherished the "Harvard ideal." Many church people urged a lower-level Bible school education. They felt that Biblical integrity and spiritual vitality were not compatible with intellectual excellence. President Luckey, on the other hand, urged that maximum effectiveness of Christianity was to be realized in a wedding of the two.

For two summers (1933 and 1934) I travelled with the Houghton College Quartet. During that time we made contact with scores of Wesleyan churches and conferences. We were troubled with the frequent complaint that "Houghton College was not spiritual." We interpreted that to mean that liberal arts college-level education was suspect as being "non- or anti-holiness" as defined by the experience-oriented Wesleyans of that day.[54]

The college did for a time offer a Christian-worker course, and an experiment in the late 1930s led to offering a bachelor of divinity degree. Only five men were ever awarded this degree, and the program ended not long after the 1939 baccalaureate convocation. Willard Smith reports, "There was a decision in the 1940s to terminate the Bible school level of ministerial training and to concentrate on the liberal arts approach. This removed a gray area that troubled the accreditation agency and was financially a burden because of the small student traffic."[55] With this decision, the college clearly established itself in the role now proclaimed by its entrance sign: "A Christian College of Liberal Arts and Sciences."

Adornment and Garment Controversy

The issue with perhaps the thorniest dimensions for the college and the Wesleyan Methodist Church was what became known as the adornment and garment controversy. At its core lay the age-old friction between arch-conservative legalists, who believed that traditional ways are best and old sanctified traditional ways (even if extra-Biblical) are best of all, and those antithetical to narrowly prescriptive approaches, who believed that sanctification and soul liberty put behavioral aspects squarely on the shoulders of the individual and that a middle road traveled in Christian love was fully as scriptural a position.[56]

Interestingly, this issue of dress and adornment was strongly addressed in the early years of the Methodist Episcopal Church in America, and the root of the Methodist position was traced directly to John Wesley himself.

Closely connected with this [characteristic, the simplicity of their manners] was the Plainness of their Dress. We are aware that there have been persons, and those strenuous contenders for evangelical religion, who have professed to think this matter of trifling importance. But the arguments by which the Founder of the Methodist Societies [John Wesley] enforced the duties of plainness of dress, were and are unanswerable. The evils of fashionable and expensive adorning of the body he attacked with considerations drawn from the Scripture, and confirmed by reason. He showed that time . . . is wasted, is murdered, while every part of a fashionable dress is adjusted. . . . He further insisted on the fact . . . that it is impossible for the mind, which resides in a body so adorned as to attract attention, to enjoy unruffled serenity. . . . *He did not strenuously enforce a particular mode of dress* [emphasis added]. . . . It will, perhaps, be regarded as a proof of his soundness of judgment, that he fixed no arbitrary standard."[57]

Wesley's posture on dress and adornment was reflected the *Discipline* of 1848: "This is no time to give encouragement to superfluity of apparel. Therefore let one be received into the church, until they have left off the wearing of gold and superfluous ornaments."[58]

Throughout early (and even more recent) Wesleyan history, the concept of dressing modestly and avoiding needless adornment waxed strong. Apparently the Allegheny Conference took the lead in this display of pious demeanor. The Rev. Orange Scott, during an extended trip on behalf of the Book Concern, visited the Allegheny Conference and observed that "the preachers [here] set a better example in point of plainness of dress than in any other conference that I have attended."[59]

In chapter 6, it was mentioned that James S. Luckey had to address the necktie issue for himself and came down on the side of modest, attractive appearance. Alumnus Ray Calhoon also mentioned this aspect of Wesleyan life, among several others:

Houghton Seminary was founded by the Wesleyan Methodist Church and since they continued to support it, the church board prescribed the rules for the student body. No student was allowed to smoke, or drink any alcoholic beverage. In fact, the deeds of all the property in the village of Houghton prohibited any liquor or beer being sold or consumed on the premises.[60] The hours of all students were regulated, whether in the dormitory or outside. No student could leave town without permission. There was no dancing permitted on campus nor could a student attend a dance off campus. Association between boys and girls was strictly limited; they could date only at an early hour at the dorm or attend a lecture or concert in the college chapel. Dress was to be very plain; the girls could wear no jewelry nor have feathers on their hats. A few of the boys went farther than the rules and considered it sinful to wear a tie.[61]

The Houghton Seminary catalogue of 1920–1921 contained the first on-campus hint of the garment and adornment controversy that was to blossom and become nearly divisive forty years later:

DRESS: The policy of the school is to encourage simplicity and modesty in dress. The Board of Education and the Faculty view with alarm the modern trend of fashion that exposes the body to the gaze of the public, and they most thoroughly approve the stand that some schools and many pulpits are taking against this evil. Hereafter students will not be permitted to attend either class exercises or the evening gatherings in dresses made with extremely short skirts, or with extremely low necks, or made of transparent material unless the body is properly covered with undergarments. All gymnasium suits must be approved by the Physical Directors.[62]

Most who were part of the greater Houghton academic milieu before 1945 had grown up in a climate of moderately-severe standards of dress and had little objection to observing Wesleyan rules while on campus. But the flood of GIs after World War II and the influx of post-WWII faculty to support the college's expansion to its doubled size led to chafing under the old rules. Stephen Paine found himself and the college administration facing such a strong clashing of positions that the institution began to suffer, and several fine faculty and staff members elected to depart.

The 1848 prohibition on wearing "gold and superfluous ornaments" was re-emphasized by the Book Committee in 1928: "The wearing of gold and jewelry for ornamentation is forbidden."[63] But the first major shot in the mid-century adornment war may have occurred in 1951 when the Ohio Conference passed a resolution expressly forbidding wedding rings for church members. The president of the General Conference rejected this rule as being unconstitutional, because it had not been endorsed concurrently by the General Conference, the annual conferences, and the local churches. The Ohio group appealed to the Board of Review but was rebuffed. The issue continued to fester, however, among the arch-conservative Ohio, Tennessee, and Allegheny conferences.[64]

One veteran staff member, a faithful Wesleyan known for her conservative demeanor, reported on her experience:

> When they hired me, I still wore my necklaces. After a year, Dr. Paine said, "You know, you're not supposed to be wearing a necklace, and you really should take it off if you plan to continue working for the college." I said, "I'll just give up the job. I don't want to go through this hassle." So I had to give up my job, and for a year I did not work at the college. Then they changed the rule, and they hired me back.[65]

But jewelry was not the only item in question. Proper dresses, especially those with long sleeves, were mandated. Our staff member continues:

> I can remember going to a program one time in the chapel just before commencement, and it was very a hot day and I wore a sleeveless dress. . . . Back then, nobody wore a sleeveless dress. . . . I can remember people staring at me like I'd committed some terrible crime. . . . I can remember feeling ostracized because I had a sleeveless dress on.[66]

Pressure for observing propriety of dress and ornamentation, especially from the Allegheny Conference, had been festering for some time. In an impassioned address delivered to the Allegheny Conference Women's Missionary Society on June 11, 1959, society president Ivah Benning Van Wormer (Houghton College class of 1927 and a member of the English faculty from 1927–1933) said:

> No, we are not going to talk about dress so much as being *undressed*. We are alarmed, amazed and horrified to see how universally men and women strut around nearly nude. . . . It is a marvel to us, that God does not strike people dead with their brazen defiance of all that is decent, moral and right. . . . What is even more alarming is the way our holiness people (even Allegheny Conference women) are taking up the trends and styles of today. For example, the sleeves are going up and up and so are the skirts since it is the way of least resistance and

brings less reproach from the world. Soon we too will be in sleeveless dresses and all that goes with it.[67]

Moving beyond dress, Mrs. Van Wormer fired off these additional comments:

We are alarmed at the *fancy, worldly hair-do's*. . . . If God made your hair straight He wants you to leave it that way. . . .We are grieved to see the *fancy hats* worn by holiness professing women. . . . We are amazed by the number of holiness women wearing *spike heels* these days. . . . We are astonished to see so many of our women wearing *highly ornamented glasses*. [These transgressions] surely do not represent old-fashioned holiness and godliness as we knew it.[68]

The adornment and garment controversy apparently reached high pitch during the 1964–1965 academic year. Late in the fall semester, the trustees had "singled out certain persons for non-cooperation." The strongly negative response by the faculty and staff led to a discussion between President Paine and trustee chair Daniel Heinz. In a "Dear Colleague" letter in January 1965, President Paine advised that the "action of the Trustees [to discipline three faculty or staff families] which was under discussion" would be laid aside until the June meeting of the full board, and that contracts would be issued "in the usual manner."[69]

In just a few days, petition sheets signed by sixty-nine faculty and staff (including nineteen who later were interviewed for this study) asked the trustees to rescind "the discriminatory action taken against three faculty-staff members" and that "the present policy of volunteerism regarding dress of members of families of faculty and staff be maintained."[70] Yet, even with strong evidence from faculty and administration that there was no workable way in which Houghton could meet the demands of the Allegheny group, Dr. Paine still felt compelled to seek campus conformity.[71]

In a June 1965 letter to his colleagues, Stephen Paine reported that the trustees had considered the petitions and a subsequent faculty recommendation of "no policy action at this time" and then had approved a presidential recommendation on the matter.[72] The board did decide to rescind the earlier disciplinary action against the three families, but the policy on dress and adornment was restated more firmly than ever. Dr. Paine attached to his letter this extract from the trustees' minutes:

1. The Wesleyan Methodist Church has historically felt that the scriptural teachings on dress and adornment reflect negatively on the use of jewelry by Christians. This attitude in our church is seen in the General Rule referring to "the wearing of gold and superfluous adornment" and in the injunction in the Special Rules to refrain from the wearing of jewelry as an example to the young and immature (*Discipline*, paragraphs 83, 86: "Should we insist on the rules concerning dress? By all means. This is no time to give encouragement to superfluity or immodesty in apparel. Therefore, let none be received into the church until they have left off the wearing of gold and superfluous ornaments and have adopted modest attire. . . . Refraining from the wearing of jewelry sets a better example for single men and women, and children. If the mature Christian men and women of the Church do not have a conscience on this matter it will be impossible for the Church to maintain its testimony against worldliness in the younger years.").

2. The Board acknowledges the observed tendency in our church toward indifference in matters of dress, particularly in new churches and with the young and immature, there being some variations in different locations and conferences.

3. The Board observes that in our other three Wesleyan Methodist colleges[73] and with the leadership of the conferences in the Houghton area an effort is still being made toward continued carefulness in dress and adornment. The Board has not heard of any official body in the church which has specifically or by implication given approval to the wearing of the engagement ring by Wesleyan Methodist pastors or members.

. . . .

6. In the present situation the Board feels that the college will most happily serve the church and maintain best liaison with it if a conservative policy on jewelry is maintained.[74]

The board document that contained the above statements, entitled "Resolution . . . Regarding the Policy on Dress," added another paragraph:

It is not our desire to depreciate the sincerity of those who may feel that the college should take a more relaxed attitude as to jewelry and clothing, but we point out that the usual procedure in such situations is to urge that in order to be consistent the

Board must either see that there is rigid and instantaneous enforcement or else relax the requirement.

Subsequent to its deliberations, the Board approved "the present policy on dress" with the following statement replacing the last paragraph:

It is requested that members of the faculty and staff endeavor to secure cooperation regarding these matters in their respective families. Wives of faculty and staff are expected to cooperate with this policy. It is realized that the college may occasionally be confronted with a case, as where an unsaved partner is involved, where the cooperation of the wife is out of the question. Matters of this kind will be decided by the Board. As a general rule the college will employ persons whose partners are in sympathy with college policy.

A copy of "Standards of Dress for Faculty and Staff" may be found as appendix L.3.

While most faculty and staff members elected to observe the decree even though they might disagree with it, not all were so complaisant. As mentioned earlier, one current Houghton staffer refused to remove her necklace and was not employed during the following year.[75] And the wearing of jewelry was definitely an issue for some spouses. It was reported that at least one resistant spouse was offered a needed job at the college as a device to get her to remove her engagement ring.[76] A long-time friend of the college, a person with many faculty connections, said, "It was a sad thing about that ring and adornment issue. You have to say that the old Wesleyans were somewhat of Puritans . . . to begin to judge other Christians is sad. . . . Really, Houghton was kowtowing to one conference that was so very strict."[77]

In another letter later that month, Dr. Paine said:

This . . . action by the Board has been accepted most gratefully by the church. . . . I do not doubt that some of our brethren [in the Allegheny Conference] may be open to criticism on the charge of legalism, but it is so much a question of point of view as to whether we are talking about "legalism" or about "Christian discipline." . . . That we have a difference of opinion here is, of course, evident. . . . Surely the Lord will enable us to maintain respect and Christian affection despite this difference.[78]

Then he added: "I ask you as my colleagues to believe that I would not stick on this present point if I did not think it important for our service to our Wesleyan Methodist constituency."

A former president of Houghton's alumni shared this impression: "They were so afraid of modernism; that was the big word they used, 'modernism.' [The Allegheny district thought that the college] strayed almost immediately when President Luckey came."[79]

Former college treasurer Willard G. Smith offered his take on the situation and its aftermath, based on his personal experience:

[The dress and adornment issue] was a difficult and stressful problem with strong emotional overtones. Basically we experienced the confrontation between two subculture groups within The Wesleyan Church. This took place in the context of liberalizing standards of dress and adornment within and without the church family. There were a few in the college and in the church who contended that the college should maintain a standard on the far right of the conservative position in these matters. In a sincere effort to appease the small church group who contended very strongly for the far right position, Dr. Paine directed the expenditure of much time and effort to this issue.

After more than ten years of serious effort to conform to the demands of the Allegheny Wesleyan Church group, the vote of [Houghton's] board of trustees terminated the effort (i.e., no wedding ring and no slacks for women on campus). During the time when an effort was being made to enforce conformity to their requirements, some good faculty and staff were lost and some students left. From my point of view, there was a terrible waste of administrative and faculty energy in this struggle. For example, as an administrative committee we spent hundreds of hours on the jewelry and slacks issue and during some of these years we did not have even an hour to study a budget of more than two million dollars.[80]

Former chemistry professor Stephen Calhoon offered his recollections of life on campus in that turbulent era:

When I went to Houghton I could see why it had a reputation in The Wesleyan Methodist Church as being liberal and hence not spiritual. That was the reputation that I had heard, but it wasn't long before I found that the true spiritual atmosphere was deeper and more meaningful than what I had been used to. I can remember during the Revival [in] the fall of '51 going up to pray with seekers at the altar, and I remember very vividly a girl wearing her jewelry, her make-up, short hair and so on dealing with a seeker out of the Bible. I said, "She knows the Bible a lot better than I do." I really had my eyes opened. It was a major change in my thinking and in my approach to things. I've appreciated that because I felt that the Houghton approach to these things was a lot more, well, to my way of thinking, Christian. Up until then the verse, "Come out from among them and be ye separate," was interpreted in terms of out-ward appearance, and I found at Houghton that it was interpreted in the way you thought, in the way you acted, and so on. To me, that was a lot more meaningful. That I always appreciated about Houghton.[81]

The thing that stands out, well, two things from this: there were three couples that were pinpointed as examples or something. The wives were not employed by the college, but they did wear an engagement ring. The president interpreted the trustees' actions of the past and, in fact, a statement in the faculty handbook to say that spouses of employees of the college were expected to conform to the rules that the faculty were expected to go by while employed by the college. If not, then there would be a change made. If they would not conform to this interpretation then the employment of the employee would be terminated. The faculty and staff rose up in arms about that.[82]

But then this engagement ring thing came up. . . . [I recall] two out of the three [who] were let go. . . . I do know that Dr. Paine con-sidered [one faculty member] a liberal. He was liberal in politics; he was a Democrat—I think [almost] the only Democrat on the fac-ulty. There were hints that Dr. Paine equated being liberal in poli-tics to being liberal theologically and then their resistance to the dress code I think just added to that. [He] was let go. [Another one] was the manager of the bookstore. Anyway, it was at their home that the first meeting took place, this first communication from Dr. Paine "following our informal meeting the other morning up at the [home of this couple], I talked with Rev. Heinz . . ." and so on. But [this couple] left after that year and went to [another college], and he was manager of their bookstore until he retired.[83]

Secessions

Oddly enough, the dress and adornment controversy was not the proximate cause of the secession of the Allegheny Conference. Other factors had even more significance: conference actions deemed unconstitutional by the denomination, disagreement concerning the potential union with the Pilgrim Holiness Church, and even the terrible tornado that destroyed Wesleyan Methodist World Headquarters in April 1965.

Lack of a headquarters building was an immediate problem, but it was felt that the pending question of union with the Pilgrim Holiness Church needed to be resolved before or concurrently with any attempt at rebuilding. Consequently, the Wesleyan Methodist quadrennial conference was moved up a year to 1966, to be concurrent with the Pilgrim Holiness session. It was at this session that the turmoil within the Wesleyan Methodist church came to a boil.

Certain of the annual conferences, most notably Allegheny and Tennessee, were against the union, fearing loss of personal rights. While they were deeply committed to an arch-conservative posture regarding adornment and dress, each conference had taken organizational actions deemed to be unconstitutional by the Wesleyan Methodist leadership and were cited for "a trend in certain conferences towards usurpation of unwarranted authority and disregard, even defiance, of the constitution of the Church."[84] In 1964, both conferences had in effect withdrawn from the Wesleyan Methodist Church by separating themselves from the authority of the General Conference. As a result, formal charges of insubordination were filed against these two conferences at the 1966 session.[85] Their response was to withdraw and form two new associations.

The dress and adornment issue did not disappear from Houghton with the secession of the Allegheny and Tennessee conferences in 1966. In 1968, Houghton's Local Board of Trustees (representing traditional denominational authority) drew up and approved this amendment to the college's statement of dress standards for faculty and staff. This rear-guard action, as applied, apparently did not produce the resistance of the earlier actions.

> The new faculty member in signing the "questionnaire for Prospective Teachers" agrees to respect certain rather well defined and clear standards of the Church. He also agrees to "conform to the church standards which call for propriety and modesty in dress and abstention from the wearing of gold and superfluous ornaments."
>
> This standard of modesty and propriety, containing as it does a reference to jewelry, follows the language of Scripture and of the

book of discipline of The Wesleyan Church, which declares the duty of the Christian to "Dress so as to adorn the gospel in the spirit of 1 Peter 3:3,4 and 1 Timothy 2:9,10, giving clear testimony to Christian purity and modesty by properly clothing the body and refraining from superfluous adornment."

Members of the Houghton College faculty and staff and their families are requested to wear clothing which modestly and properly adorns the person and to avoid excessive or showy ornamentation. It is hoped that faculty and staff will of their own preference and good judgment be wholesome examples of those things which are required by rule of the students.[86]

There is evidence that this ring-and-garment issue and its handling and confrontations came close to precipitating a major split within the college, a fracture from which the college might not have recovered. Stephen Paine is reported to have observed in later years that "this [accommodation of legalism] may have been a great mistake."[87]

In retrospect, it seems that it might have served the college well regarding these contentious issues to follow the advice of Willard Houghton to "stick to the middle of the road" or to observe A. T. Jennings's pronouncement, mentioned earlier: "It is the medium ground which contains the truth."

SIXTEEN

Looking Back, Looking Ahead

An Analysis

This book began with a description of Houghton College's 1972 graduation, and that is where the final chapter also starts.

Yes, for Dr. Stephen W. Paine and those attending the 1972 graduation, this ceremony was the culmination of an eighty-nine-year educational voyage that began in the post-Civil War dream of Willard J. Houghton and soared ever higher as it achieved state and national recognition and expanded its physical plant, academic programs, and student body. Yet the 1972 commencement also closed an era in Houghton's exhilarating history and turned a page to a fresh chapter. New hands now must carry the grand dream into the future.

What was Houghton College, on that special day in 1972? According to the sign that today graces the entrance road, Houghton was "A Christian College of Liberal Arts and Sciences."[1] The student body continued to number approximately 1,200, and most faculty still embraced the concept that their labor on the hill included a dimension of missions service.[2] Even after the building boom of the previous fifteen years, more new buildings were needed, new programs were to be developed, and new leadership was to be found and installed. But the inner Christian liberal-education character of the school would carry through, and the great ideas of providing schooling that embraced Willard Houghton's ideal of being "low in expense, fundamental in belief, and high in scholarship" would persist. Houghton College in 1972 was a sturdy academic edifice, ready to face and endure the growth and turmoil of succeeding decades.

A logical query here is the degree to which Houghton remained true to the three-point vision of founder Willard Houghton, which was officially incorporated in the college's 1948 constitution. Considering these points in reverse order, the great quality of the scholarship has been adequately demonstrated from the days of the first handful who completed their degrees off-campus, with several of this small group going on to earn doctorates, through the performance of the selected classes reported in chapter 14. Regarding constancy in core Christian beliefs, evidence may be found in the persistence of chapel life, prayer meetings, a Christian Life Emphasis Week each semester, and sustained ties to the parent Wesleyan denomination, as well as the ongoing insistence of the trustees and administration on personal Christian testimony by each faculty and staff member. In the matter of economy of tuition, however, some differences of opinion exist.

Though Houghton Seminary came into existence just as state teachers colleges with their low tuition were being founded, the rates were comparable, and Houghton offered an avowedly Christian, strongly academic preparation for teaching and other vocations. Over the years, though, as state schools of all stripe were granted increasing financial support from tax money, Houghton continued to exist (as did all private colleges) primarily on student tuition funds, with some modest assistance from the church or from endowments. Still, the faculty tended to accept Houghton service as labor for the Kingdom and bore up under the penurious pay rates, even to the point of giving back a portion in several years to help with the deficit.

The church had always lent avid philosophical support to the idea of economical education for boys and girls from the area, though "the area" quickly expanded to include most of the eastern and midwestern states. However, Wesleyan Methodists tended to be blue-collar workers, teachers, and preachers, and the denominational funding they provided was never grand. As a result, the church funding stream was less than ample, and tuition had to be maintained at least at a survival level. Still, Houghton has managed to stay price-wise in the bottom half or third of sister schools.

The Christian College

One basic characteristic that has been assumed but never described throughout this book is the answer to this question: What really is a Christian college of liberal education? In the words of distinguished Christian-college scholar William Ringenberg:

> A Christian college is a community of Christian believers, both teachers and students, who are dedicated to the search for an understanding of the divine Creator, the universe which he has created, and the role which each creature should fill in his universe. The titles of the specific courses may not differ from those in a secular college. What does differ dramatically, however, is the attitude with which Christian scholars approach their areas of investigation. To Christian learners, all truth is God's truth, and the pursuit of it is a spiritual quest to understand God better.[3]

Houghton Seminary and then Houghton College benefited from the vision and experience of Houghton's first great president, James S. Luckey. A devout Houghton Seminary graduate and subsequently a product of the liberal-education academic programs at Oberlin College[4] and later at Harvard University, Luckey's vision reached beyond the limitations of developing a Bible school or a sectarian theological seminary. He sought to educate Christian men and women who would experience the creative and active integration of faith and learning. In Luckey's eyes (and in Arthur Holmes's words from *The Idea of a Christian College*):

> The educated Christian exercises critical judgment and manifests the ability to interpret and evaluate information, particularly in the light of the Christian revelation. . . . the educated Christian must be at home in the world of ideas and men.[5]

But the concepts as expressed by Ringenberg and Holmes weren't always the accepted versions. According to Holmes, "Many suppose that the Christian college exists to protect young people against sin and heresy."[6] This concept was clearly expressed in the material published around the time of the founding of Houghton Seminary. Wesleyan Methodists sought to educate as well as indoctrinate in Christian virtues (especially of the Wesleyan Methodist variety); they wanted to provide a safe environment for Christian learning even as they sought to better mankind. And the idea of sectarian indoctrination was emphasized in the 1923 declaration by the Twenty-First General Conference that

> No school under church patronage and support shall be allowed to call into question . . . the position of the church on any point of doctrine or church polity. The province of the Church is to declare doctrine and of the school to teach what the Church declares.[7]

One can only imagine the tension that must have been felt by President Luckey, who was both a faithful Wesleyan Methodist and an enlightened educator. The challenge he was forced to embrace was immense. He saw the Christian college as being "distinctive in that the Christian faith can touch the entire range of life and learning to which a liberal education exposes students."[8]

A parallel idea in Christian schools (and especially in Bible schools) was to train people for church-related vocations.[9] Houghton Seminary offered a Bible studies track for ministerial candidates, but it never became a large part of the curriculum. As mentioned earlier, in the 1930s a separate program leading to a bachelor of divinity degree was offered, but only five men graduated and the program was discontinued early in World War II.

Academic Freedom

One pragmatic extension of the idea of seeing all learning through a Christian perspective is the idea of academic freedom. Turning again to Arthur Holmes:

> The Christian liberal arts college faces a dilemma. On the one hand, liberal education requires that we think critically about our heritage of faith and culture and wrestle honestly with the problems men in general and Christians in particular face in today's world. This requires freedom of inquiry for both teacher and student. On the other hand, Christian education implies commitment to the Word of God and responsibility to the church constituency a college serves. Liberty without loyalty is not Christian, but loyalty without the liberty to think for one's self is not education. . . . Loyalty without liberty is legalistic.[10]
>
> Academic freedom may be defined as freedom to explore the truth in a responsible fashion. . . . The Christian educator cannot

forget that his responsibility is not only to society and the church, to his students and colleagues, but also and primarily to the truth. . . . The teacher in the evangelical institution operates within the framework of belief confessed by his college.[11]

In reviewing the materials available from Houghton's history, no significant evidence of academic freedom disputes was discovered. There were other contests of will, of course, and two or three faculty were released for events of moral turpitude. A number departed more or less voluntarily as a result of the garment and adornment issue in the 1960s (see chapter 15). Of course, since any dissident faculty were usually able to find employment elsewhere at significantly better salaries than Houghton offered, the details of their departures were recorded as being elective resignations.

One faculty aspect that flowered was the arrival of a new doctoral-holding academic generation, one whose loyalties were more clearly aligned with their discipline and somewhat less with Christian education and Houghton College. These younger men and women, all of whom earned their advanced degrees elsewhere (and primarily at major secular institutions), arrived with an expectation that the pay structure, working arrangements, research and collateral education opportunities, additional duties, and employee benefits would more closely resemble their graduate institutions. To their credit, they also brought a new level of academic zeal and intellectual rigor, and their backgrounds often included a more international perspective than had their predecessors. The challenge, of course, was for the old order (and the sponsoring church) to make maximum benefit of the college's new resources.[12]

Standards of 1972

In the chapter on students, the matter of beliefs and standards was discussed, starting with early-day expectations. The faculty and students who made up Houghton College in 1972 were expected to embrace this Statement of Doctrine, as recorded in the 1971–1972 catalog:[13]

We believe that the Scriptures of the Old and New Testaments are fully inspired of God, and inerrant in the original writings, and that they are of supreme and final authority for faith and practice.

We believe there is one God, eternally existing in three persons: Father, Son and Holy Spirit.

We believe that God created man and the entire universe by special operation of divine power.

We believe in the fall of man and the consequent sinful nature of all mankind, which necessitates a divine atonement.

We believe in Jesus Christ as truly God and truly man, and in His virgin birth, His matchless teachings, His vicarious death, and His promised second coming.

We believe in justification by grace through faith and in regeneration by the Holy Spirit, Who makes the penitent believer a new creature in Christ and commences His lifelong sanctifying work.

We believe that the Christian may by filled with the Holy Spirit, or sanctified wholly, as a definite act of divine grace wrought in the heart of the believer to take full possession, cleanse and equip for service on condition of total surrender and obedient faith.

We believe in the personal existence of Satan.

We believe in the bodily resurrection of the dead—of the saved to everlasting blessedness and of the lost to everlasting punishment.

The college itself, in order to accomplish the educational mission it had declared for itself, adopted these objectives, as set forth in the college catalog for 1971–1972:[14]

As representatives of the Christian liberals arts tradition in college education, the Houghton faculty purpose to provide students with the opportunity to:

Establish a habit of intellectual pursuit, acquire a liberal arts education, reflect logically and critically on the knowledge gained and present their reflections cogently.

Develop moral excellence through understanding the bearing of Christian faith upon all knowledge and through responding in faith and love to the person of Jesus Christ as Lord of their lives.

Lay the foundation for mental, physical and spiritual health.

Learn how to function intelligently in a complex society.

Become informed and responsible citizens.

Formulate life aims and obtain the prerequisites for vocational competence.

Develop avocational interests and skills.

Understand and become sensitive to the fine arts.

Kenneth Wilson, compiler and editor of *Consider the Years 1883–1983*, concluded that summary monograph with these forward-looking words:

> Houghton College is built upon the faith of our fathers and mothers and their sacrificial achievement. But what of the faith of our sons and daughters? Now, the future is in their hands—our hands.
>
> The dream is unfinished, and that is good. Dreams must always carry individuals and organizations beyond their generation. We must always work at dreams, add to their substance, form and utility. The substance must grow and the dream must grow, always keeping ahead. At Houghton, that is the way it has been. That is the way it must continue to be.
>
> God willing and inspired human effort persevering, there will be other anniversaries—the 125th, the 150th. What Houghton sons and daughters memorialize then will depend on what we do now. Houghton College is a continuing responsibility that simply passes from one generation of loyal believers and doers to another.
>
> Today *we* are the generation. Today, Houghton is in our hands. Keep the faith![15]

Faculty

In his analysis of Christian colleges, Christian philosopher Arthur Holmes listed a number of salient points that reflect the input and effects of a Christian faculty:

- The Christian college is unique only because its faculty and administration have common commitment of a religious and moral sort, rather than the variegated commitments of a secular institution.[16]

- The Christian college is largely a community of Christians whose intellectual and social and cultural life is influenced by Christian values, so that the learning situation is life as a whole approached from a Christian point of view.[17]

- The Christian college refuses to compartmentalize religion. It retains a unifying Christian world-view and brings it to bear in understanding and participating in the various arts and sciences, as well as in the non-academic aspects of campus life.[18]

- The [Christian] educator's task is to inspire and equip individuals to think and act for themselves in the dignity of men created in God's image.[19]

- For the evangelical in education, Christian commitment does not restrict intellectual opportunity and endeavor, but rather it fires and inspires him to purposeful learning.[20]

Faculty who taught at Houghton through 1972 are listed in appendix K, and as much as is known about their academic credentials is reported. Beyond their certifications, they have been depicted by peers and by Houghton alumni as being strong examples, caring, hard-working, generous, encouraging, deeply involved, strongly religious, and friendly. Katherine Lindley '43, long-time history professor and division chair, stated the underlying credo for Houghton faculty:

Anyone who teaches at Houghton must have a higher goal than his [academic] discipline. The discipline is important and ought to be important and we ought not to be teaching here if it isn't important. But the higher importance is . . . our commitment to the Lord himself, and helping these students to know it has to be our goal.[21]

Curriculum

In chapter 12, it was mentioned that the 1879 charter of the Wesleyan Methodist Educational Society specified that the society's purpose was to develop schools what would "confer a Christian education without regard to sex or nationality." While the presumption logically was that Wesleyan Methodist funding would be used to educate Wesleyan Methodist children, in courses suitable to Wesleyan Methodist doctrine, the educational charge was not made that narrow. When Houghton Seminary opened its doors in 1883, those who enrolled were only expected to abide by the specified rules.

The curriculum that was offered to the students was one that reflected the traditional classics curriculum in other private secondary schools plus several more pragmatic subjects such as bookkeeping, and chapel was a frequent event (twice a day at times). Over the years, and especially with the quest for a college charter, the academic program was first revised from being highly prescriptive to heavily elective in structure, and the course offerings were strengthened, widened, and intensified. By the time of the granting of an absolute charter in 1927, Houghton was a solid college of learning in the Christian tradition.

Consequences of Houghton

No historical review of Houghton College would be complete without some attempt to establish the consequences of the institution in its milieu: the local area, western New York, the greater region, and even The Wesleyan Church. One significant question is this: what effects have the college and its graduates had on the western New York region? In less formal language, this might be termed the "so what?" factor.

Answers may come from three levels: intuition, as in "The college exists for good purposes and therefore must have done good"; anecdotal, or "In my experience, Houghton has done thus and so"; or some form of statistical compilation and evaluation. Even as information in the third category is almost impossible to acquire due to lack of empirical data, the first category is far too loosely impressionistic to be of value. That leaves the researcher working in the middle ground of personal statements, widened perhaps by some overall impressions and a few usable numbers. (Note: During the extensive interview effort that began several years ago in preparation for this book, a number of alumni expressed their opinion of Houghton's importance to them or its effects on their lives, and their responses may be found in appendix L.)

To solicit current opinions and anecdotes regarding the consequences of Houghton in the local area, the names of alumni residing in several communities along the Genesee River, from near the Pennsylvania line north to Rochester, were chosen. From this listing of about six hundred names, those who graduated in or before 1972 and who had usable addresses (over two hundred persons) were contacted by letter and asked these three questions:

1. How has your Houghton education affected your life since graduation?
2. How has your application of your Houghton education affected your job, your church, your community?
3. What effect do you believe Houghton as an institution has had on your church or community?

Although the number of replies was not overwhelming, the comments offered were congruent with responses made during the earlier round of personal interviews. In terms of the effects of Houghton on their lives, alumni used phrases such as:[22] "excellent academic education," "the academic material determined my career choices," "broad-based liberal arts education enabled me to keep current through many changes in my field," "gave me direction and purpose and the tools to do my job," "my Houghton education enriched my life," "gave me a passion for missionary work," "well prepared for graduate school," "solid grounding in my faith," "used my Christian education studies in missionary service," "rigorous academic standards," and "enabled me to decide my actions should be driven by virtues and not the world's values." One alumna added, "The professors' servant hearts and genuine love were inspiring." In other words, the testimony of these witnesses is that Houghton was able to achieve its proclaimed life-effect result in the lives of these alumni.

Regarding the effects that Houghton graduates have had on their communities, there is evidence that alumni have applied all dimensions of their Houghton experience throughout their personal and professional locales. Among the responses were these comments: "I strive to be honest and upright in reports to my supervisors and in contacts with other employees," "I used my Houghton education in the churches where we served and in the communities where we lived," "I have a greater sense of the importance of participation in the life of my church and a willingness to get involved in community activities," "in my community, I strive to give back more than I take," "it helped me organize and teach Bible studies to a neighborhood group for twenty-two years," "my training in social graces, culture, and commitment affected my life, my job, my church, and my community," and "Without it, I know I would not have been nearly as well prepared for my present work." Several long-time Houghton faculty commented that Houghton has had a strong influence on the educational environment in local schools, citing the fact that many who student-taught locally stayed to take district jobs.[23] Said one, "Houghton has had a significant impact on the area educational scene. The teachers may not get much recognition by a wider public, but they have a broad impact on a lot of lives."[24] Other individuals cited extensive involvement in health care, social services, churches, musical groups, and public service organizations. One alumna observed that "Wherever Houghton grads go, they spread the Good News and leave a solid witness for Christ."

Western New York has been blessed with twenty-two universities and colleges, and among them Houghton is one of the smaller institutions. Consequently, its graduates form just a small proportion of the area total. But there is some evidence that Houghton's alumni have had an influence that somewhat exceeded raw numbers.

Though Houghton was begun and continues as a denominationally-allied college, one of but eight in the area (two evangelical, six Catholic), it has gone beyond primarily furnishing pastors and laity for area churches to providing an essential cadre of faculty for regional and national primary, secondary, and post-secondary institutions. Data from surveys of selected classes (see chapter 14) suggest that 35–40 percent of each graduating class entered the teaching profession. Probably no group had a higher involvement in academe than the first eleven Houghton men who completed their final year at Oberlin: ten of them returned to Houghton to teach, and three earned doctorates.

One educator-alumnus commented:

> Houghton alumni have certainly had a positive influence on the local schools, particularly the many wives who taught at Fillmore and area schools. Also, back before every college got in the business of providing administrators for public schools, Houghton had a corner on the market. When I entered the school business in 1952, there were many superintendents who had studied at Houghton during the Depression.[25]

Much of the effect of Houghton on the local area has been expressed through the involvement of faculty, administrators, and staff in local agencies. Naturally this list includes area churches of Wesleyan and other denominations, but probably the greatest good has been done through involvement with local government, school boards, and civic organizations. Through their active participation, Houghton people have been seen as caring, practical, involved, and committed, and their efforts have been felt through community improvements to include fire department equipment, the local water system, and emergency medical technician assistance. Houghton individuals with appropriate skills and credentials have served as supply and interim pastors for many churches in a fifty-mile radius. Also, as owners of better-than-typical properties in this economically depressed region, Houghton people have been significant contributors to the tax base.

Financial Effects

Beyond the ethical, philosophical, academic, and spiritual consequences of alumni and of the college as an institution, the financial repercussions of the college have been large. The Genesee River region's central area has a meager population and a very limited economy, with small farms, local services, state and county jobs, and some light industry representing the bulk of the opportunities. Houghton College is the only major employer in a twenty-five mile radius of the village, and it is one of the largest in Allegany, Wyoming, and Livingston counties. In this milieu, the college's budget appears as large, and its effects have been growing.

As World War II was igniting, the total college expenditures were recorded as $153,336.[26] In 1972, the last year covered in this study, that sum had grown to $4,032,860.[27] According to the professional college business managers' organization, the fiscal benefits input to the community have an effective value of two to three times the actual dollar amount, indicating that total community benefits approximated ten million dollars.

Growth in college expenditures for representative years, using data drawn from available documents, is reported in Table 28.

TABLE 28	Annual Expenditures by Houghton College[28] (not adjusted for inflation)
Year	**Expenditure**
1940	$153,336*
1946	$233,774
1951	$660,308*
1956	$648,809
1961	$1,201,122
1967	$1,242,402
1972	$4,032,860

* Includes expense data for Houghton Seminary

Houghton and The Wesleyan Church

While Houghton began as a denominationally-shaped, pastor-ruled private secondary school, when James S. Luckey took office he initiated its development as a liberal arts institution rather than a Bible school. Thus began Houghton's first effect on the Wesleyans: establishing that a combination of liberal learning and evangelical theology would provide better graduates and churchmen. Though the Bible school movement did not entirely fade in Houghton's nearly ninety years of existence prior to the retirement of Stephen Paine, the Houghtonian concept of Christian liberal arts helped shape the curriculum of subsequent Wesleyan colleges.

Over the years, Houghton presidents have continued to be staunch Wesleyans, and for the most part members of the governing boards have been Wesleyan also. From this source plus faculty and staff who were Wesleyan or Wesleyan-sympathetic has come a sustained congruence with Wesleyan and broader evangelical doctrine. However, as discussed in chapter 15, dissonances and conflicts have arisen. It is a tribute to the greater campus family that most issues of contention were resolved amicably or at least subdued to the point where the academic effort could continue.

One aspect of Houghton's influence on Wesleyan thought concerns Biblical inerrancy. John Wesley reportedly never used the term "inerrant," preferring "sufficiency" or "infallible."[29] Stephen Paine, as one of the translators of the New International Version, introduced the word "inerrant" into the foundational documents for the National Association of Evangelicals and subsequently into the lexicon of the NIV translators. According to one Wesleyan source, "Our use of the word "inerrant" distinguishes us from the Nazarenes and Free Methodists of the holiness churches. . . . For some persons it conveys the idea of inspiration by divine dictation, [but] I know of no Wesleyan scholars who would accept that concept."[30]

The next major effect culminated in the garment and adornment issue of the 1960s. In the words of one denominational leader, "Houghton was influential in the challenge to legalism which prevailed in the church,"[31] an aspect discussed in chapter 15.

Asked to sum the effects of Houghton on The Wesleyan Church, a former general superintendent offered these words:

Houghton has had a tremendous impact on The Wesleyan Church. It has provided a stream of outstanding leaders, ministers, and laypersons across the years. It has brought significant leaders into the denomination because they studied at Houghton. It has maintained an appreciation for academic excellence that has been sorely needed in the church. . . . I know of no way the total impact could be measured, but it is very significant.[32]

One veteran professor and pastor expressed a more assertive thought: "Houghton with its openness to women and minorities and its emphasis on the liberal arts helped keep The Wesleyan Methodist Church from totally drifting from her roots."[33]

Staying the Course

A friend of the college recently asked, "Houghton has developed in a unique way. Not only has it retained its Wesleyan heritage, it has achieved academic excellence and national recognition? How were these twin objectives realized?"[34]

Many factors appear to have contributed, starting with Willard Houghton's decision to locate the seminary far from the lures and sin-concentrations of any major cities. On one hand, Houghton students (and faculty) have not via proximity found it convenient to immerse themselves regularly in the temptations of any surrounding or readily-accessible city. On the other, the college's relative remoteness means that the vast majority of its students reside on or very close to the campus, and the college with all its activities is central to much of their lives. Their attentions have been turned toward the college's intramural athletics, dormitory activities, service clubs and organizations, musical and dramatic performances, dating opportunities, regular chapel programs, and—perhaps not least—the pressures of rigorous academics. One side effect of the remoteness is that fads—social, theological, and academic—that blossom in livelier areas, especially on the east and west coasts, may take nearly a decade to reach Houghton. Consequently, both the fad and its effects can be observed, and any assimilation is done cautiously and based on some level of knowledge.

Another factor is stability in the college presidency. From 1908 to 2004, in essence just three men have served as president, each for a multi-decade term. (The one short-termer was a devoted Wesleyan theologian, who worked to bend the college away from any hint of liberalism and toward a more narrow sectarian track). And each of these three major leaders combined a broad Christian perspective with unusual academic capability. Under their vision, each was committed to serving the community of believers, to being true to the college's basic mission, and to sustaining Houghton's academic rigor.

A third factor involves a faculty whose members have always had as an essential credential their Christian faith and who have tended to persist in their service at Houghton. Because Houghton is a teaching college rather than a research institution, the college's faculty has had close contact with students in all grades and in multiple classroom settings, helping to build persistent bonds that sustain a conservative approach to mission definition and accomplishment. In this setting, the relationships have enhanced student academic achievements and have produced a disproportionate percentage of Houghton alumni who have earned doctoral degrees.

Because of the rather small size of the college and of the community, a condition of non-anonymity of individuals has existed. The author's experience at three major universities showed first hand how easy it is to vanish among the masses, but to do the same at Houghton is exceptionally difficult. In this island-bubble setting, the living-out of the statement of community responsibilities is rather easy to observe, giving conscience a constant audience.

Numbers have also played a role. For several reasons, Houghton has not pursued rapid expansion. Over the nearly ninety years of life examined here, seminary and college enrollment grew slowly. There has been an underlying reluctance to seek exponential growth, partly because of the funding pressures such growth would demand, partly because of the general space constraints of the current land area, partly because any enlargement of the student body must be drawn primarily from non-Wesleyan resources, and partly because of the probable dilution of Wesleyan Christian standards brought by any hurried influx of new faculty.

Can Houghton continue on its steady course? Using the records of sister institutions as a basis for extrapolation, there seems instead to be a great possibility of veering away. But the fact that Houghton purposefully continues to be Houghton will work in its favor.

A General Summary

Evangelical colleges in general, and Houghton College in particular, endured the academic revolution in the early years of the twentieth century and concurrent fundamentalist-modernist controversies, and in the last third of the twentieth century they returned at least in some degree to the educational mainstream. At the same time, those institutions with a clearer commitment to their historical roots have also maintained many of their foundational theological and ethical convictions. Existing in many ways in two worlds, committed both to Christian values and to modern learning, the evangelical colleges embrace unique opportunities and novel difficulties as they attempt to bring Christian perspectives to the citizens of the world.

William Ringenberg pronounced a hope-filled summary vision when he said, "The most obvious characteristic of the evangelical colleges in recent American history is their institutional vigor. . . . A form of higher education which seemed doomed by the educational revolution of the late nineteenth century has not only survived, but prospered." He added,

Several distinct elements have contributed to that prospering. One is the colleges' ability to provide students with the necessary educational certification for entering the major vocations and professional schools. Another is their success in cultivating the support of Christian communities which had come to distrust modern higher education but which expressed confidence in institutions that retained Christian professions and traditional behavior standards. A third is the capacity of faculty at evangelical colleges to articulate to themselves, to college administrators, and to wider Christian constituencies the theoretical and practical necessity for distinctly Christian views of the world.[35]

Alan Graffam, who examined the development of four evangelical colleges, said:

Houghton Seminary was founded as a school with religious values not as a school for the study of religion; academic subjects were central to the curriculum. An early catalog describes course offerings in sciences (chemistry, botany, physiology), mathematics (geometry, algebra), languages (Greek, Latin, German), social sciences (history, geography, civil government), and humanities (natural philosophy, rhetoric, English literature). In addition an art department and a commercial department were part of the curriculum. Obvious by its absence was a specific course in religion or biblical studies. A list of required textbooks did not include any for a course in religion. Unquestionably the faculty held strong religious views and taught with them in mind, but the subjects offered were academic and not religious in nature.[36]

Unlike many church colleges founded in the nineteenth century and blossoming in the twentieth, Houghton did not shake off its early denominational and theological roots and become secularized, however slowly or rapidly. While it began as a decidedly religious school dedicated to keeping young men and women at arms-length from the evils of the world while preparing them to change that world, it did not require its students to hold church membership or even profess Christianity. Over the decades Houghton grew and matured into a Christian college of liberal arts and sciences, where willing students could encounter all learning from a Christian perspective—and then go forth prepared to understand the world and to work, with God, to change it if they could.

Former Wesleyan general superintendent Lee M. Haines summed Houghton's status thus: "The academic excellence and national recognition [of Houghton] have come largely through the commitments of the presidents and the people they gathered around them."[37]

In Arthur Holmes's words, "The Christian college affirms that God transcends history while acting in it, and has spoken truth that lasts."[38]

Nearly one hundred years earlier, Willard J. Houghton offered this over-arching thought, an expression that encompasses both foreshadowing and benediction: "Behold what God is doing."[39] Houghton College is a vine of God's own planting.

Appendix A

Houghton Time Line

Year	Event
1703	*June 17* John Wesley born.
1735	*February 5, 1735, to Dec. 22, 1737,* John Wesley served as a missionary in Georgia.
1738	*May 24* John Wesley converted (some Moravian influence).
1775	First settler in future Allegany County area: Nathaniel Dyke.
1781	Battle of Yorktown ends the Revolutionary War.
1784	*December* Methodist Episcopal Church of America organized in Baltimore. Coke and Asbury elected as superintendents.
1787	African Methodist Episcopal Church organized in Philadelphia, in protest to discrimination in the Methodist Episcopal Church.
1791	*March 2* John Wesley died.
1797	Treaty of Big Tree opened much of western New York to settlement.
	Leonard Houghton, father of Willard Houghton, born.
1800	*February 13* Orange Scott born, Brookfield, Vermont.
	First settler established residence in future Town of Caneadea.
1806	*April 7* Allegany County formed from Genesee County.
1817	Luther Houghton (grandfather of Willard Houghton) moved from Vermont to settle in the Town of Caneadea, on the present site of the college.

1825   *July 19*   Willard J. Houghton born, on current campus site.

1826   Methodist Episcopal church organized in Short Tract.

1828   Canal route first surveyed from Rochester to Olean.

1830   Methodist Protestant Church formed by individuals expelled from the Methodist Episcopal Church in protest over the powers exercised by the bishops.

1833   Emancipation Act outlawed slavery in England's colonies.

Oberlin Collegiate Institute founded.

1836   *April*   Luther Houghton purchased three hundred acres, including current campus site.

Construction began on the Genesee Valley canal.

1837   Oberlin Collegiate Institute admitted women to the collegiate department (ladies' course).

1839   Regional conference of Methodist Episcopal Church refused to ordain two Michigan ministers (Marcus Swift and Samuel Bebbens) because they were abolitionists.

1840   Swift and Bebbens organized "Wesleyan Methodist" churches in Michigan.

1841   *October 6*   Allegany County Historical Society formed.

Oberlin College awarded first BA degrees to three women (though men had to read their graduation orations for them).

1842   *November*   Revs. Orange Scott, LaRoy Sunderland, and Jotham Horton withdrew from the Methodist Episcopal Church.

December   Revs. Luther Lee and Lucius C. Matlack withdrew from the Methodist Episcopal Church.

1843   *February 1*   Wesleyan Anti-Slavery Convention, Andover, Mass.; discussed formation of Wesleyan Methodist Church.

May 31   Utica Convention: established Wesleyan Methodist Connection.

1844   *October 2*   First General Conference of the Wesleyan Methodist Connection: committee on education recommended establishing a seminary similar to the "Oberlin Institution."

Book Concern moved from Boston to New York City; Orange Scott was Connectional publishing agent.

Methodist Episcopal Church split over slavery into North and South branches.

Albany Normal School established.

1845   Wesleyan Methodist pastor Rev. Luther Lee preached the ordination sermon for Antoinette Brown, first woman ordained in the United States.

1846   Allegheny County towns of Eagle, Pike, and Portage set off to Wyoming County; Nunda set off to Livingston County.

1847   *July 31*   Orange Scott died, Newark, New Jersey.

1848   *June*   Second General Conference elected Cyrus Prindle as publishing agent.

1851   Wesleyan Methodist churches organized in Fillmore and Short Tract.

Spiritual awakening of '51 triggered W. J. Houghton's life of service in establishing Sunday schools.

Genesee Valley Canal opened to Oramel; Erie Railroad line opened.

1852   Wesleyan Methodist Book Concern relocated from New York to Syracuse.

Houghton Wesleyan Church established in the local school house.

1954   Illinois Institute (later Wheaton College) founded by Wesleyan Methodists.

1856   Genesee Valley Canal opened to Olean.

1857   Nearly five thousand businesses failed in the Panic of 1857.

1859   Adrian College (Michigan) established; Asa Mahan president.

1860   Free Methodist Church organized in Pekin, New York, by
            Benjamin T. Roberts.

1861   *April 12*   Attack on Fort Sumter began the Civil War.

1863   *January 1*   Emancipation Proclamation issued by President
            Lincoln.

            First women admitted to Normal School in Illinois.

1864   *June*   Lockport Conference represented for the first time
            at General Conference.

            Copperhead, the last Caneadea Seneca, died.

1866   Proposed Wesleyan Methodist union with Methodist Protestant
            Church fails.

1867   *August 1*   James S. Luckey born, Short Tract, New York.

1873   Same-day failure of thirty-eight banks and brokerage houses
            started the Panic of 1873.

1875   Ninth General Conference: Wesleyans elected, for first time,
            Connection president and secretary to hold office until next
            General Conference.

1876   Willard Houghton helped build the new Houghton church with
            a heavenward-pointing hand atop its steeple, to attract passing
            canal boatmen.

            December   Dedication of Houghton Creek Wesleyan Methodist
            church building.

1877   Union of Methodist Protestant Church and Methodist Protestant
            Church South produces the Methodist Church.

1878   Genesee Valley Canal was abandoned; railroads supplanted the
            canal and made Houghton readily accessible to city dwellers.

1879   *October*   Tenth General Conference voted to organize the
            Wesleyan Educational Society and adopted a Discipline statement
            against the use of tobacco. Also, women could be licensed to
            preach but not be ordained by the General Conference as elders.

1881   *February 8* Wesleyan Educational Society is chartered.

1882   *December 5* Wesleyan Methodist Connectional Agent Dennison Smith Kinney and Willard Houghton discussed establishing a Christian school in western New York.

WNY and Philadelphia RR begins operations on tracks laid along old canal path.

1883   *February 3* First subscription taken up in village church for Houghton Seminary (first dollar reportedly contributed by Rev. Thomas K. Doty of the Allegheny Conference).

Eleven-acre plot donated for seminary grounds, south of present campus.

April 21   Houghton Wesleyan Methodist Seminary incorporated in Orleans County, under the Lockport Conference; ground broken for the seminary building.

October   Eleventh General Conference: 480 churches; 16,321 members.

1884   *August 20* Houghton Seminary dedicated.

September 15 Houghton Seminary opened for classes; Rev. William Henry Kennedy, principal.

December   James S. Luckey enrolled for the winter term.

1885   Walldorf Temperance Hotel built on Main Street (now college residence).

1886   Rev. Augustus R. Dodd, from Iowa, became principal of Houghton Seminary.

1887   First seminary diploma awarded to Melvin E. Warburton.

Bertha Grange to be paid 12.5 cents per teaching hour.

1888   Houghton Seminary organized a department for training ministers; "Bible Training Class" began.

1889   *June*   J. S. Luckey became second person to receive Houghton Seminary diploma.

Wesleyan Methodists initiated foreign mission program: physician and teacher sent to Sierra Leone.

1890 *January 7* Dr. D. S. Kinney died (born 1832).

    J. S. Luckey joined faculty of Houghton Seminary.

1891 Thirteenth General Conference: denomination incorporated as "The Wesleyan Methodist Connection (or Church) of America."

    Furnace installed in seminary building.

1892 *August 8* Willard J. Houghton resigned as agent for the seminary.

1893 Failure of Philadelphia and Reading Railroad started the Panic of 1893.

1894 J. S. Luckey became principal of Houghton Seminary.

1895 *October* Fourteenth General Conference: several members of the Book Committee were constituted as the Educational Society of the denomination, and the conference ordered that all Wesleyan Methodist educational institutions should be under its control.

    Title of Houghton Seminary "principal" changed to "president."

1896 *April 21* Willard J. Houghton died.

    June Houghton Seminary officially placed under the Wesleyan Educational Society.

1897 *June 16* "Associated Alumni of Houghton Seminary" organized.

1898 *June* Houghton Seminary asked by the Educational Society to offer four years of college courses.

1899 *September* Houghton Seminary offered first college-level courses.

    October Fifteenth General Conference required new preachers to demonstrate competence at grammar school level.

1900 *June* Willard Houghton Memorial Library Association formed.

1901 *June* John Willett was first graduate of the Advanced (collegiate) department.

1902   Rev. Sylvester Bedford purchased forty-five acres (including much of current campus); he gave the upper part for the Wesleyan Methodist campground and offered eight acres of the lower section for sale to the seminary.

Wesleyan Educational Society voted to purchase property from Bedford for $547.25.

1903   *October*   Sixteenth General Conference: union with Free Methodist Church first suggested.

1904   J. S. Luckey completed A.B. degree at Oberlin College.

1905   Work began at new campus site on Jennings Hall (later called Old Administration, and eventually Fancher Hall) and on Besse Hall, later called Women's Hall and then Gaoyadeo women's dormitory.

J. S. Luckey completed M.A. degree at Oberlin College.

1906   *June*   First graduation on the present campus in Jennings Hall (later: Fancher Hall).

First Alma Mater written by E. M. Hall (tune: "Annie Lisle").

October 15 Wesleyan Methodist Bible Institute (later Central Wesleyan College, now Southern Wesleyan University) opened.

1907   *October 17* Houghton Seminary received a New York State charter.

1908   *June*   Silas W. Bond resigned as president to become Wesleyan educational secretary.

August   J. S. Luckey, who had just received his master's degree in mathematics at Harvard, interrupted his doctoral studies to begin service as seminary president.

October 20 Stephen W. Paine born, Grand Rapids, Michigan.

October   Miltonvale College established; Silas Bond founder and first president.

1909   *February*   *Houghton Star* began publication as a monthly magazine.

Houghton students provisionally accepted with advanced standing at Oberlin and Ohio Wesleyan.

Dorm matron Vera M. Jennings was named as first dean of women.

1910   *June*   First four Houghton Seminary graduates earn degrees from Oberlin College under provisional senior-year degree completion program: H. Clark Bedford, Leland Boardman, William F. Frazier, and Ralph Rindfusz.

Laura Whitney suggested the school colors of purple and gold.

1912   Line for college gravity water system surveyed and installed.

December   Two water closets approved for women's dormitory and two for women's cloakroom in seminary building.

Summer school approved for the seminary.

1913   *July 1*   Houghton offered first summer session (six weeks).

Full-time faculty member Ralph Rindfusz given additional duty as first dean of men.

1914   *May 8*   Ground-breaking for Bedford gymnasium—H. Clark Bedford steered a plow pulled by eighty men.

1914   *June 10*   Copperhead's remains reinterred beneath the campus's Boulder.

1915   Wesleyan Methodist General Conference first held at Houghton.

1917   *October 29*   Bedford gymnasium dedicated.

Philinda Bowen became principal of Houghton Seminary.

1920   *February 11* Special Seminary chapel held to begin college charter campaign (endowment needed: $100,000).

Electricity arrived in Houghton.

Marion College organized.

1921   *May 20*   Purple and Gold competition divisions began.

S. W. Paine, at age thirteen, received his first letter from J. S. Luckey.

1922   *October*   Pilgrim Holiness Church created by merger of Pilgrim Church of California and International Holiness Church.

1923   *April 17*   Houghton College received provisional New York state charter.

June   Separate treasurers authorized for each of the Wesleyan colleges. Also, first suggestion of possible union with the Pilgrim Holiness Church.

September   Science building (later Bowen Hall, then Woolsey Hall) opened for use.

College library collection reported as holding four thousand books.

Wesleyan colleges became individual corporations, with central denominational board acting as trustees for each college. Territory of the denomination divided into districts for the four colleges.

Office of dean of the college instituted; W. LaVay Fancher named as first dean.

1924   Publication began of college yearbook, *The Boulder.*

December 11   Official inspection by NYS Board of Regents, leading to official registration as degree-granting institution in January 1925.

1925   *June*   First twenty baccalaureate degrees were awarded (Allen Baker was first to receive a degree).

July 10–21 Scopes trial over teaching of evolution, Tennessee.

1926   Swimming pool (45'x15') completed in Bedford gym.

1927   *June 30*   Houghton College received absolute state charter; college enrollment was 105.

Music department elevated from seminary to college level.

1928   *September* Former J. N. Bedford residence remodeled and opened to serve as college infirmary; two nurses hired part-time.

College education department organized.

1929   *October*   Stock market crash started the Great Depression.

1931   *A Cappella* choir organized by Wilfred Bain; Artist Series began.

LaVay Fancher named first director of Wesleyan Youth (in addition to his full-time faculty post).

1932   *June*   S. W. Paine received MA from University of Illinois.

September 26 Music faculty moved into new music building.

J. S. Luckey received LLD from Wheaton College.

1933   *February*   Houghton faculty asked to forego 10 percent of salary for 1933–1934 to help offset deficit.

June   S. W. Paine received PhD from University of Illinois and joined Houghton faculty as foreign language instructor.

1934   *January 31* All faculty required to sign oath declaring support of U.S. Constitution.

May 7   Dean W. LaVay Fancher died.

May 25   S. W. Paine appointed acting dean.

Curriculum reorganized into divisional structure: English Language and Literature; Foreign Language and Literature; Social Science; Sciences and Mathematics; Philosophy and Religious Education; Music.

December 2 New edifice dedicated for Houghton Wesleyan Church.

1935   *June*   Twenty-fourth General Conference approved "storehouse tithing" as solution to denomination's financial problems.

Summer   Two-story "arcade" addition connected Old Administration (later Fancher) with Science (later Woolsey).

July   Willard Smith began Houghton College service.

October 19 Leonard Houghton died.

November 29 Houghton College achieved Middle States accreditation.

1936   *November 28*   First Founders' Day convocation; first three honorary degrees given to Ira F. McLeister, James O. Buswell Jr., and Herman Cooper.

1937   *April 7*   J. S. Luckey died; LeRoy Fancher named interim president.

        June 16   S. W. Paine elected president.

        Final passenger train passed through Houghton.

1938   Buffalo Bible Institute founded.

1939   *June*   S. W. Paine received LLD from Wheaton.

        First business manager hired: Arthur Karker.

        Pre-war high enrollment: 426 in fall semester.

        September   Germany invaded Poland, starting World War II.

        November 12   Salary reduction finally eliminated.

        Retirement annuity program for faculty and staff (TIAA) approved.

1941   *December 7* Japanese attack on Pearl Harbor lead to U.S. entry in World War II.

1942   *February 18* Bachelor of divinity degree discontinued.

        May 23   Luckey Memorial Building dedicated.

1943   *June*   Twenty-sixth General Conference appointed committee to explore union with the Pilgrim Holiness Church.

        September   Wartime low enrollment, fall semester: 292.

1944   Rev. H. C. Van Wormer elected president of the Allegheny Conference, holding office until 1967. His leadership was characterized as showing "fervent piety, deep devotion to principles, and an aggressive evangelism."

        GI Bill of Rights enacted, laying foundation for postwar college enrollment expansion.

1945   Willard Smith named as college business manager.

        College authorized to award B.Mus. degree.

Frieda Gillette became first female division chair.

August WWII ended; returning GIs began to flood American colleges.

1946 *May 3* Rev. E. D. Carpenter, former financial secretary for Houghton Seminary, Book Committee member and Educational Society secretary, died.

Dow Hall refurbished to hold forty-eight men.

Staff manager hired to run student-operated book store.

New water system opened; 150,000 gallon reservoir.

1947 *January* Vetville's thirty-eight apartments opened to families of student-veterans.

June Twenty-Seventh General Conference: denominational reorganization established full-time office of denominational president and twenty-one-member board of administration. "The Connection . . . became a Church whose . . . programs were to be given general supervision." "Book Committee" changed to "Board of Administration."

Ruby Reisdorph became the first woman on the Board of Administration.

1948 *January* Division of Music accredited by National Association of Schools of Music.

February 18 First known college constitution ratified by trustees.

April Denominational name change to The Wesleyan Methodist Church approved.

September Fine Arts building opened; "refabricated" WWII surplus dining-hall structure.

1949 *January* Charter changed to allow awarding DFA, MusD, PdP, ScD.

1950 *Hymns of the Living Faith* published jointly by Wesleyans and Free Methodists; Charles Finney served on joint commission.

Arthur Lynip became academic dean.

1951   *February*   Social Security coverage extended to include college faculty and staff.

June   Willard G. Smith completed PhD dissertation at New York University: *The History of Church-Controlled Colleges in the Wesleyan Methodist Church.*

June   Twenty-eighth General Conference voted down proposal to merge with the Free Methodist Church; college trustees on local boards given staggered terms and increased responsibilities; S. W. Paine elected as General Conference lay vice-president.

1952   *November*   College constitution revised.

December   J. Whitney Shea completed EdD dissertation at Columbia University: *Houghton College and the Community.*

1953   *October 24*   Dedication of original section of East Hall women's dormitory.

December   Houghton College Oratorio Society joined the Buffalo Philharmonic Orchestra for the first joint performance of *Messiah.*

1954   *June*   In connection with retrenchment, all college contract employees asked to return 5 percent of salary to the college.

1955   Rev. J. Walden Tysinger became president of the newly independent Houghton Academy.

1956   *January*   Campus Heights apartments opened.

March 14   Board of Administration voted to move denomination headquarters to Marion, Indiana.

April   Plan accepted for new library and open quad.

Campus enrollment limit set at 1,200.

1957   *January 15*   Fire destroyed Publishing House building in Syracuse.

March 28   Ground broken for new chapel; cornerstone laid June 1.

Wesleyan Board of Administration approved Asbury Theological Seminary for Wesleyan ministerial students.

Houghton hand-crank phones were replaced by rotary-dial units.

June 28   New twenty-five-member board of trustees established for college.

1958   *June 20*   Board of Administration approved merger with eight congregations comprising the Missionary Bands of the World.

Buffalo Bible Institute acquired present fifty-acre campus in West Seneca.

Houghton celebrated seventy-fifth anniversary; *Consider the Years* published.

Houghton Academy began construction on separate campus, under leadership of J. Walden Tysinger.

1959   *April*   Local board of trustees authorized use of hillside for Crystal Rork Arboretum.

June   "Old Admin" (originally Jennings Hall) renamed as Fancher Hall.

June   Thirtieth General Conference revised the church's administration to include three general superintendents; a written church constitution was adopted.

December 4 First service in John and Charles Wesley Chapel.

1960   *March*   First Dictaphone units put in use at the college.

May 18   New maintenance center dedicated.

Preliminary plans developed for new library.

July   Switched from manual student filing to NCR machines.

July 19   Construction began on Shenawana dormitory.

October 25 Wesleyan World Headquarters building opened in Marion, Indiana.

1961   *March 10*   Sick leave policy adopted by trustees.

September   Shenawana men's dormitory opened.

September   Kenneth Nielsen, later vice president for finance, joined college staff.

September   Abraham Davis Jr. became first black faculty member.

1962   *April 27*   Holtkamp pipe organ dedicated by Charles Finney.

May 4   Holtkamp dedicatory recital by E. Power Biggs.

Sixty-line switchboard installed.

150-acre Stebbins farm added to college property.

Natural gas piped into Houghton.

1963   *February 16* Last freight train passed though Houghton.

May 7   Former Board of Administration chair I. F. McLeister died, Alliance, Ohio.

Stephen Paine and Charles Finney write new alma mater.

1965   *March 30*   Marion College accredited by the North Central Association of Colleges and Secondary Schools.

April 11   Tornado destroyed Wesleyan World Headquarters building in Marion, Indiana.

1966   *June*   Thirty-Second General Conference approved merger with the Alliance of Reformed Baptist Churches, from eastern Canada and Maine; Bethany Bible College became a Wesleyan institution.

Allegheny and Tennessee Conferences seceded from the Wesleyan Methodist Church.

Arthur Lynip resigned as dean.

1967   *March*   Sick leave policy approved for faculty and staff.

September   S. W. Paine sabbatical began; Robert Luckey was acting president.

Melvin Dieter elected dean for 1968, but released to become the first Secretary of Education and the Ministry of The Wesleyan Church. (The reorganization of the Wesleyan educational system placed two Bible colleges, Bethany and Allentown, in the Northeast educational zone.)

June Houghton College intercollegiate athletics approved; first intercollegiate athletics competition: Houghton vs. Roberts Wesleyan in cross-country.

November Maintenance man Leon Ovell killed while clearing snow on path below Bedford Infirmary.

1968 *January* Houghton Water District approved; college transferred control of water system to Houghton village.

June Staff manual published.

June 25 The Wesleyan Methodist and the Pilgrim Holiness churches merged to form The Wesleyan Church.

Saturday classes ended.

Community sewer system constructed.

Houghton College assisted Houghton fire company with purchase of snorkel truck.

Work began on the new Science Building.

1969 *April 10* Buffalo Bible Institute merged with Houghton College.

July Ground breaking for Reinhold Campus Center.

First administrative computing system installed.

Campus phone system integrated with Fillmore system.

1970 Paine Science and Mathematics Center completed.

1972 *May* Cornerstone laid for Reinhold Campus Center.

June 22 Genesee River overflowed as Hurricane Agnes flooded valley area.

June Stephen W. Paine and Willard G. Smith retired.

Dr. Wilber Dayton became president of Houghton.

Reinhold Campus Center completed.

1974   Lambein Learning Center completed at Buffalo suburban campus.

1975   Elizabeth Beck Feller became first female trustee.

March   John and Carolyn (Paine) Miller captured by North Vietnamese forces.

October   Millers were freed.

Hymns of Faith and Life published jointly by Wesleyans and Free Methodists; once again, Charles Finney served on the joint commissions (the only person to do so twice).

1976   *July 1*   Robert R. Luckey became president of Marion College (now Indiana Wesleyan University).

September 1 Daniel R. Chamberlain became president of Houghton.

October 5   First of three small fires damaged the Music Building.

November 17   Arson fire damaged the top floor of Luckey Building.

1978   *September 8* Ground-breaking for Physical Education Center.

1980   *October 11*   New Physical Education Center dedicated.

1983   Celebration of Houghton's centennial; *And You Shall Remember* released; *Consider The Years* reissued.

1985   Grading system modified to include "+" and "-."

1986   South Hall men's residence dedicated.

Five-unit townhouse completed at Buffalo suburban campus.

Wesleyan headquarters moved to Indianapolis.

1987   Houghton assumed sponsorship of Oregon Extension campus.

Gaoyadeo Hall razed; Fancher Hall moved 300 feet to Gao's old site.

1989   *May*   Old village church razed.

        October 7   New Academic Building dedicated.

1990   Houghton Academy received accreditation by Middle States.

1992   *February 9* Stephen W. Paine died.

        Academic structure changed from six divisions to sixteen departments.

        Houghton began adult degree completion program (called P.A.C.E.).

1993   First P.A.C.E. students graduated.

1994   Two six-unit townhouses completed at main campus.

1995   Houghton Academy, aided by the college, built a three hundred-seat theater-auditorium.

1995–1996 Town houses built (new retirement apartments).

1997   *August*   Kenneth Nielsen retired as treasurer and vice president for finance; Jeffrey Spear named as replacement.

        Laptop computers were provided for all entering students.

1998   *April 24*   Ground-breaking for the Center for the Arts.

        Stevens Art Studio dedicated.

1999   Center for the Arts occupied.

        New athletic fields opened.

        Student townhouses built.

2000   *September*   Library renovation and addition completed.

2001 $15 million gift opened door for master's degree programs in music.

2002   New apartments built for faculty, staff, students, and graduate families.

2003   First students enrolled for music master's program.

2004   Wesleyan World Headquarters moved to Noblesville, Indiana.

Appendix B

Report of the Committee
on Education, 1844

[Arthur T. Jennings, in his 1902 book *History of American Wesleyan Methodism,* presented the text of the report of the Committee on Education of the Wesleyan Methodist Connection.]

The first General conference [of the Wesleyan Connection, 1844] adopted the report of a committee on education from which we quote below:

> There is a bright, a glorious prospect before us—especially as Wesleyan Reformers. Iniquity and corruption have yielded to our attacks, and wherever we plant our standard, victory crowns our efforts. But we need to fortify our territory, extend our conquests, and urge the victorious contest even to the last and strongest entrenchment of the enemy. In our glorious warfare we must rely upon our commander and upon the instrumentality which he affords us. Among these, the preaching of the Word in its fullness and in the demonstration of the Spirit, is undoubtedly chief. The press will yield great assistance. These we are exerting with success.

But there is another instrumentality, which we are by no means at liberty to despise. We allude to the cause of literature,—sound, sanctified learning. While we would not make mere literature a test for ministerial calling, we would make it an ornament to the ministerial character—we would regard it as affording increased means of usefulness to its possessor. The world—our work especially—is demanding an educated ministry. If we cannot supply this demand, others will.

We have already a share of professional men in our ranks, who highly prize the benefits of education themselves, and who are deeply interested in the education of their families and the community at large.

Our members generally, from the causes which made them Wesleyan Methodists, have learned to appreciate the benefits of education. The literary wants of our denominational community are already demanding means of supply. But there is a peeled, degraded, restricted class, who have hitherto been, to a very great extent, excluded from the schools and seminaries of our land. For these we need institutions, men, and pecuniary assistance.

Your committee rejoice in the assurance that the spirit which led to the establishment of the Kingwood School in England, is the spirit of Wesleyan Methodism in this country. Several of our yearly conferences have already taken measures for the establishment of conference seminaries; and in one or two, Wesleyan schools are already in successful operation.

The New England conference has established a seminary in Dracut, Mass., under the name of the 'Wesleyan Institute.' Teachers are employed, and the seminary is in successful operation.

Our brethren in Michigan have taken preliminary steps for the establishment of a conference academy, with a fair prospect of success.

A committee was appointed at the last New York conference to purchase buildings located in Royalton Center [which had been offered for a Wesleyan institution] provided the requisite means could be obtained. There is a reasonable prospect that the New York institution will soon be in operation. [The buildings have been since purchased.]

Your committee would recommend that each conference take early and vigorous measures to establish, as soon as practicable, a seminary for both sexes within its limits, whose advantages shall extend equally to all colors and conditions. Perhaps it is essential to success, that but one seminary in each conference be attempted, for some time to come. This will secure concentration, efficiency and ability.

Your committee would recommend the establishment, at some central point, as soon as providence may open the way, of a "Wesleyan collegiate institution," combining the advantages of literary and theological training, on a plan, in most respect, similar to the "Oberlin Institution." For this purpose, we recommend the appointment of a committee of twelve—to be styled the "Wesleyan Literary Committee"—to whom shall be submitted all propositions for the location of a "Wesleyan Collegiate Institute," proceeding from any station and village. This committee shall have power to correspond on this subject, and decide any questions connected with the literary institution. The confirmation, commendation or revision of their decision resting with the second General conference.

We recognize the adoption of the following resolutions, Viz.;

1. Resolved, That we regard with especial favor and gratitude, that some of our preachers and ministers, in addition to the arduous labors of the pulpit, have instructed, in day school, the children of their station, who, by cruel and wicked laws, are deprived of what should be the crowning benefits of education.

2. Resolved, That we deem it essential to the character of a Wesleyan Methodist preacher, that he should spend a portion of his time in visiting the schools of his station or circuit, encouraging scholars and teachers, and dispensing to them, in school capacity, suitable advice and instruction.

3. Resolved, That we recommend to all our brethren the remembrance of colleges, academies and schools, in their devotions, both private and public, that the blessing of God may rest upon those youths who attend them, that they may become truly pious and devoted to the best interest of their fellowmen.

4. Resolved, That the supposition that the Scriptures do not require Christians, and especially Christian ministers, to study and become truly learned, when circumstances will permit, is a great and dangerous error.

5. Resolved, That the duties of the minister are such as demands of him to be as well qualified in the great truths of the Bible, and the general principles of science, as he consistently can be.

6. Resolved, That the proper improvement of the minds of young men who are called of God to the ministry, in scientific and

Biblical knowledge is a subject of as great importance, and as full of promise, as any which may be brought before our people; and the money which may be necessarily expended in its promotion will ultimately do much towards the universal triumph of every benevolent enterprise.[1]

Appendix C

Seminary Application and Incorporation, 1883

The Incorporation of the Houghton Wesleyan Methodist Seminary[1]

B e it known that we the undersigned citizens of the United States and of the State of New York; viz: Francis M. Mosher, Reuben F. Dutcher, John L. Benton, George W. Sibley, Benj. S. Laughlin, Daniel W. Ball, Henry T. Besse, Willard J. Houghton, Benton A. Hammond, Edwin R. Weaver, Alonzo Thayer, and Wesley Doty have associated ourselves together under and in pursuance of the provisions of an "Act of the Legislature of the State of New York" entitled "An act for the Incorporation of Benevolent, Charitable, and Missionary Societies," Passed April 12th, A. D. 1848, and the other acts of the said Legislature subsequently passed amendatory thereof and supplementary thereto; do hereby certify and declare as follows:

First:—That the name and title by which said society shall be known in law shall be, The Houghton Wesleyan Methodist Seminary.

Second:—That the particular business and object of the said society shall be the securement, management and disbursement of funds and property in such a manner for the Wesleyan Methodist

Connection of America, as shall confer a Christian Education without regard to sex or nationality.

Third:—That the business or particular office of such society shall be in Houghton, Allegany County and State of New York.

Fourth:—That the number of trustees of said Society shall be twelve and the names of the Trustees of said Society until the Annual Meeting in June 1883, A.D. shall be, Francis M. Mosher, Reuben F. Dutcher, John L. Benton, George W. Sibley, Benj. S. Laughlin, Daniel W. Ball, Henry T. Besse, Willard J. Houghton, Benton A. Hammond, Edwin R. Weaver, Alonzo Thayer, and Wesley Doty, and on and after which time their successors shall be elected annually.

	Henry T. Besse,
Dated	John L. Benton,
Eagle Harbor	Daniel W. Ball,
Orleans County,	Benj. S. Laughlin,
New York.	Francis M. Mosher,
April 21, 1883	George W. Sibley,
	Willard J. Houghton,
State of New York	Reuben F. Dutcher
Orleans County ss.	

On the twenty-first day of April, A.D., 1883, personally appeared before me the undersigned, a Notary Public in and for Orleans County, Francis M. Mosher, Reuben F. Dutcher, John L. Benton, George W. Sibley, Benj. S. Laughlin, Daniel W. Ball, Henry T. Besse, and Willard J. Houghton, to me known to be the same persons described in and who executed the foregoing instrument and they each and severally acknowledged that they executed the same.

A.W. Starkweather, Notary Public

I hereby approve of the foregoing Certificate of Incorporation and consent that the same may be filed pursuant to Statute.

Dated May 7th, 1883.

Albert Haight, Justice Supreme Court, 8th Judicial District, N.Y.

University of the State of New York
Charter[2]
Houghton Wesleyan Methodist Seminary

WHEREAS a petition for incorporation as an institution of the University has been duly received and

WHEREAS official inspection shows that suitable provision has been made for buildings, furniture, equipment and for proper maintenance, and that all other prescribed requirements have been fully met

THEREFORE, being satisfied that the public interests will be promoted by such incorporation, the Regents by virtue of the authority conferred on them by the law hereby incorporate with absolute charter the present trustees of the corporation created by the provisional charter granted by the Regents October 25, 1906.

Arthur T. Jennings	Edward D. Carpenter	Alfred W. Brim
Henry R. Smith	Oliver C. Indley	Martin C. Wire
Charles H. Dow	Frank Ballan	Peter P. Campbell
Homer E. Bruner	Eber Teter	Henry Cheney
Alvin W. Hall	William T. Seekins	William Barnes

and their successors and associates in office under the corporate name of Houghton Wesleyan Methodist Seminary with all powers, privileges and duties, and subject to all limitations and restrictions prescribed for such corporations by law or by the ordinances of the University of the State of New York. The first trustees of said corporation shall be the incorporators above named. The board of trustees may from time to time fix their number, which shall not be less than five no more than twenty-five.

The corporation shall be located in Houghton, Allegany County, New York, and this new charter shall take the place in all respects of the provisional charter under which the institution has been operating.

IN WITNESS WHEREOF the Regents grant this
charter No. 1834 under the seal of the University,
at the Capitol in Albany, October 17, 1907.

Signed by the Vice-Chancellor and the Commissioner of Education
Recorded and took effect 4 p.m., October 17, 1907

Appendix D

Summary of Wesleyan Methodist Church School Projects before the Civil War

H oughton historian and retired treasurer Williard G. Smith provided a summary of school projects of the Wesleyan Methodist Church in the pre-Civil War period.[1]

> The purposes of the Wesleyan Methodist Church in the establishment of the first schools were: to provide education for their children and youth in a protected environment, to further the prosecution of abolition and reform, to provide a trained and loyal ministry, and to promote the welfare of the nation.
>
> All of the school projects of the Wesleyan Methodist Church in the pre-Civil War period ended in failure: Dracut Seminary and Wasioja Seminary closed; Royalton Academy failed to open; the Michigan Conference educational interests at Leoni ran into difficulty and were transferred to Adrian; Adrian College and Illinois Institute (Wheaton College) were transferred to other church groups. The Wheaton Theological Seminary, which was opened in the post-Civil War period, also closed.

Dracut Seminary (The Wesleyan Institute) was opened at Dracut, Massachusetts, by the New England Conference in 1844. The failure of the church people to honor their pledges of support and the competition from the nearby schools of Lowell, Massachusetts, were the primary factors contributing to the closing of the academy after about two years of operation.

Royalton Academy was a project of the Rochester [New York] Conference. Land and buildings were purchased on contract and plans were made to open the school at Royalton Centre, New York, in the fall of 1845. However, the Wesleyans failed to provide the necessary funds to carry the project into operation.

Wesleyan Methodist Seminary, Wasioja, Minnesota, was an academy operated by the Minnesota Conference. A building had been provided by the community for a Free Will Baptist school in 1858. The Baptists withdrew in 1868 and the citizens induced the Wesleyans to take over in 1873. The location of the school was in a poor frontier town and away from the center of Wesleyan membership. This was an obstacle in securing students. The seminary was not given adequate church financial support and the sale of perpetual scholarships[2] deprived the school of tuition income. When the Wesleyan Education Society requested the trustees to turn over the property to the society in the 1880s as a prerequisite for denominational support, the board failed to comply. With no prospect of increasing church support and of meeting current expenses, the board closed Wasioja Seminary in 1891.

The school at Leoni, Michigan, was started by the Michigan Conference, possibly as early as 1845, although the incorporation of the Leoni Theological Institute and Seminary (academy) was in 1848. A college department was introduced in 1851 as Michigan Wesleyan University. However, when the incorporation papers were changed in 1857 to accommodate the college level work, the school was called Michigan Union College. At the same time, the Theological Institute continued to function as a unit, though perhaps without corporate entity. Although there was a good registration (323 in 1855–1856), serious financial difficulties threatened the continuation of the school. The unsound financing by the sale of [permanent] scholarships, indebtedness incurred in plant expansion, the small support of the Wesleyans, and the Panic of 1857, coupled with the personal decision of three key members of the

Leoni trustees, resulted in the moving of the Michigan Conference education interests from Leoni to Adrian, Michigan, in 1859.

Adrian College, Adrian, Michigan, incorporated in 1859, was church-related in that one-half of the self-perpetuating board of trustees were members of the Michigan Conference. The library and part of the trustees and staff from Leoni were the nucleus for the formation of the college. The campus and first buildings were provided by the city of Adrian. However, from the very beginning, building expansion and current operation exceeded available funds. Augmenting the financial difficulties, were the factors of unsound scholarship sales and Civil War inflation. The leaders of Adrian College were the key men in a movement for union of the Wesleyan Methodist and Methodist Protestant churches. After negotiations, which included a joining of the churches in the support of Adrian College, had been started, the Wesleyans officially voted down the proposal of union. The implication of the Adrian Wesleyans in the union movement caused the church to discontinue their financial support. The trustees, driven by the desperate necessity of adequate support, voted to turn the college over to the Methodist Protestants in 1867.

The Illinois Institute at Wheaton, Illinois, was organized by the Illinois Conference about 1850 and opened to students in 1853. In the beginning, the curriculum included only college preparatory courses. Some college courses were added in 1855. The school had only begun to operate when it became involved in indebtedness on its one building. The support of the Illinois Conference was not only insufficient to cover the initial cost of providing a building but also to operate the school. The sale of scholarships and the Panic of 1857 intensified the financial troubles. Recognizing their inability to support the school, the Illinois Conference transferred the Illinois Institute to the Congregationalists in 1860, who rechartered it as Wheaton College.

The Wheaton Theological Seminary was the first educational project sponsored by an agency of the central denominational body of the Wesleyan Methodist Church. The Wesleyan Educational Society in 1881 signed an agreement with the Wheaton College trustees to establish a theological department. Under the terms of the agreement, Wheaton College furnished the facilities and the Wesleyans staffed the department and paid the salaries. The burden of teaching, administration, and fund raising was left to one man [Rev. L. N. Stratton]. There was no relief for this unsatisfactory arrangement, because the church did not supply enough funds. Circumstances arose which made necessary the resignation of the professor in February, 1889. Lacking both funds and students, the Wheaton Theological Seminary project was terminated in December, 1889.

The factors contributing to the failure of the school projects of this chapter were primarily financial. In only two cases, Dracut Seminary and Wasioja Seminary, was the location a contributing factor. All of the colleges borrowed money for the construction of their buildings. This created an extra burden of indebtedness which they were unable to carry. All of the colleges and Wasioja Seminary sold scholarships to raise money for endowment and buildings. This unsound practice augmented the financial difficulties of the schools by depriving them of tuition income. The Panic of 1857 intensified the financial distress of Illinois Institute and the Leoni school. The conferences that sponsored the various schools did not have sufficient membership to carry the projects they had started and they found no effective means of gaining denominational support. In the case of Adrian College, the implication of its leaders in the union movement virtually cut off the Wesleyan support and hastened the decision of the trustees to turn the school over to the Methodist Protestants.

Appendix E

Willard Houghton's Account of the Founding of Houghton Seminary

[The early days of Houghton Seminary and college were reported by its founder, Rev. Willard J. Houghton. The following account appears in his Subscriptions and Contributions book, preserved at the college. Rev. Houghton's original spellings, abbreviations, and punctuation have been retained.]

Rev. D. S. Kinney[1] then Agent of the W. M. Connection in the night following the Dedication of the W. M. Church at Short Tract Allegany County N.Y. in the month of Oct. 1882, stated to me, that we as a Denomination very much needed a school in the Western N.Y. as it was a central place where we as a church would school our children away from the environments of the large Towns and Cities. And said that Houghton would be a good place as it was free from the evils of the larger Towns and Cities. Also said that if I would take hold of the work he would do all that he could to put an Endowment on it so as to make it easey for the poor and an object for our people to send their children from a distance to their own Christian school.

After much prayer and consultation with D. S. Kinney, Rev. N. Wardner then Editor of the Wesleyan Methodist and also with the Lockport

Conference in the bounds of which the Seminary is located, and the Church and friend of Christian Education at Houghton all agreeing to stand by and help on the work, Feb. the 3rd. 1883, the first subscription was taken in the Houghton Church . After about one months work by Rev. D. W. Ball, W. J. Houghton, Alonzo Thayer, and John Parker within a radius of five miles of Houghton our sub Books footed up to about $1,000.

In the month of Apr. 1883 the peticion for the Incorporation papers[2] was completed at Eagle Harbor Seat of Lockport Conf. that year. And the following persons ware the charter members. W. J. Houghton, D. W. Ball, H. T. Besse, W. Daughty, R. F. Dutcher, J. L. Benton, G. W. Sibley, F. M. Mashier, B. S. Laughlin, B. A. Hammond, E. R. Weaver, and A. Thayer.

The grounds that the Seminary stands on with Eleven acres was the liberal donation of Mr. and Mrs. Harry Tucker. The first money paid in to the Building fund was by Rev. T. K. Doty of the Allegany Conf.

In the month of Apr. 1883 the ground was broken By Alonzo Thayer and Rev. D. W. Ball who had charge of excavating for the foundation and bringing the water to the grounds. At the Spring Conferences in the year 1883 the subscription for Building and Endowment came up to about $1500. And the job of Building the Houghton Wesleyan Methodist Seminary was let to Mr. Armstrong of Cuba to do the stone and brick work. C. P. Lapham to put on the roof and enclose and Walter Arnold to do inside work.

The principle men in locating the Building on the Hill whare the Building now stands was Revs. N. Wardner, D. S. Kinney, H. T. Besse. Time would fail to speak of the many interesting Providences connected in the planting of this school Heaven seemed to smile upon it from the beginning. Soon after the job was let and the Building commenced thare came a financial pressure and crops were blasted so that it was imposable to collect subs that was counted good and in the fall of 1883 it looked dark as though it must founder. But the W. M. General Conference in cession at Syracuse lifted the cloud by a cash subs of over $800 and much paid down, so the work went on.

In Sep. 1884 the Building was parcialy finished so it was thought best to open the school, yet thare was $1800 debts, yet subs suficant to pay when colected Rev. W. H. Kennedy was selected as Principle Luther Grange Assistent, Miss Allis Boardman Teacher, Sister Mary Depew, Primary Teacher, Miss Eva Davis to take the oversight of the Lady studance and to give them weekley lectures. So the school opened in Sept. 1884.

After four years and five months hard struggle in colecting money to make improvements on the Building and paying debts and Teachers, I was able in June 1887 to report to the Board of Trustees that the building was free from debt. And a nomber Thousand of uncolected subs, from Apr. 12th, 1883 to June 15th 1887 all the money labor and material. The amount in cash and estimated value of material and labor is set opasit each name in this Book. At this time June 15th 1887 our work as regular Agent ceased. Since this time many have given just as worthy to be credited in carrying on this work, and verily, verily they will have their reward in the world called heaven.

[signed] W. J. Houghton[3]

Appendix F
Nathan Wardner's Houghton Seminary Dedicatory Address[1]

[A handwritten note at the top of the archive copy of this address says, "Houghton Seminary Dedicatory address published in The Wesleyan Methodist August 27, 1884, but never delivered. The Reverend Mr. Nathan Wardner laid aside this prepared address and spoke extemporaneously."]

This is an hour for grateful thanksgiving and mutual congratulation. We gather today to dedicate to God this magnificent building, reared in the interests of a divinely consecrated culture. First of all, and above all, it becomes our duty to acknowledge "the good hand of God" upon this work. Its inception was clearly his inspiration. This enterprise was first begotten in devout minds and hearts by the Holy Spirit's impulses. These towering walls first rose complete before the vision of their faith. Confident of the divine call, profoundly impressed with the necessity and possibility of so grand an enterprise, obedient hands and hearts gave heed to, not an unfamiliar voice, as it gave command: "Arise and build!" God never bids to impossibilities. Though to merely human calculation, the magnitude of the work seemed overwhelmingly appalling, that faith which "laughs at impossibilities, and cries, "it shall be done!" put its hands toward heaven and to this work, and the Aarons and the Hurs held them up, while God himself gave success. The gratitude of the heart would pause right here and sing,

> Praise God from whom all blessings flow,
> Praise him all creatures here below;
> Praise him above, ye heavenly host,
> Praise Father, Son and Holy Ghost.

There are conclusive evidences that a gracious providence selected, and secured at the hand of friendly and generous impulses, the charming and commanding site on which, as "a city set on a hill," this Seminary is reared. Like "Mount Zion in the sides of the north," it is indeed, "beautiful for situation."

The earnest prayers that have been offered on the behalf of this educational enterprise, God has heard, the tears of solicitude that have been shed are in his bottle, the wakeful night vigils, he has seen; the sacrifices that have been made, he has written in his book. The possible advantages of intellectual culture are such as to justify the greatest measure of labor and sacrifice in furnishing youth with the best possible facilities for its acquirement. There is an important sense in which essential truth inheres in the old couplet:

> 'Tis education forms the common mind;
> Just as the twig is bent the tree's inclined.

Apprehended in its proper sense, and in its legitimate relations to the moulding and controlling power of religious thought and experience, Phillips has very fitly and forcibly said: "Of all the blessings which it has pleased Providence to allow us to cultivate, there is not one which breathes a purer fragrance or bears a heavenlier aspect, than education. It is a companion which no misfortune can depress, no crime destroy, no enemy alienate, no despotism enslave; at home a friend, abroad an introduction; in solitude a solace, in society an ornament; it chastens vice, it guides virtue, it gives at once a grace and government to genius. Some one has said: "A bar of iron worth five dollars, worked into horse-shoes, is worth ten dollars and fifty cents; made into needles, it is worth three hundred and fifty-five dollars; made into penknife blades, it is worth three thousand two hundred and eighty-five dollars; made into balance springs for watches, it is worth two hundred and fifty thousand dollars. What a drilling the poor bar must undergo to reach all that! But hammered and beaten and pounded and rolled and polished, how was its value increased! It might well have quivered and complained under the hard knocks it got, but they were necessary to draw out its fine qualities, and fit it for higher offices. So, children, all the drilling and training which you are subject to in youth, and which often seems so hard to you, serve to bring out your nobler and finer qualities, and fit you for more responsible posts, and greater usefulness in the world."

Addison has said: "What sculpture is to a block of marble, education is to the human soul. The philosopher, the saint, or the hero, the wise, the good, or the great man, very often lies hid and concealed in a plebian, which a proper education might have disinterred, and have brought to light. It is, therefore, an unspeakable blessing, to be born in those parts of the world where wisdom and knowledge flourish. To return to our statue in the block of marble, we see it sometimes only begun to be chipped, sometimes rough-hewn, and but just sketched into a human figure; sometimes we see the man appearing distinctly in all his limbs and features; sometimes we find the figure wrought up to great elegancy; but seldom meet with any to which the hand of a Phidias or a Praxiteles could not give several fine touches and finishings." The skillful chisel can bring out the statue. An accomplished master's hand can polish the granite.

It is said of Michael Angelo, that passing through an obscure street in Florence, he discovered a block of marble half concealed in rubbish. He at once flew to clearing away the filth that covered it. On being asked by a friend the cause of his strange course, he replied: "Ooh! there is an angel in the stone and I must get it out." He had the coarse block removed to his studio, and "with mallet and chisel he got the angel out."

There is many an angel in nature's mental quarries that culture never lets out. Education is very fitly defined to be: "The art of drawing out or developing the faculties; the training of human beings for the functions for which they are destined." As a rule the foundation of a cultured life is laid under the years of majority, or a sublime intellectual structure is never reared. Though:

> Our needful knowledge, like our needful food,
> Unhedg'd lies open in life's common field,
> And bids all welcome to the common feast.

The feast is seldom relished unless an early taste for the sweets of knowledge is cultivated. Youth-time is largely the hope of after years; it is the seed-time of life. He who in sloth sleeps away the morning, spoils the day. If spring is not improved, the fall gathers no harvest. History may record exceptions to this general rule, but the exceptions are not sufficient to invalidate its force. Plutarch began the study of Latin when between seventy and eighty years of age. Cato, at eighty, mastered the Greek language. Ogilby, the translator of Homer and Virgil, was unacquainted with Latin and Greek until he was past fifty. Franklin did not fully commence his philosophical pursuits before he had reached his fiftieth year.

It is not assumed that mere intellectual culture, is, in itself, the means of either usefulness or happiness. The greater the attainments, when these are sold to work—as is frequently the case—all manner of wickedness, the greater the possibilities of evil in character and influence. It is equally true that the more perfect the intellectual development, the greater the possibilities of personal happiness and instrumental blessing. Hence, the necessity of sanctified education that embraces the development of the heart, as well as that of the head; an education that tends to kindle the fires of moral and spiritual, as well as mental illumination. That culture which seeks to merely transform the head into a brilliant lighthouse, and leaves the heart a dungeon of moral darkness, lies under the serious accusation of neglecting that moral culture which can alone sanctify human capabilities to the accomplishment of those high and holy purposes divinely allied to human existence.

God's ideas of the equilibrium of human character embraces both mind and morals, both the intellectual and spiritual. Education is necessarily a blessing to its possessor, and to the world, only, as what God in his economy of development "has joined together," no man "puts asunder." The highest intellectual attainments, divorced from the moral and spiritual, may prove a life and death curse, while lesser developments of intellectuality coupled with grace may bless both their possessor and the world, living or dying. The legitimate thought and purpose of true culture is to join the mightiest attainments of intellectual development with the matchless experimental power of divine grace, in bringing forward a symmetrical character in harmony with the divine ideal.

These thoughts are not of today, merely; they came to these shores in the Mayflower, coupled in the minds and hearts of the Pilgrim fathers. Immediately on landing, in 1620, one of the first acts of the Plymouth colonists was to build both a meeting-house and a school-house. The necessity of the union of the religious and the scientific, by which the scientific is sanctified by the religious, is, at least, in theory sanctioned by the interest taken in education by the churches of the land.

Take one fact as illustrative. By the report of the U. S. Commissioner of Education, there is shown to be 377 universities and colleges in the

United States. All but seventy-eight of these are under the auspices of the religious denominations or sects of the country. Add to this the 124 Theological Seminaries all under the same patronage, and the general prominence given to the necessity of a religiously moulded education is still more clearly seen. Whatever may be the failure of reducing this theory to practice it is the one central thought of christendom, apprehended and fostered, however, only under the revealings of the cross. Says Dr. McClintock: "The ancient Spartans educated their youth in a stern and severe drill, beginning with the earliest infancy, and tending to make the body elastic, vigorous, and firm to the last degree. For the mind and heart, it cared nothing. A young man who could neither read or write might yet be the flower of the Spartan youth if he could hurl the discus farther than his fellows, or wield the javelin with more vigor and grace; or if he could endure, without a groan, the savage discipline of the lash, inflicted, not in punishment, but as a test of honor, and with all the sanctions of a heathen religion, before the altars of the gods. Nor was the Athenian culture, with all its boasted superiority of refinement, intrinsically better. It was an intellectual discipline, to be sure, and, as such, in many respects superior to our own; but it took little heed to the spiritual nature, and left the culture of the heart to accidental agencies to a great extent. The Persians, perhaps more than any other nation of antiquity, took pains to implant moral principles in the minds of children, yet their morality was of the earth earthy. It sought the advantages of virtue rather than its beauty."

It remains for Christianity alone to develop the perfect man, while that moral and spiritual perfection is reached only through the merit of that cleansing blood that flows through its system of atoning grace. Even the best intellectual culture which Christianity, with its superior advantages of light and knowledge can import, is powerless to purify the heart and life, only as faith is inspired to venture on infinite merit. Dr. T. Watson is credited with the following truthful saying: "Education doth much cultivate and refine nature; education is a good wall to plant the vine of grace against, but it is not grace." Arnot gives in a quaint manner, some seasonable and sensible advice bearing upon this question: "Don't cram your children with unreal forms, like blown bladders, which occupy all the room, and collapse on the first rude rub on real life. In pity to your children, seek to put something into them that will last and wear. Don't expend all your energies in trying ornaments on them to attract the gaze of the curious in the street; get into them, if you can, some of that ornament which is, in the sight of God of great price. Mothers, if your hearts have been quickened by the Spirit, take your fashions from the Word of God. Occupy yourselves mainly in moulding the heart and life of your children after the pattern which Jesus showed and taught. This will give you most enjoyment at the time, and more honor afterwards."

Spurgeon, one of the greatest of living ministers, counsels the young: "O young man! build thy studio on Calvary; there raise thine observatory, and scan by faith the lofty things of nature. Take thee a hermit's cell in the garden of Gethsemane, and lave thy brow with the waters of Siloa. Let the Bible be thy standard classic, thy last appeal in matters of contention; let its light be thine illumination; and thou shalt become more wise than Plato, more truly learned than the seven sages of antiquity." Dr. Beaumont uttered sentiments akin to the following: "And shall we cultivate for the sake of having a collection of beautiful flowers, to wither in a day? And shall not the mind and heart be cultivated, when the harvest is to be reaped in spiritual beauty, moral excellence, eternal advantages?"

The importance of looking to heart purification in this educational work grows upon our conceptions. Horace had in mind a very plain and positive truth when he said, "Unless your cask is perfectly clean, whatever you pour into it turns sour." The eloquent and gifted Blair, in discoursing to the youth, embodies our central thought in glowing words: "Whatever ornamental or engaging endowments you may possess, virtue is a necessary requisite, in order to their shining with proper lustre. Feeble are the attractions of the fairest form, if it be suspected that nothing within corresponds to the pleasing appearance without. The Author of your being had enjoined you to take heed to your ways: to ponder the paths of your feet; to remember now your Creator in the days of your youth. Let not then the season of youth be barren of improvements so essential to your future felicity and honor. It is too common with the young, even when they resolve to tread the path of virtue and honor, to set out with presumptuous confidence in themselves. Trusting to their own abilities to carry them successfully through life, they are careless of applying to God, or of deriving any assistance from what they are apt to reckon the gloomy discipline of religion. Alas, how little they know of the dangers that await them! Neither human wisdom nor human virtue, unsupported by religion, is equal to the trying situations which often occur in life. Correct then, this ill-founded arrogance. Expect not that your happiness can be independent of him who made you. By faith and repentance apply to the Redeemer of the world. By piety and prayer seek the protection of the God of Heaven."

The mightiest grasp of human thought, separated from humble piety, is not necessarily the precurser of happiness either for life, death, or eternity, while far less of mental or acquired gifts, if joined in sanctified devotion, to God, make happiness and usefulness in their sphere and measure complete and heaven sure. The gifted bard, with lyre tuned to lofty strains, fitly sings the contrast:

> There was a man large of understanding,
> Of memory infinite, of judgment deep,
> Who knew all learning, and all science knew,
> And all the phenomena in heaven and earth,
> Traced to their causes; traced the labyrinths
> Of thought, association, passion, will;
> And all the subtile, nice affinities
> Of matter traced; its virtues, motions, laws;
> And most familiarly and deeply talked
> Of mental, moral, natural, divine.
> Leaving the earth at will he soared to heaven,
> And read the glorious visions of the skies;
> And to the music of the rolling spheres
> Intelligently listened; and gazed far back
> Into the awful depths of Deity.
> Did all that man assisted most could do;
> And yet in misery lived, in misery died,
> Because he wanted holiness of heart.

And now the contrast:

> One man there was—and many such you might
> Have met—who never had a dozen thoughts
> In all his life, and never changed their course;
> But told them o'er, each in its 'customed place,
> From morn till night, from youth till hoary age.
> Little above the ox, which grazed the field,
> His reason rose; so weak his memory,
> The name his mother called him by he scarce
> Remembered; and his judgment so untaught
> That what at evening played along the swamp,
> Fantastic, clad in robe of fiery hue,
> He thought the devil in disguise, and fled
> With quivering heart and winged footsteps home.

The word philosophy he never heard,
Or science; never heard of liberty,
Necessity, or laws of gravitation,
And never had an unbelieving doubt;
Beyond his native vale he never looked,
But thought the visual line, that girt him round,
The world's extreme; and thought the silver moon
That nightly o'er him led her virgin host,
No broader than his father's shield. He lived—
Lived where his father lived—died where he died;
Lived happy, died happy, and was saved;
Be not surprised; he loved and served his God.

The one central purpose of the Almighty, as allied to human development, is, to bring forth from the mental, moral, and spiritual possibilities of our being, the most perfectly moulded, rounded, and polished character, meet both for the Master's best use and service here, and for heaven hereafter. This is the overmastering thought, the vital inspiration of Houghton Seminary. I see in the opening visions of the future, a youthful multitude climbing this hill of sanctified science, until from its sun light summit they go forth one by one to shine as intellectual and spiritual luminaries in a dark world.

There is a sense which exalts human privilege to the skies, in which those who are burnished for God, are the lights of the world, "A city that is set on a hill which cannot be hid." Candles, light of the Almighty never seek to hide under the secret seclusion of a bushel, advertising professedly hidden wisdom on sale for a fee. Such lights are the rather set on a golden candlestick to blaze their illumination in full view of the darkness of a world's ignorance and sin. He who has learned anything which possesses the essential elements of blessing for a world, brands himself as the foe of universal humanity by a refusal to shed the revealing light of its glory on a poor, blind, benighted race.

The divinely appointed business of sanctified science is the revelation, and not the concealment of truth, whether embraced in the realm of the purely scientific, or the intrinsically religious. The light of truth, either in the intricate workings of natural, or spiritual dispensations, is God's own patrimony to men; and he who would seek its concealment, rather than its development, seeks to thwart the beneficent purposes of that God who is the center and source of all light, and who seeks to flood our dark world with its divine radiance.

This citadel of consecrated lore is heaven-ordained to stand with open gates, to shine on all surrounding darkness the light and heat kindled from heaven on its sacred altars, and to invite the world to revel in the brightness of that rising which bathes its summit in God's own free sunshine. Divinely ordained agencies, either in science or salvation, are commissioned to bring forth, whatsoever things are true, whatsoever things are pure, whatsoever things are of good report, in short, to bring forth and make manifest the truths of science and salvation, as they are in Christ Jesus, in the spirit of that early gospel exhortation: "Behold the Lamb of God!" A city that God sets by the hand of his own building on a hill cannot be hid. In instituted contrast with the darkness-seeking systems of human devising, the bard of song tuned again his lyre, and poured forth the truth in golden numbers:

> The christian faith,
> Unlike the timorous creeds of pagan priests,
> Was frank, stood forth to view, invited all,
> To prove, examine, search, investigate,
> And gave herself a light to see her by.

The foundational thought of Houghton Seminary,—we, this day, give to God, impleading his divine acceptance—is, the sanctification and union of mental and spiritual culture in the preparation and development of agencies to bless themselves, and to bless the world. Faith in the issues of this heaven-approved enterprise—in sending forth characters moulded into meetness as co-workers together with God—scarce falls below the standard of life efficiency and eternal glory sung by the poet:

> Needy, poor
> And dying men, like music, heard his feet
> Approach their beds; and guilty wretches took
> New hope, and in his prayers wept, and smiled,
> And blessed him, as they died forgiven; and all
> Saw in his face contentment, in his life
> The path to glory and perpetual joy;
> Deep-learned in the philosophy of heaven,
> He searched the causes out of good and ill,
> Profoundly calculated their effects
> Far past the bounds of time; and balancing,
> In the arithmetic of future things,

The loss and profit of the soul to all
Eternity; a skillful workman he
In God's great moral vineyard; what to prune
With cautious hand he knew; what to uproot;
What were weeds, and what celestial plants
Which had unfading vigor in them, knew;
Nor knew alone but watched them night and day,
And reared and nourished them, till fit to be
Transplanted to the paradise above.
Oh, who can speak his praise! great humble man!
He in the current of destruction stood
And warned the sinner of his woe; led on
Immanuel's members in the evil day;
And, with the everlasting arms embraced
Himself around, stood in the dreadful front
Of battle, high, and warred victoriously
With death and hell. And now was come his rest,
His triumph day. Illustrious like a sun,
In that assembly, he, shining from far,
Most excellent in glory, stood assured,
Waiting the promised crown, the promised throne,
The welcome and approval of the Lord;
Nor one alone, but many—prophets priests,
Apostles, great reformers, all that served
Messiah faithfully, like stars appeared
Of fairest beam; and round them gathered, clad
In white, the vouchers of their faithfulness,
The souls their care had nourished fed and saved.

Appendix G

New York State Charters
for the College

Provisional Charter of Houghton College

This instrument witnesseth That the Regents of the University of the State of New York Have granted this provisional charter incorporating Edward G. Dietrich, Rev. Edward D. Carpenter, Rev. John S. Willett, Rev. Frank A. Butterfield, Rev. T. P. Baker, L. H. McMillan, Rev. G. L. Densmore, Rev. Charles Sicard, Fleming Perrine, Rev. A. B. Hotchkiss, O. N. Carnahan, Rev. Walter L. Thompson, O. S. Ballinger, Rev. John Clement, Joe Lawrence, and their successors and associates, as a College of liberal arts and science, for the promotion of science, literature, art, history, and other departments of knowledge under the corporate name of Houghton College, to be located in the village of Houghton, Allegany county, and State of New York, with fifteen trustees, to be at first the persons named herein as incorporators, to hold until the next General Conference of the Wesleyan Methodist Connection (or Church) of America, to be held in June 1923, and until their successors shall be elected at such General Conference, to serve for terms of four years each, the election of trustees to be held quadrennially thereafter at the General Conference of the said Wesleyan Methodist

Connection (or Church) of America, with power in them to increase or decrease its membership in such manner and upon such terms as shall be provided for by the general rules of its trustees and with power in them, from time to time, by a unanimous vote of their full board, to fix their terms of office and their number, to be not more than twenty-five nor less than five; and with the provision that this provisional charter will be replaced by an absolute charter, authorizing the college to confer upon its graduates the usual degrees, subject to the restrictions and the requirements of the University, if within five years the corporation shall acquire resources and equipment of the value of at least $500,000 available for its use and support and sufficient and suitable for its chartered purposes in the judgment of the Regents of the University and be maintaining an institution of educational usefulness and character satisfactory to them; and that until the granting of the absolute charter suitable degrees of The University of the State of New York will be conferred upon the graduates of the college who, in the judgment of the Regents, shall have duly earned the same.

Granted April 7, 1923, by the Regents of the University of the State of New York executed under their seal and recorded in their office.

Number 3253

Chester S. Lord, Chancellor
Frank P. Graves, President of the University[1]

Absolute Charter of Houghton College

The University of the State of New York
Absolute Charter of Houghton College

This instrument witnesseth that the Regents of the University of the State of New York being satisfied that the required conditions have been met, have granted to Houghton College the absolute charter to replace the provisional charter which was granted April 7th, 1923, and continue the corporation with all its powers, privileges and duties.

Granted June 30th, 1927, by the Regents of the University of the State of New York executed under their seal and recorded in their office.

Number 3677.

Chester S. Lord, Chancellor
Frank P. Graves, President of the University and
Commissioner of Education[2]

Amendment to Allow Awarding Honorary Degrees

The University of the State of New York
Amendment to the charter of Houghton College

This instrument witnesseth that the Regents of the University of the State of New York have awarded the charter of Houghton College, located at Houghton, Allegany Co. which was provisionally incorporated by the Regents on April 7, 1923 such provisional charter having been replaced by an absolute charter on June 30, 1927 by authorizing said corporation to confer the degrees of Doctor of Laws, LL.D., and Doctor of Divinity, D.D., honoris causa.

Granted July 17, 1936, by the Regents of the University of the State of New York executed under their seal and recorded in their office.

Number 4370.

Chester S. Lord, Chancellor
Frank P. Graves, President of the University and
Commissioner of Education[3]

Amendment to Allow Additional Honorary Degrees

The University of the State of New York
Amendment to the charter of Houghton College[4]

This instrument witnesseth that the Board of Regents for and on behalf of the Education Department of the State of New York has amended the charter of Houghton College, located in Houghton, Allegany County, which was incorporated by the Board of Regents under a provisional charter on April 7, 1923, such charter having been made absolute by the action of the Regents on June 30, 1927, and having been amended on July 17, 1936, by authorizing said corporation to confer the honorary degrees of doctor of laws (LL.D.) and doctor of divinity (D.D.), by authorizing the corporation to confer the honorary degrees of doctor of fine arts (D.F.A.), doctor of letters (Litt.D.), and doctor of pedagogy (Pd.D.), in conformity with the rules of the Regents of the University and the regulations of the Commission of Education for the registration of institutions of higher education.

Granted September 14–15, 1950, by the
Board of Regents for and on behalf

of the State Education Department,
executed under the seal of the said
Department and recorded therein,
Number 5929.

(signed) William J. Wallin
Chancellor

(signed) Lewis A. Wilson
Acting President of the University and
Commissioner of Education

Appendix H

Why the Christian College?
by Stephen W. Paine

The desire of the editors of *Eternity*[1] to have a concise statement of the case for the Christian college deserves commendation. The term "Christian college" is here used not as an equivalent for the term "church-related college," but in the narrower sense as referring to that comparatively smaller group of colleges which (1) have an evangelical statement of faith and take it very seriously, and (2) endeavor to maintain a standard of campus life in harmony with the statement of faith and with the standards of Bible-believing Christians generally—granted that the matter of evangelical standards of life does not fall easily into an exact formula.

I shall mention three crucial areas of service rendered by the Christian college to the evangelical cause. First, the Christian college confronts its young people with the evangelical world view. Perhaps a student's most important quest in college should be a proper perspective of the universe and his relation to it. He studies the sciences to learn something of the physical nature of his world. Psychology, sociology, history, and ethics give him some insights into the personal elements of his environment—how people behave and why. Foreign languages also, besides being tool subjects, are excursions into the thought patters of people. And English shares the same values.

But Christian people believe that the most important factor in any man's life is his relationship to the God who created him, and who sustains him in life, and further, that none of these other fields of learning are seen in their right perspective when viewed apart from God. Dr. R. B. Kuiper, former president of Calvin College, well illustrated this point when he said, "One may look at a window pane in one of two ways. Either he may stare at the pane itself and make it alone the object of observation, or he may look through the pane up at the heavens. So there are two ways to studying nature and history. One may lose himself in the bare facts, or one may look up through the facts at God, who is revealed in all the works of his hands, and in the guidance of the destinies of men and nations."

The Christian college, through its direct classroom approach, through the freely declared and known faith of its teachers, and through the central importance assigned to spiritual matters in college life, puts God at the center of his universe.

This is something which other colleges do not and cannot do. The *Harvard Report* frankly admits this inability. Pointing out the lack of a unifying central view in the colleges, the report says, "Sectarian, particularly Roman Catholic, colleges have, of course, their solution, which was generally shared by American colleges until less than a century ago, namely, the conviction that Christianity gives meaning and ultimate unity to all parts of the curriculum, indeed to the whole life of the college. . . . But whatever one's views, religion is not now for most colleges a practical source of intellectual unity." All which reminds us so forcefully of Paul's words, "The world by wisdom knew not God." (1 Cor. 1:21)

This secularism of the schools and colleges generally, this omission of God from his universe by those who are supposed to be communicating their wisdom about the most important matters in their respective fields, is more than likely to leave its mark in the thinking of the student. He may have friends—or a pastor, or parents—who tell him that God is the greatest factor of life. But these tend to be considered mere laymen in comparison with the professors.

Dr. Bernard Iddings Bell, commenting upon the secularism of the schools, said, "If a child is taught in school about a vast number of things—for twenty-five hours a week, eight or nine months of a year, for ten to sixteen years or more—and if for all this time matters of religion are never seriously treated, the child can only come to view religion as, at best, an innocuous pastime preferred by a few to golf or canasta" (*Life*, October 16, 1950).

As though this silent treatment were not bad enough, there are often deliberate efforts to nullify by open opposition whatever vestiges of faith the students happen to have. A science professor in an eastern college, whose name we refrain from mentioning, was fond of a little demonstration which he was wont to "pull" on his beginning class about once every year. Lecturing on the continuity of natural law, he would ask if there were anyone in the class who believed that there is a God who can be appealed to by prayer and who will actually answer such prayer and "do something about it"—change things around.

The professor would wait for a response from the class, and often there would be in the group a few young people from Christian homes who would raise their hands in response to the professor's question. The teacher would make an indulgent remark or two on the naivete of persons holding such outmoded views and would then come to his "pitch": "Well, I'll tell you what we'll do. Now I have here in my hand a glass test tube. I'm going to release my hold on the test tube and a force called *gravitation* will take effect, causing the test tube to drop toward the concrete floor in the laboratory. Now in the meantime, you just pray that this test tube won't break, and we'll see what happens." He would then drop the test tube, which would splinter on the hard floor.

This type of deliberate, cleverly graphic, and wholly unfair effort on the part of a seasoned academic infidel to overthrow any favorable tendencies of his immature hearers toward the Christian faith is a perhaps extreme but by no means an un-duplicated situation.

For every such determined type of faith-wrecker there are scores who confine themselves to a more polite and incidental heckling of the historic Christian point-of-view and, more recently a growing number who are ready to praise Christian values like the power of prayer, with the added note that one need not be an obscurantist Bible-believer ("bibliolator") to have these.

Now a person may quickly point out this or that student who, by God's help, and perhaps with the help of Christian church connections or of a small group of evangelical fellow-students, has been able to weather the storm in a secular college, perhaps even to emerge the stronger for having done so. For this we say, "Thank the Lord." But human society is organized upon the basis that man is susceptible to influence, that propaganda tends to affect people's attitudes and points of view. Subversive ideologies go on this basis and are able to win a surprising number of converts in spite of their basic error. Industrial corporations go on this basis and pour millions of dollars into sales organization and advertising—with justifying returns.

The Christian church recognizes this principle and maintains a weekly preaching of the Word, a teaching ministry, and an evangelistic and missionary outreach. Christians are warned by the Scriptures not to forsake the assembling of themselves together, but to exhort one another daily. It seems entirely reasonable to suppose that, in spite of shining exceptions, a persistent espousal of the secular point of view will have an effect upon those who come under its influence.

Anyone who has had any contact with such matters and has kept his eyes open knows that this is precisely the say things often go. William H. Buckley discusses some of his observations by the way of "results" of this kind. Typical is the comment on Professor K——- who, he says, "held forth at Yale for a great many years, teaching a basic course in one of the most important fields of social science, and revealing an unswerving contempt for religion in general and Christianity in particular. To my personal knowledge, he thus subverted the faith of numbers of students who, guilelessly, entered the course hoping to learn sociology and left with the impression that faith in God and the scientific approach to human problems are mutually exclusive." (*God and Man at Yale,* p. 17)

In this connection it should be kept in mind that most young people entering college from Christian homes are from sixteen to eighteen years old. Many of them are very naive in their acceptance of Christian presuppositions. Some are from less than the strongest of Christian backgrounds. They may even be half ready to consider other points of view and other ways of life. They are usually fairly susceptible to majority social pressure. They are a bit overawed to be in college. They tend to admire the academic proficiency and the urbanity of their teachers. Their purpose in being at college is to learn from their teachers. Often these teachers are winsome of personality and take a genuine interest in their students. It is the exceptional young person who can simply keep his personal admiration and his religious faith in separate compartments, to say nothing about having the intellectual background and the strength of personality to rise up and confound his teachers in their learned unbelief.

Against such a background the Christian college presents a bright contrast, with its positive espousal of the Christian world view, its frequent answering of intellectual difficulties, and its effort to win the non-Christian or wavering students to a constant faith in Christ. Happily, a high proportion of these Christian liberal arts colleges are members of the standard regional accrediting agencies. This does not necessarily mean that they are as large or as wealthy as some of the institutions accredited, but if we can place any dependence on the accrediting agencies that are received as standard the country over, then the membership of many of our Christian colleges in these associations should encourage us to feel that the colleges are doing good work academically. There is no reason to suppose that the accrediting agencies would be partial in their favor.

The other contributions of the Christian college are closely related to the one already mentioned. Let us consider a moment the fact the Christian college imparts to many of its students a Christian character. We do not mean to discount for a moment the transforming power of the new birth in life and conduct, but we would point out that even recognizing this, the development of personal ideals and ways of life is influenced by example. As Christians, we have the Holy Spirit in our hearts to guide us. He often does this by sending us to the Word of God for the basic principles of our behavior, and by referring us to the example of godly men and women for the spelling out of the details. Some have felt that the most important contribution of the Christian college to its students—more important than any proposition values imparted, however valuable—is this impact of Christian character on character. The very word "character" of course means originally an imprint or impression received from a stamp or seal.

Relatively few basic and deep-seated changes are wrought in us through our own determination and effort. Most such changes are effected by influences outside ourselves. A man with a deep-seated disorder may realize that he needs to be operated upon. He can choose the surgeon whom he will let work upon him, but once the decision is made and the anesthetic administered, the desirability of the change is, to a great extent, out of his own hands.

So it is with reference to the factors which shape our characters and influence the direction of our lives; the really crucial decision often concerns the question as to which factors we will permit to operate upon us. Once they have begun to operate, the chooser himself—and the quality of those choices—is changed. A young man who had attended a certain school where his basic point of view had been radically reversed said to one with whom he had earlier associated and had been at basic agreement, "Well, I'll admit I've changed completely, and now that I am convinced that your point of view is wrong, I wouldn't want to go back to it. But I will say that a young fellow going to a school should pick one that teaches what he wants to believe and go to such a school, because that's the way he will be when he comes out."

One of the most potent of character molding forces is that of association. Solomon said, "He that walketh with wise men shall be wise" (Prov. 13:20). It is true that the Christian must ultimately rub shoulders with the world and witness to it by being different from it. But for the formative years of his life God has graciously provided Christian homes—and Christian schools.

Looking back at my own undergraduate life, I thank the Lord heartily that my leaders in thought development and intellectual growth, those persons who deserved and received the admiration and approval of myself and my fellow students, were devout and consistent Christians. The athletic coach, admired by everyone for his own record as an athlete and his sports-wisdom, was a deacon in the church. The coach of debate, who helped us to concoct those forensic booby traps and atomic bombs which promised "sudden death" for the opponents, was a kindly and affectionate Christian gentleman who often filled the pulpit of a Sunday.

My classmates too made a wonderful contribution to my life. Some of them were far ahead of me in spiritual depth, a fact to which even then I was not blind. I admired the fellows on the basketball squad. Most of them had a ready testimony for the Lord, and they were just as much at home conducting a gospel service as when "burning up" a hardwood court. I admired my colleagues of the cross country team. Our captain easily won the state intercollegiate championship. And he it was who would get us together in his room in the hotel to read the Word and have our prayers together in the evening.

A young person can, of course, find Christian example elsewhere than in a Christian college. But he ought to have all of this he can get, and the Christian college is in this respect an unparalleled resource.

All of which leads me to the next and closely related idea. The Christian college affords a Christian social life. We are not now thinking of character impact so much as the fact of one's simple wholesome acceptance as a member of a group to which the student can feel he "belongs."

In the non-Christian college a Christian student will tend to find this social life in some evangelical church group or with the small number of his fellow students who are found to be believers. He can often thus "make it through" although feeling himself betimes a sort of outcast insofar as the bulk of the student body are concerned. This is good, so far as it goes, but a young person in the late teens needs a better situation than this. He needs a sense of security in his relationships with the group, a sense of "belonging," of being socially acceptable. Young people naturally accept one another, and they need themselves to feel accepted.

Almost everyone is familiar with the type of inferiority complex which often goes with feeling oneself a member of a "minority group." It issues negatively in feelings of persecution, in touchiness, supersensitivity, and attitudes of suspicion. It issues positively in over-assertiveness, belligerence and a desire to dominate. This in not to say that these factors operate fully in all young persons who have to stand alone. Some individuals adjust more wholesomely than do others. But at college age it is good if the Christian young person can feel himself at once a whole-hearted and an acceptable part of the social life of the school. And in the Christian college he finds this a glorious possibility. He finds that, by and large, he can enter unreservedly into activities. He finds in himself a feeling of kinship for the other splendid young people with whom he is working, and he realizes that they feel the same way toward himself.

College friendships tend to be lasting friendships. Yes, and we might as well add that it is a widely understood fact that a large number of young people find their life partners in college—be it secular or Christian. What a privilege, then, to be part of a group of young people comprising the very cream of Christian young manhood and young womanhood, gathered from widely scattered communities and families, often representing individually the very best that a given family or community can send. And I may also say, from the teachers' point of view, it is a rare privilege to have the opportunity of working with such young people and of making some contribution to their lives.

Finally I would like to point out that the Christian college fosters a Christian vision of service. Persons of like objectives tend to consort together, and persons who spend much time together tend to have similar objectives. A departmental professor, desiring to recruit his students for service in a given area, will establish a departmental club for study and discussion of matters pertaining to that area. He will take them to professional meetings where they will meet leaders in the field.

In a Christian college the student has the example of Christian faculty members, working sacrificially as Christian teachers. He observes that despite modest salaries, they seem to get along financially and to have their needs met. Time and again it works out that he feels in his heart a call to do likewise. Again, as foreign missionaries visit campus and speak in chapel, the Christian students are confronted from time to time with the imperative of Christ's commission to go into all the world. Many of their student friends are feeling the call to full-time Christian service. There is a tendency to be open and thoughtful about one's life plans in view of Christ's just demands. And it is only natural that from such colleges there is a steady stream of young people whom God calls to the pastorate, the mission field, and to other phases of his work.

As I think over the friendships of college days I rejoice to name over many of my schoolmates who are now out in the work of the Lord, many of them filling places of considerable responsibility and trust.

In summary, then, many of us feel that because the Christian college confronts its students with the Christian view of God and man, because it mediates a positive urge to Christian Character, because it provides for its young people a Christian social life and invites them to consider a Christian life calling, evangelical people ought to feel like using to the greatest possible extent these advantages, and supporting these schools enthusiastically with their prayers and with their means.

Appendix I

Senior Administrators of Houghton, 1883–1972

Academic Year	Principal	Academic Dean	Dean of Men	Dean of Women	Dean of Students	Chair of Trustees
1884–85	W. H. Kennedy	—	—	—	—	—
1885–86	W. H. Kennedy	—	—	—	—	—
1886–87	A. R. Dodd	—	—	—	—	R. F. Dutcher
1887–88	A. R. Dodd	—	—	—	—	R. F. Dutcher
1888–89	A. R. Dodd	—	—	—	—	R. F. Dutcher
1889–90	A. R. Dodd	—	—	—	—	G. W. Sibley
1890–91	A. R. Dodd	—	—	—	—	R. F. Dutcher
1891–92	A. R. Dodd	—	—	—	—	R. F. Dutcher
1892–93	E. W. Bruce	—	—	—	—	R. F. Dutcher
(1893)	J. R. Hodges	—	—	—	—	R. F. Dutcher
1893–94	J. S. Luckey	—	—	—	—	R. F. Dutcher

Academic Year	President	Academic Dean	Dean of Men	Dean of Women	Dean of Students	Chair of Trustees
1894–95	J. S. Luckey	—	—	—	—	R. F. Dutcher
1895–96	S. W. Bond	—	—	—	—	A. T. Jennings
1896–97	S. W. Bond	—	—	—	—	A. T. Jennings
1897–98	S. W. Bond	—	—	—	—	A. T. Jennings
1898–99	S. W. Bond	—	—	—	—	A. T. Jennings
1899–00	S. W. Bond	—	—	—	—	A. T. Jennings
1900–01	S. W. Bond	—	—	—	—	A. T. Jennings
1901–02	S. W. Bond	—	—	—	—	A. T. Jennings
1902–03	S. W. Bond	—	—	—	—	A. T. Jennings
1903–04	S. W. Bond	—	—	—	—	A. T. Jennings
1904–05	S. W. Bond	—	—	—	—	A. T. Jennings

Academic Year	President	Academic Dean	Dean of Men	Dean of Women	Dean of Students	Chair of Trustees
1905–06	S. W. Bond	—	—	—	—	A. T. Jennings
1906–07	S. W. Bond	—	—	—	—	A. T. Jennings
1907–08	S. W. Bond	—	—	—	—	A. T. Jennings
1908–09	J. S. Luckey	—	—	V. M. Jennings	—	A. T. Jennings
1909–10	J. S. Luckey	—	—	V. M. Jennings	—	A. T. Jennings
1910–11	J. S. Luckey	—	R. E. Rindfusz	C.E. Carroll	—	A. T. Jennings
1911–12	J. S. Luckey	—	R. E. Rindfusz	B. Thurston	—	A. T. Jennings
1912–13	J. S. Luckey	—	R. E. Rindfusz	B. Thurston	—	A. T. Jennings
1913–14	J. S. Luckey	—	—	B. Thurston	—	E. G. Dietrich
1914–15	J. S. Luckey	—	—	B. Thurston	—	E. G. Dietrich
1915–16	J. S. Luckey	—	—	B. Thurston	—	E. G. Dietrich
1916–17	J. S. Luckey	—	—	G. B. Thurston	—	E. G. Dietrich
1917–18	J. S. Luckey	—	H. B. Hester	F. B. Kelly	—	E. G. Dietrich
1918–19	J. S. Luckey	—	H. B. Hester	F. B. Kelly	—	E. G. Dietrich
1919–20	J. S. Luckey	—	H. L. Fancher	F. B. Kelly	—	E. G. Dietrich
1920–21	J. S. Luckey	—	F. H. Wright	—	—	E. G. Dietrich
1921–22	J. S. Luckey	—	F. H. Wright	—	—	E. G. Dietrich
1922–23	J. S. Luckey	W. L. Fancher	F. H. Wright	—	—	E. G. Dietrich
1923–24	J. S. Luckey	W. L. Fancher	F. H. Wright	A. J. Hampe	—	E. G. Dietrich

Academic Year	President	Academic Dean	Dean of Men	Dean of Women	Dean of Students	Chair of Trustees
1924–25	J. S. Luckey	W. L. Fancher	F. H. Wright	A. J. Hampe	—	E. G. Dietrich
1925–26	J. S. Luckey	W. L. Fancher	F. H. Wright	H. F. Davison	—	E. G. Dietrich
1926–27	J. S. Luckey	W. L. Fancher	F. H. Wright	H. F. Davison	—	E. G. Dietrich
1927–28	J. S. Luckey	W. L. Fancher	F. H. Wright	H. F. Davison	—	E. G. Dietrich
1928–29	J. S. Luckey	W. L. Fancher	F. H. Wright	A. L. Fillmore	—	J. S. Willett
1929–30	J. S. Luckey	W. L. Fancher	S. W. Wright	A. L. Fillmore	—	J. S. Willett
1930–31	J. S. Luckey	W. L. Fancher	S. W. Wright	A. L. Fillmore	—	J. S. Willett
1931–32	J. S. Luckey	W. L. Fancher	S. W. Wright	G. Kartevold	—	J. S. Willett
1932–33	J. S. Luckey	W. L. Fancher	S. W. Wright	G. Kartevold	—	J. S. Willett
1933–34	J. S. Luckey	W. L. Fancher	S. W. Wright	G. Kartevold	—	J. S. Willett
1934–35	J. S. Luckey	S. W. Paine	S. W. Wright	G. Kartevold	—	J. S. Willett
1935–36	J. S. Luckey	S. W. Paine	S. W. Wright	G. Kartevold	—	I. E. McLeister
1936–37	J. S. Luckey	S. W. Paine	S. W. Wright	I. Driscal	—	I. E. McLeister
1937–38	S. W. Paine	R. W. Hazlett	S. W. Wright	I. Driscal	—	I. E. McLeister
1938–39	S. W. Paine	R. W. Hazlett	S. W. Wright	I. Driscal	—	I. E. McLeister
1939–40	S. W. Paine	R. W. Hazlett	S. W. Wright	L. Hatch	—	I. E. McLeister
1940–41	S. W. Paine	R. W. Hazlett	S. W. Wright	L. Hatch	—	I. E. McLeister
1941–42	S. W. Paine	R. W. Hazlett	S. W. Wright	—	—	I. E. McLeister

Academic Year	President	Academic Dean	Dean of Men	Dean of Women	Dean of Students	Chair of Trustees
1942–43	S. W. Paine	R. W. Hazlett	G. E. Moreland	R. W. Prentice	—	I. E. McLeister
1943–44	S. W. Paine	P. F. Ashton	F. H. Wright	E. Beck	—	F. R. Eddy
1944–45	S. W. Paine	G. E. Moreland (acting)	F. H. Wright	E. Beck	—	F. R. Eddy
1945–46	S. W. Paine	P. E. Woolsey (acting)	F. H. Wright	E. Beck	—	F. R. Eddy
1946–47	S. W. Paine	P. E. Woolsey	F. H. Wright	E. Beck	—	F. R. Eddy
1947–48	S. W. Paine	L. A. King	F. H. Wright	E. Beck	—	R. S. Nicholson
1948–49	S. W. Paine	L. A. King	F. H. Wright	E. Beck	—	R. S. Nicholson
1949–50	S. W. Paine	L. A. King	F. H. Wright	E. Beck	—	R. S. Nicholson
1950–51	S. W. Paine	A. W. Lynip	F. H. Wright	E. Beck	—	R. S. Nicholson
1951–52	S. W. Paine	A. W. Lynip	H. R. Brandt	V. Blake	—	R. S. Nicholson
1952–53	S. W. Paine	A. W. Lynip	H. R. Brandt	V. Blake	—	R. S. Nicholson
1953–54	S. W. Paine	A. W. Lynip	H. R. Brandt	V. Blake	—	R. S. Nicholson
1954–55	S. W. Paine	A. W. Lynip	R. O. Ferm	V. Blake	—	R. S. Nicholson
1955–56	S. W. Paine	A. W. Lynip	—	V. Blake	R. O. Ferm	R. S. Nicholson
1956–57	S. W. Paine	A. W. Lynip	—	V. Blake	R. O. Ferm	R. S. Nicholson
1957–58	S. W. Paine	A. W. Lynip	—	E. Rennick	B. T. Hall	R. S. Nicholson
1958–59	S. W. Paine	A. W. Lynip	—	E. Rennick	R. O. Ferm	R. S. Nicholson

Academic Year	President	Academic Dean	Dean of Men	Dean of Women	Dean of Students	Chair of Trustees
1959–60	S. W. Paine	A. W. Lynip	J. H. Mills	E. Rennick	—	R. S. Nicholson
1960–61	S. W. Paine	A. W. Lynip	J. H. Mills	E. Rennick	—	B. H. Phaup
1961–62	S. W. Paine	A. W. Lynip	—	E. Rennick	J. H. Mills	B. H. Phaup
1962–63	S. W. Paine	A. W. Lynip	—	E. Rennick	J. H. Mills	B. H. Phaup
1963–64	S. W. Paine	A. W. Lynip	—	L. Haller	J. H. Mills	B. H. Phaup
1964–65	S. W. Paine	A. W. Lynip	—	L. Haller	R. T. Fraser (Mills on leave)	B. H. Phaup
1965–66	S. W. Paine	A. W. Lynip	—	L. Haller	J. H. Mills	B. H. Phaup
1966–67	S. W. Paine	none listed	none listed	L. Haller	J. H. Mills	B. H. Phaup
1967–68	S. W. Paine (on sabbatical; R. R. Luckey acting president)	B. H. Hall (acting)	none listed	L. Haller	J. H. Mills	B. H. Phaup
1968–69	S. W. Paine	M. E. Dieter	none listed	I. Rogato	J. H. Mills	B. H. Phaup
1969–70	S. W. Paine	C. W. Thomas	—	I. Rogato	P. Steese	B. H. Phaup
1970–71	S. W. Paine	C. W. Thomas	—	—	J. H. Mills	M. H. Snyder
1971–72	S. W. Paine	C. W. Thomas	—	—	J. H. Mills	M. H. Snyder

Appendix J

Honorary Degree Recipients, 1937–1972

Alphabetical Listing of Honorary Degree Recipients, 1936–1972

A college is defined by the persons it graduates and by the
individuals chosen for honrary degrees.

— Anonymous

Date	Name	Degree	Date	Name	Degree
1969	John D. Abbott	DD	1946	D. Leigh Colvin	LLD
1972	John B. Anderson	LLD	1965	Robert A. Cook	PdD
1966	Myron Shenk Augsburger	LLD	1955	James Francis Cooke	DFA
1949	H. Clark Bedford	DD	1936	Herman Cooper	LLD
1952	James N. Bedford (Sem.)	DD	1958	Ernest L. Crocker '27	DD
1965	Allyn R. Bell, Jr.	LLD	1969	Alton M. Cronk '30	DFA
1939	Gordon Knox Bell	LLD	1964	Malcolm R. Cronk '35	DD
1950	Frank R. Birch	DD	1946	Rutherford Decker	LLD
1951	John Bolten	LLD	1943	Harold Dieter	DD
1961	Harold W. Boon '36	LLD	1964	Melvin Easterday Dieter	LLD
1942	Philinda S. Bowen (Sem.)	LLD	1953	Glen Donelson '36	DD
1959	Myron F. Boyd	LittD	1945	Enoch C. Dryness	LLD
1968	Charles Wesley Bradley	DD	1956	Everett Dyer '29	PdD
1945	J. Wesley Bready	LLD	1962	Ruth E. Eckert	LittD
1971	William R. Bright	LittD	1937	Francis R. Eddy	DD
1959	H. Clifford Bristow '32	DD	1941	V. Raymond Edman	LLD
1969	H. Myron Bromley '48	LittD	1967	Elmer William Engstrom	LLD
1936	J. Oliver Buswell	LLD	1960	George E. Failing '40	LittD
1958	Charles Irving Carpenter	DD	1946	Charles V. Fairbairn	LLD
1971	Joel H. Carroll	LLD	1953	Mark Fakkema	LittD
1940	Russell Carter	LLD	1937	Paul Fall '08 Sem	LLD
1951	Mary Lane Clarke	LittD	1956	Bess M. Fancher	PdD
1965	Arthur M. Climenhaga	LLD	1955	H. LeRoy Fancher	LittD

Date	Name	Degree	Date	Name	Degree
1948	Dwight Ferguson	DD	1943	Robert Jones, Jr.	LLD
1952	Robert Findley*	LittD	1963	Walter H. Judd	LLD
1962	Leighton Ford	DD	1949	Kenneth S. Keyes	LLD
1965	Harry C. France	PdD	1966	Eugene L. Kierstead	DD
1960	Frank E. Gaebelein	LLD	1956	Paul L. Kindshi	DD
1963	Gustav-Adolf Gedat	LLD	1971	Dennis F. Kinlaw	LLD
1963	Kenneth E. Geiger	DD	1958	Wesley L. Knapp	LLD
1959	Charles Goodell	LLD	1972	Stanley Sebastian Kresge	LLD
1956	Woodrow I. Goodman	LLD	1970	Harold Barnes Kuhn	DD
1950	William F. Graham	LLD	1952	Robert G. Lee	LittD
1938	Frank Peirpont Graves	LLD	1960	Alton E. Liddick	DD
1970	Wilson Greatbatch	ScD	1968	Carl Wesley Lovin	DD
1938	Joe Hanley	LLD	1945	Walter A. Maier	LLD
1957	William K. Harrison	LittD	1939	Leslie R. Marston	LLD
1959	Mark O. Hatfield	LLD	1954	B. Joseph Martin	LLD
1942	Herbert E. Hawkes	LLD	1940	Harold C. Mason	LLD
1957	Ray W. Hazlett	LittD	1938	E. F. McCarty	DD
1972	Orley R. Herron	LittD	1939	William F. McConn	DD
1950	Ward M. Hopkins	LLD	1936	Ira Ford McLeister	DD
1945	C. N. Hostetter	DD	1951	Herbert S. Mekeel	LLD
1937	Phillip E. Howard	LLD	1952	Ted Mercer	LittD
1968	George A. Huff '42	DD	1964	Virgil A. Mitchell	DD
1963	James Roger Hull	LLD	1964	W. Stanley Mooneyham	LittD
1948	J. H. Hunter	LLD	1966	George Edward Moreland	PdD
1971	Adolph H. Hutter	LLD	1950	Rhett C. Mullinax	DD
1947	T. Christie Innes	LLD	1968	George A. Newbury	LLD
1964	Mabel Hinde James	PdD	1944	Roy S. Nicholson	DD
1948	Z. T. Johnson	DD	1947	Harold J. Ockenga	DD

*not in alumni list

Date	Name	Degree	Date	Name	Degree
1966	Stephen Frederick Olford	LittD	1950	John Robert Swauger	DD
1962	John Ottley Percy	DD	1972	A. Wingrove Taylor	DD
1954	Daniel T. Perrine	DD	1960	Clyde W. Taylor	LLD
1937	Frederick C. Perry	LLD	1947	Herbert J. Taylor	LLD
1957	Paul P. Petticord	LLD	1958	J. Paul Taylor	LittD
1961	Bernard H. Phaup	DD	1940	Theos Thompson '12 Sem	LLD
1961	Alan Redpath	DD	1952	A. W. Tozer	LLD
1941	Daniel A. Reed	LLD	1955	David T. Tsutada	DD
1954	David A. Rees '27	DD	1956	H. Park Tucker	DD
1953	Paul S. Rees	LittD	1955	Harry L. Turner	DD
1951	Rufus Reisdorph	DD	1954	Frank L. Tuthill	PdD
1968	Athol Railton Richardson	LLD	1962	John Walden Tysinger	DD
1965	Claude A. Ries	DD	1969	Roger John Voskuyl	LittD
1956	George Beverly Shea	DFA	1944	Kenneth P. Wesche	DD
1953	Harold K. Sheets	DD	1956	George M. Wilson	LittD
1972	Thomas Skinner	DD	1957	Kenneth Lee Wilson '41	LittD
1946	Oswald J. Smith	LLD	1949	Oliver G. Wilson	DD
1967	Timothy Lawrence Smith	LittD	1950	Frank Herbert Wright	DD
1972	Willard G. Smith '35	LLD	1941	William H. Wrighton	LLD
1961	Edwin G. Spahr	DD	1970	Luther W. Youngdahl	LLD
1962	Frank Bateman Stanger	LLD			

Analysis of Honorary Degrees Awarded by Houghton College, 1936–1972			
Degree Recipients	**1936–48**	**1949–60**	**1961–72**
Wesleyan Officials	5	11	7
Officials: Other Denominatons	6	8	3
Officials: Other Colleges	12	6	9
Officials: Special Ministries	4	7	3
Missionaries/Evangelists	0	4	4
Public Officials	5	7	6
Civic/Business Figures	1	3	8
Major Donors	0	0	1
Houghton Figures	1	6	7
Miscellaneous/Insufficient Biographical Data	2	3	2
Total Degrees Awarded	36	55	50
Houghton Alumni*	2	6	6

*These individuals are included above.
Note: Data are not precise, due to incomplete details, multiple options, and some assumptions.

Date	Recipients of Honorary Degrees from Houghton College (The charter of Houghton College was amended on July 17, 1936 to allow it to grant honarary degrees.)	
Date	**Name**	**Degree**
1936	**Ira Ford McLeister,** Wesleyan pastor; Wesleyan Methodist Sunday school secretary and editor, 1919–1927; editor of *The Wesleyan Methodist* 1927–1943; president of the Book Committee and president of Houghton's board of trustees, 1935–1943.	D.D.
	Herman Cooper, PhD, Assistant Commissioner of Education for the State of New York.	LL.D.
	James Oliver Buswell Jr., PhD, Northern Presbyterian pastor; chaplain in World War I; president of Wheaton College, 1926–40 (including Stephen W. Paine's undergraduate days).	LL.D.
	[Note: These three honorary degrees were the only ones conferred by Houghton president J. S. Luckey, who died on April 7, 1937.]	
1937	**Francis R. Eddy,** Chair, Wesleyan Committee on Education, 1923–1927; Connectional evangelist, 1927–1931; Sunday School secretary and editor, 1931–1935; publishing agent, 1935–1939; president, Wesleyan General Conference, 1939–47; agent, Wesleyan Methodist Publishing Association, 1939–1959; served on committee to examine union with Pilgrim Holiness Church.	D.D. LL.D.
	Phillip E. Howard, Publisher, Sunday School Times.	LL.D.
	Paul H. Fall, '08 (Sem.); PhD, Cornell, Science teacher (chemistry) at Houghton (1909-13), Oberlin, Kent State; president, Hiram (Ohio) College 1940–1957.	LL.D.
	Frederick C. Ferry, NYS Board of Regents; active supporter of Houghton's state charter. D.D.	LL.D.
1938	**Frank Pierrepont Graves,** Commissioner of Education for the State of New York and president of the University of the State of New York; author, history of education text.	LL.D.
	Elmer F. McCarty, Wesleyan pastor; Foreign Field Secretary, 1919–23; Foreign Mission Secretary 1923–44; missionary to Sierra Leone 1944–47.	D.D.

	Joe R. Hanley, Minister; lawyer; state senator, 44th district, New York.	LL.D.
1939	**Gordon Knox Bell,** Industrialist.	LL.D.
	Leslie Ray Marston, PhD, Univ. of Illinois; Free Methodist bishop; president of Greenville College 1927–1936; NAE president; chaired World Relief Commission.	LL.D.
	William F. McConn, President of Miltonvale College, 1924–1931; president of Marion College, 1932–1960.	D.D.
1940	**Russell Carter,** Supervisor of public school music, New York State Education Department.	LL.D.
	Harold C. Mason, DD, Huntingdon College; EdD, Indiana University; pastor and bishop, Church of the United Brethren in Christ; professor at Asbury Seminary and at Northern Baptist Theological Seminary; author.	LL.D.
	Theos J. Thompson, '12 (Sem.), Professor of chemistry; dean of student affairs, University of Nebraska.	LL.D.
1941	**Daniel A. Reed,** Former football coach at Cornell; Congressman, 43rd district, New York.	LL.D.
	V. Raymond Edman, PhD, Clark; professor of political science; president of Wheaton College, 1940–65; a founder of NAE.	LL.D.
	William H. Wrighton, Pastor; chair, philosophy department, University of Georgia.	LL.D.
1942	**Philinda Sprague Bowen,** Widow of Rev. James Henry Bowen; Seminary teacher 1908–17; Seminary principal 1917–1942. First woman to receive a Houghton honorary doctorate. Honored as one of Houghton's Centennial 100.	LL.D.
	Herbert E. Hawkes, PhD, Yale; dean, Columbia University; "champion of liberal arts education"; president, Association of Colleges and Universities, 1934–35; chair, American Council of Education, 1938–39.	LL.D.

1943	**Harold Dieter,** President of Allentown Bible Institute (later United Wesleyan College) for thirteen years; secretary of first committee established to discuss merger with Pilgrim Holiness Church.	D.D.
	Robert Jones, Jr., Acting president of Bob Jones University.	LL.D.
1944	**Roy Stephen Nicholson Sr.,** Pastor, North Carolina conference, 10 years; WYPS Superintendent, 1931–35; Wesleyan Methodist Sunday School secretary and editor, 1935–39; Home Missionary secretary, 1939–43; Connectional editor, 1943–47; General Conference president, 1947–1959; chair, Houghton board of trustees, 1947–1960 ; chair, Division of Religion, Central Wesleyan College, 1959–1968; author, *History of the Wesleyan Methodist Church.*	D.D.
	Kenneth Paul Wesche, DD, Asbury Seminary; professor of missions and church history, Asbury Theological Seminary; missionary to China 1932–1944.	D.D.
1945	**Walter A. Maier,** Radio speaker, Lutheran Church (Missouri Synod).	LL.D.
	Enoch C. Dryness, Registrar, Wheaton College.	LL.D.
	John Wesley Bready, Historian, British; author of *England Before and After Wesley* and *This Freedom Whence.*	LL.D.
	Christian N. Hostetter Jr., President, Messiah Bible College.	D.D.
1946	**Mrs. D. Leigh Colvin,** National president of the Women's Christian Temperance Union.	LL.D.
	Charles V. Fairbairn, Free Methodist bishop.	LL.D.
	Oswald J. Smith, Pastor of People's Church, Toronto; missions proponent; speaker, writer.	LL.D.
	Rutherford L. Decker, Pastor, Temple Baptist Church, Kansas City, Missouri; a founder of Denver Rescue Mission and Conservative Baptist Foreign Mission Society (degree conferred in absentia).	LL.D.

Year	Recipient	Degree
1947	**T. Christie Innes,** Pastor; evangelist; general secretary, American Tract Society.	LL.D.
	Harold J. Ockenga, (Taylor '27) PhD, Univ. of Pittsburgh; pastor, Park Street Congregational Church, Boston, for thirty-three years; a founder and the first president of NAE; co-founder and president of Fuller Theological Seminary; president, Gordon College.	D.D.
	Herbert J. Taylor, President of Club Aluminum; president, Rotary International; originator of Rotary's "Four-Way Test."	LL.D.
1948	**Dwight H. Ferguson,** BA, Asbury College; evangelist; Wesleyan and C&MA pastor.	D.D
	Z. T. Johnson, President, Asbury College.	D.D.
	J. H. Hunter, Author; editor of *Evangelical Christian,* Toronto.	LL.D.
1949	**Kenneth S. Keyes,** Businessman; president, Keyes Company, Realtors of Miami (Fla); president, National Institute of Real Estate Boards.	LL.D.
	Oliver G. Wilson, Teacher at Miltonvale College, 1929–43; Wesleyan Methodist Sunday school secretary and editor, 1943–47; editor of *The Wesleyan Methodist,* 1949–1959; elected a general superintendent in 1959.	D.D.
	Henry Clark Bedford, Seminary '02, MA, Seminary teacher for thirteen years; president of Alumni Association 1902–06; president, Central College (S.C.), 1915–19; first president of Marion College (1919–22); spearheaded construction of Bedford gym. Honored as one of Houghton's Centennial 100.	D.D.
1950	**Frank Richard Birch,** Missionary to Sierra Leone, 1919–1944; Wesleyan world missions secretary, 1943–1959.	D.D.
	William F. "Billy" Graham, International evangelist; 1950 commencement speaker.	LL.D.
	Rhett Clifton Mullinax, MA, Wesleyan pastor; member, Board of Administration 1947–1951; President, Central Wesleyan College, 1948–1968.	D.D.

	John Robert Swauger, BS, Asbury; Wesleyan Methodist Home Missionary Secretary, 1943–1955; Editor, *The American Holiness Journal;* President, Allegheny Conference, 1935–1943.	D.D.
	Frank Herbert Wright, BD, Alfred University, Professor of theology and chair of the Division of Theology and Christian Education; Houghton service 1921–1952. Honored as one of Houghton's Centennial 100.	D.D.
	Ward Morris Hopkins, BA, University of Michigan, Allegany County judge, 1936–1958; founding member of Houghton development committee, 1949; president, First National Bank of Cuba (N.Y.).	LL.D.
1951	**Rufus D. Reisdorph**, BA, Marion; MA, Vanderbilt; Wesleyan Methodist Sunday school secretary and editor, 1937–1943 and 1947–59;chaplain, U.S. Army, 1943–46; president, Miltonvale College, 1946–1948; editor of Sunday school literature, 1947–59; general superintendent, 1959–1963; later served in Philippines.	D.D.
	Herbert S. Mekeel, Former NAE president; pastor of First Presbyterian Church, Schenectady.	LL.D.
	John Bolten, German immigrant; Christian author and speaker; founder of the Bolta Co., Lawrence, Massachusetts.	LL.D.
	Mary Lane Clarke, Seminary teacher '95–'00; first Houghton Seminary missionary (Sierra Leone); edited Limba dictionary. Honored as one of Houghton's Centennial 100.	Litt.D.
1952	**A. W. Tozer**, Pastor, C&MA church in Chicago; author and lecturer; editor of *The Alliance Weekly*.	LL.D.
	Ted Mercer, Vice president, Bob Jones University; president, Bryant College, Tennessee.	Litt.D.
	Robert E. Lee, Pastor, Bellevue Baptist Church, Memphis.	Litt.D.
	James N. Bedford, President of Buffalo Bible Institute at time of merger with Houghton. LL.D.	D.D.

1953	**Paul Stromberg Rees,** MA, University of Southern California; DD, Asbury College; pastor, Evangelical Covenant Church; author, conference speaker; revivalist.	Litt.D.
	Mark Fakkema	Litt.D.
	Harold K. Sheets, MA, Phillips; Wesleyan pastor; general secretary, Wesleyan Youth, 1943–1955; Home Missions secretary, 1955–1959; general superintendent, 1959–1968.	D.D.
	Glen Donelson '36, Methodist pastor; superintendent of United Methodist Erie district for sixteen years.	D.D.
1954	**Frank L. Tuthill,** Principal, Fillmore High School, 1907–1918; Allegany county school superintendent 1918–1953; Houghton charter advocate before Wesleyan Educational Board, 1923.	Pd.D.
	B. Joseph Martin, President, Wesleyan College (Macon, Ga.); president, Taylor University.	LL.D.
	Daniel T. Perrine, Wesleyan pastor; president, Michigan Conference 1923–1952.	D.D.
	David A. Rees '27, MA (Syracuse), President of Rochester Conference; associate Publishing Agent 1945–; sixty-four years of Wesleyan pastoral service.	D.D.
1955	**Herbert LeRoy Fancher,** Sem '10; BA Oberlin; MA, Cornell, Professor of German forty-three years; Houghton vice president for academics. Honored as one of Houghton's Centennial 100.	Litt.D.
	David T. Tsutada, Japanese Christian leader; incarcerated for his faith during World War II; founder of Immanuel General Mission (affiliated with Wesleyan Church); first Japanese national to be honored (son John honored in 1984).	D.D.
	Harry L. Turner, Free Methodist pastor; author and lecturer.	D.D.
	James Francis Cooke, Editor of *Etude* for forty-three years; president of Presser Foundation for thirty-seven years; recipient of fourteen other doctorates.	D.F.A.

1956	**Paul L. Kindshi,** Graduate of Miltonvale College; Wesleyan pastor; president, Iowa Conference 1949–1954; executive director, National Holiness Association, 1954–1960; executive secretary, Sunday Schools, 1959–1972.	D.D.
	Woodrow I. Goodman, MA, Wheaton, Registrar at Houghton; founding president of Bethel College, 1947 –1960; president of Marion College, 1960–1976; concurrently president of Owosso College 1969–70.	LL.D.
	Bess M. Fancher, MA, Univ. of Chicago, Professor of education; Houghton service 1918–1955. Honored as one of Houghton's Centennial 100.	Pd.D.
	Everett Dyer '29, Executive director, New York State School Boards Association; trustee, Green Mountain College.	Pd.D.
	George Beverly Shea '32, Sacred recording artist; soloist with Billy Graham Evangelistic Association; 1973 Alumnus of the Year (family). Honored as one of Houghton's Centennial 100.	D.F.A.
	H. Park Tucker, Attended Houghton after losing an arm in a coal mining accident; chaplain, U.S penitentiary in Atlanta.	D.D.
	George M. Wilson, Business manager, Billy Graham Evangelistic Association; a founder, Youth for Christ.	Litt.D.
1957	**William K. Harrison,** Lt. Gen., US Army (Ret.); former chief of staff for Far East and United Nations Command; negotiator of Korean armistice.	Litt.D.
	Paul Parker Petticord, President, National Association of Evangelicals; president, Western Evangelical Seminary.	LL.D.
	Ray William Hazlett, Sem. '14, MA, Oberlin, professor of English at Long Island U; professor of English and chair of the Division of English; Houghton service 1923–1926, 1938–1957. Honored as one of Houghton's Centennial 100.	Litt.D.
	Kenneth Lee Wilson '41, Christian writer and editor of *Christian Herald.* Honored as one of Houghton's Centennial 100.	Litt.D.

1958	**J. Paul Taylor,** Free Methodist bishop; long-time speaker on "The Light and Life Hour," Free Methodist radio program.	Litt.D.
	Charles Irving Carpenter, MA, Drew, Maj. Gen.; chief of chaplains, U. S. Air Force.	D.D.
	Ernest L. Crocker, Wesleyan pastor; Houghton trustee; president, Western Michigan Conference 1952–1962.	D.D.
	Wesley L. Knapp, Wesleyan pastor and educator; president of Miltonvale College, 1952–1969.	LL.D.
1959	**Myron F. Boyd,** Free Methodist bishop; radio speaker, "The Light and Life Hour."	Litt.D.
	Mark O. Hatfield, MA, Stanford, Christian layman; Governor of Oregon; U.S. Senator from Oregon.	LL.D.
	Charles I. Goodell, Christian layman; U.S. Representative from N.Y. thirty-fourth district (Houghton area).	LL.D.
	H. Clifford Bristow, Chaplain, USAF; served in Europe and Africa in World War II.	D.D.
1960	**George E. Failing '40**, MA, Duke; PhD, Syracuse, Wesleyan minister; HC instructor and director of public relations 1947–53; editor of *The Wesleyan Methodist* 1959–68 and of *The Wesleyan Advocate* 1973–84. Honored as one of Houghton's Centennial 100.	Litt.D.
	Clyde W. Taylor, an NAE founder; secretary, Evangelical Foreign Missions Association; missionary in Colombia and Peru.	LL.D.
	Alton E. Liddick, Wesleyan minister and missionary in India; executive secretary, Wesleyan World Missions, 1959–1968, HC Book Store manager and director of public relations 1952–54. Honored as one of Houghton's Centennial 100.	D.D.
	Frank E. Gaebelein, Educator; founder, Stony Brook School.	LL.D.
1961	**Bernard H. Phaup,** Graduate of Central Wesleyan; Wesleyan pastor; 1932–1953; general superintendent, The Wesleyan Church, 1959–1973.	D.D.

	Alan Redpath, Pastor in Surrey, England; top rugby player; trustee, Columbia (N.C.) Bible College; pastor, Moody Memorial Church, Chicago.	D.D.
	Edwin G. Spahr, Accountant for Girard Trust (Philadelphia), then of Standard Oil; became missionary in Manila.	D.D.
	Harold W. Boon '36, PhD, HC alumni field representative and instructor; professor and president of Nyack Missionary College. Honored as one of Houghton's Centennial 100.	LL.D.
1962	**John Ottley Percy,** General secretary, Interdenominational Foreign Missions Association; SIM missionary to Nigeria; head of SIM US.	D.D.
	John Walden Tysinger, Wesleyan pastor; Houghton Academy principal at time of separation of campuses.	D.D.
	Frank Bateman Stanger, President, Asbury Seminary; professor, evangelist, Methodist administrator.	LL.D.
	Ruth E. Eckert (Paulsen), Educator; chair, Department of Higher Education, University of Minnesota; native of Buffalo.	Litt.D.
	Leighton Ford, Evangelist; Billy Graham's brother-in-law.	D.D.
1963	**Gustav-Adolf Gedat,** YMCA leader for Germany; arrested by Gestapo; in 1953 elected to German Bundestag; helped found International Christian Leadership in Germany.	LL.D.
	Walter H. Judd, Christian layman; U.S. Representative from Minnesota.	LL.D.
	Kenneth E. Geiger, General superintendent, United Missionary Church; president, National Holiness Association.	D.D.
	James Roger Hull, President, Mutual of New York Insurance Co.	LL.D.
1964	**Malcolm R. Cronk** '35, Minister and teacher, Wesleyan churches; Wheaton Bible Church; Church of the Open Door; professor at Trinity Seminary. Honored as one of Houghton's Centennial 100.	D.D.

	Virgil A. Mitchell, BTh, Central Wesleyan; Wesleyan pastor; president of South Carolina Conference 1949–1957; executive secretary of church extension, 1959–1963; general superintendent 1963–1984.	D.D.
	W. Stanley Mooneyham, Special assistant to Billy Graham	Litt.D.
	Melvin Easterday Dieter, PhD, First Wesleyan Educational Secretary; president, Allentown-United Wesleyan College; provost and vice president, Asbury Seminary; chair, Houghton College trustees.	LL.D.
	Mabel Hinde James, Conservation activist; helped establish Moss Lake sanctuary.	Pd.D.
1965	Arthur M. Climenhaga, (Taylor '38) President, Upland (Calif.) College, Brethren in Christ missionary to Rhodesia; NAE executive secretary; dean, Western Evangelical Seminary; president, Messiah College.	LL.D.
	Robert A. Cook, President, Youth for Christ; president, The King's College.	Pd.D.
	Claude A. Ries, ThD, Wesleyan minister, professor of Greek and Bible, and chair of the Division of Theology and Christian Education; Houghton service 1924–1963. Honored as one of Houghton's Centennial 100.	D.D.
	Harry C. France, Investment counselor; author, "Investors' Forum" newspaper column; faculty, NYU; U.S. Treasury officer.	Pd.D.
	Allyn R. Bell Jr., Pew Foundation officer.	LL.D.
1966	George Edward Moreland, PhD, professor of zoology and chair of Division of Science and Mathematics; Houghton service 1941–1966. Honored as one of Houghton's Centennial 100.	Pd.D.
	Stephen Frederick Olford, Author; pastor, Calvary Baptist Church, New York City.	Litt.D.
	Eugene L. Kierstead, BTh, Marion College, 1934; Wesleyan pastor; president of Indiana Conference 1949–59; business manager, Wesley Press 1959–1968.	D.D.

	Myron Shenk Augsburger, Evangelist; author; president, Eastern Mennonite College; president, Christian College Coalition.	LL.D.
1967	**Timothy Lawrence Smith,** Professor of history at The Johns Hopkins University; author of *Revivalism and Social Reform: American Protestantism on the Eve of the Civil War*; was giving Houghton commencement address as Israeli Six-Day War broke out.	Litt.D.
	Elmer William Engstrom, CEO of RCA Corporation.	LL.D.
1968	**Athol Railton Richardson,** Judge, Supreme Court of New South Wales, Australia; general synod member, Church of England	LL.D.
	Carl Wesley Lovin, Graduate of Central Wesleyan; Wesleyan pastor; Department of Extension and Evangelism, The Wesleyan Church 1963–1968; National Wesleyan Youth President; district superintendent, North Carolina.	D.D.
	Charles Wesley Bradley, Wesleyan pastor; district superintendent, Middle States; secretary, Houghton trustees.	D.D.
	George A. Huff '42, Missionary to Sierra Leone, 1945–59 ; district superintendent, Western Michigan; HC development director.	D.D.
	George A. Newbury, Buffalo attorney, businessman, civic leader; executive vice president of M&T Bank.	LL.D.
1969	**John D. Abbott,** Pastor, Pilgrim Holiness Church; district superintendent, Eastern District 1953–1960; secretary, Sunday Schools and Youth 1960–62; general secretary and treasurer 1962–68; general superintendent, Pilgrim Holiness and Wesleyan Churches 1966–88.	D.D.
	Roger John Voskuyl, President, Westmont College; head, Council for Advancement of Small Colleges (now CIC).	Litt.D.
	H. Myron Bromley '48; PhD, Yale, Linguist; C&MA missionary to West Irian; did pioneer work on Bible translation.	Litt.D.

	Alton M. Cronk '30, Chair, Houghton College music division; chair, music department, Wheaton College.	D.F.A.
1970	**Wilson Greatbatch**, BA, Cornell; MS, SUNY at Buffalo, Inventor of the implantable heart pacemaker; adjunct professor of physical science; Houghton service since 1968.	Sc.D.
	Harold Barnes Kuhn, Wesleyan pastor; professor, Asbury Seminary; editorial board, *Christianity Today.*	D.D.
	Luther W. Youngdahl, Judge, U.S. District Court, Washington D.C., since 1951; three-term governor of Minnesota.	LL.D.
1971	**William R. Bright**, Founder, Campus Crusade for Christ.	Litt.D.
	Dennis F. Kinlaw, President, Asbury College; evangelist; Bible teacher.	LL.D.
	Adolph H. Hutter, Austrian emigrant; special attorney, U.S. Justice Department; a founder of Evangelical Adoption and Family Service and Faith Heritage School (Syracuse).	LL.D.
	Joel H. Carroll, Central N.Y. businessman; trustee, Keuka College; major Houghton donor.	LL.D.
1972	**John B. Anderson**, Christian layman; U.S. Representative from Illinois.	LL.D.
	Thomas Skinner, African-American evangelist.	D.D.
	A. Wingrove Taylor, Wesleyan pastor; district superintendent, Caribbean; general superintendent of Carribean Provisional Conference 1974–1994.	D.D.
	Willard G. Smith '35, PhD, business manager and treasurer; Houghton service 1935–1972. Honored as one of Houghton's Centennial 100.	LL.D.
	Orley R. Herron, President, Greenville College (Illinois).	Litt.D.
	Stanley Sebastian Kresge, Founder and board chair, S.S. Kresge Company; chair, Kresge Foundation; instrumental in getting matching grants for several Houghton College buildings.	LL.D.

Legend

DCS	Doctor of Commercial Science	LHD	Doctor of Humane Letters
DD	Doctor of Divinity	MusD	Doctor of Music
DFA	Doctor of Fine Arts	PdD	Doctor of Pedagogy
LittD	Doctor of Letters	ScD	Doctor of Science
LLD	Doctor of Laws	STD	Doctor of Sacred Theology

Appendix K

Faculty Directory, 1884–1972

Faculty names were extracted from a set of cards assembled by Dr. W. G. Smith prior to his retirement in 1972. Degree information was taken from extant Houghton College catalogs. Degree shown is highest held (where known) during Houghton service. Class numerals, if shown, indicate Houghton alumnus.

Agee, Vance G. '71
BA Houghton College
1967–1969 German

Ahnell, Emil G.
MMus Northwestern Univ.
1952–1953 Piano Theory

Ahnell, Carol
*BMus New England
Conservatory of Music*
1952–1953 Flute

Alderman, Richard J. '52
MS Alfred University
1971–1985 Admissions,
Registrar, Alumni Affairs

Alexander, Helen I. '66
BA Houghton College
1967–1968 English

Alger, H. Raynard '46
*MAMusEd Teachers College,
Columbia Univ.*
1946–1951 Brass

Allen, Jane McMahon '61
*MMus Eastman School of
Music*
1964–1967 Piano

Allen, William T.
PhD Eastman School of Music
1953–1995 Piano; Composer
in Residence

Andrews, John M.
*MMus Eastman School of
Music*
1935–1979 Violin

Andrews, Lila M.
*BMus Eastman School of
Music*
1936–1971 Piano, Woodwinds

Angell, Edward
BD Capital Univ.
1953–1956 Theology
Pastor, Houghton Wesleyan
Church

Apel, Herbert E. '61
BA Houghton College
1961–1962 German and
English

* Archibald, A. R.
1920–1921 Theology

Arlin, Edith E. Noss
MA Univ. of Cincinnati
1930–1938 Latin and French

Ashton, Philip F.
PhD Univ. of Washington
1942–1944 Psychology
1943–1944 Dean of College

Austin, Robert C.
MA Middlebury College
1955–1966; 1972–1974
German

* Ayers, John
1941–1942 Biology

Bachus, Nancy
*MMus Eastman School of
Music*
1969–1974 Piano and Voice

Bailey, Donald L.
DA Univ. of Northern Colorado
1967–1982 Voice; Chair Div
of Fine Arts

Bain, Mary Freeman '31
BA Houghton College
1932–1939 Registrar

Bain, Wilfred C. '29
MA New York Univ.
1931–1938 Voice and Theory

Baker, Allen M. '25
BA Houghton College
1923–1932 French

Baker, Herman
BMus Northwestern Univ.
1926–1930 Voice

*‡ Baker, Susan J.
1888–1889 English.

Ball, Abbie A.
Emerson College of Oratory
1913–1915 Oratory

Ballard, Emelene (Hollenbach)
BA Houghton, RN
1931–*1932* Biology
1941–1943 Nurse

Bancroft, Peter
PhD Univ. of Colorado
1971–1976 Math

Barcus, James E. '59
PhD Univ. of Pennsylvania
1964–1980 English; Chair, Div
English and Speech

Barcus, Nancy
MA SUNY College at Geneseo
1964–1980 English

Barker, Vera
MLit Univ. of Pittsburg
1946–1951 History (Seminary)
1951–1952 History (College)

Barth, Elizabeth A. Samuelson '63
MA Univ. of Buffalo
1965–1967 Sociology

Basney, Eldon
Peabody Conservatory of Music
1951–1979 Music

Basney, Lionel '65
PhD Univ. of Rochester
1968–1985 English

Bean, Stanley '48
BA Houghton College
1950–1951 Sociology and
Economics

Beck, Elizabeth (Gilbert; later Feller)
MA University of Michigan
1944–1951 Dean of Women

Bedford, Frederick G. '50
MA Middlebury College
1960–1965 French

Bedford, H. Clark Sem '02
BA Oberlin College 1910
1901–1915 English, Math,
Greek, Latin

Bedford, John Nelson
A.M. Wheaton, D.D.
1897–1908 Theology

Bemis, Jack
MMus Eastman School of Music
1956–1958 Woodwinds

Benton, J. L. (Rev.)
1892–1895 Theology

Bisgrove, Mildred '42
MAMusEd Univ. of Pennsylvania
1943–1945 Piano

Blake, Viola '48
BA Houghton College
1951–1957 Dean of Women

* Boardman, Alice (later Smith)
1885–1887 Elocution and
Rhetoric

Boardman, Leland J. Sem '09
PhD Cornell Univ.
1923–1929 Physics, Math.,
Supt. of Bldgs.

* Boardman, Willard C.
1893–1894 Latin and History

Bolton, Charles A.
BD Louvain Univ.
1963–1966 French

Bond, Hattie West
BA, BS Wheaton
1896–1906 Ancient Languages

Bond, Silas W. (Rev.)
MA Wheaton
1895–1908 Principal,
President

† Boon, Harold '36
BA Houghton College
Social Science and Economics

Boon, J. Kenneth '62
PhD Kansas State Univ.
1964–2002 Biology

Bowen, Philinda Sprague
*Geneseo Normal School; LLD
Houghton College*
1889–1943 Latin, English;
Seminary Principal

† Bowen, Ward C.
MA
1916–1918 Science

Bowman, Allen
PhD Univ. of Michigan
1941–1942 History

* Brackett, Gertrude L.
BA
1931–1932 Mathematics

Brandt, Henry '47
PhD Cornell Univ.
1951–1954 Dean of Men

Bridgeman, Loraine I.
PhD Indiana Univ.
1968–1969 Linguistics

Bruce, Erwin W. (Rev.)
1892–1893 Principal, English
1905–1911 Theology

Budensiek, Mary E.
MA Univ. of Minnesota
1946–1954 Voice

* Buffington, Miss
1922–1923 Dean of Women

Burke, Ernest Douglas
MA Syracuse Univ.
1958–1994 Physical Education

Burnell, Dorah
MA Univ of Nebraska
1926–1955 Chemistry

Butler, Ruth
*MLS SUNY College at
Geneseo*
1969–1985 Librarian (BSC)

† Button, Gertrude
MSLS Albany State Univ.
1953–1954 Library

Butterworth, Donald
*MMus Eastman School of
Music*
1945–1950 Voice

‡ Caley, Wendell
1959 Physics and Mathematics

Calhoon, Stephen W. '53
PhD Ohio State University
1956–1973 Chemistry

Campbell, Alfred
BA Wheaton College
1961–1973 English

Carapetyan, Caro M.
MS Columbia Univ.
1941–1945 Voice

† Carapetyan, Edna G.
New York Piano Conservatory
1941–1945 Organ

Carey, Mary Harris '49
MSLS Pratt Institute
1968–1972 Library

Carpenter, Victor W. '63
MA Middlebury College
1963–1985 German, French

Carr, Robert A. '65
MS SUNY College at New Paltz
1969–1971 Mathematics

Carrier, Esther Jane
PhD Univ. of Michigan
1950–1979 Library

Carroll, Clarice E. (later Cofield)
BS
1911–1912 Dean of Sem Women; Hist, Bio.

Chen, James Pai-Fun '55
PhD Pennsylvania State Univ.
1960–1966 Chemistry

Cheney, L. Keith
MS Univ. of Michigan
1963–1975 Education

Christensen, Larry W.
PhD Purdue University
1969– Chemistry

Christy, W. Oliver '28
BA Houghton College
1928–1929 Mathematics

Clader, Durwood '40
BA Houghton College
1940–1942 Biology

Clark, Keith C.
U.S. Army Band
1966–1981 Brass

† Clarke, George H.
1906–1907 Business

Clarke, Mary L. Lane
1895–1896 Elementary
English and History
1896–1900 Rhet. Lit., German
(resigned 27 Jan 00 to go to Africa)
1902–1904 Rhetoric and Literature
1920–1923 Missionary Course

Clawson, Jennie E. Reid
1905–1907 Literature and English

Coen, Judith K.
BMus Eastman School of Music
1965–1969 Voice

Cole, Corinne E. '29 (later Frith)
BA Houghton College
1929–1932 Latin and French

* Cole, Joy B.
1922–1923 Voice

Coleman, John J. (Rev.)
BD
1912–1920 Theology

Cook, Arnold W. '43
MA East Tennessee State Univ.
1960–1985 Business Administration

Cook, E. Elizabeth '62
MS St. Bonaventure Univ.
1964–1985 Biology

Cory, Janice E.
MMus Univ. of Oklahoma
1969–1970 Organ

Coughlin, Joseph W.
PhD Michigan State Univ.
1971–1975 Education

Cox, P. Wayne
MA Univ. of Iowa
1971–1986 Sociology (BSC)

Cronk, Alton M. '30
MAMusEd New York Univ.
1931–1948 Piano

Cronk, Wenona Ware '34
BA Houghton College
1941–1948 English

Crosby, Norva Bassage '38
BA Houghton College
1963–1977 Spanish

Crosby, Robert L. '38
MA Universidad Internacional
1966–1977 Spanish

Crossley, Noralyn '62
BA Houghton College
1965–1967 English

* Crossman, Theodore E. '55
BA Houghton College
1958–1959 Botany

*‡ Crow, Effie
1890–1892 Music

Cummings, Robert L. '50
MA Univ. of Rochester
1962–1988 German

Davis, Abraham Jr. '55
PhD Univ. of Indiana
1961–1975 English

* Davis, Arthur
BA Houghton College
1950–1951 German

Davis, Charles M.
MA Univ. of Chicago
1953–1963 English

* Davis, Eva L.
1885–1887 English Dept.

Davis, Mildred J.
1918–1919 Oratory and Music

Davison, Rachel (see Fee)

Davy, Ralph
1895–1900 Sciences, Math
and History
1911–1912 Math

* Depew, Mary
1885 Governess

Dilks, Edith
MEd Rutgers Univ.
1935–1938 Education and
English

‡ Dirkes, Gilbert
1958–1959 English

Dodd, Augustus R. (Rev.)
1886–1892 Principal; Greek,
Higher Math

* Dodd, Mrs. Gussie C.
1886–1888 Art Dept and
Preceptresss

* Dodd, Nellie C.
1889–1890 German, Rhetoric,
Physiology

Doig, Donald C. '61
MMus Eastman School of Music
1964–1968 Voice

Doolittle, Charles E.
BS Pennsylvania State Univ.
1966–1969 Biology

Douglas, DeLeo S.
MA Univ. of Michigan
1940–1942 Latin

Douglas, Raymond E.
PhD Cornell University
1924–1940 Biology
Chair, Div. of Sciences and
Math

Dow, Elizabeth Hall
1901–1912 German

Dow, Mabel
1910–1911 Phys Geog, Ele
Alg, Physiol
1911–1912 Latin

Downs, Ralph A.
MS Brown Univ.
1969–1970 Biology

Driscal, Ione '27
BA Houghton College
1936–1940 English;
Dean of Women

† Dumm, Ruth
BA Asbury College
1947–1948 History

Duncan, Bryan L.
PhD Wayne State Univ.
1970–1972 Biology

Dunkle, Roberta M.
MA Wheaton College
1971–1881 Dean of Women

Eastman, Daniel R. '55
PhD Pennsylvania State Univ.
1962–1965 Physics

* Easton, Adella
1887–1893 Latin, Physiology,
German

Eastwood, Coralie F.
New England Conservatory
1911–1913 Voice

Ebner, Frederick A. '32
BA Houghton College
1931–1932 German

Eddy, Hazel M.
1919–1921 Voice, Piano

Edwards, Kamala D.
MA Jabalpur Univ.
1967–1969 English

* Eldridge, Beatrice
1919–1920 Oratory

Elliott, James W.
1915–1917 English, Greek

‡ Elliot, Everett (Rev.)
1958 Bible

Ellis, Malcolm E.
MA Butler Univ.
1969–1971 Bible

† Emerson, Wallace L.
*PhD Univ. of Southern
California*
1947–1948 Psychology

Erhard, Betty J. (later Groat)
BMus Houghton College
1947–1950 Voice

Eyler, Marvin H. '42
BA Houghton College
1946–1947 Physical Education

Failing, George E. '40
MA Duke Univ.
1947–1954 Theology, Public
Relations

Fair, Roberta G.
*MEd Indiana Univ. of
Pennsylvania*
1959–1971 Education

Fall, Paul H. Sem '13
PhD Cornell Univ.
1912–1916 Chemistry
(1909–1913?)

Fancher, Bessie M.
MA Univ. of Chicago
1918–1956 Mathematics,
Education

Fancher, Herbert LeRoy Sem '10
MA Cornell Univ.
1912–1955 French and German
1919–1922 Dean of Men
1954–1955 Vice Pres.

Fancher, Willard LaVay Sem '13
PhD Cornell Univ.
1919–1934 Science,
Economics
1923–1934 Vice President

Fancher, Zola K. '26
BA Houghton College
1929–1957 Economics,
Mathematics, Education

Farnsworth, Bessie V.
1908–1911 Music

Farwell, Richard '34
BA Houghton College
1960–1963 Registrar

Fee, Rachel Davison '25
MA Oberlin College
1925–1959 Mathematics;
Registrar

Fenton, Clara Tuttle
1906–1908 Music

Ferm, Lois M. Roughan '39
BA Houghton College
1957–1959 Education

Ferm, Robert O. '39
ThD Central Baptist Seminary
1954–1959 Dean of Men,
History

Fern, Terry
MMus Univ. of Louisville
1971–1974 Voice

Fillmore, Anna L.
1929–1932 Dean of Women

Finch, Judith B.
MS Canisius College
1969–1986 English (BSC)

Finney, Charles H.
PhD Eastman School of Music
1946–1979 Organ; Chair, Div.
of Fine Arts

* Fissher, Issalina
1890–1892 Art

Fitts, Grace
BMus Syracuse Univ.
1914–1916 Voice

Fletcher, Beatrice M. '48 (later
Benedict)
BMus Houghton College
1948–1949 Piano

Foust, Ethel L.
*MRE Biblical Seminary (New
York)*
1945–1950 Christian
Education.

Fraser, Robert L.
JD Univ. of Buffalo
1963–1971 Business Law
1964–1967 Dean of Students

Frazier, William F. Sem '09
BA Oberlin College 1910
1912–1915 Philosophy and
History

Gares, Carol E. '65
BA Houghton College
1967–1969 Physical Education

‡ Garrison, Clifford '57
EdD SUNY at Buffalo
1970–1972 Academic Dean
(BSC)

Gillette, Frieda A.
PhD Cornell Univ.
1923–1969 History
1944–1950 Acting chair, Div.
of History and Social Science
1951–1969 Chair, Div. of
History and Social Science

Gordon, Raymond '62
BA Houghton College
1963–1964 Linguistics

* Gott, Evelyn A.
1953–1954 Piano

Gould, Richard A. '61
PhD Princeton Univ.
1968– Classics

Graham, Mary Clark
BSLS
1944–1950 Library

† Green, Beulah M.
MA Univ. of Illinois
1948–1949 English

† Greenberg, Hannol (later Tarrell)
1912–1913 Latin

Greenway, William N.A.
MA Stetson Univ.
1962–1999 English

Greer, Norris
MMus Univ. of Michigan
1958–1968 Voice

† Griffiss, Mary Lou
BA Asbury College
1947–1948 Piano

† Grimes, Luta
New England Conservatory
1910–1911 Voice

† Gugger, Edward
MA Middlebury College
1958–1961 French

† Guiterrez, Melchor Reyes
*MS Kansas State Teachers
College*
1962–1964 Spanish

Hagwood, Thomas R.
MA Univ. of Virginia
1968–1970 English

Hale, Virgil '50
MMus Indiana Univ.
1951–1953 Voice

* Hall, A.W.
1899–1903 Spring terms
1905–1906 no info on position

Hall, Bert H. '42
*ThD Northern Baptist
Theological Sem.*
1947–1973 Theology,
Philosophy
1964–1965 Acting Dean of
Students
1965–1969 Acting Academic
Dean
1970–1973 Chair, Div. of
Religion and Philosophy

Haller, Lola
EdD Michigan State Univ.
1963–1968 Dean of Women
1969–1991 Education
1979–1985, Chair, Div of
Education and Psychology.

* Hamilton, James E. '63
BA Houghton College
1969–1970 Philosophy

† Hamilton, Margaret J.
BSMusEd Houghton College
1944–1945 Piano

‡ Handyside, Hattie
1888 Reading

Harding, Thomas
*MS Case-Western Reserve
Univ.*
1968–1973 Physics

Hazlett Ray W. Sem '14
MA Oberlin College
1923–1926 English
1938–1957 English
1938–1943 Dean of College
1952–1957 Chair, English
Division

Henry, Carol J.
MMus Indiana University
1969–1971 Piano

Herr, Helen Louise
*BMus Westminster Choir
School*
1937–1938 Voice

Hester, Harold H.
BA Oberlin College 1914
1916–1919 Philosophy,
History, Greek
1918–1919 Dean of Men

* Hester, Maud
1918–1919 no other info

Heydenburk, David H.
BMus Oberlin College
1945–1951 Organ and Theory

Higdon, James M.
MMus Northwestern Univ.
1970–1973 Voice, Piano,
Organ

* Hildreth, D. M.
1923–1925 Music

Hill, Margaret J. Hamilton '44
BSMusEd Houghton College
1944–1947 Piano and Sacred
Music

* Hill, Pearl
1928–1929 Dean of Women

Hillpot, Ella M.
New England Conservatory
1911–1944 Piano
1934–1944 Chair, Music
Division

Hirsch, Helen K. Hubbard
EdD University of Pittsburgh
1960–1980 Christian
Education

Homan, Robert L. '39
BSMusEd Houghton College
1939–1946 Instr Brass and
Woodwind

Hopkins, Howard M.
1892–1895 Commercial,
Shorthand, Typing

Hostetter, Sarah '61
BMus Houghton College
1962–1964 Piano

Howard, David A.
PhD Duke Univ.
1969– History

Howard, Irmgard K.
PhD Duke Univ.
1970– Chemistry

* Hubbard, Dorothy E.
1923–1924 Music

† Hubbard, Helen K.
1960–1961 Christian education

* Hubbard, Junia
1926–1929 Art

* Huffman, Joseph A.
1932–*1933* Bible

Huibregtse, Richard A.
MA Univ. of Michigan
1970–1972 Political Science

Huizenga, C. Nolan
AMusD Univ. of Michigan
1958–1989 Piano

Hutchison, D. Warner
*MMus North Texas State
College*
1955–1958 Brass

Hutton, Lindol H. '57
MBA SUNY at Buffalo
1969–1975 Business Admin

Hutton, Ruth Fancher '43
MA Wheaton College
1962–1988 English and
Speech

Hynes, Gilbert S.
*MMus Boston Univ. College of
Music*
1953–1958 Voice

† Jackson, Ina R. '45
*MRE Asbury Theological
Seminary*
1951–1955 Christian
Education

Jacobson, Richard A.
*MA South Dakota School of
Mines*
1966– Mathematics

Jeffrey, Robert J. J.
1894–1895 Sciences

* Jennings, Etta
  1914–1917 Library

Jennings, Vera M.
  1907–1911 Elementary Course
  1908–1911 Dean of Sem
  Women; Art

Johannsen, Andrea
  BS New York Univ.
  1935–*1937* Voice

‡ Johnson, David
  1960–1961 Music/Organ

† Johnson, Royce O.
  1958–1959 Education

Johnson, Paul F.
  MEd Rhode Island College
  1972–1994 French
  1975–1985 Chair, Div. of
  Foreign Languages

‡ Johnson, Royce O.
  1958–1959 Education

Jones, Charles E.
  PhD Univ. of Wisconsin
  1969–1971 History

Kartevold, Gudrun
  *MRE Biblical Seminary of
  New York*
  1932–1937 Dean of Women

Kaufman, Willis M.
  MA Duke Univ.
  1966–1968 Chemistry

Kellogg, Marjorie Lawrence '60
  MA Middlebury College
  1960–1963 French

Kelly, Florence B.
  MA Univ. of Michigan
  1918–1921 Dean of Women,
  Eng and Hist
  1953 Library

Kennedy, William Henry (Rev.)
  1885 Principal

Killian, Charles D.
  BD Asbury Seminary
  1965–1967 Homiletics and
  Speech

Kimball, Roland C.
  MA Univ. of New Hampshire
  1957–1961 English

‡ Kindt, Charles N.
  1960–1961 English and
  History

King, J. Stanley
  *BMus Eastman School of
  Music*
  1933–1936 Instr Violin and
  Orch Inst.

King, Lauren A.
  PhD Ohio State Univ.
  1930–1931 English
  1946–1950 English; Dean of
  College

Kingdon, Douglas '57
  MS Buffalo State College
  1960–1963 Elementary
  Education

Kingdon, Harold E. '57
  DMin Bethel Seminary
  1967– Bible and Theology
  1998– Chair, Dept. of
  Religion and Philosophy

Kinlaw, Lorine
MA Duke Univ.
1949–1953 English

Kinney, Mrs. Dennison S.
1893–1894 Elocution and
English
1894–1895 English and
History

* Kitamura, Mitsuo
1968–1970 Voice

Kleis, Harold J.
MA Univ. of Michigan
1967–1969 Education

Kreckman, Alfred D.
*MMus Eastman School of
Music*
1930–1958 Piano and Choral
Music

Kreckman, Ellen E. '59
MSLS Syracuse Univ.
1961–1998 Library

Krehbiel, Carolyn
BA Otterbein College
1949–1951 Physical Education

Kutchukian, Sylvia
*MMus Eastman School of
Music*
1968–1972 Voice

Lane, Leila
1904–1905 Literature

Lane, Mary L. (see Clark)

‡ Langlie, Warren
1960–1961 Piano

Laughlin, B. S. (Rev.)
1888–1892 Bible Training
Class
1895–1897 Bible Training
Dept.

Lawless, Leo B.
BMus Syracuse Univ.
1927–1930 Piano and Theory

* Lawrence, Alexander
1922–1923 Greek and Science

* Lawrence, Elvira
1914–1915 Registrar

Leax, John R. '67
MA Johns Hopkins Univ.
1968– English; Poet in
Residence

* Lee, Harold
1921–1923 Science

Lennox, Edna E. Culp
MA Emerson College
1920–1925 Oratory, Public
Speaking
1944–1963 Public Speaking

Lennox, Ian H. '51
BA Houghton College
1956–1957 Sociology
1977– Trustee

Leonard, Frank L
BA Ohio Wesleyan Univ.
1935–1937 Physical
Education.

Lewis, Helen
MA Western Reserve Univ.
1964–1968 Elementary
Education.

Lienard, Estelle Reid
1905–1907 Music

Lindley, Katherine Walberger '43
PhD Univ. of Wisconsin
1963–1989 History
1974–1986 Chair, Div of
History and Social Science

Lindley, Kenneth E.
PhD Univ. of Iowa
1963–1989 Physics; Chair, Div
of Science and Mathematics

Livenspire, Edith Stearns '32
BMus Houghton College
1941–1946 Voice

† Lucas, W. Hugh
1952–1953 Voice

Luckey, James S.
MA Harvard College
(LLD Wheaton College)
1890–1895 Shorthand, Typing,
Greek, Math
1894–1895 Principal, then
President
1908–1937 President; Math,
Physics

Luckey, Robert R. R. '37
PhD Cornell Univ.
1942–1976 Mathematics
1954–1961 Public Relations
1961–1976 Vice President for
Development
1967–1968 Acting President

* Luckey, Ruth Brooks '45
BA Houghton College
1952–1954 History

* Lugendorf, Claude
1905–1907 Commercial

Lusk, Franklin L.
MMus American Conservatory
(Chicago)
1961–1966 Voice

Lynip, Arthur W. '38
PhD New York Univ.
1950–1966 Dean of College;
English

Madwid, Anne '40 (later Farwell)
BA Houghton College
1940–1944 Registrar

Mack, Marcile D.
MMus Cleveland Institute of
Music
1945–1952 Piano

Mack, Philip J.
MMus Cleveland Institute of
Music
1945–1952 Voice

MacLean, Sara
MA Northwestern Univ.
1960–1967 English

Markell, Ruth Wilde '49
BA Houghton College
1944–1950 German

† Mason, Harold C.
EdD Indiana University
1941–1942 English

Mattke, Robert A.
MA State Univ. of Iowa
1969–1988 Bible and
Theology (BSC)

* Maxey, Margaret BS
1933–*1937* Phys Ed.

* McAnnich, Ethel M.
1923–1924 Exposition and
History

McCallum, Floyd F.
EdD Michigan State Univ.
1967–1981 Psychology; Chair,
Div. of Psychology and
Education

‡ McCone, Clyde
1960–1961 Religion

McConn, Maynard
MSMusEd Butler Univ.
1948–1950 Music Education

McCord, Marie M.
MMus Indiana Univ.
1955–1960 Piano

McDowell, G. Tremaine
MA
1917–1919 English

McDowell, Howard W.
AM
1899–1902 Ancient Lang, Hist
1902–1903 Polit Sc and Logic
1903–1909 Polit Sc and Logic
and Soc Sc.
1909–1911 Philos, Hist Treas,
Librarian
1911–1912 Philos, Theology
and Librarian
1912–1915 Field Worker,
Librarian
1915–1916 Philos, Hist.,
Librarian

McMaster, Gloria
*MMus Eastman School of
Music*
1971–1975 Music

McMillen, Alice J. Hampe '25
BA Houghton College
1922–1926 Dean of Women
1924–1925 Asst. Theol Dept.
1943–1964 Bible

McMillen, Sim I
MD Univ. of Pennsylvania
1951–1968 College Physician;
Missions

McNeese, Harold
BSE Geneva College
1937–1946 Physical Education

McNiel, Harold E.
*DMA Eastman School of
Music*
1958–2002 Brass

‡ McNiel, Carol
1959 Mathematics

Miller, Carlene
BS Gordon College
1964–1967 Physical Education

Miller, Elke J. '66
BA Houghton College
1966–1967 German

Miller, Florence G.
MA Bob Jones Univ.
1953–1956 Piano

Miller, Myron M.
MA Wheaton College
1963–1967 Philosophy

* Miller, Ruth
  1925–1926 Voice and Piano

Mills, James H. Jr.
  STM Temple Univ.
  1959–1973 Psychology; Dean
  of Students

Molyneaux, J. Maxwell
  BA Oberlin College *(later,*
  PhD Cornell)
  1925–1926 Chemistry

Molyneaux, Roberta (later Grange)
  '29
  BA Houghton College
  1929–1931 Science and
  German

Montgomery, Martha H.
  MA Univ. of Michigan
  1923–1924 Biology

‡ Montzingo, Lloyd
  1960–1961 Mathematics

Moon, Blanche G. '33
  BA Houghton College
  1947–1951 Mathematics

Moore, Charlotte
  PhD Univ. of Pennsylvania
  1931–1932 Prof. English

Moore, Ralph
  MA Western Reserve Univ.
  1951–1953 Brass

Moore, Rebecca
  BS Pennsylvania State Univ.
  1951–1953 Piano

Moreland, George E.
  PhD Cornell Univ.
  1941–1966 Biology; Chair,
  Div. of Science and Math

* Morgan, Maxine B.
  BMus
  1929–1931 Violin and Theory

Morrow, Robert R.
  MS Univ. of Illinois
  1964–1965 Brass

Moses, M. Belle Sem '16
  AB Univ. of Michigan
  1914–1919 Science and
  Drawing
  1930–1938 Librarian

† Moxey, Margaret
  BS Univ. of Pennsylvania
  1934–1936 Physical Education

Mullen, Laurence K.
  MA Boston Univ.
  1966–1993 Bible and
  Theology

Munro, Donald W.
  PhD Pennsylvania State Univ.
  1966–1994 Biology

Musser, Anne Louise (later
  Honeywell) '58
  MMus Univ. of Michigan
  1961–1968 Organ

Nash, Ronald H.
  MA Brown Univ.
  1960–1963 Philosophy

* Neighbor, Mary
  1937–1944 Library

Nelson, Marven O.
  EdD Univ. of Buffalo
  1948–1956 Psychology

Neu, David '58
  MS Cornell Univ.
  1960–1961 Mathematics

Neu, Martha J. '68
  BS Houghton College
  1968–1975 Chemistry

Newhouse, Edward B.
  EdD Ball State Univ.
  1970–1980 English; Education

Nielsen, Doris J. '71
  MSEd SUNY at Buffalo
  1971–1997 Physical Education
  and Recreation

Nielsen, Kenneth L.
  *MDiv Faith Theological
  Seminary*
  1963–1966 Manager of Dining
  Hall
  1966–1972 Business management
  1972–1984 Treasurer and Bus.
  Manager
  1984–1997 Vice President for
  Finance

* Nilson, K.
  PhD
  1947–1948 Psychology

Noble, Robert T. Jr. '50
  BMus Houghton College
  1950–1951 Brass

Noether, James L. '65
  MA Alfred Univ.
  1968–1971 Psychology

Noether, Rita S. '67
  BA Houghton College
  1967–1970 French

North, Maynard J.
  MA Univ. of Vermont
  1952–1953 English

Norton, Edgar R.
  *MS MusEd Potsdam State
  Teachers College*
  1956–1993 Music Education.

Nussey, Wesley B.
  MA Syracuse Univ.
  1964–1977 Registrar

Ortlip, Aimee
  *Pennsylvania Academy of Fine
  Arts*
  1941–1959 Art

Ortlip, H. Willard
  *Pennsylvania Academy of Fine
  Arts*
  1947–1958 Art

Ostlund, Harry J.
  1908–1913 Library, English

* Paddock, Millie June
  1915–1922 Piano

Paine, S. Hugh Jr.
  MS Texas A&M Univ.
  1960–1976 Physics

Paine, Stephen William
  PhD Univ. of Illinois
  1933–*1937* Greek, Latin; Dean
  of College
  1937–1972 President of
  College

Palmer, Jean Burmaster '68
1969–1976 Library

Pardoe, (Miss) Franc
1906–1908 Elementary Course

* Parsons, Mary A.
1922–1923 Greek

* Pendleton, Hattie
1889–1890 Art

Perison, Harry Donald '49
BMus Houghton College
1949–1954 Piano

Piersma, Bernard J.
PhD Univ. of Pennsylvania
1971– Chemistry

Pinckney, Geneva S. '62
MA Univ. of Connecticut
1962–1964 Botany

Pitt, Joseph R.
1929–*1933* Bible

Pocock, Betty Jane Goodwin '56
BA Houghton College
1962–1964 English

Pocock, Richard C. '55
EdD Columbia Univ.
1959–1995 Mathematics

Pool, Alice M. '29
Doctor of Letters, Univ. of Mexico
1935–1974 French and English; Spanish

Prentice, Ruth W.
BA
1942–1943 Dean of Women

Price, Richard W. '52
MA Pennsylvania State Univ.
1953–1957 Math and Physics

Prinsell, Gustave G.
MD Columbia Univ.
1965–1974 College Physician

Pryor, Marvin J.
MA Amherst College
1929–1943 Physics and Astronomy

Redman, Edith P. Barringer '42
MSLS SUNY College at Geneseo
1967–1987 Library

Rees, Arland B. '50
PhD Syracuse Univ.
1965–1972 History

Reese, Floyd E.
PhD Purdue Univ.
1948–1956 Chemistry

Reist, Irwin W. '57
ThM Northern Baptist Theological Sem.
1965–1979 Bible

Rennick, Elizabeth (Bessie)
1952–1963 Registrar; Dean of Women

Reynolds, Melvin F.
MEd Miami Univ.
1967–1972 Sociology

Rhoades, Robert W.
MS Brockport State College
1967–1983 Physical Education

Richardson, Roger
BFA Syracuse Univ.
1971–1979 Art

Rickard, Josephine '25
PhD Cornell Univ.
1926–1969 English; Chair,
Div. of English

Riegel, Dwight L.
BS Univ. of Rochester
1958–1960 Elementary
Education

Ries, Claude A.
ThD Northern Baptist
Theological Sem.
1924–1965 Hebrew, Greek,
Bibical Literature
Chair, Div. of Religion

Riggall, Norah M. (m. A. Ray
Calhoon '15)
BA Northwestern Univ.
1914–1918 Oratory

Rindfusz, Ralph
AB Oberlin College 1910
1910–1914 Science

* Rishell, Lois
1925–1926 Oratory

Ritson, John William
National Diploma in Design
1958–1964 Art

Robertson, James D.
PhD Univ. of Cincinnati
1944–1946 Education and
Psychology

‡ Rodeheaver, Reuben
1958–1959 Music

Roederer, Jean-Louis Marie
Jose '64
MA Middlebury College
1966– French

Roeske, William A. '56
MA Univ. of Buffalo
1965–1990 Mathematics; Data
Processing and Computer
Science

Rogato, Isabelle (m. Robert Weir)
MEd Boston Univ.
1968–1971 Dean of Women

Rork, Crystal L.
PhD Cornell Univ.
1923–1959 Botany

Rosenberger, Harry E.
PhD New York Univ.
1937–1943 Philosophy

Rothermel, Bertha M. '30
BA Houghton College
1926–1933 Oratory

Russell, C. Belle
AB
1914–1917 Latin, Greek
1926–1927 English

Saufley, Duane C.
PhD Purdue Univ.
1965–1998 Physics

* Saunders, Jean D.
1971–1974 Education

‡ Saunders, Vernon
1959 Mathematics

Saxon, Esther
MMus George Peabody College for Teachers
1953–1955 Piano and Theory

Schaible, Linda
BS Greenville College
1969–1972 Physical Education

Schonhard, Gertrude L'Arronge
Advanced private voice training
1952–1953 Voice

Schram, Eugene C., Jr.
BMus Westminster Choir College
1938–1942 Voice

Schram, Grace C.
BMus Westminster Choir College
1938–1941 Voice

Schroer, Albert W.
MA Ohio State Univ.
1953–1956 Voice

Schultz, Carl '53
PhD Brandeis Univ.
1965– Bible and Theology
1976– 1997 Chair, Div. of Religion and Philosophy

‡ Schwartz, Morton
1959 Mathematics

Scott, Robert A. '59
MS Syracuse Univ.
1963–1966 Biology

Scott, Robert D.
BS Purdue Univ.
1961–1965 Mathematics

Sentz, Georgiana D.
MS SUNY College at Buffalo
1960–1979 Art

* Sergeant, Ina Jackson '45
BA Houghton College
1951–1953 Mathematics
1953–1954 Piano
1954–1955 Christian Education

Shannon, Frederick D.
PhD Univ. of Akron
1958–1987 Chemistry
1973–1985 Academic Dean

Shea, Aileen Ortlip
Pulitzer Prize in Art 1935
Degree Normal, the Sorbonne
1936–1947 Instr in Art

Shea, J. Whitney '33
EdD Columbia Univ.
1934–1974 Economics and Sociology
1942–1946 Army
1969–1974 Chair, Div. of Social Sciences

Shewan, Nancy
BS Indiana State Teachers College
1960–1967 Piano

Shewan, Robert
MS Ithaca College
1960–1967 Music

‡ Shigley, E. Harold
EdD Indiana Univ.
1969–1970 Academic Dean (BSC)

Sibley, Verner H.
1887–1895 Commercial Dept.;
Math

Sicard, Lynford
BA Wheaton College
1931–1932 Latin and French
1932–1934 Asst. to Pres.

Skillings, Ralph
MA Ball State Univ.
1971–1975 Psychology

Small, Samuel A.
PhD Johns Hopkins Univ.
1932–1943 English

*‡ Smith, Ella
1887 English

Smith, Lois B. (Mrs. Henry R.)
1921–1948 Drawing and
English

Smith, Henry Richey Jr.
MA Cornell Univ.
1907–1924 Literature and
English.
1923–1924 Supt of grounds

Smith, Paul N. F.
BA Pasadena College
1962–1963 Philosophy

Smith, Willard Garfield '35
PhD New York Univ.
1935–1972 Treasurer and
Business Manager

Snell, Charles J.
EdD Calvin Coolidge College
1957–1973 Psychology

Sorensen, Hans
Prague Conservatory
(Bohemia)
1931–1933 Violin and
Orchestra

Sperzel, Katherine
1908–1913 Registrar

Spofford, Marguerite
New England Conservatory
1913–1914 Voice

* Sprague, George
1919–1921 teacher

* Sprague, Mrs. George
1919–1921 Librarian

Stark, Helen F. Davison '25
BA Houghton College
1926–1929 Dean of Women
1929–1931 English, Bible,
Civics

Steese, Paul A '27
1932–1934 Education and
Physical Training
1969–1970 Dean of Students

† Stearns, Edith M. '41
BSMusEd Houghton College
1941–1942 Voice

Steinacker, Erma
BA Marion College
1949–1950 Spanish

Stevenson, Lena '33
BA Houghton College
1934–1944 Registrar, Bursar

Stewart, Donna J. '67
  BA Houghton College
  1968–1970 Mathematics,
  Computer Science

Stockin, Bruce C. '56
  PhD Univ. of Buffalo
  1956– ? Psychology
  1963–1967 Psychology

Stockin, Frank Gordon Jr. '37
  PhD Univ. of Illinois
  1938–1981 Latin; Classics
  1964–1975 Chair, Div. of
  Foreign Lang. and Literature

Stockin, Marjorie Ortlip
  BS Columbia Univ.
  1939–1956 Art
  1963–1978 Art

Stone, Elwood W.
  BSLS Syracuse Univ.
  1946–1951 English

‡ Swardstrom, John
  1959–1960 Physics

* Sweeten, Alice M.
  1887–1889 Art.

* Sweeten, E. Grace
  1888–1889 English.

Talbot, Gordon G. '49
  MA Wheaton College
  1957–1960 Christian
  Education

* Tatsch, Paul A. '68
  BA Houghton College
  1971–1972 Economics

Terrey, Robert J.
  *BSME Pennsylvania State
  College*
  1955–1958 Mathematics and
  Physics

Thomas, Clifford W.
  EdD Michigan State Univ.
  1969–1974 Academic Dean;
  Education

Thomas, Katherine T.
  MA Michigan State Univ.
  1969–1971 Education

Thomas, Paul Milton
  MA Univ. of Michigan
  1959–1964 Biology

Thurston, Blanche
  1913–1918 Dean of Sem
  Women; Registrar; Voice

Traore, Irma D. Cashie '62
  BA Houghton College
  1965–1968 French

Trenkle, Rose W.
  1900 English

Trexler, Frederick D. '64
  PhD Pennsylvania State Univ.
  1969–1998 Physics

Tropf, Gordon H. '49
  BA Houghton College
  1949–1950 Biology

Troutman, Richard L. '53
  PhD Univ. of Kentucky
  1958–1969 History and
  Political Science.

* Tucker, Miss
  1898–1899 Private Lessons,
  Instr. and Vocal

Tucker, Perry L. '28
  MA Columbia Univ.
  1931–1946 Geology

Vandenbergh, David P. '67
  BA Houghton College
  1967–1972 German and Classics

Van Vlack, Steven C.
  MBA Syracuse Univ.
  1968–1969 Business
  Administration

Van Wormer, Ivah Benning '27
  BA Houghton College
  1927–1933 English

Wacker, Martha Woolsey '44
  BA Houghton College
  1944–1945 Prep

* Walldorf, Etta
  1892–1894 Art and Music

* Warburton, Edith (later Pocock)
  1923–1925 French
  1967–

Weese, Wightman
  MA Syracuse Univ.
  1971–1975 English

* Weinsheimer, Herbert G.
  1969–1977 Greek (BSC)

* Wells, A. Lois
  1926–1927 Mathematics and
  English

Wells, George R. '47
  EdD Univ. of Buffalo
  1947–1988 Physical Education

Wessell, Lynn R.
  MA Univ. of Southern Illinois
  1967–1970 Political Science

Whitaker, Charles B. (Rev.)
  *Bonebrake Theological
  Seminary*
  1921–1932 Theology;
  Religious Education

Whiting, Anne M.
  PhD Pennsylvania State Univ.
  1968–1990 Biology

Whitney, Laura A.
  *Hamilton (Ontario) Normal
  School*
  1908–1911 French

Wightman, E. Russell
  PhD Univ. of Michigan
  1948–1951 Physics

Willett, Edward J. '39
  EdD SUNY at Buffalo
  1962–1985 Economics

* Willett, John S.
  1932–1933 Evangelism

Williams, Oliver H.
  MA Boston Univ.
  1949–1951 History

Wilson, Charles R.
  PhD Vanderbilt Univ.
  1959–1965 Bible and
  Theology

‡ Wilson, Kenneth L.
  1960–1961 English

Wilson, Lucele Hatch '31
  BA Houghton College
  1939–1942 Dean of Women

Wilt, Lloyd P. '46
*PhD Indiana Univ. of
Pennsylvania*
1968–1985 English

Wilt, Lois Jane Hardy '46
MA Western Reserve Univ.
1968–1988 Music

* Wolter, Gerald A.
1965–1968 Chaplain; Asst.
Registrar

Wood, Lawrence W.
1973–1976 Philosophy

Woods, Robert W.
DMus Greenville College
1958–1962 Voice

Woolsey, Pierce E. Sem '16
PhD Cornell Univ.
1923–1958 Latin, French
1933–1945 Chair, Div. of
Languages
1945–1958 Dean of College

Woolsey, Warren M. '43
*STM Lutheran School of
Theology*
1958–1959 Philosophy
1966–1994 New Testament
and Missions

Worthington, James K.
PhD Syracuse Univ.
1971–1979 Education

* Woughter, Gerald
1950–1951 Voice

* Wright, Florence
BA Houghton College
1938–1943 Librarian

Wright, Frank Herbert (Rev.)
BD Alfred University
1921–1951 Theology,
Philosophy
1921–1929, 1943–1951 Dean
of Men
1935–1951 Chair of Div. of
Philosophy and Religion

Wright, Stanley W.
AB Oberlin College
1930–1943 Biblical Literature
1929–1942 Dean of Men

Yorton, Florence '25
AB
1902–1905 Latin and Greek

Zahniser, Clarence H.
PhD Univ. of Pittsburgh
1963–1965 Religious
Education

* Zehr, Dorothy M.
1921–1922 Vocal

Zernov, Riza
*MRE Asbury Theological
Seminary*
1955–1957 Christian
Education

Zimmerman, Ruth (Steese)
BFA Univ. of Nebraska
1929–1931 Instr. Voice and
theory

---

* Found in Smith cards but not in
catalog listings
† Found in catalog but not in
Smith cards
‡ Found only in trustees' minutes

Appendix L

Interviewees Sum Up Houghton

During most of the interviews he conducted, the interviewer posed this question: "I'm going to ask you to sum up Houghton in one sentence. Tell me what that one sentence would be." What follows is an extended selection of the responses.

Fred Parker, faculty: Boy, that's hard to come up with, but maybe this comes as close as anything. God loves to work at Houghton College. Let's keep giving him the chance.

Dr. Harold McNiel, faculty: The words that began to form, I don't have a sentence. . . . Loved by God, an organization, a school, a college that shows God loves us. I think that's what Houghton is.

Dr. Ed Willett '39, faculty: From my perspective, Houghton still is and has been God's staging area, one of God's staging areas to send men and women out to serve him wherever he pleases.

Mary (Harris) Carey '49: As to its influence on me or in general, because I was about to say that it was by far the happiest years of my life, and I learned more there than any other single place that I went. That's as far as I am concerned. As far as Houghton is concerned, in the early days it was a great glory to God and a very respected and well-run institution, academically. I don't think people could do any better as far as learning.

Marilyn (Tucker) Byerly '54, staff: I think Houghton is an exciting, wonderful place in the United States. It's probably unique in the fact that almost everyone in the community is part of the college. The students here are great, the music is superb, the Artist Series is wonderful.

Dr. George Failing '40: I thank God for Houghton College. It filled a niche in my life that I don't know how better that niche could have been filled on all levels.

Warren Woolsey '43, faculty: I struggle for words about that. It would seem to me a thoroughly respectable academic community with basically Christian motivation and a place where a person can explore new ideas, do some thinking, maybe a little bit conservative.

Ella (Phelps) Woolsey '43: For me, Houghton was the place where I met Jesus Christ as personal savior and was nurtured by caring faculty and loving friends and should probably have majored more on the academic than I did but found it a good place to develop.

Margaret Wynn '52, staff: I feel it's a place where God is honored, where they're striving to really make servant-scholars. Sometimes I think the scholar is more emphasized than the servant. But for me it was a place of learning more about God and a place where I gave my life to the Lord to serve him wherever he would have me go, and it was a place that taught me Christian values.

Dr. Duane Saufley, faculty: I think that we have judged ourselves by ourselves and called ourselves excellent where we may not be.

I think because of who we are and because we are Christians seeing God's creation in everyone that we need to think more unilaterally about all of our students, all of our faculty, all of our staff, and to increase the human relationship which sometimes is lacking in terms of arrogance and exclusiveness.

Dr. Willis Beardsley '60, faculty: People trying to live Christian lives in an academic community.

Dr. James Bence '37: Houghton College is not the perfect school, but it does have a tremendous ministry in preparing young people to go out into the world and to live Godly lives before the world.

Florence (Lytle) Bence '35: Houghton College is a wonderful institution. I've been very proud that our children and many of our grandchildren have been able to go there. I have very few regrets.

Edna (Woodworth) Shaffner '49: It would take a long time to get into a sentence. It is a touchstone for me. It's a place where I learned to grow. The people meant so much to me, and if you hear the word Houghton you know they're your friend. I think that's what I have to say.

Douglass Shaffner '40: There were really a lot of good people who helped me expand my mind. I enjoyed that and appreciate it.

Eileen (Griffen) Spear '52, staff: Providential. Providential. I really felt that I was led here by the Lord, and I feel that my life was changed and directed and as I come back I feel it's still providential.

Dr. Clinton Strong '41: A pleasant memory of an excellent time in my life.

Mary (Tiffany) Strong '40: Educationally and spiritually sound.

Olson Clark '46: Let me think. To me Houghton College speaks of a depth of spiritual reality that is basic to my whole way of living. I've had some criticisms and yet, when you come right down to it, I don't know of a place where I'd rather see my energies devoted because it was here my spiritual roots were established, and I had an awful lot of encouragement. I had more opportunities afforded me as a young person growing up in this community than I would have in any other place.

Dr. Daniel Kauffman '67: There is so much good about Houghton. It's got such a fine heritage, fine people. You can't do much without a good history, without a good background. Houghton has got such a fine rich background.

Dr. Fred Shannon, faculty: Best thing that ever happened to me, troubles and all.

Alton Shea '36: I would say the four years of college are a shining experience, and the educational experience; friendships and the whole milieu of what happened is quite the center of a person's life over the years.

Marjorie (Ortlip) Stockin, faculty: I know some people think it's terrible to be off here in the boondoggles, but I think its a wonderful place where you can get off and put things together without being too much influenced by the cities and the Internet, which is coming in as fast as anything.

Richard Alderman '52, staff: I think it was a caring place that wanted to direct you both academically and spiritually to the betterment of yourself and society.

Rev. William Calkins '44: It was a good school, I got a good education, a good background in the beginning. I'm glad I went there.

Anne (Madwid) Farwell '40: Having come from a cow college (when we were there) it has made a lot of progress in lots of ways: quality of education, quality of the plant, the buildings, and I think that they've come a long ways and that they are going to go further.

Richard Farwell '34: I hope that Houghton never loses its spiritual distinctives because Harvard, Yale, they all started with this thing and lost it completely.

William Greenway, faculty: Overall, a wonderful, spiritual, academic place to serve, to work with students and faculty members that, in general, has been very pleasurable with a few blips along the way.

Ellen Kreckman '59, library: Well, I feel very fortunate to have been here and had this experience. I think it's something that a good many people don't have, and I don't think I, up until fairly recently, have realized what a privilege it has been.

Dr. Fred Trexler '64, faculty: I think for me Houghton has been a place of ministry where I've been free to learn new things and then teach them to my students and try to teach them from a Christian perspective.

Dr. Willard Smith '37, administrator: To me the capstone of Houghton's character is its co-emphasis on Christian service and academic excellence as expressed in the phrase "servant scholars."

Dr. Stephen Calhoon '53, faculty: [The most positive thing about Houghton] was the balanced approach that I encountered: balance of spirituality with academics, and although the almost cliche of integration of faith, learning, and living had not come into use, I believe that it was in practice even when I was there as a student. I felt that when a person graduated from Houghton they were well prepared to enter the world knowing what they believed, being prepared to put their knowledge into action and to live their lives as Christians ought to.

Richard Sandle '42: I would say that Houghton College as a college is a great testimony to the people of the United States because of their earnestness and administration.

Janice (Strong) Sandle '43: Houghton is founded on the rock spiritually, and the knowledge that we got in our field is special. It's top notch.

Ruth (Brooks) Luckey '45: I think it was the answer to my prayers educationally, marriage-wise and spiritual.

Dr. Robert Luckey '37, faculty: First, it's my educational home and as such it was a wonderful place to both grow up and become educated and be involved in education.

Ralph Traber '50: I believe that the experience that has stayed with me about Houghton is that they brought out the total person. They were interested in developing a Christ-like person that knew how to handle himself and knew what was required to live a Christian life. The academic side was very important because as a student that was interested in going on to future education they were interested in developing the total person. They wanted a person that was a total being. They weren't interested in just getting the education poured down the throat, but they wanted the person who knew the values that would carry them through their life here on earth.

Helen (Paul) Paine '37: When I think of my overall years here I think I'd say the most outstanding thing would be the people that I got to know here in Houghton. . . . [it was] the people that I met while I was here that had the most impression, made the biggest impression, maybe had the most influence on my life.

Philip Stockin '68: We have a foundation of Christian education that's serving people and making a difference in people's lives, holding on to fundamental truth, with a capital T, and that can't change, and that's what Houghton has modeled for me as a kid growing up—a life of service. We talk about scholar/servants, and I believe that with all my heart and that's what it showed me, and that's what I think we have to hang on to; we can change the packaging but we'd better not change what's on the bottom of it all.

Lyndell (Sheldon) Harter '71: When I was in Houghton as a student, Houghton to me was a group of older people, teachers, who really cared about what we were doing with our lives. You knew they cared about you. You knew they prayed for you. You knew they wanted you to have success. You knew it was a place that you wanted to be at that point in your life. It was a time when you made very good friends who cared about you. There were sad times but mostly it was happy times. I think that Houghton, when I look back now, that's what I got out of being here. It was the people that I met, that I knew cared about me—adults who still now care about me when I'm back here as an adult, meeting them on an adult basis.

Bruce Brenneman, faculty: I would say that Houghton College is a community of committed, devoted scholars who daily live out their faith and profoundly affect the lives of students and colleagues alike.

Lois (Munger) Hurlburt '35: I think probably I would equate growing up like maybe making a cake or whatever, and I feel that the training I had at home was good but that Houghton was the frosting on the cake. It really made me, I think, what I am. I'm all for it. I'd send anybody there because I think it could help anybody.

Russell Hurlburt '50: I changed from a boy to a man in a short time in the Marine Corps. I came back to Houghton thinking that I was a man and I was a little bit, not discouraged nor oppressive to their straight-laced way of thinking and living, but thinking that they were a little too narrow and a little too demanding. That would be all right for college kids but I wasn't a college kid any more. I had grown up and gone past that stage, I thought I had. So there was some resentment in my life at that time.

[My view has changed in the intervening decades. Now] I respect their high standards. They lived by them from all appearances and expected their students to, and that's good. There aren't many colleges that are that way any more. The few that used to be, I think Houghton's one of the few that's left.

Lois (Hardy) Wilt '46, faculty: I feel probably that the strongest influence that Houghton's had on my life is spiritually. I think that we were taught when I was here the power of prayer. Throughout the whole time, let's face it, it changed my life. I met my husband here. My best friends are Houghton graduates. The thread of spiritual training; an excellent preparation for life as far as the courses we got, the teachers, the individual attention. It certainly made the direction of my life much clearer.

Elisabeth (Anderson) Veazey '44: I found Houghton to be a very whole-some, enjoyable place and a very nurturing environment also.

Philip Anderson '33: It was a major influence in my young life. I had come from a Christian background which was a strong background. Houghton put me into an environment where I was comfortable, and I learned to be comfortable while I was there at Houghton. I appreciated Houghton so much for that. It was reinforcing the way I had been brought up all through the years.

Dr. Bernard Piersma, faculty: I think Houghton is a school founded and dedicated to serving the Lord to make servants of Jesus Christ who would also be scholars. I think we have in recent years tended to drift a little bit away from that; but our students are tremendous, well-pre-pared. I have great hope that we will turn back to some of the heritage that I think we've lost.

Isabelle Rogato Weir, dean of women: When I think of Houghton College, I think of three wonderful years with a lot of wonderful people that I had opportunity to work with and a place that I was able to make a contribution. I really look back on it with a great sense of satisfaction.

Ruth (Kupka) Merz '52: I am truly grateful to God for my years at Houghton and feel that it left me with a challenge to serve my genera-tion, in obedience to God.

Dr. Lola Haller, faculty: As dean of women and as faculty member, I always thought of Houghton as having very high academic standards which I really appreciated, but most of all the opportunity and the privilege to have the spiritual dimension that you didn't have in a sec-ular college and that you were able to work with kids spiritually as well as academically.

Lois (Harris) Gilliland '50: As a missionary kid in 1946–1950 it was a home-away-from-home.

Dr. Dean Gilliland '50: Houghton is the place where I was able to focus on my life and make a point for my future, and it has stayed there. That's what Houghton did for me.

Arnold Cook '43, faculty : Houghton stands as a personal illustration, permanently to me, of what God can do to bring about circumstances that, had I failed to obey, I would have missed so much in life.

Betty Cook '62, faculty: Houghton did something for me personally in the realm of learning, in the realm of teaching (since I started them both later than the average person), in giving me confidence in myself, in learning enough so that I could go ahead with the writing that has opened up to me, the photography that's opened up to me, the correspondence with the students, the spiritual relationship with God. I think all of that put together would make up Houghton for me.

Dr. William Olcott '40: Houghton was an excellent facilitator in that it gave us a good, sound understanding of what we should have known about our various curriculum courses, and it gave us the background to understand the make-up for what came next and not to be bamboozled and fuzzled and put off-base by it. It also was an excellent place to meet and make life-long friends which, really, education is all about.

Dr. Stanley Sandler '60: Houghton was a transforming experience for me, a callow youth who had a real interest in history but no discipline involvement in it and who knew almost nothing about good music, and by the time I was finished these two things were a very important part of my life. I have to thank Houghton for that.

Richard Hart '69: Houghton provided me with an overview of world history, economy, and industry that enabled me to learn how to think and execute creatively, Christianly, and practically, so that I would be able to collaborate with church and community the rest of my life.

Velma Harbeck Moses Hewson '36: I think Houghton College is a wonderful school for a student to attend to get a good basis for Christian living, academic training, fellowship with people, and preparation for life in general.

Kenneth Motts '50: I think that Houghton is founded on the Rock. I think they have followed through, and just what they have just campus-wise right now it has paid off. I think they're still where they were. I don't think they've lost it.

John De Brine '47: The college was a place then where you got a high academic, respected education but with the emphasis of the spiritual so that when you graduated you left with biblical balance: A, with a good working knowledge of your major, but B, with a realization that all history is designed to demonstrate there is a God. I would say that was their big contribution. I have great respect for them because of that.

Dr. James E. Barcus '59, faculty: Houghton in my life has been a situation in which the sum is more than its parts. It gave me an academic basis for my life but not just an academic basis. It certainly contributed to my spirituality in a number of ways, because as a seventeen-year-old I was not tough. It gave me a broader vision of the world. It's all of those things put together, that synthesis which is much, much greater than any individual part. Many of the faculty members represented that synthesis of mind, vision, heart, soul. That synthesis is more important than any individual part.

Dr. Esther Jane Carrier, librarian: Houghton was a wonderful experience for me. Memories of the administration, faculty, and students still linger. Perhaps most of all I remember many of the spiritual church and chapel services. I learned much from many, matured, and still carry much of this influence as part of my life.

Dr. Clifford W. Thomas, academic dean: Houghton College is an outstanding Christian college. They have attained recognition and achievement in academic fields, which I think reflect what they are doing for the students. And at the same time, they have retained their Christian emphasis, their background, and have done a masterful job of blending together a liberal arts program with a Christian background, influence, that comes through. It is possible to do it and they have proved it. I think that's where I see them.

Dr. Ian H. Lennox '51, trustee: How has Houghton (and I include there the college and the community, its constituency, students, faculty and the whole thing) influenced my life and my life of the family? The Lennox family—my wife, our family, our children, my mother, my father—is what is it because of Houghton, intellectually, spiritually, relationally. Houghton and all it stands for is infused into the very thread of our being. I cannot imagine our family being anything apart from Houghton College.

Elizabeth Beck Gilbert Feller, former dean of women and Houghton's first female trustee: After doing all my work in secular institutions, it [being a Christian] curbs your social life, really, because you don't do the things they do. In Houghton there is that opportunity of being a whole person and enjoying it. When I went to school, it was study, and I could see in Houghton it was not only study but it was association with others in learning on another area of your life. Now, I'm not condemning the actual education at the university, but I don't think it was complete.

Dr. Lee M. Haines Jr., former trustee: Houghton College is our oldest [Wesleyan] educational institution. It's the most highly regarded one academically. It's an institution that has served the denomination well, and the relationship between the two is at the best that it's been and it's going to get bettr.

Dr. Bert H. Hall '43, former faculty and acting dean: I think Houghton has provided a quality of education for professionals that has given the professional world a Christian flavor. As I've met Christians, graduates, over the years I've felt they were well prepared not only in their field but as Christians for the work that they were doing.

Dr. Richard C. Pocock '55, faculty: Houghton gave me an opportunity in a career which was far beyond anything I had ever dreamed of and pushed me to succeed and was the most wonderful place in the world for bringing up kids.

William Davis '69: Probably for me the spiritual foundation that developed at Houghton, because so many years as a [missionary] kid you were challenged as to why did you believe, and Houghton just affirmed strongly by the teachers and the good Christian kids that were here that I was in the right place. The second thing was the spiritual participation back then. Even the bad kids went to the weekly class Bible study/prayer meetings and participated. Chapel was a lot of fun. So the spiritual emphasis was great.

Jill Davis, '71: What I remember is just that being such a very spiritual place. The class prayer meetings did an awful lot for me and then grace before every meal in the dining hall and the singing and prayer at every single class. It was just a wonderful spiritual experience being here. It opened up a whole new world to me that I had not seen before because I came from a small town and I came to this school with a lot of Christians from different backgrounds that I learned a lot and grew a lot from just from the interaction with the Bible studies and the prayer meetings and things like that. The teachers impressed me so much with their spirituality, and I guess that it just gave me a world view that I didn't have.

Gloria (Kleppinger '65) Huizenga, faculty spouse: Houghton College opened my eyes to a wider world of learning, to a greater challenge for personal spiritual growth, and to committed participation in kingdom work and service to others.

Appendix M

Campus Anecdotes

No one would presume for a moment that student life is devoid of humorous escapades, and the author elected to include some even in such a serious tome as this. Though the subject of college anecdotes, pranks, and shenanigans almost deserves a separate book, a short collection forms an appendix to the chapter on students and student life. The following stories have been selected from a list that seems to be nearly endless.

One colorful class of '39 alumna (who admits to having been engaged three times during her four years at Houghton), shared a number of anecdotes about student life.

> Those were the days when the shenanigans were great on campus. It was a small school. Worth Cott, who was in charge of the whole campus at that time, lived in that house in back of where Gao used to be. One Halloween night, some of the rascally boys had sounded the fire alarm. So Worth Cott came out and demanded that we all get out of Gaoyadeo, which was a fire trap and the only dorm we had then. (The fellows used to stay in the houses around.) He came in the hall, called up and down the stairs because they didn't know

that there wasn't a fire. Here we all are in our pajamas and robes and curlers all standing out on the front lawn, and it was a false alarm. About half an hour later after we went in we had an earthquake. Things did begin to jiggle. I had brought my doll to college and the thing slipped off the bed and broke the head. We thought the kids were playing jokes on us again. Worth Cott came in the front hall again and we wouldn't move. We thought that the boys were up to something, but it really was an earthquake. We finally all got out and it didn't damage anything. As I was going around a corner in the building there was a clock hanging down and I got a black eye. I was going with George Hillman, and two days later I had the biggest black eye and, of course, everybody blamed George. They said that he was the cause of all the trouble in the dorm.

Then we had Alice Pool living in the dorm. She was an unmarried faculty member. These people didn't have places to live around town. So some of these crazy guys opened the window at the end of the stairway, and they took a crate of chickens and let them loose in the dorm. They flew all over the dorm but some of them landed in Alice Pool's room sitting on her bed posts when the lights came on. You never heard such a racket in your life as she screamed up and down that hall. Then they got some girl's clothes and put them on a line between the flag pole and something—girls' panties out there and bras.

I don't know if it was that year but the next year they took Prof. Stanley [Wright]'s cow and put it up in the chapel. Anyway, they took Prof. Stanley's [Jersey] cow and put in the old chapel and when they got it up there they couldn't get it down. The cow wouldn't move. They had a terrible time. They were theological students, too. They were in great trouble.[1]

I think it was my sophomore year when Merritt Queen and his buddies, all preacher-boys, stole the bell off the campground, where your gym is now, that was the Wesleyan Campground. Every summer they had a big do up there. They had a big auditorium and a great big bell that they rang. These guys stole the bell but coming down Woolsey hill there they stumbled and fell and it rolled all the way down the hill. You could hear it for ten city blocks and everybody knew who stole the bell.

Another story, when [my husband] Bob was dean of students there: they took the clapper from the bell in Fancher Hall a long time ago, but some of the students who were there when my husband was dean didn't know the clapper was gone. One time while he was dean, they climbed up there and they were going to ring the bell. Somebody reported it to Bob but he didn't go up and make them come down, he locked the door and made them stay up there all night. The only way they could come down was break the door down. When they broke the door down everybody knew who did it, and his punishment was they had to replace the door out of their own pockets.[2]

I still remember Doc Jo [Rickard], when we had to wear hose. She would come up behind you going up the stairs and pull on the back of your hose to be sure you had it on. We'd draw lines down our legs where the seam goes. It didn't bother me as a student as much, but it bothered me as a faculty member because I thought that I had a certain dignity of my own and I wasn't abusing anything that I thought was unchristian.

When Bob was dean of students [1953–1959], the boys were not allowed to wear mustaches or facial hair. We had this one boy who was absolutely not going to abide by that. Bob called him in and said, "Have you had any psychological problems?"

He said, "No."

Bob said, "Have you ever had to see a counselor?"

He said, "No."

Bob said, "Well, I want you to come into my office tomorrow morning, and I want to take you to Buffalo to a counselor."

He said, "Why, Dr. Ferm?"

Bob said, "Well, we've asked you not to wear facial hair, and you absolutely refuse to follow the code, and I want you to go up there with me to see this man. He's a Christian counselor and maybe you can make him understand why you cannot fit into the way life is in Houghton."

The boy came the next morning with it all shaved off.

There was a couple that was very amorous, and one day as Bob was walking through the connection between Fancher and Woolsey, this guy grabbed this girl's hand—only Bob slipped his hand into the fella's hand. All of a sudden this guy realizes he's squeezing this great big hand which he had thought was his girl friend's, and we didn't have any problem with him any more.[3]

Another alumnus adds these:

At Halloween Paul [Titus '35] used to like to go to Stanley Wright's barn and get that cow out and bring the cow up and put it by the girls dormitory at Gaoyadeo dorm. Gudrun Kartevold was the dean of women at that time. He'd bring that cow up and tie it by the stairs and call out, "Gudrun, Gudrun," then run.

I can remember another good one at Halloween. We had a bunch called the Hillbillies. There were about six or seven of us together. G. D. Kellogg was a carpenter, kind of an elderly man. He lived up on one of those roads where the science building is now. He had a garage downtown, and he had this old truck. At Halloween one time we went down and got that truck and shoved that thing way up that hill and put it up on the stairs of the administration building. That was quite a job. The next morning after Halloween everybody saw that and didn't know what to do. Of course, not any of the fellows that had worked to get it up was interested in getting it down. They watched all these others work together to get that thing down.[4]

Willard Smith, long-time Houghton administrator, recalled a couple of pranks from the pre-WW II years, and he identified the perpetrator as Merwin "Red" Ellis. In one case, Red had gotten at cross purposes with the librarian, who lived in Gaoyadeo dorm, and decided on revenge. Near midnight on Christmas eve, he entered the unlocked dorm, took the ring of room keys from the office, and turned off the master electric switch for the building. Then he went from room to room and set all the radios he could find to a Buffalo radio station and turned the volume all the way up. Downstairs, in the dining area, he loaded the contents of a box of cigars (purchased in Fillmore) into the three pop-up toasters and pushed the levers down. Before exiting the building, he turned the electricity back on. As soon as the radios warmed up they began blaring, and soon the smell of well-toasted cigars filled the building. The dean was called out, and quiet was not restored until the janitor and his master key were located. A bit of investigation by the dean led to the culprit, and when confronted Red confessed.[5]

Red Ellis later returned to his Gao-dorm venue for another prank. One fall night, around two in the morning, a couple of loud explosions awakened the sleeping Gao girls. Again the dean was called, but his walk-around inspections revealed nothing, so he headed for home. Before he passed the old infirmary, another resounding "boom" rolled along the Genesee hills. He sprinted back but again found nothing. Half way home again . . . another boom. Thirty minutes of checking still turned up nothing, so he gave up and went home. He learned days later that Red had been hiding in the wide eaves-trough near the corner of the building, lighting large firecrackers and dropping them into the downspout.[6]

During the librarian tenure of Esther Jane Carrier, and shortly after the new library opened in 1964, a collection of students pulled on of the larger pranks in library history. In Dr. Carrier's words,

> There were all those big plate glass windows [separating the main desk from the reading area], and I had a helper who felt you didn't need to be that strict with kids to keep discipline. It was one Tuesday night . . . Jean [my helper] came running back [to my office] and said, "Oh, Miss Carrier, come out, come out!"
>
> I went out and I have no idea what was in that reading room. There were birds flying around, there were chickens running around, there were mice running around, there were girls standing up screaming. The whole place was wild. . . . The animals were not much happier about being there than I was about having them. [I promptly closed the library.] People went out holding chickens by the legs.[7]

A member of the class of 1960, a writer of military history, volunteered two anecdotes from his days at Houghton:

> Dr. Paine once said in chapel that the student labor that built the old Fine Arts Building wasn't too professional, and "I'll bet if you could find the one main spike the whole thing would come crashing down." A few days later in chapel there was a tremendous *crash!* and a student ran up to Dr. Paine on the chapel platform and, holding up a large railroad spike, yelled, "I found it, Dr. Paine!" (A group of pranksters had rolled some trash cans down the chapel stairs.)
>
> And then there was the chapel evangelist whose tongue worked on occasion faster than his brain. He started out, "There's entirely too much freedom between boys and girls in Bible school. And unless we clean this up, we'll all wind up in the gutter—bless His holy name!"[8]

Appendix N

Miscellaneous Documents

Willard Houghton's Appeal for Books and Materials, 1884

A Proposition

When young people marry and are about to commence housekeeping, their friends very often make a reception for them and bring presents that are necessary to make them comfortable and happy. Now, the Wesleyan Methodist Seminary at Houghton is just commencing; it is wedded to Christ, truth and reform, and is strongly tied to the Wesleyan Methodist Connection of America; and we hope its friends in some way will remember this young institution, and make the hearts happy that daily tread these halls, by untying their hands, in presenting them with gifts necessary for the great work committed to their trust.

Rev. W. H. Kennedy, Principal, is the originator of this thought, to put a good library in this school, by friends sending a book or more from their libraries. Books that are seldom used, might be of great use to the coming young gentlemen and ladies that in the future are to mould to a great extent the character of the church and the world. In this way we can speak after we are dead. This work has already commenced. The first book was given by W. King, of Michigan, *Wilford's Microcosm*. The following have also contributed: W. H. Kennedy, Principal, *Chamber's Encyclopedia*; W. J. Houghton, *Kitto's Bible Illustrations*, four volumes; J. E. Tiffney, Chapel Bible. We hope the friends will very soon send in a library that will be a lasting benefit to this new institution. Some can donate papers to be pasted on a reading case, and in this way silently talk to the coming boys and girls, and sow seed on this good ground.

We also need at once a chemical apparatus, and for physiology a skeleton. We are living in an age of object teaching. Nothing will impress the intellect like what comes through the sense of seeing.

Now, I ask our friends in the name of reason, what can you do to live forever and speak even after you are dead, more than to put books, papers, and helps to enlighten and elevate the rising generations?

Those sending books, papers, or other help, will please address Rev. W. H. Kennedy, Houghton, Allegany county, N. Y.

W. J. Houghton

(December 1884; probably published in the Wesleyan Methodist*)*

Willard Houghton's Letter to the Wellsville Editor, 1885

Dear Sir:

Thought perhaps a few lines from Houghton might be interesting to the readers of your paper:

Our little village is growing rapidly notwithstanding the pressing times. Seven new buildings are contracted to go up before winter and we are looking for others. The new Waldorff Temperance Hotel is doing a fine business.

The first school year of Houghton Seminary closed cheeringly July 1st. Most of the students are to return in the fall to continue their studies, and evidently there will be a large increase in scholars. It will be pleasing to many in this vicinity to learn that there is to be a commercial course added this coming year. Mr. Luther Grange, professor of this department, is a young man of twenty-six years, a graduate fresh from Elmira College. Let all of the young gentlemen and ladies who are looking to commercial life come to this school. The trustees have also secured the services of Mrs. Mary Depew as governess whose duty it will be to take the place of mothers to the coming girls, visit their rooms often to give counsel and instruction there, and also to gather all the female students by themselves once a week to give lectures on proper conduct and behavior in their associations with the sexes. We are confident that every mother knowing this highly cultivated Christian lady will be pleased to know that their girls are to be under the watchful eye care of this mother in Israel. Every effort will be made by the faculty to make this one of the best Christian schools in the land. Hoping that this school may be a lasting benefit to this section of the country we ask the patronage of the people. Let the boys and girls begin to pack their trunks the first week in September will soon roll around.

W. J. Houghton[1]

Janitor's Contract,[2] 1895

This agreement entered into this 13th day of June 1895. Between R. F. Dutcher President of the Board of Trustees, Houghton Seminary, N.Y. party of the first part; said

R. F. Dutcher resident of North Cohocton, N.Y. and Thomas M. Patterson of Houghton N.Y. party of the second part.

Witnesseth that for and in consideration of the sum eighty seven ($87.00) dollars, to be paid to the said Thomas M. Patterson, in the manner following: to wit, commencing on the first of September and working three months said Patterson shall receive $21.75 at the end of said three months service; and shall receive a like sum of $21.75 at the duration of each three months service for the year ending Aug. 31st 1896. Said $87.00 shall be paid to said Thomas M. Patterson for his services as janitor for the year ending August 31st 1896. Said Thomas M. Patterson agrees with said R. F. Dutcher that he will perform the work of janitor for said seminary for the term of one year, in the following manner.

First by taking the entire over-sight of all the Seminary grounds, all the walks leading to the Seminary Building, and to the Privies and out buildings; keeping them clean from dirt or filth; or snow or any other obstruction.

Keeping the privies clean and the grass or weeds mown down along the side of all the walks during the entire year.

Second by taking the entire Seminary building under his care during the entire year, above mentioned, to mop each room in the building before the commencement of each period of five weeks of school. To wash the windows outside and inside, to sweep each room daily, at night, which is occupied, and dust the same each morning; to keep the entire building under lock and key, at all times, except during school hours. To keep the cellar locked at all times and to allow no student in the cellar except by consent of the party of the first part. To sift all the ashes and carry the same outside of the building, to keep the cellar clean and in good order constantly; to take good care of the furnaces by keeping them clean from ashes or by not allowing them to be overheated, to take the cold air from the hall most of the time and when taking the cold air from the hall to keep out-of-door air boxes closed, to use one or the other of the out-of-door air boxes, when the air is vitiated by use from the inside, to deliver and stow away in the cellar not more than thirty tons of coal during the year and in the spring, as soon as fire is no longer needed in the furnaces to take down the pipes and clean out the furnaces, clean up the cellar, and have the same neat and tidy, at the time of the Annual Board Meeting. To furnish water for the scholars to drink by keeping fresh drinking water in the pail in the Seminary at all times, during the school hours, to build fires in the furnaces on Monday morning by five o'clock if necessary, and let them go out on Friday nights, to keep the rooms at the temperature of about 68 degrees if possible, and to light the building for all meetings held in the Seminary by order of the Board of Trustees, to open and light up the Neosophic Society room at 7:00 p.m. each evening of the society meeting, and to ring the bell as heretofore practiced.

Signed by R. F. Dutcher President of and in behalf the Board of Trustees.

(Signed) Thos. M. Patterson as Janitor

Standards of Dress for Faculty and Staff, circa 1965

Each year there are a number of persons newly joining the faculty and staff of Houghton College, some of whom are not members of the Wesleyan Methodist church and who are thus not fully cognizant of some of the matters in which their cooperation is desired.

The matter of standards of dress and adornment as one meets the public is one of these. The prospective faculty member in signing the doctrinal statement agrees to respect certain rather well defined and clear standards of the church. He also agrees to "conform to the church standards which call for propriety and modesty in dress and for not wearing gold or useless ornaments."

This standard of "modesty and propriety" is one which appeals to all spiritual Christians and they understand in general that this will call for some deviation from the world's extremes of dress and adornment. But as to the details thus implied there is still a great variety of ideas even among spiritual Christian people.

On the Houghton campus all of us agree on the general principle that we as Christian staff members and as examples to the students should dress with simplicity and modesty. We endeavor to avoid too much specification of details but always in institutional life some basic understandings are found helpful because not only personal but institutional testimony is involved. The principle of simplicity, it seems to us, precludes the "wearing of gold and superfluous ornaments" (1 Tim. 2:8,9; 1 Peter 3:3). This we do not understand to apply to useful articles such as watches and eye glasses. Neither is it construed to apply to the wedding band. It is construed to refer in general to jewelry (e.g., rings other than the wedding band, necklaces, earrings, bracelets, and the like) and to expensive and ostentatious dress.

Amid the world's extremes of changing styles of clothing the sincere and careful Christian will desire to be on the conservative side. Women on the faculty and staff are asked to be especially careful that their dress styles be above question. For instance, there are certain types of so-called "cap sleeves" and extremely short sleeves which we request not be worn at our employment on the campus or in public. This applies as well to the wearing of "shorts," It is also requested that stockings be worn in public. This attention to matters of dress is not because it is thought that one's personal modesty or spirituality can be made matters of rule, but because in institutional life a general understanding is needed for the sake of the witness of the group.

It is felt that the staff and faculty will be desirous to cooperate in the above matters as they realize that this is one of the implications of service for Christ under the auspices of a Christian college. It is one of those points in which for the sake of group strength the individual voluntarily sacrifices a small amount of liberty in personal taste.

Regarding the families of staff and faculty members, it is realized that sometimes there may be instances where other members of the family are not fully sympathetic with the standards of the college and of the Wesleyan Methodist Church. As a rule, staff and faculty families are found to be understanding in these matters and thus they become examples to the student body, greatly helping in maintaining wholesome standards of life on the campus. Naturally, it is hoped that members of the staff and faculty will be successful in securing cooperation regarding these matters in their respective families.

Pastors of the Houghton Wesleyan (Wesleyan Methodist) Church

1852–1876	John Watson, L. W. Khral, Mr. Pepper (circuit preachers)	1912	William Frazier
		1912–1917	Charles B. Whittaker
		1917–1921	Charles Sicard
1876–1880	George W. Cooper	1921–1937	Joseph R. Pitt
1880–1884	Daniel W. Ball	1937–1942	Ernest W. Black
1884–1887	James E. Tiffany	1942–1951	Chauncey I. Armstrong
1887–1891	Benjamin S. Laughlin		
1891–1892	George W. Sibley	1951–1956	Edward D. Angell
1892–1895	Edwin W. Bruce	1956–1961	Martin W. Cox
1895–1897	J. Robert Jeffrey	1961–1968	Edward D. Angell
1897–1903	Sylvester Bedford	1968–1969	Karl K. Wilson
1903	Howard W. McDowell	1969–1970	Oliver Dongell
		1970–1973	Melvin Shoemaker
1903–1904	Mrs. Jennie Ayers	1973–1976	Morton W. Dorsey
1904–1905	J. Hughes	1977–1982	H. Mark Abbott
1905–1909	Charles H. Dow	1982–1995	J. Michael Walters
1909–1910	William Clow	1995–1996	Paul Shea (Interim)
1910–1912	Dean Sumner Bedford	1996–	Wesley D. Oden

Information Concerning Students, circa 1972[3]

Dr. Lois Roughan Ferm was graduated from Houghton in 1939, then returned to the campus from 1953 to 1959 with her husband, Dr. Robert O. Ferm, who served as professor of history and dean of students. As part of her doctoral program at the University of Minnesota, Lois wrote a dissertation entitled "Student Characteristics and Environments for Learning in Wesleyan Colleges." Her study opens with these statements:

Almost every phase of American society has changed [over the decade of the '60s] and practically all of its institutions have been involved in these [near cataclysmic] shifts. Higher education, including the church-related college, has felt the pressures. Student unrest, an abundance of over-specialized people, shortage of funds for private education, and the questioning of the Judaeo-Christian basis of our American tradition have all caused deep concern to church-sponsored colleges. . . .[4]

As restless, discontented young Americans have been flowing into colleges and universities, their ire has been vented against what they consider to be tragic weaknesses of the total society. Coupled with this is their indignation over what they believe to be long over-due need for changes in collegiate education. . . .[5]

Added to the general problems in society and higher education, the church-related college has special ones of its own. The demand now being placed upon these schools is that they provide an intel-lectually-based view of the historic Christian faith.[6]

Students Shape Colleges

Ferm cites two studies of college matriculant characteristics that assert that students have a strong tendency to select the church college that suits their vocational and religious needs. Says Ferm, "The implication of these studies is that the atmosphere of a college may be determined in large meas-ure by the students it enrolls."[7] In fact, one assessment device, the College Student Questionnaire, assumes that a college's environment is a product of its size and the intelligence and personal characteristics of its students and that the students who comprise the college develop distinctive subcultures. In other words, students themselves uniquely define the college.

Some Specific Characteristics

Dr. Ferm's 1972 report of her study of students at Wesleyan colleges involved 1374 individuals from the (then) five Wesleyan institutions: Bartlesville, Central, Houghton, Marion, and Miltonvale. Some 45 percent came from Houghton alone; another 30 percent were from Marion. Because of proportionate skewing of the sample toward these two larger and rea-sonably similar units, her finding would seem to be of analytical validity for anyone attempting to analyze Houghton.

According to Ferm, Wesleyan liberal arts colleges have not drawn the bulk of their students from metropolitan areas. Her data (collected in 1969) indicate that 75 percent of entering freshmen came from communities with fewer than fifty thousand persons; nearly 48 percent were from villages of under ten thousand or farming areas.[8] Also, students came from smaller high schools: about 50 percent graduated in a class of fewer than two hundred, with slightly more than half of that group in classes of under one hundred.[9] And well over a third came from a blue-collar background, with another eighth from homes of full-time Christian workers.

She goes on to say that "The tendency [is] for students to select the church college which suits their vocational and religious need. . . . The implication of the studies [cited: Darley, 1962; Goldsen and others, 1962; Heist, 1958; and Astin, 1965, 1968] is that the atmosphere of the college may be determined in large measure by the students it enrolls. . . . Several [investigators] operate on the theory that students make the college and thus develop distinctive student subcultures."[10]

On parental educational background, Ferm reports that slightly more than half of the fathers of liberal arts freshmen had no college training, with nearly 60 percent of the mothers also in that category. Little can be drawn from this, however, as she reported almost identical percentages for the parents of freshmen in other American liberal arts colleges.[11]

One interesting fact from her data was that less than 25 percent of the homes subscribed to any non-religious periodicals.[12]

"Not surprisingly, the largest percentage (41.6 percent) of the liberal arts freshmen came from Wesleyan homes—the denomination sponsoring the colleges. The next largest percentage (18.2 percent) reported a Baptist affiliation."[13] [Note: over the next twenty-five years, those percentages were reversed; analysis of this shift lies beyond the chronological scope of this work.]

"The homes of Wesleyan students apparently observed most of the religious practices inquired about in this study. Five in six (85 percent) of the liberal arts freshmen said they had been encouraged to attend church and Sunday school . . . Approximately 80 percent reported grace before meals and parents' attendance at church and Sunday school. Nearly three-fourths (74.3 percent) noted that a religious periodical was received in their home. About 70 percent said they had attended church camp or Daily Vacation Bible School."[14]

From Ferm's summary: "With most of these [Wesleyan] homes observing the religious practices queried in this study, students judged them to have exerted a strong spiritual influence upon them. Churches, too, were thought to have had a considerable influence on these students' development."[15]

"Two-fifths of Wesleyan liberal arts freshmen reported high school averages of B+ or above, which was a higher percentage than for freshmen generally. . . . "[16]

"Participation in high school, musical, athletic, language, and social organizations was characteristic of liberal arts students. . . . Wesleyan liberal arts students held a substantial number of leadership roles in scholastic and athletic organizations [as did freshmen throughout the U.S.]"[17]

Generally these Wesleyan students came from small cities and towns and from lower middle-income homes. "These homes and the churches exert a strong influence upon the students. In the main they are good students and participate in high school activities which are in accord with their religious background."[18]

Why did students choose to attend Wesleyan colleges? "Liberal arts learning and vocational preparation are the prime reasons . . . The majority of students had made at least a tentative choice of a career before coming to college, with these clustering around teaching or Christian work. Their main reasons for a particular career were a desire to be helpful to others and to use their special abilities. . . .

". . . Parents, other relatives, and high school teachers were the persons chiefly mentioned as having helped students make their choice. Generally, liberal arts fields and specified areas of education and Christian work were the predominant selections in majors specified by these students."[19]

In the arena of religious beliefs, "There was general consensus among students that God was Divine, the Creator of the universe, who knows the thoughts and feelings of an individual, and to whom each person would one day be accountable. More than nine-tenths of the freshmen had reached these views about God before coming to college."[20]

Concerning views of Biblical authority, "More than half of the liberal arts freshmen (54.9 percent) accepted the plenary inspiration view [a view identified by Ferm as generally being regarded by theologians as being "better based intellectually"]. A smaller percentage felt that the verbal dictation was the acceptable one."[21] By the senior year, another ten percent endorsed plenary inspiration. And, notes Ferm later, the vast majority of all students had adopted their view of the Bible before coming to college.

"Since students come to college with their special problems and hopes, it is important for both administrators and faculty to be aware of how satisfied students are with what the institution offered them."[22]

Just over half of freshmen surveyed (near the end of their first semester) said they were "satisfied" or "very satisfied" with their academic experience thus far. Nearly a third, however, reported being "dissatisfied" or "very dissatisfied," a large enough portion to be of serious concern.[23]

More than a third [of freshmen] commended one or more of their faculty for showing concern for students or "for their innovative or motivating styles of teaching. The instructor's scholarship did not seem to be a primary concern in describing superior faculty members."[24]

"Relatively few [students] noted favorable features of their general education courses. . . . Few . . . expressed satisfaction with the courses in religion, Bible, and religious education."[25] "An opportunity to correlate academic studies with the Bible is often stated as a basic purpose of a church-related institution. Yet very few students . . . noted this satisfaction."[26]

"Nearly half (47.3 percent) . . . of freshmen said they were satisfied with [the non-academic aspects] of college life, and another 16.1 percent apparently felt very satisfied. . . . When specific reasons . . . were probed, small group life beyond the dormitories" [including organized clubs, student government, sports, and friendships] was cited by nearly a third of freshmen. Next in importance for 30 percent was "chapel and other opportunities for spiritual growth and commitment." One-sixth cited "general encouragement toward self-expression, self-understanding, and independence."[27]

Because more than one-fourth of freshmen were dissatisfied their academic experience, students were asked to specify the nature of their dissatisfactions. . . . The most frequently mentioned gripes related to faculty, "including such things as inadequate preparation, mediocre teaching, poor testing, assignment of busy work, and inability to correlate Biblical teaching with academic studies."[28] The primary dissatisfactions with non-academic aspects involved "the rules, particularly those relating to dormitory living, compulsory class attendance, and dress." Some felt that "college life involved too many traditions and did not require enough personal thought and decision-making."[29]

Other Observations Concerning Church Colleges

Interestingly, according to a 1966 Danforth-funded study by Manning M. Pattillo and Donald M. Mackenzie, "the investigators agreed that the way in which the faculty expressed the religious emphasis of the college was the most significant factor in determining denominational impact upon the student. Effective faculty members appeared to be those who were in close accord with denominational views and who did not play down the church relationship of the college, but rather frequently emphasized the alliance."[30]

Also, "the religious impact of the college is more dependent on the place of religion as an 'all-pervasive' force than it is upon particular programs. This suggests that specific courses in Bible and theology will not affect students as much as the personal religious commitment of the faculty and administration."[31]

Myron Wicke (1964), after investigating specific elements in the religious environment of the church college, contends that the "content" of the religious heritage must be part of the program, but that its expression cannot be coerced by chapel or any other specific activities. From his findings he concluded that the most successful church college is one where the religious atmosphere itself causes people to be sensitive to social, political, and international problems and, as a result, to risk themselves in behalf of these causes. In this manner, materialism is resisted and the religious purposes of the church come through with a "prophetic" voice.[32]

Ferm's Conclusions

1. The students who select Wesleyan colleges generally come with rather limited types of social and educational experiences.
2. The largest percentages of students attending Wesleyan colleges come from spiritually-oriented homes and churches.
3. Wesleyan colleges attract students who have achieved well academically in their high school work with a good many also giving evidence of participation and leadership in non-class activities.
4. Senior students strongly motivated and supported by parents come to college with two dominant aims, namely to gain liberal learning and preparation for a vocation.
5. Senior students in these colleges do not differ from freshmen in their goals and outlooks.
6. Most students are satisfied with their choice of a small coeducational and religiously-oriented college, and say that they would make the same choice again.
7. Wesleyan colleges rank lower than other denominational and private (independent) colleges in students' perceptions of the learning environment provided for intellectual growth and development.
8. These colleges rank between the denominational and the private colleges in the climate furnished for out-of-class activities.[33]

Alumni among the Centennial 100

In the May 1983 issue of *Milieu*, the centennial reunion coordinator presented a list of one hundred Houghton-connected individuals selected by an alumni team as best representing the ideals of Houghton. Of that group, eighty-four were alumni, as listed here. Descriptive information is drawn from that 1983 listing and may be outdated.

Richard Alderman '52	High school teacher and principal; college administrator; alumni association president.
Gordon S. Anderson '43	Minister; president of Christian Radio Broadcasters Association.
John M. Andrews, Jr. '58	Physicist, Bell Laboratory.
Wilfred C. Bain '29	Founder of the Houghton College Choir; dean of School of Music at Indiana University; '81 Alumnus of the Year.
James E. Barcus '59	Houghton professor and English division chair; professor of English and department chair, Baylor University.
John Bechtel '62	Christian and Missionary Alliance missionary in Hong Kong; missionary administrator in U.S.
H. Clark Bedford, Sem.'87	Seminary teacher for thirteen years; first president of Marion College.
Marilyn Birch '44	Wesleyan missionary physician in Sierra Leone; '67 Alumnus of the Year.
Marion Birch '44	Wesleyan missionary teacher and administrator in Sierra Leone.
Harold W. Boon '36	Professor and president of Nyack College.
Stephen W. Calhoon '53	Houghton professor of chemistry; academic dean of Central Wesleyan College.
Benjamin Chan '65	Head of Christian School in Hong Kong.
James P. Chen '55	Houghton associate professor of chemistry; professor and researcher at University of Tennessee Memorial Research Center and Hospital.
Kenneth Clark '48	HIBA minister and missionary in Japan (32 years).
Mary Lane Clarke, Sem '93	First Houghton Seminary missionary (Sierra Leone); edited a Limba dictionary.

Malcolm Cronk '35	Minister and teacher; professor at Trinity Seminary.
Wilber Dayton '38	Wesleyan minister and teacher, president of Houghton College '72–'76.
John DeBrine '47	Radio minister, Youthtime director; '70 Alumnus of the Year.
Robert Dingman '50	National personnel-search executive; formed his own company in '79; '82 Alumnus of the Year.
Ione Driscal '27	High school teacher; Wesleyan missionary in Sierra Leone.
John Edling '44	Wesleyan missionary and surgeon in Haiti.
John Essepian '55	Dentist; member of the New York State Board of Dental Examiners.
Marvin Eyler '43	Professor of physical education and dean at University of Maryland; '72 Alumnus of the Year.
George E. Failing '40	Wesleyan minister; editor of *The Wesleyan Methodist* and of *The Wesleyan Advocate.*
Bessie M. Fancher, Sem '09	Houghton College teacher for thirty-seven years.
H. LeRoy Fancher, Sem '10	Houghton professor of German forty-three years; vice president.
W. LaVay Fancher, Sem.'13	Houghton professor of economics and academic dean.
Zola Kitterman Fancher '26	Part-time college teacher; seminary teacher until retirement.
Rachel (Davison) Fee '25	Associate professor of mathematics; registrar 1944–1958.
Robert O. Ferm '39	Minister and author; Billy Graham Team, thirty years; '74 Alumnus of the Year.
Homer J. Fero '31	Dentist; Houghton board of trustees.

Bert Hall '43	Houghton professor of philosophy and academic dean; professor at Azusa University.
John (Pete) Hammond '59	Specialized ministries and director of evangelism for InterVarsity Christian Fellowship for sevemteen years.
Ray W. Hazlett, Sem. '03	Professor of English at Long Island University; Houghton professor of English; division chair.
Marilyn J. Hunter '59	Resident physician and surgeon at Wesleyan Hospital on La Gonave, Haiti.
Morris Inch '49	Professor and department chair for Bible, Religion and Archeological Studies, Wheaton College.
Diane H. Komp '61	Professor of pediatrics and chief pediatric hematologist-oncologist at Yale University School of Medicine.
Paul A. Krentel '42	President and co-founder of The Melmark Home for Children with Down's Syndrome.
Paul LaCelle '51	Professor and chair of radiation biology and biophysics department, University of Rochester Medical Center.
Ian H. Lennox '51	President of Citizens' Crime Commission in Philadelphia.
Alton Liddick '37	Wesleyan minister and missionary in India; head of Wesleyan World Missions Department.
Katherine W. Lindley '43	Houghton professor of history; chair of Division of History and Social Science.
Robert Longacre '43	Missionary with Wycliffe; professor of linguistics, University of Texas at Arlington.
James S. Luckey, Sem. '89	Seminary teacher and principal 1994–1996; seminary and college president and math professor 1908–1937.
Robert R. Luckey '37	Houghton professor of math and vice president in development; president of Marion College; '76 Alumnus of the Year.

Arthur W. Lynip '38	Houghton professor of English and dean; professor at Westmont College.
Robert N. Lytle '39	Wesleyan minister and missionary; head of Wesleyan World Missions Department.
Robert MacKenzie '60	President of the Benson Company; involved in Gaither Music company.
Alice J. McMillen '25	Wesleyan missionary in Sierra Leone; Houghton dean of women and instructor in Bible.
Carolyn (Paine) Miller '60	Wycliffe missionary; prisoner in Vietnam; '77 Alumnus of the Year.
John D. Miller '57	Wycliffe missionary; prisoner in Vietnam; '77 Alumnus of the Year.
Silas R. Molyneaux '36	Colonel USAF, ret.; professor at West Point and USAF Academy; chief, Research and Analysis Division, Office of Secretary of Air Force, Pentagon; president of alumni association.
Wesley B. Nussey '40	Wesleyan minister; Central New York district superintendent; Houghton registrar.
Henry Ortlip '40	Wesleyan minister; missionary and field superintendent of Wesleyan Church in Haiti.
Paul Pang '64	Principal of United Christian College in Hong Kong (1,300 students).
Alice Pool '29	Houghton professor of Spanish; faculty secretary.
Josephine G. Richard '25	Houghton professor of English and chair of the English Division.
James Ridgeway '55	Wesleyan minister and teacher; superintendent of Wesleyan Churches in Australia; principal of Kingsley College.
Claude A. Ries, Sem. '18	Wesleyan minister; Houghton professor of Bible and chair of Division of Religion and Philosophy.

Herschel Ries '47	Missionary electronics engineer with Radio ELWA in Liberia; Houghton plant engineer.
Priscilla Ries '50	Medical records and office manager, Cook County TB Dist. (Illinois); president of alumni association.
Crystal L. Rork '27	Seminary teacher; Houghton professor of biology.
Benjamin C. Saoshiro '55	Minister of Immanuel Church in Japan; professor at Immanuel Bible Training College; superintendent of East Greater Tokyo Area of Immanuel Church.
Carl E. Selin '62	Specialist in nuclear medicine; professor at UCLA Medical Center.
Alton J. Shea '36	Wesleyan minister and missionary in Sierra Leone; evangelist and soloist; '73 Alumnus of the Year (family).
George Beverly Shea '32	Sacred recording artist; soloist with Billy Graham Evangelistic Association; '73 Alumnus of the Year (family).
Eila Shea '66	Wesleyan missionary nurse in Sierra Leone; staff nurse and part-time director of nursing.
J. Whitney Shea '33	Houghton professor of sociology and chair of Division of History and Social Science; '73 Alumnus of the Year (family).
William A. Smalley '45	Missionary anthropologist/linguist; professor of linguistics at Bethel College.
Allen R. Smith '43	Manager of Houghton College Press.
Willard G. Smith '35	Houghton business manager and treasurer; general treasurer of Wesleyan Church Headquarters.
Paul A. Steese '27	Houghton instructor in Math; high school math teacher and vice principal in Rochester City Schools; president of alumni association; '68 Alumnus of the Year.

Herbert H. Stevenson '38	Engineer with Eastman Kodak; member, then chair of Houghton trustee board.
Hollis Stevenson '29	Dentist; director of Wesleyan Men; Houghton board of trustees; '65 Alumnus of the Year.
F. Gordon Stockin '37	Houghton professor classics and chair of division; '79 Alumnus of the Year.
Philip G. Stockin '67	Teacher and business manager in Wesleyan Academy, Puerto Rico; Houghton Academy principal.
H. Park Tucker '40	Minister and chaplain in state and federal prisons.
Asuquo Epke Udo '56	Principal of secondary school and teacher training college in Nigeria; member of Nigerian Parliament.
Bruce Waltke '52	Minister and teacher; Old Testament Department head at Regent College; member of Committee on Bible Translation for NIV.
George R. Wells '47	Houghton professor of physical education and department head, director of Youth in One Accord revival ministry.
Kenneth L. Wilson '41	Christian writer and editor of *Christian Herald*.
Warren M. Woolsey '43	Wesleyan missions teacher in Sierra Leone; Houghton professor of New Testament and missions.
Frank H. Wright, Sem. '06	Houghton professor of theology and division chair.
Stanley W. Wright, Sem.'05	Wesleyan minister; teacher at Central Wesleyan College; Houghton professor of Bible and dean of men.

Alma Mater

(tune: Annie Lisle)

Ernest M. Hall '06   H.S. Thompson

1. When the east-ern sun is sink-ing Toward the crim-son west,
2. Hon-ored lives for thee have fal-len, Hearts that broke and bled,
3. Oth-er schools may claim their thou-sands; We're a smal-ler band.
4. Soon from out our halls of learn-ing All must take our leave,
5. When o'er earth thy fame has ris-en Like the morn-ing light,

Thoughts of thee, fond Al-ma Ma-ter Fill our loy-al breast.
Have been wrung thy cause to pros-per And thy light to shed.
But for God and right-eous-ness we Take a no-ble stand.
But thy mem-ory still we'll cher-ish, To thy pre-cepts cleave.
'Twill but rise the earth to glad-den And dis-pel the night.

Chorus

1-4. Hough-ton, Hough-ton, now and e'er, May thy name be dear,
5. Hough-ton, Hough-ton, now and e'er, Let us pray that we,

Ev-er on through life to con-quer, And our hearts to cheer.
All her sons, be firm and loy-al Till e-ter-ni-ty.

Written for the 1906 Commencement and dedication of Jennings Hall, the new Administration Building (now Fancher Hall).

Alma Mater

Ernest M. Hall (v. 1, 2, 4)
Stephen W. Paine (v. 3, 5)

Charles H. Finney

1. When the east - ern sun is sink - ing Toward the crim - son west,
2. Hon - ored lives for thee have fal - len, Hearts that broke and bled,
3. Soon from out thy halls of learn - ing All must take our leave,
4. When o'er earth thy fame has ris - en Like the morn - ing light,
5. Hough - ton, Hough-ton, now and ev - er Let us pray that we,

Thoughts of thee, fond Al - ma Ma - ter Fill our loy - al breast.
Have been wrung thy cause to pros - per And thy light to shed.
But thy mem - ory still we'll cher - ish To thy pre - cepts cleave.
'Twill but rise the earth to glad - den And dis - pel the night.
All her sons, be firm and loy - al Till e - ter - ni - ty.

Music and new verses written in August 1963

Bibliography

Individuals Interviewed by the Author

C lass numerals, where shown, indicate year of graduation from Houghton College. Other numbers indicate years of service at the college. Spouses are listed with spouses, even if out of alphabetical order.

Richard J. Alderman '52, 1971–1991

William T. Allen, 1953–1992

Philip F. Anderson '33

Elisabeth A. Veazey '44*

John M. Andrews Sr., 1935–1974

James E. Barcus '59, 1964–1980

Eldon Basney, 1951–1978

Willis Beardsley '60, 1980–

Evelyn "Dindy" Bence '74

James E. Bence '37

Florence (Lytle) Bence '35

Fay (Hunting) Bennett '43

Ehrmann Bennett

Mary Boomhower, 1952–1997

Bruce Brenneman, 1982–

E. Douglas Burke, 1958–1994

Marilyn Byerly '54*

A. Ray Calhoon '16

Stephen W. Calhoon '53, 1956–1978

William S. Calkins Jr. '44

Mary (Harris) Carey '49, 1960–1963

Esther J. Carrier, 1950–1979

Daniel R. Chamberlain, 1976–

Philip H. Chase '44

Marion (Schoff) Chase '43

Robert W. Childs '53

Olson Clark '46*

Ray M. Coddington '47, 1971–1989

Arnold W. Cook '43, 1960–1989

Elizabeth (Park) Cook '62, 1964–1988

Robert L. Cummings '50, 1962–1988

Abraham Davis Jr. '55, 1961–1974

William Davis '69

Jill Wallace Davis '71*

Wilber T. Dayton '38, 1972–1976

John D. DeBrine '47

George E. Failing '40, 1947–1953

Lowell Fancher, 1948–1991

Lois Fancher

L. Roscoe Fancher '35

Elizabeth (Coe) Fancher '34

Richard D. Farwell '34, 1960–1963

Anne (Madwid) Farwell '40

Elizabeth Beck Gilbert Feller,
1943–1951

Lois (Roughan) Ferm '39

Anne Finney (faculty spouse
1946–1979)

Dean S. Gilliland '50

Lois (Harris) Gilliland '50

Harold Grant, 1964–1993

Evangeline Grant

William N. A. Greenway, 1962–1999

Richard A. Gould '61, 1968–

Lee M. Haines Jr.,
general superintendent

Bert Hall '43, 1947–1973

Lola Haller '57, 1963–1997

Richard K. Hart '69

Lyndell Harter '71

Velma (Harbeck) Moses Hewson '32

Lois (Munger) Hurlburt '35

Russell Hurlburt '50

Ruth Fancher Hutton '43, 1962–1988

Gloria (Kleppinger) Huizenga '65

Raymon Irish (lifetime area resident)

Daniel C. Kauffman '67

Harold I. E. Kingdon '57, 1967–1903

Ellen E. Kreckman '59, 1959–1960;
1961–1998

John R. Leax '66, 1968–

Ian H. Lennox '51, 1977–

Dean A. Liddick '60, 1964–2001

Katherine (Walberger) Lindley '43,
1963–1989

Kenneth E. Lindley, 1963–1989

Robert R. R. Luckey '37, 1942–1976

Ruth Luckey '45

Arthur Lynip, 1950–1966

Harold McNiel, 1958–2002

Evan Molyneaux '29

R. Silas Molyneaux '36

Kenneth C. Motts '50

Lawrence K. Mullen, 1966–1993

Kenneth L. Nielsen, 1962–1997

William V. Olcott '40

Stephen J. Ortlip '42

Doris Armstrong Ortlip '44

W. Henry Ortlip '40

Helen (Paul) Paine '37

Frederic C. Parker, 1976–1998

Bernard J. Piersma, 1971–

Richard C. Pocock '55, 1959–1995

Herschel C. Ries '47, 1946–1949,
1972–1989

Ruth (Samuels) "Sammie" Ries

Priscilla Ries '50*

John Robb, 1961–1982

David E. Robbins Jr. '47

Richard Sandle '42

Janice (Strong) Sandle '43

Stanley L. Sandler '60

Duane C. Saufley, 1965–1998

Carl Schultz '53, 1965–

Douglas D. Shaffner '40

Edna (Woodward) Shaffner '49

Frederick D. Shannon, 1958–1993

Alton J. Shea '36

Aileen (Ortlip) Shea, 1936–1946

Paul W. Shea '69, 1994–

Allen R. Smith '43, 1946–1986

Esther (Fulton) Smith '43, 1955–1986

Guendolen (Stuart) Smith '49

Howard Smith '50

Willard Smith '37, 1937–1972

Eileen (Griffen) Spear '52, 1989–1999

Marjorie (Ortlip) Stockin, 1939–1959; 1963–1978

Philip G. Stockin '68

Clinton H. Strong '41

Mary (Tiffany) Strong '40

Clifford W. Thomas, 1969–1974

Virginia (Blowers) Totman '50

Floyd E. Totman '50

Ralph E. Traber Jr. '50

Frederick D. Trexler '64, 1969–1998

Layton F. Vogel '36

Isabelle (Rogato) Weir, 1968–1971

George R. Wells '47, 1947–1988

Edward J. Willett '39, 1962–1985

Lois (Hardy) Wilt '66, 1968–1988

Warren M. Woolsey '43, 1958–1959, 1966–1994

Kenneth W. Wright '34

Margaret Wynn '52, 1974–1989

*individual did not graduate

Interviews Conducted by Others

Interviewee (Interviewer)

John Andrews Sr. (K. Lindley)

Wilfred Bain (E. Willett)

Frieda Gillette (K. Lindley, B. Hill)

Frieda Gillette (R. Rozendal)

Frieda Gillette: 1951 Revival (R. Miller)

Robert Luckey (K. Lindley; F. Gillette)

Roy Nicholson (E. Willett)

Ortlips on family history and art

Stephen Paine and Arthur Lynip

Kenneth Wilson (D. Liddick)

Chapels and Other Taped Programs

William Allen (chapel: Andrews and Finney)

Robert Fiegl (Anna Houghton Daughters)

Robert Fiegl (WJSL interview)

Robert Fiegl (chapel: campus building)

Timothy Fuller (two Heritage chapels)

Lee M. Haines Jr (chapel: reform and piety)

Maxine L. Haines (chapel: Wesleyan women ministers)

Walter Hobbs (chapel: J. Whitney Shea)

Katherine Lindley (chapel: the war years)

Arthur Lynip (chapel: F. Gordon Stockin)

Stanley Sandler '60 (chapel: Houghton in the 1950s)

Gordon Stockin (lecture: *Logos Americanus*)

Gordon Stockin (chapel: bio, anecdotes)

Gordon Stockin (chapel: liberal arts educ.)

Other Primary Sources

Houghton College, *Data Presented for Consideration of the Commission on Institutions of Higher Education, Middle States Association of Colleges and Secondary Schools,* January 12, 1953.

Houghton College, *Houghton College Middle States Report and Self-Surve*y, 1965.

Houghton College, *Houghton College Bulletin*, Vol. VII, No. 7, June 1942, "A Glimpse of Houghton's Revival," by Stephen W. Paine.

Houghton College catalogs, 1887 to 1972.

Middle States Association of Colleges and Secondary Schools. *Evaluation Report of Houghton College, Houghton, New York, for the Commission on Institutions of Higher Education of the Middle States Association of Colleges and Secondary Schools*. March 16–18, 1953.

Middle States Association of Colleges and Secondary Schools, Commission on Institutions of Higher Education. *Report on Houghton Colleg*e, February 21–24, 1965.

Minutes of the Book Committee of the Wesleyan Methodist Connection (Wesleyan Archives)

Minutes of the Houghton Athenian Society (Houghton College Archives)

Minutes of the Houghton Faculty (Houghton College Archives)

Minutes of the Houghton Neosophic Literary Society (Houghton College Archives)

Minutes of the Local Board of Managers (Houghton College Archives)

Minutes of the Trustees of Houghton College (Wesleyan Archives)

Minutes of the Wesleyan Methodist Board of Administration (Wesleyan Archives)

Palmer, Edmund. *The Autobiography of Edmund Palmer Written for His Children*. Houghton, New York, 1916. Monograph.

Books and Dissertations

Allen, Richard Doyle. *An Investigation of the Religious Climate at Four Liberal Arts Colleges Related to the Wesleyan Church*. Unpublished doctoral dissertation, Michigan State University, 1984.

Beck, Elizabeth. *Planning a Women's Residence Hall for Houghton College*. Unpublished master's thesis, University of Michigan, 1946. Copy in Houghton archives.

Beers, F. W., and Co. *History of Allegany County, N.Y., 1806–1879*. New York: Press of George McNamara, 1879.

Calhoon, Alvin Raymond. *Just One in a Million*. Interlaken, N.Y.: Heart of the Lakes Publishing, 1986.

Carpenter, Joel A. and Kenneth W. Shipps. *Making Higher Education Christian*. Grand Rapids, Mich.: Christian University Press (Eerdmans), 1987

Crooks, Mrs. E. *Life of Rev. A. Crooks*. Syracuse: Wesleyan Methodist Publishing House, 1875.

Dieter, Melvin E. (ed.), *The Nineteenth Century Holiness Movement*. Kansas City, Mo.: Beacon Hill Press, 1998

Douglass, Harl R.. *Secondary Education in the United States*. New York: Ronald Press, 1964.

Ferm, Lois. *Student Characteristics and Environment for Learning in Wesleyan Colleges*. Unpublished doctoral dissertation, University of Minnesota, 1972.

Fletcher, Robert. *A History of Oberlin College: From Its Foundation Through the Civil War*, 2 vols. Oberlin, Ohio: Oberlin College, 1943.

Gillette, Frieda A., and Kathering W. Lindley. *And You Shall Remember . . . a Pictorial History of Houghton College*. Houghton, N.Y: Houghton College, 1982

Graffam, Alan Edward. *On the Persistence of Denominational Evangelical Higher Education: Case Studies in the History of Geneva College, Roberts*

Wesleyan College, Nyack College, and Houghton College. Unpublished doctoral dissertation, SUNY at Buffalo, 1986.

Hockin, Frederick. *John Wesley and Modern Methodism.* London: Rivingtons, 1887

Holmes, Arthur F. *The Idea of a Christian College.* Grand Rapids, Mich.: Eerdmans, 1975

Jennings, Arthur T. *History of American Wesleyan Methodism.* Syracuse: Wesleyan Methodist Publications Association, 1902.

Johnson, Curtis D. *Islands of Holiness: Rural Religion in Upstate New York, 1790–1860.* Ithaca, N.Y.: Cornell University Press, 1989.

Larson, Arlin T. *A College's Purposes: The Idea of Education at Oberlin College.* Unpublished doctoral dissertation, University of Chicago, 1976.

Lemcio, Mirian Paine. *Deo Volente: A Biography of Stephen W. Paine.* Houghton, N.Y.: Houghton College Press, 1987.

MacLear, Martha. *The History of Education of Girls in New York and New England 1800–1870.* Washington:Howard University Press, 1926.

Martin, Joel. *The Wesleyan Manual, or History of Wesleyan Methodism.* Syracuse; Wesleyan Methodist Publishing House, 1889

McLeister, Ira F., and F. R. Eddy, eds. *Wesleyan Standards.* Syracuse, N.Y.: The Wesleyan Methodist Publishing Association, circa 1930.

McLeister, Ira Ford. *History of the Wesleyan Church in America.* 3rd ed.— Rev. by Roy Stephen Nicholson. Marion, Ind.: Wesley Press, 1959.

McLeister, Ira F. and Roy Stephen Nicholson. *Conscience and Commitment: The History of the Wesleyan Methodist Church in America.* (4th ed: Lee M. Haines Jr. and Melvin E. Dieter, eds.) Marion, Ind.: The Wesley Press, 1976.

Mead, Frank S. *Handbook of Denominations in the United States.* Nashville: Abingdon Press, 1995.

Minard, John S. *Allegany County and Its People: A Centennial History 1795–1895.* Alfred, N.Y.: W. H. Ferguson and Co; 1896.

Nichols, Timothy Jay. *For the Good of the World: Education and Salvation at the Houghton Wesleyan Methodist Seminary and the Oberlin Collegiate Institute.* Unpublished doctoral dissertation, SUNY at Buffalo, 1996.

Pierce, William. *The Ecclesiastical Principles and Polity of the Wesleyan Methodist Church.* London: Hamilton, Adams, and Co., 1868.

Reid, Daniel G. ed., *Dictionary of Christianity in America.* Downers Grove, Ill.: InterVarsity Press, 1990.

Ringenberg, William C. *The Christian College:A History of Protestant Higher Education in America.* Grand Rapids, Mich.: Christian University Press (Eerdmans), 1984.

Rudolph, Frederick. *The American College and University: A History*. New York: Vantage Books, 1962.

Rule, William Harris. *Wesleyan Methodism Regarded as the System for a Christian Church*. London: Aylott and Jones, 1846.

Russell, John Dale, and Charles H. Judd. *The American Educational System: An Introduction to Education*. Cambridge, Mass.: Houghton-Mifflin, 1940.

Scott, Rev. Orange. *The Grounds of Secession from the M. E. Church, or, Book for the Times: Being an Examination of Her Connection with Slavery and Also of Her Form of Government*. New York: The Wesleyan Connection of America, 1851.

Shea, J. Whitney. *Houghton College and the Community*. Unpublished doctoral dissertation, Columbia University, 1952.

Smith, Timothy Lawrence, *Revivalism and Social Reform: American Protestantism on the Eve of the Civil War*. Baltimore: Johns Hopkins Press, 1980

Smith, Willard G. *The History of Church-Controlled Colleges in the Wesleyan Methodist Church*. Unpublished doctoral dissertation, New York University, 1951.

_____ *90 Plus: the Willard G. Smith Story*. Self-published. 2002

Strong, Douglas M. *Perfectionist Politics: Abolition and the Religious Tensions of American Democracy*. Syracuse: Syracuse University Press, 1999.

Taylor, Charles W. *History of the (Higher) Educational Movement of the Wesleyan Methodist Church of America*. Unpublished doctoral dissertation, Indiana University, 1959.

Taylor, Leslie O., Don R. McMahill, and Bob L. Taylor. *The American Secondary School*. New York: Appleton, Century Crofts, 1960.

Tewksbury, Donald G. *The Founding of American Colleges and Universities Before the Civil War*. New York: Columbia University (Anchor Books [1968]), 1932.

Thomas, Erma Anderson. *The Man of the Hour, a Biography of Dr. J. S. Luckey*. Houghton, N.Y.: Houghton College Press, 1937.

Thomas, Paul Westphal, and Paul William Thomas. *The Days of Our Pilgrimage: The History of the Pilgrim Holiness Church*. (Eds: Melvin E. Dieter and Lee M. Haines, Jr.) Marion, Ind.: The Wesley Press, 1976.

Tuttle, Robert G. Jr. *John Wesley: His Life and Theology*. Grand Rapids: Zondervan, 1978

Wing, R. L., and Lois G. Wing. *Directory of Houghton College Baccalaureate Graduates, 1925–1972*. Houghton, N.Y.: Houghton College Quick Print, 2001.

Wood, Arthur Skevington. *The Burning Heart: John Wesley, Evangelist*. Grand Rapids: Eerdmanns, 1967

Woody, Thomas. *A History of Women's Education in the United States* (2 vols.). New York: Octagon Books, 1929 (reprinted 1966).

Bibliography of Works for Shea Essay, Chapter 14

Carter, Charles W. *A Half Century of American Wesleyan Missions in West Africa*. Syracuse, N.Y.: Wesleyan Methodist Publishing Association, 1940.

Clarke, George and Mary Lane. *American Wesleyan Methodist Mission of Sierra Leone, W. Africa* (no publication data)

Fyfe, Christopher. *A Short History of Sierra Leone*. London: Longman, 1962.

Hall, A.W. *Three Hundred Miles in a Hammock or Six Weeks in Africa*. Houghton, N.Y.: Wesleyan Methodist Publishing Association, 1989.

Maclure, Hugh L. *Letters from the White Man's Grave: Pioneering on the Medical Missionary Frontier*. White Rock, B.C.: CREDO Publishing Corp., 1994.

Sanneh, Lamin. "Africa." In *Toward the 21st Century in Christian Mission*, ed. James M. Phillips and Robert T. Coote. Grand Rapids: Eerdmans, 1993.

Shea, Paul W. "Years of Decision: The Houghton College Experience and Missionary Motivation and Preparation." Unpublished D. Miss. major project, Trinity Evangelical Divinity School, 1994.

Steffan, Tom A. "Storytelling," in *The Evangelical Dictionary of Missions*, ed. A. Scott Moreau. Grand Rapids: Baker, 2000.

Walls, Andrew F. *The Cross-Cultural Process in Christian History*. Maryknoll, N.Y.: Orbis Books, 2002.

Other Resources

Brackney, William H. "Church Union Dialogue in the Come-Outer Tradition Wesleyan Methodists and Methodist Protestants 1858-1876: Methodist History, Vol. XXI, No. 2, January 1986, 82–97.

Conway, Jill K. "Perspectives on the History of Women's Education in the United States." *History of Education Quarterly*, 14 (Spring 1974).

Grange, Roberta Molyneaux. *My Book*. Unpublished personal journal (6 manuscript vols.) (Houghton Archives)

Kipp, David L. *Locking the Heights: The Rise and Demise of the Genesee Valley Canal*. Monograph published by the Canal Society of New York State, 1999.

Liddick, Dean (ed.). *Houghton Wesleyan Church Sesquicentennial, 1852–2002*. New York: Houghton Wesleyan Church, 2002.

President's Commission on Higher Education, *Higher Education in American Democracy* (6 vols.). Washington, D.C.: Government Printing Office, 1947.

Smith, Timothy. *Uncommon Schools: Christian Colleges and Social Idealism in Midwestern America, 1820–1950*. Copyright by author, 1952. Monograph printed by Indiana Historical Society.

Smith, Willard G., and R. L. Wing. *Directory of Faculty Who Served Houghton College Before 1972*. Houghton, N.Y.: Houghton College Quick Print, 2001.

Van Wormer, Idah Benning. "White Raiment or Nakedness," a message delivered at the fifty-third session of the (Wesleyan Methodist) Allegheny Conference Women's Missionary Society, June 11, 1959. Printed and distributed by the Women's Missionary Society.

Wilson, Kenneth L. *Consider the Years 1883–1983*. Houghton, N.Y.: Houghton College Press, 1982.

Wright, Kenneth W. *A Brief History of the Development of the Infrastructure of Houghton Seminary and Houghton College*. Unpublished monograph, 2001. (Houghton Archives)

Wright, Kenneth W. *Brief Account of the Development of Houghton Seminary with a Biographical Sketch of Philinda Sprague Bowen*. Unpublished monograph, 2001. (Houghton Archives)

Notes

Preface

1. Alan Graffam, On the Persistence of Denominational Evangelical Higher Education: Case Studies in the History of Geneva College, Roberts Wesleyan College, Nyack College, and Houghton College, 198.

Chapter 1

1. Kenneth Wilson, *Consider the Years: Houghton College 1883–1958*, 2.
2. P. F. Kluge, *Alma Mater—A College Homecoming*, 2.
3. Willard J. Houghton, as recorded in the covers of his ledger book for contributions.
4. Josephine G. Rickard to Katherine Lindley, postmarked Sept. 19, 1981.

Chapter 2

1. Orange Scott, in *The Grounds of Secession from the M. E. Church, or, Book for the Times: Being an Examination of Her Connection with Slavery and Also of Her Form of Government,* presented two arguments which underlay the necessity for individual and congregational separation from the Methodist Episcopal Church. The first regarded the status of slavery in the church. His points:

> 1. John Wesley was against slavery.
> 2. The Methodist Episcopal Church, organized in 1784, was against slavery.
> 3. However, slavery came to be accepted as slave owners and their sympathizers became a majority in the church.
> 4. In 1837, the Georgia Conference passed a resolution stating that "slavery is not a moral evil." This statement was subsequently sanctioned by the M.E. General Conference; Bishop Hedding argued that "The right to hold a slave is founded on this rule: 'Therefore, all things whatsoever ye would that men should do to you, do ye even so to them, for this is the law and the prophets.'" [Note: Timothy Smith quoted unnamed "Princeton professors" as the originators of a "maddeningly ingenious defense of slavery," with roots in Calvinism: "God had chosen some to be masters and some to be servants . . . in much the same way as certain men were elected to be saved and others to be damned." *Revivalism and Social Reform,* 186.]
> 5. The Bible exhorts Christians to separate themselves from evil doers, either by casting them out of the church or, if evildoers constitute the majority, by seceding from the church.

The second argument addressed the political structure of the M. E. church, most especially the power of the bishops.

> 1. John Wesley did not appoint Thomas Coke and Francis Asbury as bishops; Coke and Asbury elevated themselves to this rank.
> 2. They and others organized the Methodist Episcopal Church in America. It was not an agency of Wesleyan Methodism.

3. The seven bishops, elected by their pastoral subordinates to life-long sinecures, arrogated to themselves all power in the church, and they exercised their powers in a dictatorial manner. Their leadership was of a sovereignty which did not involve scriptural underpinnings or congregational election and decision making.

4. The bishops barred any discussion of abolitionism, and they dismissed pastors and churches who acted in opposition to this edict.

5. Again, the only possible redress was secession and separation.

2. A picture of D. S. Kinney comes from I. F. McLeister, *History of the Wesleyan Church in America* (3rd ed.), 108–109: "Speaking of [D.S. Kinney's] large vision and ability in finances, Rev. W. J. Houghton said: 'We have only to open our eyes to see the monuments reared chiefly by his hands—the Publishing House and Houghton Seminary. Although he never gave a dollar out of our Connectional funds to plant the Seminary building, yet indirectly he has solicited and put thousands of dollars into that school, and really, under God, has planted that moral lighthouse.'

"After speaking of their travels together, Mr. Kinney as [Connectional] Agent and Mr. Houghton representing the Seminary, when they attended seventeen conferences, he continued, 'Often after spending a day on the conference floor, he would go to his room to spend sleepless nights in answering pressing correspondence. Long after the midnight hour the moving of his chair or the scratching of his pen has awakened me. I would say to him that he must drop that pen and go to his rest, or he would surely die; but he would say, "Brother Houghton, what shall I do? This work is upon me, no one can do it for me." After going through the excitement and overwork of one conference he would take the cars for the next, and the changes mostly in the night. Instead of taking the sleeping-car, like the aristocracy of the land, he would use for his pillow the iron arm of the seat or the window-sill, thus saving the money for the connection. He often spoke of the struggling missionaries on the frontiers, and the poor in the churches, for whom he was so willing to deny himself. How often he would breathe out, 'Jesus, blessed Jesus! Brother Houghton, what would we do without Jesus?'"'"

3. Arthur T. Jennings, *History of American Wesleyan Methodism*, 2. Also, Robert G. Tuttle, *John Wesley: His Life and Theology,* 38.

4. Ira F. McLeister, *History of the Wesleyan Church in America* (1934), 1.

5. A. S. Wood, *The Burning Heart: John Wesley, Evangelist*, 24

6. Ibid., 13.

7. Ibid., 14

8. Ibid., 51, 54.

9. Ibid., 60–67.

10. Jennings, Loc. cit.., 3.

11. Wood, op. cit., 72.

12. Frank Mead, *Handbook of Denominations*, 173–174.

13. The hymnody output of Charles Wesley equalled that of another famous hymn writer, Fanny Crosby (1820–1915): both produced words for more than 8000 pieces of music. (Source: essay by John Tyson, "Charles Wesley, Preacher, Teacher, and Singer of Revival," *The Preacher's Magazine,* June-August 1987, 54–60.)

14. Wood, op. cit., 28

15. Jennings, Loc. cit., 5–6.

16. Ibid., 6–7.

17. Ibid., 15.

18. Graffam, op. cit., 153.

19. Ibid., 154.

20. Wood, Loc. cit.., 22.

21. Floyd H. Benham, "The Anti-Slavery Party." *Historical Wyoming*, Warsaw, NY, April 1998; 110.

22. Ibid.

23. Jennings, Loc. cit., 21 and 25–26. Orange Scott, in his 1851 book, *The Grounds of Secession from the M. E. Church,* describes at some length the half-century struggle by pastors and laymen for congregational participation in the decisions of the Methodist Episcopal bishops, even to the point of asserting that the "M.E. form of government is a gross violation" of the church polity principles recorded in scripture (145). "None but those blinded by ignorance . . . can fail to see the *seeds of Popery* in the M. E. polity" [italics in the original].

24. Ibid., 20.

25. As quoted in McLeister and Nicholson, 26.

26. Donald Strong, *Perfection Politics*, 19.

27. Ibid., 25. Later in the "Pastoral Address" document, the authors say: "The history of the past shows that the members of any religious community are wont to feel less friendship for seceders from their own communion, and their general policy is apt to be more bitter and persecuting towards such than towards other branches of the Church, who are much further removed from their communion views."

28. McLeister and Eddy, eds. *Wesleyan Standards,* 4.

29. Joel Martin, *The Wesleyan Manual, or History of Wesleyan Methodism*, 60.

30. Willard Smith, *The History of Church-Controlled Colleges in the Wesleyan Methodist Church*, 93.

31. This conference was later divided into three parts, with the Syracuse Conference covering most of central New York and the Lockport Conference embracing the western portion. Houghton Seminary was founded under the Lockport Conference.

32. Martin, *op.cit.*, 19. By 1902, says Martin (194–195), there were twenty-four conferences: Alabama, Allegheny, Central Ohio, Champlain, Dakota, Illinois, Indiana, Minnesota, Nebraska, New York, North Carolina, North Michigan, Pacific, Rochester, Iowa, Kansas, Lockport, Miami, Michigan, South Kansas, Syracuse, Tennessee, West Iowa, and Wisconsin.

33. Jennings, op. cit., 81–84.

34. McLeister (1934), 49.

35. McLeister (1934), 91, 98, 103, 104.

36. From the private papers of F. R. Eddy, as quoted by Charles W. Taylor, *History of the (Higher) Educational Movement of the Wesleyan Methodist Church of America*, 9.

37. For more information on revivalism and the holiness movement, see Melvin E. Dieter, *The Nineteenth Century Holiness Movement*, and Timothy Lawrence Smith, *Revivalism and Social Reform: American Protestantism on the Eve of the Civil War.*

38. Melvin E. Dieter *et al.* "Evangelicalism: An Alternative Perspective. A Report on the Research Project." *The Asbury Herald*, Spring 1988, 8.

This statement of Wesleyan Holiness Theology was presented in "A Report on the Research Project," cited above.

Historically, evangelicals hold basic beliefs concerning the Trinity, humanity, Holy Scripture, salvation, the Church, and Christian ethics. In addition, the Wesleyan Holiness Movement adheres to some very basic points central to Wesleyan theology. With a few slight variations, these points can be summarized as follows:

1. That God calls all believers to entire sanctification in a moment of full surrender and faith subsequent to their new birth in Christ. Through sanctifying grace the Holy Spirit delivers them from all rebellion toward God, and makes possible wholehearted love for God and others. This grace does not make believers

faultless nor prevent the possibility of their falling into sin. They must live daily by faith in the forgiveness and cleansing provided for them in Jesus Christ.

2. That believers are assured that they are children of God by the inward witness of God's Spirit with their spirits, by faith in the gracious promises of God's Word, and by the fruit of the Spirit in their lives.

39. Strong, op. cit., 48.

40. Whitney Cross, *The Burned-over District*, 3.

41. Curtis D. Johnson, *Islands of Holiness: Rural Religion in Upstate New York, 1790–1860*, page 42.

42. Mark A. Noll, "Christian Colleges, Christian Worldviews, and An Invitation To Research," introductory essay to *The Christian College* by William C. Ringenberg, 14–15.

43. Robert Fletcher, *A History of Oberlin College: From Its Foundation Through the Civil War*, 2 vols, 1:207. (Quoted in Larson, op. cit., 54–55)

44. Frederick Rudolph, *The American College and University*, 48–49.

45. Ibid., 54.

46. Willard J. Houghton to Orrin T. Higgins, March 5, 1883.

47. Harl Douglass, *Secondary Education in the United States*, 8–10; Leslie O. Taylor, Don R. McMahill, and Bob L. Taylor, *The American Secondary School, 9–10*.

48. Taylor, McMahill, and Taylor, op. cit., 10.

49. Douglass, op. cit., 9–10.

50. Russell and Judd, *The American Educational System*, 271–278 .

51. Ibid., 150–151

52. Rudolph, Loc. cit., 57.

53. Lawrence B. Davis, draft manuscript in Houghton archives, 1981, n.p.

54. Ibid.

55. Ibid.

56. From an undated newspaper clipping found in the Houghton archives, probably from the 1920s.

57. R. L. Wing was a student at Pike Seminary High School when it burned.

58. Taylor, *History of the (Higher) Educational Movement of the Wesleyan Methodist Church of America*, 10.

59. Taylor, op. cit., 18, quoting from *The True Wesleyan*, III, November 29, 1843, 189.

60. McLeister and Nicholson, *Conscience and Commitment: the History of the Wesleyan Methodist Church of America* (4th ed: Haines and Dieter, eds.), 480. The authors drew some of their cited material from the *Wesleyan Methodist Discipline* (1854), 115–116.

61. Luther Lee. *Wesleyan Manual* (no date), 1.

62. Willard Smith, *The History of Church-Controlled Colleges in the Wesleyan Methodist Church,* 93–97. The text of this section from his dissertation appears as appendix D.

63. Ibid., abstract.

64. Details of the life of Edmund Palmer come from "The Autobiography of Edmund Palmer Written For His Children" (1916) and from "A Blessing to Thousands: The Life of Edmund Palmer," unpublished essay by Robert Cunningham.

Chapter 3

1. The essay, "Houghton in Days of Yore" by John S. Minard, has been credited to the Rochester Post Express, ca. 1903.

2. F. W. Beers and Co. *History of Allegany County, N.Y., 1806–1879.*

3. From a chapel talk given by Willard G. Smith, April 1958.

4. Willard Houghton to Frank Higgins, March 24, 1880. Frank Higgins later served for one term as governor of New York.

5. Gillette and Lindley, *And You Shall Remember . . . A Pictorial History of Houghton College*, 25 and following.

6. Willard Houghton to O. T. Higgins, November 26, 1878.

7. Willard Houghton to O. T. Higgins, December 28, 1880.

8. Willard Houghton to O. T. Higgins, June 21, 1881.

9. Thomas, *The Man of the Hour*, 26.

10. Ibid., 27.

11. W. J. Houghton to O. T. Higgins, March 5, 1883.

12. Gillette and Lindley, Loc. cit., 29.

13. Willard Houghton to Amos Hopkins, February 9, 1865 (edited for spelling, etc.)

14. Willard Houghton to O. T. Higgins, October 10, 1881.

15. Quoted in McLeister, *History of the Wesleyan Methodist Church in America*, 235.

16. Willard Houghton to O. T. Higgins, March 5, 1883.

17. Ibid.

18. McLeister, Ibid.

19. Copies of Grange's journals are in the Houghton Archives.

20. Kenneth Wright to author, November 18, 1998.

21. Funeral tribute by the Rev. A. T. Jennings, April 1896; Houghton Archives.

22. Wilson, *Consider the Years 1883–1983*, no page numbers.

Chapter 4

1. American *Wesleyan*, Vol. L, Nov. 22, 1882, 5.

2. Willard Houghton's Subscription and Contribution Book, 1884–1887, 1–2.

3. Taylor, *History of the (Higher) Educational Movement of the Wesleyan Methodist Church of America*, 30.

4. Loc. cit.

5. Willard J. Houghton to "Bro. O. T. Higgins," March 5, 1883.

6. Willard J. Houghton, Subscription and Contribution Book, 1884–1887, 1–2.

7. Willard J. Houghton, Subscription and Contribution Book, 1884–1887, 1–2.

8. Loc. cit.

9. Minutes, Executive Board, Wesleyan Educational Society, 1910–1912 (old minutes record by special order), 125.

10. Willard J. Houghton to "Bro. O. T. Higgins," March 5, 1883.

11. Willard J. Houghton, Subscription and Contribution Book, 1884–1887, 1–2.

12. A copy of charter, *Wesleyan Methodist*, Vol. LV, May 11, 1898, 3.

13. Loc. cit.

14. *Wesleyan Methodist*, Vol. LII, Aug. 27, 1884, 3.

15. Ibid., Sept. 3, 1884, 3.

16. Willard J. Houghton, Subscription and Contribution Book, 1884–1887.

17. Willard J. Houghton to "Bro. O. T. Higgins," Dec. 18, 1884.

18. *Wesleyan Methodist*, Vol. LII, Dec. 31, 1884, 4.

19. Willard J. Houghton, Subscription and Contribution Book, 1884–1887, 1–2.

20. Ibid., 208.

21. Willard J. Houghton to "Bro. O. T. Higgins," Dec. 16, 1884.

22. Willard J. Houghton, Subscription and Contribution Book, 1884–1887, 208.

23. Resolution of the Board of Trustees, Houghton Seminary, *Wesleyan Methodist*, Vol. LIV, June 29, 1887, 3.

24. *Wesleyan Methodist*, Vol. LIII, May 27, 1885, 4–5.

25. Minutes, Executive Committee, Trustees of Houghton Seminary, 1887–1895, 55 and 64.

26. *Wesleyan Methodist*, Vol. LV, Mar. 16, 1898, 1.

27. Ibid., Vol. LVI, June 7, 1899, 4.

28. Ibid., Vol. LVII, Oct. 2, 1889, 3.

29. *Wesleyan Methodist*, Vol. LXIII, Feb. 28, 1906, 4.

30. Ibid., Vol. LVII, April 18, 1900, 9.

31. Ibid., Vol. LVII, July 4, 1900, 9.

32. Record Book, Treasurer, Willard Houghton Memorial Library Association, 1900–1915.

33. *Wesleyan Methodist*, Vol. LXI, June 18, 1902, 8.

34. Ibid., Vol. LX, May 20, 1903, 4.

35. Ibid., Vol. LX, Sept. 9. 1903, 9.

36. Ibid., Vol. LXII, June 21, 1905, 8.

37. *Wesleyan Methodist*, Vol. LXIII, Aug. 15, 1906, 4.

38. Minutes, Book Committee, Wesleyan Methodist Connection (or Church) of America, 1890–1911, 44.

39. *Wesleyan Methodist*, Vol. LVI, Aug. 29, 1888, 5.

40. "Historical Notes," Record Book, Houghton Bible Training School, 1890–1908, 3.

41. "Historical Notes," Record Book, Houghton Bible Training School, 1890–1908, 3.

42. *Wesleyan Methodist*, Vol. LII, Sept. 25, 1895, 9.

43. "Standing Rules," Student Register and Record Book, Houghton Bible Training School, 1890–1908, 26.

44. *Wesleyan Methodist,* Vol. LI, June 20, 1894, 8–9.

45. *Wesleyan Methodist*, Vol. LXIV, July 10, 1907, 8.

46. Minutes, Executive Committee, Trustees of Houghton Seminary, 1887–1895, 75.

47. Emily Moore, a letter published in *Wesleyan Methodist*, Vol. LI, Feb. 28, 1894, 14.

48. Minutes, Executive Committee, Trustees of Houghton Seminary, 1887–1895, 76.

49. J. R. Hodges, letter of resignation, *Wesleyan Methodist*, Vol. LI, Jan. 17, 1894, 2–3.

50. *Wesleyan Methodist*, Vol. LXX, June 17, 1908, 8.

51. Minutes, Executive Committee, Trustees of Houghton Seminary, 1887–1895, 20.

52. *Wesleyan Methodist*, vol. LXI, July 27, 1904, 3.

53. "Obituary of Willard J. Houghton," *Wesleyan Methodist*, Vol. LXI, July 27, 1904, 3.

54. Loc. cit..

55. *Wesleyan Methodist*, Vol. LV, Sept. 7, 1887, 3.

56. *Wesleyan Methodist*, Vol. VL, Sept. 7, 1887, 3.

57. *Wesleyan Methodist*, Vol. LIX, Oct. 29, 1902, 4.

58. Ibid., Vol. LVI, Apr. 5, 1899, 4.

59. Ibid., Vol. LVII, June 13, 1900, 9.

60. Hand-written copy of constitution of Houghton Seminary Neosophic Society on loose paper in the Society's Record Book, 1884–1891.

61. *Wesleyan Methodist*, Vol. LV, Oct. 12, 1898, 4.

62. Ibid., Vol. LXIV, Feb. 28, 1906, 4.

63. Ibid., Vol. LIX, July 9, 1902, 2.

64. Minutes, Associated Alumni of Houghton Seminary, 1897–1907, 1.

65. Loc. cit.

66. *Wesleyan Methodist*, Vol. LII, Aug. 6, 1884, 4.

67. A report on Houghton Seminary, *Wesleyan Methodist*, Vol. LIV, Mar. 7, 1888, 4–5.

68. Willard J. Houghton, a letter, *Wesleyan Methodist*, Vol. LIV, June 30, 1886, 7.

69. The shortfall in funds to pay faculty was temporarily resolved by issuing notes of credit which the faculty could redeem at the Fillmore Bank. At the same time, denominational officials were paid in full, leading to this entry in the minutes: "The question was raised about the fairness of paying denominational officials in full while teachers were not paid in full." Minutes of the Book Committee, June 28, 1911, 167

70. Willard J. Houghton to "Bro. O. T. Higgins," Dec. 1, 1886.

71. A report, *Wesleyan Methodist*, Vol. LI, Man. 31, 1894, 14–15.

72. Willard J. Houghton, a report, *Wesleyan Methodist*, Vol. LII, May 27, 1885, 4–5.

73. *Wesleyan Methodist*, Vol. LI, Dec. 3, 1893, 15.

74. Ibid., Vol. LV, Aug. 23, 1899, 5.

75. Ibid., Vol. LXIII, June 20, 1906, 8.

76. *Wesleyan Methodist*, Vol. LXIV, July 10, 1907, 4.

77. Book Committee Report, *Wesleyan Methodist*, Vol. LXIV, May 15, 1907, 12.

78. *Wesleyan Methodist*, Vol. LVII, Oct. 2, 1889, 3.

79. Ibid., Vol L, Mar. 9, 1892, 3.

80. A. R. Dodd, a news item, *Wesleyan Methodist*, Vol. LVIII, Sept. 17, 1890, 4.

81. *Wesleyan Methodist*, Vol. L, Sept, 14, 1892, 3.

82. Ibid., Vol. LI, July 12, 1893, 14.

83. Ibid., Vol. LXIII, Aug. 29, 1906, 4.

84. Willard J. Houghton, Subscription and Contribution Book, 1884–1887, 207.

85. Educational Society Report, *Wesleyan Methodist*, Vol. LXIII, June 20, 1906, 8.

86. Minutes, Executive Committee, Board of Trustees, Houghton Seminary, 23.

87. *Wesleyan Methodist*, Vol. LXX, Jan. 15, 1908, 4.

88. These last few paragraphs of text were added by R. L. Wing.

89. McLeister and Nicholson, *Conscience and Commitment*, 123.

90. Ibid., 124.

91. Minutes of the Book Committee, June 8, 1.

Chapter 5

1. The authorization came from the Book Committee: "A motion was made to raise Houghton Seminary to the grade of college as soon as the condition of the seminary will warrant such action." *Minutes of the Book Committee of the Wesleyan Methodist Connection*, 24 Jun 1898, 26.

2. Fifteenth Annual Catalogue of the Houghton Seminary and Announcement of Houghton College, Houghton, N.Y, 1898–1899

3. Ibid., no page.

4. *Catalogue of Houghton Wesleyan Methodist Seminary, 1907–1908*, 12.

5. Charles William Eliot, inaugural address, October 19, 1869. Quoted in Rudolph, *The American College and University*, 293.

6. Rudolph, op. cit., 294.

7. Ibid., 305.

8. Ibid., 302.

9. *Catalogue of Houghton Wesleyan Methodist Seminary, 1908–1909,* 36–37.

10. Thomas, op. cit., 38.

11. Willard G. Smith and R. L. Wing, *Directory of Faculty Who Served Houghton College Before 1972*. Houghton, N.Y: Houghton College Quick Print, 2001.

12. Thomas, op. cit., 39.

13. Roberta Molyneaux Grange, *My Book*, Vol. 4, 14

14. Willard Smith, op. cit., 15 and 17.

15. Kenneth W. Wright, *A Brief History of the Development of the Infrastructure of Houghton Seminary and Houghton College*, 30; the motion to install electricity for lighting was reported on May 17, 1920, in the Advisory Board Record, 179.

16. Wright, op. cit., 1.

17. Note, Stanley Sandler, 24 Feb 04.

18. Advisory Board Record, May 21, 1918, 165.

19. Wright, Loc. cit., 9.

20. Record book of the Houghton Seminary Advisory Board, 1908–1922, 50.

21. Ibid., 53.

22. Wright, op. cit., 9–10.

23. Advisory Board Record, July 16, 1915, 109.

24. Advisory Board Record, January 13, 1913, 58.

25. Ibid., 107.

26. Ibid., 110–115.

27. Minutes of the Educational Society, 1912–1924, 18.

28. Advisory Board Record, January 13, 1913, 67.

29. Advisory Board Record, August 22, 1922, 196.

30. Wright, op. cit., 12.

31. *Catalogue of Houghton Wesleyan Methodist Seminary, 1888–1889*, 15.

32. Advisory Board Record, January 26, 1915, 99.

33. *Announcements of Houghton College for 1923–1924*, 17.

34. Minutes of the Trustees of Houghton College, September 7, 1927, 28. Dr. A. H. Lyman of Fillmore was contracted (for $500) to provide two health lectures plus two physicals per student per year and one hour of medical services per student per year.

35. *Catalogue of Houghton College, 1927–1928*, 18.

36. There was also denominational constraint. In 1919, the Educational Society stipulated these rules on employment for teachers:

> The Wesleyan Methodist Church believes in the fundamental doctrines as outlined in the following questions, and also believes that a Christian life should be manifested by abstaining from secret societies and from such worldly amusements as dancing, card playing, theater going, etc. The Board of Managers believe that teachers while employed should respect these principles and should also conform to the Discipline of the Church in respect to the wearing of gold. This does not apply to eyeglasses and useful articles, but does apply to rings, bracelets, and needless ornaments.
>
> Prospective teachers are requested to answer the following questions:
>
> Do you believe in the inspiration of the Holy Scriptures?
>
> Do you believe in the unity and the trinity of the God head—God the father, God the Son, and God the Holy Ghost?
>
> Do you believe that God created man and the entire universe by a direct and special operation of divine power?
>
> Do you believe in the deity of Jesus Christ, in the miraculous conception and virgin birth, and in the crucifixion and resurrection of Jesus?
>
> Do you believe in a personal devil, hell, and the eternal punishment of the wicked?
>
> Do you believe in the fall of man and the consequent sinful nature of all mankind, which necessitates a divine atonement?
>
> Do you believe in the new birth as a miraculous and instantaneous work of the Holy Spirit through faith in Jesus Christ?

Do you believe in entire sanctification and the baptism of the Holy Ghost as a distinct work of grace subsequent to regeneration?

If employed as a teacher, will you cooperate with the president and the administration of the work of the school?

If employed as a teacher, will you support the doctrines and principles of the Wesleyan Methodist Church, as outlined above, by precept and example?

Minutes of the Educational Society, October 15, 1919, 123

37. Advisory Board Record, 44.

38. Ibid., 49.

39. Ibid., 135.

40. *Catalogue of Houghton Wesleyan Methodist Seminary, 1916–17*, 23.

41. Advisory Board Record, July 1920, 180–182.

42. *Catalogue of Houghton Wesleyan Methodist Seminary, 1908–1909,* 12 and 15.

43. *Catalogue of Houghton Wesleyan Methodist Seminary, 1888–1889*, 12.

44. *Catalogue of Houghton Wesleyan Methodist Seminary, 1903–1904*, n.p.

45. Numbers drawn from Houghton Seminary catalogs for the respective years.

46. Alan Graffam, *On the Persistence of Denominational Evangelical Higher Education: Case Studies in the History of Geneva College, Roberts Wesleyan College, Nyack College, and Houghton College*, 166–167.

47. Roberta Molyneaux Grange, *My Book*, Vol. 3, 30.

48. Ibid., 32.

49. Kenneth Wilson, *Consider the Years* (1983), no page numbers. Interestingly, section 1099 of the Education Law of 1909 stipulated "No institution shall be given power to confer degrees in this state unless it shall have resources of at least five hundred thousand dollars."

50. Willard Smith, op. cit., 117.

51. Minutes of the Educational Society, February 1923, 183.

52. Augustus Downing to James Luckey, February 1, 1922

53. In 1926, the trustees approved this pay scale for Houghton College:

    Instructor—1st year—$1,000

    Instructor—2nd year—$1,075

    Instructor—3rd year—$1,150

    Instructor—4th year—$1,200

    Instructor—5th year—$1,200

    Assistant professor—$1,300–1,400

    Associate professor—$1,500–1,600

    Professor—$1,700–1,800

Minutes of the Trustees of Houghton College, February 2, 1926, 15.

54. Downing letter, op. cit.

55. Ibid.

56. Willard Smith, Loc. cit., 128.

57. Minutes, Wesleyan Educational Society, 1912–1924, 166.

58. Ibid., 183

59. *Houghton College Bulletin of General Information, 1923*, 23.

60. Ibid., 22.

61. Willard Smith, op. cit., 126.

Chapter 6

1. Erma Anderson Thomas, *The Man of the Hour*, 21.

2. Ibid., 22.

3. Ibid., 23.

4. Houghton Seminary catalogues 1894 to 1898; Thomas, *op cit.*, 32.

5. Thomas, op.cit., 24.

6. From a letter of tribute (1937) by W. D. Cairns, professor of mathematics, Oberlin College, as quoted in Thomas, op. cit., 80.

7. Thomas, op. cit., 37.

8. Interview, Willard Smith, March 1996, 18.

9. Interview, Ray Calhoon, August 1996, 2.

10. Fifteenth Annual Catalogue of the Houghton Seminary and Announcement of Houghton College, 1898–1899.

11. Charles W. Taylor, *History of the (Higher) Educational Movement of the Wesleyan Methodist Church of America*, 177, citing *Wesleyan Methodist*, May 1916, 12.

12. Catalogue of Houghton Seminary and Houghton College, 1909–10.

13. Ibid., 40–41.

14. Ibid., 41.

15. Ibid., 40 and 42.

16. Robert Molyneaux Grange, *My Book*, vol. 3, 37.

17. Interview, Willard Smith, March 1996, 3–4.

18. Interview, Willard Smith, July 1998, 9.

19. Interview, Willard Smith, March 1996, 18.

20. Interview, Ray Calhoon, August 1996, 4.

21. Interview, Olson Clark, March 1998, 2.

22. Interview, Lois Ferm, April 1996, 2.

23. Interview, Herschel Ries, January 1997, 8.

24. Interview, Ruth Hutton, March 1997, 4.

25. Interview, Silas Molyneaux, March 1997, 23.

26. Interview, Helen Paul Paine, September 1996, 4.

27. Thomas, op. cit., 44.

28. A. Ray Calhoon, *Just One in a Million*, 72.

29. Ibid., 73.

30. Silas Molyneaux, op. cit., 17.

31. Ibid., 57.

32. Taylor, Loc. cit., 201–210.

33. Ibid., 73.

34. Thomas, Loc. cit., 73.

35. Interview, Wilber Dayton, April 1997, 10.

36. From a letter of tribute (1937) by Frank Pierrepont Graves, president of the University of the State of New York and Commissioner of Education, as quoted in Thomas, op. cit., 81.

37. Calhoon, *Just One Life in a Million*, 112.

38. Interview, Ray Calhoon, August 1996, 112.

39. McLeister and Nicholson, Loc. cit., 489.

Chapter 7

1. Willard G. Smith, *The History of Church-Controlled Colleges in the Wesleyan Methodist Church*, 159.

2. Thomas, *The Man of the Hour*, 59.

3. Houghton College *Bulletin of General Information* (1923), 12–14.

4. Minutes of the 21st Wesleyan Methodist General Conference, June 1923, 80 (as quoted in McLeister and Nicholson, 161).

5. Thomas, op. cit., 59.

6. Roberta Molyneaux Grange, *My Book* , Vol. 4, 15.

7. Kenneth Wilson, *Consider the Years 1883–1983*, 14.

8. From Bishop Charles V. Fairbairn, "I Call to Remembrance," publication and date unknown, 8.

9. Ibid.

10. The trustee minutes for 1927 record that "At the regularly called meeting of the Board of Trustees of Houghton College, held at Houghton on June 21, 1927, it was unanimously voted to petition the Board of Regents [of New York State] for a permanent charter for Houghton College."

Assets listed: campus, $10,879.49; buildings, $131,202.84; school furniture, $9,280.39; apparatus, $6,621.88; library, $8,610.47; total, $166,595.07

Farm, $23,078.12; mortgages and bonds, $4,090.50; rentals, $99,968.80; printing plant, $3,629.10; water works for village, $6,021.01; endowment notes, $13,364.40; total, $150,151.93.

Guaranteed interest on $387,500 pledged as annual payment of the Wesleyan Methodist Connection, as per guarantee.

Total productive assets: $ 537,651.93

Liabilities: $24,136.03

Minutes of the Trustees of Houghton College, 26.

11. Smith, op. cit., 137–138.

12. The effects of the Depression were felt in another way on campus. In February 1933, faculty were asked to forego 10 percent of salary due to tuition shortfall. This "voluntary" reduction was lowered to five percent for 1939–1940 and in November 1939 was finally eliminated. Minutes of the Trustees, 66, 104, 113.

13. "Annual Report of the President and Treasurer of Houghton College for 1932," 3–15.

14. Thomas, op. cit., 60–61.

15. Kenneth Wilson, *Consider the Years* (1983), no page numbers.

16. Smith, op. cit., 150.

17. Data from Smith, *History*, 149.

18. Alan Graffam, *On the Persistence of Denominational Evangelical Higher Education: Case Studies in the History of Geneva College, Roberts Wesleyan College, Nyack College, and Houghton College*, 166–167.

19. Kenneth L. Wilson, *Consider the Years*, 1983, no page numbers.

20. Adam Leroy Jones, Chairman of the Middle States Commission on Higher Education, to President J. S. Luckey, November 29, 1930.

21. Smith, op. cit., 144 and 150.

22. *Tenth Annual Catalogue of Houghton College, 1932–1933*, 10–12.

23. 1932 Annual Report, 2–3.

24. *Eleventh Annual Catalogue of Houghton College, 1933–1934*, 16.

25. *Fiftieth Annual Catalogue of Houghton Wesleyan Methodist Seminary* (included in the Houghton *Catalogue* for 1933–1934), 98 and 100.

26. From the minutes of the Middle States Commission on Higher Education meeting, November 24, 1933.

27. From S. W. Paine's diary, quoted in Lemcio, op. cit., 92.

28. Ibid.

29. From the minutes of the Middle States Commission on Higher Education meeting, November 13, 1935.

30. See appendix G.

31. Stephen W. Paine, quoted in Thomas, op. cit., 82.

Chapter 8

1. From the Wheaton College Web site.

2. Miriam Paine Lemcio, *Deo Volente*, 46. In her book, Lemcio quotes frequently from the extensive diaries of her father. These diaries are closely held by the family and were not accessible for this study.

3. Ibid., 50.

4. *Who's Who in America, 1984–1985*; quoted during Stephen Paine's funeral.

5. Lemcio, op. cit., 45.

6. Wood, *The Burning Heart: John Wesley, Evangelist,* 33.

7. Ibid., 52.

8. Interview, Timothy Nichols with Helen Paul Paine, summer 1996, 1.

9. Data drawn from Lemcio, op. cit.

10. Ibid.

11. Ibid., 70.

12. Interview, Edward Willett, October 1996, 7.

13. Interview, Willard Smith, March 1996, 6.

14. Quoted by Lemcio, op. cit., 77.

15. Quoted in Lemcio, op. cit., 192.

16. Lemcio, op. cit., 82–85.

17. Interview, Katherine Lindley with Robert Luckey and Frieda Gillette, summer 1980, 10.

18. Material adapted from a Houghton College press release, December 1, 1958.

19. The trustees' minutes for May 18, 1937, record that H. L. Fancher was named acting president (subsequent to the death of J. S. Luckey), because a "qualified college official" was needed to sign diplomas. Minutes of the Trustees of Houghton College, 94.

20. Minutes of the Trustees of Houghton College, June 16, 1937, 95.

21. Interview, Edward Willett with Roy S. Nicholson, January 1984, 6–7.

22. Willard Smith, *90 Plus*, 71.

23. Interview, Edward Willett, October 6, 1996, 12–13.

24. Interview, Silas Molyneaux, March 1997, 11.

25. Lemcio, *op cit.*, 102.

26. From Arthur Lynip's concluding remarks, Founders' Day 1992.

27. Kenneth Wilson, *Milieu*, July 1972, 2.

28. Smith, op. cit., 7–8.

29. Interview, Edward Willett, October 8, 1998, 15.

30. Lemcio, op. cit., 130.

31. Willard Smith reported: "During July [1970], Dr. Stephen Paine was confined to his home because of a serious back problem. This meant the Administrative Committee meetings were held at his bedside." Smith, *90 Plus*, 213.

32. Medical details drawn from Lemcio, op. cit., 222–223, and other Paine documents.

33. Minutes of the Trustees of Houghton College, November 23, 1943, 147.

34. Interview, Dean Liddick with Stephen Paine, November 1978, 1.

35. Stephen W. Paine, speech to the NAE's Bible Translation Committee, August 27, 1966, 1.

36. Liddick interview, op. cit., 2.

37. Paine speech, op. cit., 8.

38. Ibid., 8. It is interesting to note that, according to one campus Wesley expert, Wesley never used the term "inerrant"; he characterized the Scriptures as "infallible."

39. Liddick interview, op. cit., 4.

40. Lemcio, op. cit., 213.

41. Ibid., 215–221.

42. Liddick, op. cit., 6.

43. Interview, Timothy Nichols with Helen Paine, Summer 1996, 11.

44. Wilson, *Milieu*, July 1972, 2.

45. Interview, Lee M. Haines, March 2002, 3.

46. Interview, Robert Luckey, September 1998, 17.

47. Robert Luckey, written response to question submitted by Dean Liddick, undated (circa 1984).

48. Arthur Lynip, untitled eulogy to Stephen Paine delivered in February 1992, 3.

49. Lemcio, op. cit., 9.

50. Bruce Gallup, chapel remarks, May 16, 1972.

51. Quoted in Lemcio, op. cit., 228, citing the *Milieu* for July 1972.

52. Interview, Silas Molyneaux, March 1997, 11.

53. Interview, Robert Danner with Robert Luckey, November 1985, 4.

54. Interview, Richard Alderman, March 1998, 9.

55. Interview, Helen Paine, September 1996, 12.

56. Quoted in a letter from Carolyn Paine Miller to Dean Liddick, March 12, 1992.

57. From "A Tribute to Stephen W. Paine," by Wesleyan general superintendent Virgil A. Mitchell (undated).

58. Quoted by John Hartman in the funeral oration, February 14, 1992.

Chapter 9

1. *Catalog of Houghton College*, 1937–1938, 9–12.

2. Willard G. Smith, *The History of Church-Controlled Colleges in the Wesleyan Methodist Church*, 150.

3. Ibid., 134.

4. Ibid., 160.

5. But the fiscal duress was loosening a bit: the salary reduction system begun in 1933 was cut from ten to five percent and then eliminated in 1939. Also, 1939 was the year when a retirement annuity program (under TIAA) was begun for faculty and staff, with contributions of five percent from the individual and five percent from the college. Retirement was optional at age sixty-five and was mandatory at age seventy.

6. Smith, Loc. cit., 135.

7. Interview, Olson Clark, March 1998, 20; interview, William Calkins, May 1998, 13. Calkins also provided a photograph of the outhouse.

8. Interview, Katherine Lindley with Robert Luckey and Frieda Gillette, summer 1980, 24.

9. Stephen Paine, *The Building God Showed Us in the Creek*, undated pamphlet.

10. Smith, op. cit.,

11. Data for the years 1937–1938 and 1938–1939 from Smith, *History*, 149; for the years 1939–1940 through 1945–1946 Ibid., 150.

12. Smith, *90 Plus*, 87.

13. The war also brought some unexpected benefits. As reported by public information chief Dean Liddick in the October 1991 *Houghton Milieu* (24), "Asked today about the war's impact on the college, alumni of that period said that dedication notwithstanding, some pre-war faculty were less than scintillating. One faculty child of those days observed, 'Because enrollment went down, the number of teachers had to go down. I remember hearing an aside quite a few years later, that World War II allowed the college to remove the poorest professors. It was not done maliciously, but it was done with good judgment . . . and it was a way to upgrade the quality of instruction.'"

14. Ibid., 96.

15. This event came from the contemporary comic strip, "Li'l Abner," drawn by Al Capp. It was the day when single girls from Dogpatch were allowed to chase single boys.

16. Katherine Lindley, Houghton Heritage chapel talk, February 14, 1996.

17. E-mail from Benjamin Armstrong to *Houghton Milieu*, April 5, 2002.

18. Stephen W. Paine, *"A Glimpse of Houghton's Revival." Houghton College Bulletin*, Vol. VII, No. 7, June 1942.

19. Kenneth Wilson, *Consider the Years* (1958), n.p.

20. Woolsey, cited in Paine, op. cit., 33.

21. Ibid., 34.

22. Ibid., 35.

23. Paine, op. cit.

24. Alan Graffam, *On the Persistence of Denominational Evangelical Higher Education: Case Studies in the History of Geneva College, Roberts Wesleyan College, Nyack College, and Houghton College*, 170–17.

25. Robert Molyneaux Grange, *My Book*, vol. 4, 58.

26. Ibid., 60.

27. Ibid., 6.

28. Ibid., vol. 5, 1–3.

29. Ibid., 5.

30. Ibid., 18.

31. Interview, Robert Cummings, February 1997, 5.

32. Ibid., 6.

33. Interview, Evan Molyneaux, April 1997, 17–19.

34. Interview, William Olcott, September 1999, 22.

35. Interview, Warren Woolsey, April 1997, 18–19.

36. Interview, Lowell Fancher, March 1997, 4–8.

37. Those who lost their lives in World War II were Richard F. Bennett, Robert M. Danner, Warren T. Dayton, Walter F. Ferchen, Merril W. McKinley, J. Merton McMahon, Ralph L. Norton, Henry E. Samuels, John H. Smith, and Carl M. Wagner. (Listing from Kenneth Wilson, *Consider the Years* [1983].)

38. Smith, *History,* op. cit., 136.

39. Smith, *90 Plus*, 102.

40. Smith, *History,* op. cit., 138.

41. Lemcio, *Deo Volente,* 91–92; Smith, *History (*op. cit.*)*, 150.

42. Thomas A. Askew, "The Shaping of Evangelical Higher Education Since World War II." From Joel A. Carpenter and Kenneth W. Shipps (eds.), *Making Higher Education Christian,* 138–147.

43. Ibid., 141.

Chapter 10

1. Thomas DeLoughry, *Cornell Magazine,* September 1995, 24.

2. Smith, *History*, 144.

3. Willard Smith, "Recollections of Veterans' Housing Efforts at Houghton College," unpublished essay written September 30, 1989.

4. Ibid.

5. Quoted by Dean Liddick, "They Changed Houghton College Forever," *Houghton Milieu,* January 1990, 6–7.

6. Smith, *History*, 134.

7. Liddick, op. cit., 6–7. This building stood until 1999, when it was razed to make room for the new Center for the Arts.

8. *Houghton Star*, November 11, 1955, 4.

9. *Houghton College Bulletin*, March 1948.

10. C. Douglas Darling, professor of clinical medicine at Cornell University, quoted in DeLoughry, op. cit., 24.

11. Interview, Katherine Lindley with Josephine Rickard, summer 1982, 9.

12. Interview, Bert Hall, May 2002, 18.

13. Extracted from an edited ditto copy of Houghton College Constitution, 1, ink-dated as being ratified by the trustees on February 18, 1948; Houghton Archives. Other notes indicate it was ratified by the faculty on January 7, 1948, and by the Local Advisory Board on January 8, 1948.

14. Shea, *Houghton College and the Community*, 24.

15. Quoted from *Higher Education in American Democracy*, 7, by Shea, op. cit., 6.

16. Data for these five years from Smith, op. cit., 150.

17. Then-librarian Esther Jane Carrier commented on the declining numbers: "It [1952] was a hard time for Houghton because the GIs had graduated and the Korean War had started and their enrollment kept falling. They cut budget unbelievably." Interview, Esther Jane Carrier, February 2001, 11.

18. Enrollment numbers for 1950–1961 provide by the Houghton College Financial Aid Office.

19. Interview, Elizabeth Beck Feller, April 2002, 6–8. Her 1946 thesis was titled, *Planning a Women's Residence for Houghton College*.

20. Willard Smith, *History*, 127, quoting the Houghton Star for October 1911, 12.

21. Smith, *90 Plus*, 108.

22. Ibid., 112.

23. Ibid., 133.

24. Then-librarian Esther Jane Carrier commented on the 1953 study: "They were accredited in the '30s, and they were supposed to have a ten-year review or something but they were way behind, and this was their first reaccreditation, I think. It was [in] the year of 1952." Interview, Esther Jane Carrier, February 2002, 11.

25. E-mail from Oswald Ratteray, September 4, 2002.

26. *Evaluation Report of Houghton College, Houghton, New York, for the Commission on Institutions of Higher Education of the Middle States Association of Colleges and Secondary Schools*. March 16–17–18, 1953; 3.

27. Ibid., 5.

28. Ibid., 15.

29. Ibid., 4.

30. Ibid., 13.

31. Ibid., I-4.

32. Ibid., 9.

33. Ibid., 15.

34. There also apparently was no sick leave policy. On March 10, 1961, a sick leave policy was finally adopted by the trustees. But there was one item of relatively good news: in 1951, the provisions of the Social Security Act had been extended to college faculty and staff, providing a retirement foundation. Minutes of the Trustees, February 15, 1951, 249.

35. Dr. Bert Hall received the first Houghton sabbatical in 1959–1960, for a full year at half salary. Interview, Bert Hall, May 2002, 19.

36. *Evaluation Report (1953)*, op. cit., 6.

37. Ibid., 10.

38. Ibid., 4.

39. Ibid., 17. Several of those interviewed (who will remain anonymous) agreed with the statement that Houghton over the years has been willing to pay too little and in return expect too much of its faculty and staff. Also, shortly after the Middle States team's 1953 visit, all contract employees were asked to return five percent of salary to the college, in connection with a retrenchment effort. Minutes of the Trustees, June 26, 1954, 319.

40. Ibid., 9.

41. Ibid., 16.

42. Ibid., 16.

43. Ibid., 11.

44. Ibid., 2.

45. Ibid., 17.

46. Esther Jane Carrier observed, "I believe it was this accreditation visit in March when there were almost no hard-top roads or walks in Houghton and mud was nearly ankle-deep that the chairman suggested less mud would be a big improvement. Someone later commented that the improved walks were one of the best results of the accreditation visit." Letter, Esther Jane Carrier to the author, June 5, 2001.

47. Almost simultaneously with the start of planning on the chapel/auditorium came this statement by the trustees of the "Philosophy of Dramatics":

"The college does not admit drama that is essentially of history, of social problems, of social satire, of mystery, of comedy, of horror, etc., not because all drama is base or ignoble but because it is administratively impossible to maintain a demarcation between that which is acceptable in evangelistic circles and that which is unacceptable." Minutes of the Trustees, February 15, 1955, 325.

48. Smith, *90 Plus*, 131.

49. From a manuscript in the Stephen Paine file, Houghton College Office of Public Relations.

50. Smith, *90 Plus*, 140.

51. Ibid., 147.

52. Smith, *History*, 144.

53. *Catalog of Houghton College*, 1949–1950, 11–13.

54. Houghton College catalog, 1950–1951, 11.

55. Interview, Elizabeth Feller, April 2002, 19.

56. *Houghton Star*, April 18, 1958, 1.

57. George Wells, "Our Land Was Healed." Houghton College Press, March 1952, 3.

58. Interview, Arthur Lynip, March 1996, 14–15.

59. Details drawn from Wells's pamphlet (op. cit.) and from a news release from the Houghton College Office of Public Relations.

60. Smith, *90 Plus*, 144.

61. *Houghton College Catalog*, 1945–1946, 1997–1999.

62. Smith, *History*, 139.

63. *Data Presented for Consideration of the Commission on Institutions of Higher Education, Middle States Association of Colleges and Secondary Schools*, January 12, 1953, 101–104.

Chapter 11

1. These numbers furnished by the Houghton College Financial Aid Office.

2. Format and data for first three columns drawn from Willard Smith, *The History of Church-Controlled Colleges in the Wesleyan Methodist Church*, 144. Data in columns four and five (continuing the Smith pattern) came from the catalogs of Houghton College for 1959–1960 and 1969–1970.

3. Smith, *90 Plus*, 163–164.

4. Ibid., 160.

5. Interview, Esther Jane Carrier, February 2001, 15.

6. *Houghton College Self-Survey*, 1965, 20.

7. Carrier, op. cit., 17.

8. Ibid., 18–19.

9. Ibid., 26.

10. Paraphrased from Smith, *90 Plus,* 173.

11. Smith, *90 Plus*, 172.

12. Smith, *90 Plus,* 184.

13. Smith, *90 Plus*, 185.

14. Smith, *90 Plus*, 188.

15. *Self-Survey*, 1965, 52.

16. Interview, Fred Shannon, September 2002, pg. 1. The issue was discussed in the Local Board of Trustees meeting on October 16, 1969 (book of minutes, 87).

17. Lemcio, *Deo Volente*, 220–221.

18. *Self-Survey*, 1965, 28.

19. *Houghton College Self-Survey*, 1965, 3.

20. Carrier, Loc. cit., 27.

21. *Self-Survey*, 29.

22. Middle States Association of Colleges and Secondary Schools, Commission on Higher Education, "Report on Houghton College," February 21–24, 1965, 22.

23. Stephen W. Paine to Middle States, February 24, 1967.

24. Letter, Dean Liddick to author, Sept. 10, 2002.

25. *Self-Survey*, 1965, 10.

26. Paine letter, op. cit., 1.

27. Minutes of the Local Board of Trustees, January 6, 1971, 154.

28. Houghton College response to report by Middle States visiting team, 2

29. Minute book of the Local Board of Trustees, 1968–1972, 148.

30. Houghton College response to Middle States, 3.

31. Smith, *90 Plus,* 161.

32. Smith, *90 Plus*, 167.

33. Smith, *90 Plus*, 178.

34. Letter, Dean Liddick, 15 May 2003.

35. Smith, Loc. cit., 191.

36. Ibid., 173.

37. Ibid., 185.

38. Ibid., 199.

39. Ibid., 195.

40. Ibid., 188.

41. Lemcio, *Deo Volente,* 159.

42. Paul Westphal Thomas and Paul William Thomas, *The Days of Our Pilgrimage: The History of the Pilgrim Holiness Church* (eds.: Melvin E. Dieter and Lee M. Haines Jr.), 2.

43. Ibid., 18.

44. Ibid, 5, quoting J.B. Chapman, *A History of the Church of the Nazarene* (Kansas City, Mo., 1926), 19.

45. Ibid., 13, 29.

46. Ibid., 55.

47. Ibid., 236.

48. Ibid., 285–286; 307.

49. Ibid., 305, 307.

50. Ibid., 317, 320. McLeister and Nicholson, *Conscience and Commitment,* 318.

51. *Buffalo Evening News*, April 19, 1969.

52. From a summary of Houghton College charter activities provided by the State Education Department in January 2003.

53. BBI Business Office report, October 22, 1968.

54. J. N. Bedford to BBI supporters, May 23, 1969.

55. Robert Luckey to James Bedford, March 25, 1968.

56. Per data furnished by the state Education Department, op. cit.

57. Houghton College Buffalo Campus *Newsletter*, October 1969, 1.

58. HCBC *Newsletter*, September 1970, 1.

59. Beardsley and Beardsley, *Site Study Report*, July 27, 1970.

60. Program, "Founders' Club Banquet Presenting a Master Plan for Buffalo Campus," November 5, 1970.

61. Alan Graffam, *On the Persistence of Denominational Evangelical Higher Education: Case Studies in the History of Geneva College, Roberts Wesleyan College, Nyack College, and Houghton College*, 172.

62. *Houghton College Catalogue 1971–1972*, page 30.

63. Minutes of the Local Board of Trustees, June 2, 1971, 182.

64. Lemcio, op. cit., 223.

65. Ibid., 182.

66. Ibid., 183.

67. Ibid., 206

68. Ibid., 208

69. Interview, Wilber Dayton, April 26, 1997, 20.

70. LBT minutes, op. cit., 213

71. Stephen Paine to Arthur Lynip, July 6, 1972; quoted in Lemcio, op. cit. 230.

Chapter 12

1. Ira McLeister, *History of the Wesleyan Methodist Church of America* (1934), 1940–1941

2. Ibid., 53.

3. Ibid., 56.

4. Ibid., 90.

5. Ibid., 99.

6. Charles W. Taylor, *History of the (Higher) Educational Movement of the Wesleyan Methodist Church of America.*, 234, citing the charter of the Wesleyan Educational Society.

7. Ibid., 234.

8. McLeister, op. cit., 113.

9. McLeister and Nicholson, *Conscience and Commitment*, 106.

10. Taylor, op. cit., 235.

11. McLeister, op. cit., 122.

12. McLeister and Nicholson, op. cit., 132.

13. *Discipline of the Wesleyan Methodist Connection (or Church) of America* for 1923, 253.

14. *Discipline of the Wesleyan Methodist Connection (or Church) of America* for 1927, 256.

15. Ibid., 243.

16. Ibid., 160–161.

17. McLeister and Nicholson, op. cit., 211.

18. Taylor, Loc. cit., 242–243, citing the *Discipline of the Wesleyan Methodist Church of America*, 1955, 148–149.

19. McLeister and Nicholson, op. cit., 250; Lee Haines to author, November 30, 2002.

20. Middle States visiting team report, February 21–24, 1965, 2–3.

21. At the Wesleyan Methodist General Conference in 1864, a small group (unauthorized by the Connection) called for a convention of non-Episcopal Methodists to explore a potential union with the northern, anti-slavery branch of the Methodist Protestant Church. But widespread antipathy to the proposed union soon developed among Wesleyan Methodists, who feared disruption of denominational unity. At a special union conference in 1866, Methodist Protestants outnumbered Wesleyan Methodists by about four to one, and the resulting proposed program of union disregarded Wesleyan sensibilities against liquor consumption and secret societies and did not support other reform issues. When the Wesleyan Methodist annual conferences rejected the proposals, feeling ran high among the defeated pro-union group, and a number of preachers (including pioneer Wesleyan Methodist pastors such as Luther Lee, Lucius Matlack, John McEldowney, and Cyrus Pringle) and several congregations subsequently reunited with the Methodist Episcopal Church. In the words of Arthur Jennings, "Very many of the men who once led the battle which Wesleyan Methodists were supposed to be fighting against iniquity ceased to command the confidence of the people, but for lack of the right kind of machinery they were permitted to lead away some of the most valuable interests of the Connection." (Jennings, *History of American Wesleyan Methodism.*, 91).

22. Lee M. Haines to author, November 30, 2002.

23. Minutes of the Houghton Local Board of Trustees, January 2, 1973, 292.

24. McLeister and Nicholson, 58.

25. Ibid., 482.

26. Ibid, 59.

27. Ibid., 492–493.

28. Ibid., 480–481.

29. Lemcio, *Deo Volente,* 17.

30. Taylor, Loc. cit.., 231–233.

31. Ibid., 141.

32. Ibid., 133.

33. Ibid., 142.

34. Ibid., 143.

35. Ibid., 146 and 148.

36. Edited ditto copy of Houghton College Constitution (Houghton Archives), ink-dated February 18, 1948, 5.

37. Ibid., 5–6

38. Shea, *Houghton College and the Community*, 72–75.

39. Graffam, *On the Persistence of Denominational Evangelical Higher Education: Case Studies in the History of Geneva College, Roberts Wesleyan College, Nyack College, and Houghton College*, 172.

40. Interview, Daniel Chamberlain, October 2002, 13–14; Lee Haines to author, November 30, 2002.

41. Smith, *90 Plus*, 75–76.

42. Ibid., 91–92.

43. Ibid.; Haines letter, November 30, 2002.

44. Interview 2, Willard Smith, July 1996, 11.

45. Ibid., 12.

46. McLeister and Nicholson, *Conscience and Commitment*, 210.

47. Houghton College, *Data Presented for Consideration of the Commission on Institutions of Higher Education, Middle States Association of Colleges and Secondary Schools,* January 12, 1953, III-3.

48. Constitution of Houghton College, 1951 revision, 10.

49. Constitution of Houghton College, 1956 revision, 5.

50. Constitution of Houghton College, 1962 revision, 4–5.

51. Ibid., 6.

52. Interview, Robert Danner with Robert Luckey, November 1985, 1.

53. McLeister and Nicholson, op. cit., 282.

54. 1972 *Boulder*, 49.

55. Daniel Chamberlain to author, December 12, 2002.

56. McLeister and Nicholson, op. cit., 497–498.

57. Smith, *90 Plus*, 137.

58. Data from the *Catalogue of Houghton College for 1934–1935*, 10–11.

59. Interview, Edward Willett, October 3, 1996, 14.

Chapter 13

1. From "Willard Houghton's Account of the Founding of Houghton Seminary." (See appendix E).

2. Data compiled from *Houghton College Catalogs* for 1925, 1935, 1945.

3. Data compiled from *Houghton College Catalogs* for 1955 and 1965.

4. Data extracted from Willard Smith, *The History of Church-Controlled Colleges in the Wesleyan Methodist Church*, table XV, 153.

5. Miriam Lemcio, *Deo Volente*, 210.

6. Data extracted from Table 4:07, in Lois Ferm, *Student Characteristics and Environments for Learning in Wesleyan Colleges*, 61. The five colleges were Bartlesville Wesleyan College (Oklahoma), Central Wesleyan College (South Carolina), Houghton College, Marion College (Indiana), and Miltonvale Wesleyan College (Kansas).

7. Data extracted from *Houghton College Fact Book* for 1984, I-11.

8. Interview, Arthur Lynip, March 1996, 18.

9. Harold Kingdon to author, April 25, 2002.

10. *Catalogue of Houghton Seminary, 1886–1887*, 10.

11. Ibid., 15.

12. *Houghton Seminary Circular*, 1886–1887, 2–3.

13. Ibid.

14. Roberta Molyneaux Grange, *My Book,* vol. 2, 13–14.

15. Ibid., vol. 1, 21–22.

16. *Catalogue of Houghton Seminary*, 1908–1909, 26.

17. *Catalogue of Houghton Seminary,* 1905–1906, 9.

18. Ray Calhoon, *Just One Life in a Million*, 51.

19. Ibid., 53.

20. *Catalogue of Houghton Seminary* for 1907–198, 7.

21. Unrecorded conversation with former dean Elizabeth Beck Gilbert Feller, April 2002.

22. Advisory Board Record, 190.

23. Lemcio, op. cit., 193.

24. Smith, *90 Plus*, 98.

25. Anecdote and letter provided by an alumnus who wishes to remain anonymous.

26. *Houghton Star*, October 23, 1956, 5.

27. Smith, *90 Plus*, 139.

28. Not all evangelical leaders were sold on the importance of revivals, and some leaders warned that planned events that dealt primarily with emotional awakenings were not the ideal religious activity. According to his biographer Clyde Kilby, Jonathan Blanchard (who was president of Wheaton College and Stephen Paine's great-grandfather), preferred no revivals at all if the work of the church could be realized without them. "When they are successful," Blanchard said," they tend to make us vain and conceited because we do so much. Then they beget disrelish for ordinary labors in the church and make them seem tedious, and they also exalt religious activity above the grace of God. If unsuccessful, they produce discouragement, faintness of heart, and fretfulness in the church." (Clyde Kilby, *Majority of One: The Biography of Jonathan Blanchard*, 84.)

29. The issue of intercollegiate athletics was addressed often by the governing boards. The Educational Society minutes for 1912 report: ." . . The rules governing athletic sports on the grounds do not permit matched games between the students of the Seminary and outside teams." (31) This proscription was amplified in 1914: "That the rule forbidding our school athletic teams playing games with outside athletic teams apply to the individual student playing with outside teams or attending games played by outside teams." (June 18, 1914, 46)

The issue appeared again in 1922: "The presidents of our schools do not feel that interscholastic athletics would work to the advantage of our schools" (169).

In 1934, as Houghton was striving for Middle States accreditation, the question was again raised. From the Book Committee minutes: "[Received] A petition from Houghton College asking that they be permitted to engage in athletics to the extent of entering into games with Cheseborough Junior College. The Book Committee by unanimous vote expressed themselves as being opposed to intercollegiate games on the part of any of our schools" (February 1, 1934, 215).

Apparently there was more agitation following World War II: "The Educational Society requested that the Board of Administration reappraise the previous stated policy on interscholastic athletic competition. The Board surveyed the colleges and elected to retain the old policy" (June 17, 1959, 254).

Even as late as 1961 the policy remained: "It is the sense of the Board that action taken in 1959 pertaining to intercollegiate activities means no intercollegiate activities under any circumstances" (June 7, 1961, 273).

But a year later the first sign of loosening appeared:

> 2. The historic policy of the Church in its opposition to regular conference athletics is to be maintained.
>
> 3. Occasional inter-school games for recreation and fellowship with other Christian schools may be permitted at the discretion of the Local Board of Trustees subject to the right of review of the Board of Administration and the following regulations:" The stipulations included a limit of nine contests per year, no football, and expenses to be paid from student fees. (June 6, 1962, 283)

30. Unrecorded comment made prior to an interview, A. Ray Calhoon, August 1996. This incident was also reported by Roberta Molyneaux Grange, *My Book*, vol. 3, 37.

31. A. Ray Calhoon, *Just One in a Million*, 112.

32. Smith, *90 Plus*, 130.

33. Arthur Lynip, op. cit., 21.

34. Alan Graffam, op. cit., 179.

35. Minutes of the Educational Society, February 7, 1961, 269.

36. Advisory Board Record, 186.

37. *Catalogue of Houghton Wesleyan Methodist Seminary,* 1921–1922, 23.

38. Minutes of the Book Committee, February 1, 1934, 215.

39. Interview, Layton Vogel, August 28, 1996, 14.

40. Lemcio, *Deo Volente,* 81.

41. Graffam, op. cit., 180.

42. Interview, A. Ray Calhoon, August 1996, 71.

43. Stanley Sandler, "Houghton in the 1950s," 1–2.

44. Ibid., 4.

45. Ibid., 4–5

46. Ibid., 7–8.

47. Interview, Bert Hall, May 2002, 18.

48. From remarks by Elwood Zimmerman, "Remembering Dr. Stephen Paine," September 25, 2001.

49. Lois Ferm, *Student Characteristics and Environment for Learning in Wesleyan Colleges,* 193–197.

Chapter 14

1. One strong but quite secular voice played a role in attracting missionaries abroad, particularly to the Far East. According to the minutes of the Executive Committee of the Book Committee, "Dr. Nicholson brought a very interesting report of his attendance at the meeting of the American Bible Society held in New York City on December 3, explaining the worldwide need for Bibles and the urgent request of General MacArthur for missionaries in Japan" (December 4, 1947, 382).

2. Numbers developed by counting names listed in *Directory of Houghton College Baccalaureate Graduates 1925–1972.*

3. Data drawn from *Data Presented for Consideration of the Commission on Institutions of Higher Education, Middle States Association of Colleges and Secondary Schools,* January 12, 1953, page 107.

4. Data provided by Katherine Lindley '43 and friends.

5. Data assembled from Houghton records and other sources by Dean '60 and Carmen VanderVeen '60 Liddick.

6. Houghton *Milieu,* May 1983, 18–20.

7. Data extracted from two sources. First, class survey response forms: these forms were sent to about 190 addressees; twenty-one sets were returned for incorrect address and thirty-six were returned with data. Second, Barbara (Robbins) Bates '72 discovered some old alumni office records and drew from them data for nearly 80 percent of the class.

8. Andrew F. Walls, *The Cross-Cultural Process in Christian History,* 95.

9. A. W. Hall, *Three Hundred Miles in a Hammock or Six Weeks in Africa,* 139

10. Clarke (*American Wesleyan Mission of Sierra Leone*) and Carter (*A Half Century of American Wesleyan Missions in West Africa*) list dates of arrival on the field. According to them, Houghtonian Hattie Brooks arrived in November 1899 and Mary Lane in June 1900, making the latter technically the second Houghton alumna to arrive.

11. Paul W. Shea, "Years of Decision: The Houghton College Experience and Missionary Motivation and Preparation."

12. See lists in Gillette and Lindley, *And You Shall Remember*; Carter, *A Half Century of American Wesleyan Missions in West Africa*; and Clarke, *American Wesleyan Methodist Mission of Sierra Leone, W. Africa*.

13. Missionaries had a vital role, but the great spread of the gospel in Sierra Leone to a great degree was done by national evangelists. One of Andrew Wall's ringing declarations is that "Most Africans have always heard the gospel from Africans, and virtually all the great movements towards the Christian faith in Africa have been African led" (Walls, op. cit., 45).

14. Hugh Maclure, M.D., *Letters from the White Man's Grave: Pioneering on the Medical Missionary Frontier,* 170.

15. Missionary educator Dr. Evvy Campbell of Wheaton Graduate School and Houghton alumna Eila Shea, both nurse colleagues who labored alongside Dr. Marilyn in her later years, are working on collecting and publishing Dr. Birch's stories from Sierra Leone. This much-anticipated narrative will be a most profound and valuable narrative on missionary medicine.

16. Tom A. Steffan, "Storytelling," *Evangelical Dictionary of World Missions,* 909.

17. Marion Birch to Daniel Chamberlain, 1983.

18. Maclure, Loc. cit.., 206.

19. In a 1994 survey of 380 Houghton missionaries, nearly one in five respondents named Warren Woolsey as the most helpful professor in their preparation to serve on the mission field, tying the number naming Warren's predecessor, the distinguished Claude Ries. What is astounding is that from the late 1940s on missionary alums listed eighty different Houghton faculty as being the most helpful in their preparation for missions!

20. E-mail, Paul Shea to author, January 15, 2003.

21. Warren Woolsey, "Are Foreign Missionaries Still Needed?" *Milieu* (Fall 1986)

22. Lamin Sanneh, "Africa," James M. Phillips and Robert T. Coote, *Toward the 21st Century in Christian Mission.* (Grand Rapids: Eerdmans, 19.

Chapter 15

1. It is interesting to note that four of the founders of the Wesleyan Methodist Church were members of the Masonic order: Orange Scott, Leroy S. Sunderland, Jotham Horton, and Luther Lee. (Source: Arthur T. Jennings, *History of American Wesleyan Methodism,* 61.) Though the secret society debate was long and hot, it was not until 1879 that members of secret societies were officially excluded from membership in all Wesleyan churches. (Source: Joel Martin, *The Wesleyan Manual, or History of Wesleyan Methodism,* 27.) Another dimension of this ban was reported by Kenneth Wright in a 1997 monograph; "The Wesleyan Church was so opposed to [secret societies] that its adherents were adjured to refrain even from membership in the Grange (the popular name of the Patrons of Husbandry) . . . or the Grand Army of the Republic, a fraternal society founded . . . by Civil War veterans for the commemoration of their dead comrades."

2. Greek-letter societies were apparently a serious issue for Wesleyan Methodist officials. According to the Minutes of the Wesleyan Methodist Educational Society for 1928, "Resolved that no Greek letter fraternities nor fraternities of a similar character be permitted to exist in connection with any of our educational institutions" (209). One 1931 alumnus, who admitted he had studied within the premises of a fraternity house (but had never joined) while at Syracuse Medical College, was rejected as a missionary candidate partly because of that association.

3. I. F. McLeister, *History of the Wesleyan Church in America* (1943), 97; 1879 General Conference.

4. Curtis D. Johnson, *Islands of Holiness: Rural Religion in Upstate New York, 1790–1860*, 53.

5. Martha MacLear, *The History of Education of Girls in New York and New England 1800–1870*, 6.

6. Jill K. Conway, "Perspectives on the History of Women's Education in the United States," *History of Education Quarterly*, 14 (Spring 1974), 2.

7. Thomas Woody, in *A History of Women's Education in the United States*, vol. 1, 101, citing Charles Butler's *The American Lady*, 1851.

8. Jennings, op. cit., 119–120.

9. Ibid., 124.

10. Interview, Lee M. Haines, March 2002, 8–9.

11. Details from *Brief Account of the Development of Houghton Seminary with a Biographical Sketch of Philida Sprague Bowen*, by Kenneth W. Wright, n.p..

12. McLeister and Nicholson, *Conscience and Commitment: The History of the Wesleyan Methodist Church in America*, 202, 332, and 350.

13. Interview, Elizabeth Beck Gilbert Feller, April 2002, 19.

14. McLeister and Nicholson, op. cit., 304. McLeister (1934; 98) states, "It was decided [at the 1879 General Conference] that it would be the polity of the Connection to license [women] to preach but not to ordain them as elders."

15. Chapel talk, Rev. Maxine Haines, March 20, 2002.

16. Interview, Ray Calhoon, August 1996, 2.

17. Minutes of the Wesleyan Methodist Educational Society, June 27, 1912, 5.

18. Interview, Raymon Irish, November 1998, 4.

19. Unrecorded pre-interview comments, Kenneth Wright, March 1997.

20. Willard Smith, April 1996 written responses, 5–6.

21. Interview, Marilyn Byerly, April 1997, 13.

22. Interview, Willard Smith, July 1997, 18–19.

23. Whitney Shea, *Houghton College and the Community*, vi.

24. Ibid., 69.

25. Ibid., 76.

26. Ibid., 77.

27. One current dictionary cites these as the five points of Calvinism: the supremacy of the Scriptures, the omnipotence of God, the sinfulness of man, the salvation of the elect by God's irresistible grace alone, and adherence to a rigid moral code. Arminianism, in contrast, holds that Christ died for all men and that salvation is regeneration by grace through faith and as such is a matter of personal election.

28. Johnson, op. cit., 42.

29. From the minutes of the Book Committee, February 1, 1934: "A resolution from some brethren in the Champlain Conference protesting against the employment of some Calvinistic evangelistic workers at Houghton College was presented to the [Book] Committee. Rev. I. F. McLiester was authorized to make written reply to the brethren." (215) No further details of the matter were located.

30. Interview, Robert Childs, April 1997, 10.

31. According to McLeister and Nicholson, op. cit., (73), membership in the two churches at the time was approximately 35,000 for the Methodist Protestants and 15,000 for the Wesleyan Methodists.

32. McLeister (1934), 71–78. He also comments: "The activity of these men in trying to destroy the Church they helped to establish became a grievous matter to the denomination."

33. Ibid., 77.

34. McLeister and Nicholson, op. cit., 193.

35. Ibid., 204–205.

36. Ibid., 216 and 228.

37. Van Wormer, Loc. cit., 6.

38. Ibid., 232.

39. Stephen Paine diary entry for June 23, 1955; quoted in Lemcio, op. cit., 169. General Conference president Roy Nicholson earlier had passed to Stephen Paine a note saying that members of the joint commission should be awarded an "ecclesiastical purple heart."

40. Ray Calhoon, *Just One Life in a Million*, 80–81.

41. Interview, Willard G. Smith, March 1996, 22–23.

42. Interview, Willard G. Smith, July 1996, 19–20.

43. E-mail, Harold Kingdon, April 2002.

44. Jennings, op. cit., 81.

45. Whitney Cross, *The Burned-over District*, 202.

46. Wesleyan Methodist Education Committee report of 1844 (see appendix B).

47. "Willard Houghton was narrow-minded in a sense, really. He wanted a Bible school at that time. He wasn't thinking of a college the way we think of a liberal arts college with an evangelical turn to it." Interview, Silas Molyneaux, March 1997, 25.

48. Timothy Smith, *Uncommon Schools: Christian Colleges and Social Idealism in Midwestern America, 1820–1950,* 27.

49. From the minutes of the Twenty-First General Conference (1923), 80, as reported in McLeister and Nicholson, 161.

50. Interview, Edward J. Willett, October 1996, 2.

51. Interview, Willard Smith, July 1998, 8–9.

52. Ibid.

53. Interview, Willard Smith, March 1996, 4.

54. Willard Smith, written response to interview questions, March 1996, 1–2.

55. Ibid., 3.

56. James A Connor, writing in *Kepler's Witch* (San Francisco: Harper Collins, 2004) observed, "Repression follows orthodoxy like a jackal," 55.

57. From "On the Character of the Early Methodists," in vol. 1 of the 3rd series of *The Wesleyan Methodist Magazine*, March 1822.

58. *The Discipline of the Wesleyan Methodist Connection*. New York: L. C. Matlock for the Wesleyan Methodist Connection, 1848, 74.

59. Reported in McLeister and Nicholson, op. cit., 46.

60. Note: Evidence is lacking to support the contention that *all* deeds contained a no-liquor covenant. However, the deeds to lots on the southwest side of Houghton Creek, sold by Houghton College during World War II, contained this covenant: "The manufacture or sale of intoxicating beverages shall not be permitted upon any lot in this sub-division. Violation of this clause will cause the property to revert to Houghton College." Minutes of the Trustees of Houghton College, February 18, 1942, 147.

61. Calhoon, op. cit., 55.

62. *Houghton Seminary Catalogue*, 1920–1921.

63. Minutes of the Book Committee, February 7, 1934, 175.

64. McLeister and Nicholson, op. cit., 270.

65. Interview, Marilyn Byerly, April 1997, 4.

66. Ibid, 21.

67. From a message delivered at the fifty-third session of the (Wesleyan Methodist) Allegheny Conference Women's Missionary Society, June 11, 1959, by the president, Mrs. Ivah B. Van Wormer, 7. Printed and distributed by the Women's Missionary Society.

68. Ibid., 7–8.

69. S. W. Paine to "Colleagues," January 21, 1965.

70. Copies of petition sheets, 25 January 1965.

71. Written responses, Willard G. Smith, April 1996, 3.

72. S. W. Paine to "Dear Colleague," June 9, 1965.

73. Inked sidenote by a senior faculty member on archival copy: "[these three] currently allow eng[agement] rings!"

74. Minutes of the Local Board of Trustees, June 4, 1965.

75. Byerly, op. cit., 4.

76. Interview, person wished to remain anonymous, March 1997.

77. Interview, Alton and Aileen Shea, February 1998, 20–21.

78. S. W. Paine to "Dear Colleague," June 17, 1965.

79. Interview, Silas Molyneaux, March 1997, 25.

80. Willard Smith, written response to interview questions, July 1996, 3–4.

81. Interview, Stephen Calhoon, April 1997, 12.

82. Ibid., 18.

83. Ibid., 24–25.

84. McLeister and Nicholson, op. cit., 294.

85. Ibid., 294–296.

86. Minutes of the Local Advisory Board, 1968–1972, 8.

87. Unrecorded pre-interview comments by Helen Paine.

Chapter 16

1. In her doctoral dissertation, *Student Characteristics and Environment for Learning in Wesleyan Colleges*, Lois Ferm defines a Christian liberal arts college as "a college offering studies in a number of areas of inquiry, all of which are, at least in theory, interpreted in the light of the Christian faith. The college may be affiliated with one denomination or may be interdenominational in character" (11).

2. From William Ringenberg, *The Christian College*, 72–73: "Historically, college professors have been willing to work for moderate or low pay because of the deep sense of satisfaction inherent in their work. They are free to use their creative skills in dealing with the great issues of life, and they have opportunities to influence young people in a life-changing manner. Christian college instructors frequently view their vocation as a calling from God equally sacred as that of a call to the ministry. . . ."

3. Ibid., 215.

4. Oberlin was already well into its drift toward secularization when the first Houghton Seminary students entered that college to complete their degrees. According to William Ringenberg, op. cit., (135–136), "Secularization occurred at Oberlin somewhat earlier than at most church colleges. The steps in the process of change . . . included (1) a gradual acceptance by professors and students of the theory of evolution and a gradual decline in their confidence that the biblical record was divinely inspired; (2) a gradual acceptance of the liberal Protestant interpretation of the Christian faith; (3) a gradual willingness to hire non-Christians as instructors; (4) the abandonment of the senior Bible requirement; and (5) a gradually increasing desire to upgrade the general academic quality and reputation of the institution without a concurrent and equivalent desire to sustain the previous religious zeal."

5. Arthur F. Holmes, *The Idea of A Christian College*, 15.

6. Ibid., 14.

7. Minutes of the 21st Wesleyan Methodist General Conference, 80. (See chapter 7 for further discussion.)

8. Holmes, op. cit., 46.

9. Ibid., 15.

10. Ibid., 77.

11. Ibid., 85.

12. See Thomas A. Askew, "The Shaping of Evangelical Higher Education Since World War II," in Joel A. Carpenter and Kenneth W. Shipps (eds.), *Making Higher Education Christian*, 147.

13. *Houghton College Catalogue 1971–1972*, 8.

14. Ibid., 7.

15. Kenneth Wilson, *Consider the Years 1883–1983*, last page.

16. Holmes, op. cit., 87.

17. Ibid., 93.

18. Ibid., 19.

19. Ibid., 24.

20. Ibid., 26.

21. Interview, Robert Danner with Katherine Lindley, November 1985.

22. The reported statements were taken from individual written responses. Since none of the respondents had formally granted permission to use their names, no source identification will be given. All responses are filed in the Houghton Archives.

23. During the author's several years of supervising Houghton student teachers in area public schools, he was constantly impressed by the positive comments of school administrators and cooperating teachers regarding the preparation, ethics, decorum, and appropriate dress of the Houghton student teachers.

24. Letter, Dean Liddick, January 27, 2004.

25. E-mail, Richard J. Alderman, February 10, 2004.

26. Houghton College Annual Report for 1939–1940, 15.

27. Houghton College Financial Report 1971–1972, 15.

28. Data drawn from *Houghton College Annual Report for 1939–1949*, 15; *Houghton College Financial Report for 1945–1946*, 15; *Houghton College Report of Audit for 1950–1951*, H-4; *Houghton College Report of Audit for 1955–1956*, K-3; *Houghton College Report of Audit for 1960–1961*, 11; *Houghton College Financial Report for 1966–1967*, 18; *Houghton College Financial Report for 1971–1972*, 15.

29. E-mail, John Tyson, October 3, 2003.

30. E-mail, Lee M. Haines, January 16, 2004.

31. E-mail, Carl Schultz, January 28, 2004.

32. Haines, op. cit.

33. Schultz, op. cit.

34. Letter, Dow Chamberlain, September 18, 2003.

35. Mark Noll, "Christian Colleges, Christian Worldviews, and an Invitation to Research," in William C. Ringenberg, *The Christian College*, 32.

36. Alan Graffam. *On the Persistence of Denominational Evangelical Higher Education: Case Studies in the History of Geneva College, Roberts Wesleyan College, Nyack College, and Houghton College*, 172.

37. Haines, op. cit.

38. Holmes, op. cit. 115.

39. Attributed to Willard Houghton; quoted by Willard Smith, *90 Plus*, 195.

Appendix B

1. Jennings, Arthur T. *History of American Wesleyan Methodism.* Syracuse: Wesleyan Methodist Publishing Association, 1902: 82–84.

Appendix C

1. Copied from a transcript in Houghton College Archives (original document missing) by Nichols in *For the Good of the World: Education and Salvation at the Houghton Wesleyan Methodist Seminary and the Oberlin Collegiate Institute*, appendix I. Note: The term *seminary*, in the context of the nineteenth century, meant a private secondary academy, precursor to the private high school of the next century. The denotation of *seminary* as higher education for ministers is a later-developed meaning.

2. This document, not found in the Houghton archives, appeared in Charles W. Taylor, *History of the (Higher) Educational Movement of the Wesleyan Methodist Church of America*, page 328. No copy of the provisional charter mentioned herein has been found.

Appendix D

1. Willard Smith. *The History of Church-Controlled Colleges in The Wesleyan Methodist Church*, 93–97.

2. These perpetual scholarships, available for perhaps $50, guaranteed one student's tuition for a number of years or in perpetuity. The problems were that the funds were often received via a promissory note and that donors believed they could educate their children (in sequence) and anyone else they might designate forever.

Appendix E

1. From McLeister and Nicholson (*Conscience and Commitment*, 102): Rev. Dennison Smith Kinney was born in Dresden, New York, in 1832, and died in Syracuse, New York, January 7, 1890, in his fifty-eighth year. His education . . . was received at Leoni Wesleyan Seminary in Michigan and in Oberlin College. "Rev. Kinney was several inches over six feet, and built proportionately. He was a powerful man, and of magnificent appearance."

2. See appendix C for full text of the incorporation petition.

3. Material quoted was drawn from the version reported by Timothy Nichols in *For the Good of the World: Education and Salvation at the Houghton Wesleyan Methodist Seminary and the Oberlin Collegiate Institute*, appendix D.

Appendix F

1. Typescript in Houghton College archives.

Appendix G

1. From the framed copy hanging in the office of Houghton's president.

2. Quoted in Thomas, *The Man of the Hour*, 60.

3. From *The Houghton Star*, 18 September 1936.

4. This document, not found in the Houghton archives, appeared in Charles W. Taylor, *History of the (Higher) Educational Movement of the Wesleyan Methodist Church of America*, 331.

Appendix H

1. This article was published in *Eternity* magazine, May 1956, pages 8–9, 38–41.

Appendix M

1. This anecdote was confirmed by Willard Smith, who had to assist in the removal of the cow and of the evidence the cow left behind, and by Kenneth Wright, son of Prof. Wright.

2. Interview, Lois R. Ferm, April 1996, 11–12.

3. Ibid., 15–16.

4. Interview, Layton Vogel, 9.

5. Willard Smith, *90 Plus: the Willard G. Smith Story*, 80.

6. Smith, op. cit., 83.

7. Interview, Esther Jane Carrier, February 2001, 37–38.

8. Note, Stanley Sandler, February 24, 2004.

Appendix N

1. Willard J. Houghton, Letter to the Editor, *The Wellsville Spectator*, July 17, 1885 (Original document is in Houghton College Archives).

2. Minutes of the trustees of Houghton Seminary, 1895.

3. Information extracted from Lois Roughan Ferm, *Student Characteristics and Environments for Learning in Wesleyan Colleges*.

4. Ibid., 1.

5. Ibid., 1–2.

6. Ibid., 3–4.

7. Ibid., 33.

8. Ibid., 51.

9. Ibid., 52.

10. Ibid., 33–34.

11. Ibid., 55.

12. Ibid., 59.

13. Ibid., 60.

14. Ibid., 62.

15. Ibid., 76.

16. Ibid., 77.

17. Ibid.

18. Ibid., 78.

19. Ibid., 107–108.

20. Ibid., 121.

21. Ibid., 123.

22. Ibid., 138.

23. Ibid., 141.

24. Ibid.

25. Ibid., 143.

26. Ibid., 144.

27. Ibid., 46–147.

28. Ibid., 150.

29. Ibid., 154.

30. Ibid., 17.

31. Ibid., 18.

32. Ibid., 18–19.

33. Ibid., 195–197.

Index

G

H

T